# DEMOCRACY'S SPECTACLE

# DEMOCRACY'S SPECTACLE

Sovereignty and Public Life in Antebellum
American Writing

JENNIFER GREIMAN

Fordham University Press
NEW YORK   2010

FORDHAM
UNIVERSITY
LIBRARY
BRONX, NY
ROSE HILL

© 2010 Fordham University Press

All rights reserved. No part of this publication may be reproduced, stored in a retrieval system, or transmitted in any form or by any means—electronic, mechanical, photocopy, recording, or any other—except for brief quotations in printed reviews, without the prior permission of the publisher.

Fordham University Press has no responsibility for the persistence or accuracy of URLs for external or third-party Internet websites referred to in this publication and does not guarantee that any content on such websites is, or will remain, accurate or appropriate.

Library of Congress Cataloging-in-Publication Data

Greiman, Jennifer.
   Democracy's spectacle : sovereignty and public life in antebellum American writing / Jennifer Greiman. — 1st ed.
      p.  cm.
   Includes bibliographical references and index.
   ISBN 978-0-8232-3099-0 (cloth : alk. paper)
      1.  American literature—19th century—History and criticism.   2.  Politics and literature—United States—History—19th century.   3.  Democracy in literature.   4.  Sovereignty in literature..   5.  Literature and society—United States—History—19th century.   6.  Democracy—Psychological aspects.
I. Title.
PS217.P64G74    2010
810.9′358735—dc22

                                                                    2009036158


Printed in the United States of America

12  11  10      5  4  3  2  1

First edition

THE
AMERICAN
LITERATURES
INITIATIVE

A book in the American Literatures Initiative (ALI), a collaborative publishing project of NYU Press, Fordham University Press, Rutgers University Press, Temple University Press, and the University of Virginia Press. The Initiative is supported by The Andrew W. Mellon Foundation. For more information, please visit www.americanliteratures.org.

*To the memory of my father, Harley Greiman*

# Contents

# Acknowledgments

This book has been inspired and sustained by family, friends, and colleagues to whom I owe so much more than thanks.

The University at Albany, State University of New York, the College of Arts and Sciences, and the United University Professions provided research support for travel to libraries and archives during the summers of 2006 and 2007. I was able to complete the majority of work on the manuscript during a spring 2007 leave funded by the Nuala McGann Drescher Affirmative Action/Diversity Leave Program, and a fall 2007 writing leave granted by the University at Albany Department of English. In the earliest stages of this project, my research was supported by a dissertation grant from the Mellon Foundation and by the Chancellor's Dissertation Fellowship at the University of California, Berkeley.

Begun as a dissertation in Berkeley's Department of Comparative Literature, this project has not shaken its comparatist roots, and for that I thank Nancy Ruttenburg. An enthusiastic, patient, generous, and rigorous dissertation director, Nancy models a range of expertise and a genius for close reading to which I will always aspire. I can trace the origins of this project to a seminar taught by Sam Otter more than a decade ago, and in the intervening years he has continued to guide my readings in and of American literature. It has been my great good fortune that Nancy and Sam regard their commitment to their students as a long-term one, and I thank both of them for their ongoing mentorship. This project also benefitted in its dissertation stage from the support and guidance of Judith Butler, whose insights and encouragement helped to shape its current form. I am deeply grateful for the example of three such inspired teachers.

The University at Albany English department has provided me a stimulating intellectual home, and I owe thanks to all of my colleagues in this dynamic department. Two chairs—Steve North and Mike Hill— have been unwavering in their support and, along with Liz Lauenstein and Regina Klym, have helped me to secure funding and leave. Branka Arsić, Rick Barney, Bret Benjamin, Eric Keenaghan, Marjorie Pryse, Helene Scheck, and Charlie Shepherdson have all generously read and engaged with my work and provided invaluable guidance and insight. I also remain indebted to the talented group of graduate students in my fall 2004 seminar on "Antebellum Spectacle," whose discussions helped to shape this project at a crucial phase.

I have been very fortunate to work with Helen Tartar and Fordham University Press, and to enjoy the support of the American Literatures Initiative. In addition to Helen, whose enthusiasm for the project spurred me to finish, I'd like to thank Tim Roberts, Ruth Steinberg, and Thomas Lay for their efficiency, skill, and professionalism. The book also owes an immeasurable debt to the recommendations and insights of the two readers Helen secured. I am particularly grateful to Jonathan Elmer, who offered as comprehensive and discerning a reading of this book as I could hope to have. An early version of Chapter 2 was published in the *Arizona Quarterly* 60.1 (2004) as "Racial Violence and the Theatrics of Opinion in Beaumont's *Marie*."

I feel incredibly lucky to have found in my colleagues at both the University of California, Berkeley, and at the University at Albany, the most supportive of communities and the dearest of friends. To those once together at Berkeley, and now scattered all about, I send my warmest thanks for many years of friendship: Amir Banbaji, Ayelet Ben-Yishai, Promita Chatterji, Gil Hochberg, James Ker, Jo Park, Allison Schachter, and Laura Schattschneider. At Berkeley, I also had the pleasure of serving as an editor of *qui parle* with brilliant colleagues and friends—in particular, Arianne Chernock, Lilya Kaganovsky, Ben Lazier, John Ronan, and Catherine Zimmer.

In Albany, an already welcoming community has continued to grow, and for sustaining me with food, drink, and friendship, I thank: Elisa Albert and Ed Schwarzschild, Branka Arsić and David Wills, Rick Barney, Joel Berkowitz and Esther Nathanson, Bret Benjamin and Laura Wilder, Leona Christie, Pat Chu and Andrew Hoberek, James and Sharon

Danoff-Burg, Pierre Joris and Nicole Peyrafitte, Cricket Keating and Larin McLaughlin, Eric Keenaghan and Jeffrey Lependorf, James Lilley and Lauren Sallata, Ineke Murakami, Angela Pneuman, Helene Scheck, Paul Stasi, and Lisa Thompson.

To my expansive and widespread family, I owe pretty much everything. Kim Sauvageot, Adam Braun, and, most recently, Linh-Mai, have shown me such love and generosity over so many years that by now we must be related. Harvey and Ellie Trachtenberg have warmly welcomed me into the fold. Jeannie Masquelier and Tom Esgate have sustained me in every conceivable way, and I am so grateful to them for my California home. I thank my amazing brother, Paul Schwabe, for talking me into more welcome distractions from work—from skiing to running marathons—than I can count. For three decades, George Robertson has offered me boundless love, support, and patience, while keeping roofs from Charlottesville to San Francisco to Albany from falling in on my head. My mother, Judy Robertson, first inspired my fervor for words and with unyielding love and good humor has been my most stalwart champion. Finally, to my partner and dearest friend, Barry Trachtenberg, I owe endless love and thanks. From that cold, upstate New York winter day when he made me hike in the snow, fed me falafel, and sang Dead Milkmen, he has made my life a joy and a delight.

I dedicate this book to my father, Harley Greiman, who did not live to see me begin it or finish it, but from whom I learned to love and live my work.

# Introduction

"Could the kind reader have been quietly riding along the main road to or from Easton, that morning, his eyes would have met a painful sight." Midway through *My Bondage and My Freedom*, Frederick Douglass longs for an impossible spectator: a witness to the daily abominations of slavery who is in no way implicated by them.[1] A writer more keenly attuned than almost any of his contemporaries to the ethical complexities that such "painful sights" entail, Douglass pauses to imagine such a spectator more than once—one who is both present and not present, capable of standing witness to atrocities but hovering almost spectrally outside of them.[2] Such viewpoints are emphatically hypothetical in Douglass's writing, emerging through the fiction of counterfactual clauses—"if any one wishes to be impressed with the soul-killing power of slavery . . . ," "could the kind reader have been quietly riding by . . . "—and standing in marked contrast to the "painful sights" that serve instead as repeated moments of "initiation" into slavery's regime.[3] Indeed, on the morning in question, scores of people did stand along the Easton road to watch as Douglass and four other men were arrested and dragged to prison on charges of plotting escape; but none of them could fill the role of the quiet rider Douglass envisions, because everyone whom he sees watching him is either a fellow slave or one of his persecutors. On that morning, Douglass and his friends become the occasion for a peculiar, impromptu public spectacle that marks yet another moment in his perpetual initiation, another passage through what he calls in 1845 the "bloodstained gate."[4] Douglass's language of initiations and gates, as well as his longing for a witness who can see without passing through them, echoes through his autobiographies as an expression of hope for a clear, locatable "outside" to slavery. But the relentlessness with which such initiations recur suggests that slavery is instead a regime of thresholds, forever rendering indistinguishable "outside" from "inside," and making of every spectator a participant.

In its combining of "all manner of ribaldry and sport" with calls for the torture and execution of Douglass and his friends, the spectacle along the Easton road begins with a lost distinction between punishment and entertainment, as an eager crowd gathers around the scene of the men's capture as if it were a public hanging. But, strictly speaking, no "law" has been applied to the men, aside from the blanket exception from all legal protection and right of the enslaved. Before the men reach the prison, before they face that farce of law which could hang them even though Douglass protests to the constables that no crime has been committed, their conviction is pronounced and their punishment begins. Even once they are clearly in the state's custody, locked in prison and under its jurisdiction, the men remain partially outside of the law that holds them, since, as well as the presumed agents of an uncommitted crime, they are still the salable property of others. Convicted of guilt by the spectators before their imprisonment, assessed for sale after it, neither presented with the evidence against them nor put to trial, and held by the state until their confinement becomes unprofitable to their masters, the men are suspended on a bloody threshold that cannot be said to coincide exactly with the realms of law, public, private, or state. Douglass describes the brutal absurdities of this indecipherable position with characteristic irony, mocking both the "moral vultures" in the crowd and the baseless charges against him and his companions, so that the full measure of the violence done only becomes evident in a strange and haunting passage that appears near the end of the episode:

> We were literally dragged that morning, behind horses, a distance of fifteen miles, and placed in the Easton jail. We were glad to reach the end of our journey, for our pathway had been the scene of insult and mortification. Such is the power of public opinion, that it is hard, even for the innocent, to feel the happy consolations of innocence, when they fall under the maledictions of this power.[5]

Given the abuse the men suffer on the road, Douglass's sense of relief at reaching the relative safety of the jail is perhaps unsurprising, but it comes as something of a shock to read of his susceptibility to "the power of public opinion." Douglass is obviously subject to force—to the force of law that permits constables to arrest men with no evidence that a crime has been committed and that recognizes their personhood only insofar as it renders them punishable, and to the "combined physical force" of the community that keeps him enslaved. But Douglass would seem to stand outside the reach of the more intimate and coercive effects of these authorities. What is most surprising about his reflection is that, despite his knowledge of the justice of his plot, and his disdain for the spectators who revel in his arrest, the opinion of a "public" somehow gets to him, unsettling "the happy consolations" of an innocent man. How are we to understand such a "public"? Is it limited to that metonymic crowd of "vultures," "tormenters," and "imps" who harass him along the Easton road? Or does it refer to the combined power of legal force and social abuse to which he is subjected that day? This is obviously not a public to which Douglass belongs voluntarily, nor does his relationship to it confer anything on him but total subjection. But neither is this a public of enfranchised citizens from which he is simply excluded, irrelevant, or immaterial. Indeed, as Douglass describes the repeated "scene[s] of insult and mortification" of which he is the center, and the absurd lengths to which these people go to abuse him, it becomes clear that this is a public that requires *him*—one that constitutes itself through the spectacle of his abuse and punishment, one whose authority is marked by its capacity to instigate or suspend the application of law to him. Finally, though the authority of such a public is derived by force, what Douglass means when he speaks of its "power" is clearly not limited to physical violence alone. If it is impossible to say for certain whether Douglass is inside or outside of this public, it also becomes uncertain whether that public lies inside or outside of him.

The chapters that follow make a study of such spectacles, uncovering through them a wide-ranging critique of the paradoxes of a democratic public sphere whose ambivalent gestures of inclusion and exclusion create startling forms of association in the United States of the nineteenth-century—associations that are involuntary and unanticipated, that are not limited by restrictions of legal citizenship, and that often make of public belonging a kind of violation. From the sight of the jeering crowd to the strangely intimate effect of public opinion on an innocent man, Frederick Douglass's account of the events along the Easton road captures the complexity of defining the public sphere of the United States in the antebellum period. Indeed, Douglass calls into question the appropriateness of speaking of the public in terms of a "sphere" at all, since it incorporates those whom it also expels and resists all efforts to locate it. On the morning he describes, the "sphere" of the public would seem to be everywhere, overlapping with spaces from which it should appear to be distinct—the law, the state, the private sphere of "property," and the solitary reflections of an imprisoned slave. Traditionally, political thought has defined the public sphere through precisely such distinctions. In antiquity, Hannah Arendt argues, it referred to the space outside of the household, conferring freedom from the essentially dominative structure of domestic life, the realm of family and slaves.[6] In Jürgen Habermas's influential account of the bourgeois public sphere, eighteenth-century Europeans understood it as a realm of freedom from the state, a space of political critique where private citizens gathered in rational deliberation and debate, and where "domination itself was dissolved."[7] Writing in 1855 about "the power of public opinion," Douglass registers a profound and jarring difference between the public with which he finds himself entangled and the theoretical models that have become most familiar to contemporary scholarship, especially those rooted in assumptions of the separateness and non-dominative character of the public sphere. Instead, Douglass's remarks on "the power of public opinion" give evidence of a public that lacks the character of freedom from domination, as it gradually begins to converge with the realms of privacy and intimacy and takes on the sovereign authority once associated primarily with the state.

If Douglass invokes a meaning of the word "public" that has not been fully accounted for by recent scholarship in U.S. literary studies, it would nonetheless be misleading to suggest that there is clear consensus on the concept or the formation of the public sphere, or to suggest that Habermas's model remains predominant in the field. A generation of Americanists has thoroughly engaged the Habermassian thesis, first contesting its reliance on print mediation, rationality, and independence, and later pointing to the ways in which the public cannot be said to presume private subjects, but regulates and forms them through affective forces like desire and persuasion.[8] But even as the debates with Habermas have reinvented his model for the U.S. context, they have also shaped U.S. public sphere theory in particular ways. In the two decades since Michael Warner's *Letters of the Republic* introduced a Habermassian reading of the early United States, the public sphere models that have developed in American literary studies retain many of the same basic concerns with privacy, intimacy, and abstraction. Americanist public sphere theory remains principally concerned with the structure of citizenship—its purportedly abstract form and its corresponding need for the excessive embodiment of non-citizen subjects—describing a public that is largely defined by political belonging, even as it is also characterized as politically impotent in the face of the state. As scholars have refuted Habermas's presumption of public rationality, demonstrating the centrality of sentiment and affect in nineteenth-century public life and arguing that the U.S. public is indeed a space of intimacy, they have ultimately read into that intimacy signs of a passive and depoliticized public sphere.[9] When Douglass speaks of a "public" in Easton that day, he describes one whose bonds are clearly affective and whose effects are chillingly intimate—but it is also far from passive. The crowd that first gives this public a form and a face is spontaneous and spectacular in ways that the structure of citizenship fails to explain, while its relationship to the state seems at once confrontational and collaborative. Though it would be difficult to speak of a "politics" in this spectacle, the crowd that Douglass encounters comports itself with a punitive authority that approximates political or sovereign right. The scene that Douglass describes appears strange under the lens of current public sphere theory, and that strangeness points to the need for a different set of concepts in which to capture more precisely the era's own complex sense of the term.

Two histories of public life in the United States have sought to do just this, but while they share the same basic point of departure—that "nineteenth-century America was a *public* society in ways hard to imagine after the invention of twentieth-century privacy"[10]—William Novak and Mary Ryan offer strikingly different portraits of that public. In *The People's Welfare*, Novak proposes the concept of the "well-regulated society" as a corrective to the long-standing assumption that the United States in its first century was characterized by minimal government and virtual statelessness. But rather than countering that narrative with an insistence on a powerful, centralized state, Novak traces a network of local governance, regulation, and policing that created the early U.S. public sphere, making it the space where, he argues, governance was most directly performed and lived. Ryan's *Civic Wars* reiterates Novak's contention that the public was the basic concept organizing collective life in the nineteenth century, but she shifts her focus away from formal regulation and official institutions to examine the public that develops in parallel with the spheres of citizenship and governance. In particular, she describes an urban public filled with improvised places and occasions of association—city streets, entertainment venues, riots, and parades—to argue that the public was experienced primarily as a fractious, diverse, impromptu spectacle.[11] If Novak's network of regulation and policing seems incompatible with Ryan's space of improvisation and agitated, unregulated association, these two models of the antebellum public nonetheless go a long way toward contextualizing Douglass's use of the term, as he finds himself neither inside nor exactly outside a punitive, spectacular public that is also neither inside nor outside of him.

Taken together, the accounts by Novak and Ryan of how nineteenth-century Americans understood the public sphere also coincide with the work of one of that public's original theorists, Alexis de Tocqueville, whose study of democratic government and culture in the U.S. is notable for its recognition of precisely such contradictions. Frequently cited for its celebration of the United States as a democracy "of associated peoples, of voluntary organizations . . . of public sociality,"[12] *Democracy in America* is equally famous for the varieties of involuntary association that it details, from majority tyranny to public opinion. Though in its form, *Democracy in America* attempts to institute a split between the political and cultural life of democracy (volumes 1 and 2 of the text, respectively), it perpetually frustrates its own distinctions, demonstrating the ways in which government has migrated out of state control and how political power has become a basic feature of social life. As Claude Lefort writes, Tocqueville's recognition of the blurred distinctions between the state and the social, between politics and culture, even between public and private, follows from one of his major theses: "his realization that democracy is a form of society."[13] Tocqueville is able to pursue the changes wrought by democracy "in every direction," from political institutions to cultural phenomena to the psychological makeup of subjects, because democracy inaugurates a politics that is coextensive with the social, through a power which "appears to belong to no one."[14] Against the model of aristocratic societies—where the basis of the social order and the origins of political power are radically external and transcendent—Tocqueville imagines democratic society as one "that acts by and for itself," one with "no authorities except within itself."[15] However, all the while democracy appears to enclose everything within it, Tocqueville argues, popular sovereignty also converts the immanence of authority into a kind of transcendence, in an original blurring of inside and outside that makes possible the public of improvised but absolute authority with which Douglass finds himself entangled: "The people reign over the American political world as God rules over the universe. It is the cause and the end of all things; everything rises out of it and is absorbed back into it."[16]

Staging belonging and exception to that belonging in the same moment, the spectacle that Douglass describes is peculiarly democratic, one that could only occur at the point where sovereign right enters into an expansively defined public sphere. As the subject for whom the protections of law are suspended, Douglass marks the law's sovereign force. As the occasion for which a crowd has collected itself into a judging, punitive public whose opinion gets inside him, Douglass also marks the limit case of inclusion in an ostensibly democratic public. In both cases, he is included insofar as he can be punished and expelled, situated at the point where the inside and outside of law, politics, and the strange, coercive power of the public become indistinct. In this, the problem at stake in Douglass's haunting account of the power of public opinion over an imprisoned slave is closely linked to the problem at stake in Tocqueville's circular formulation of popular sovereignty in the United States. The questions that both raise involve the highly contested place of sovereign power in democratic societies: Are sovereignty and democracy antithetical, or is democracy dependent upon sovereignty? Or, alternately, does democracy depend upon a sovereignty that is nonetheless antithetical to it? What Tocqueville's image does propose is that the popularization of sovereignty has created a public sphere so transformed by its empowerment that, to describe it, he must first reimagine the very shape of a "sphere." Rather than a geometric enclosure that contains the public, marks it off from private life and state power, and clearly designates its membership, he envisions a circular system that constantly produces and reincorporates its own outside. Only in the context of such a strange and shifting space can Douglass's position with respect to the public of Easton begin to become legible. Only by accounting for public scenes such as Douglass describes, I argue in *Democracy's Spectacle*, can popular sovereignty in the antebellum era be understood *as* a sovereignty that both constituted and burdened the public sphere.

## Tocqueville's Sphere: Democracy and Sovereignty

So enigmatic is Tocqueville's spherical model of popular sovereignty that theorists from Carl Schmitt to Jacques Derrida have cited it as the very image of democracy's vexed reinterpretation of sovereign power. However, a common recourse to Tocqueville has yielded anything but agreement on Tocqueville's meaning, and this warrants a brief detour through the image's afterlife in twentieth- and twenty-first-century critical theory. Conventional sovereignty is commonly described as a "borderline" concept, one concerned with "thresholds" and "bans," inclusion and exclusion, and thus peculiarly disposed to spatial metaphors. But the question of what constitutes the power of exception, and thus the question of where, exactly, its thresholds and borders lie, varies widely among its major twentieth-century theorists. For Carl Schmitt, the "borderline" of sovereignty lies between normalcy and emergency; for Michel Foucault, it lies between life and death; and for Giorgio Agamben, sovereignty marks a border so fundamental to the origins of political life that "life and law, outside and inside become indistinguishable."[17] Carl Schmitt opens his 1922 defense of transcendent political authority with a deceptively simple definition: "Sovereign is he who decides upon the exception."[18] Schmitt effectively makes the sovereign self-defining, created in and by the act of deciding upon an exception. Because the sovereign comes into being in the act of suspending the law, its form lies outside of law and cannot be codified juridically. The border Schmitt speaks of is thus the line between the normal functioning of a political and juridical order and its total suspension in a state of emergency, decided upon by a sovereign who is "personal" and yet who acts with almost divine transcendence. Schmitt insists upon both the personal element of the sovereign and its transcendence; the power of exception, he argues, is analogous to the miracle in theology, a kind of magic that cannot be accounted for by such paradigms of normalcy as the formal regulation of law. In Schmitt's classic formulation, therefore, sovereignty is at odds with the efforts of constitutional democracies to oppose personal rule with the impersonal rule of law and to "banish the miracle from the world."[19]

Schmitt's narrative of sovereignty from the eighteenth century on is largely one of declension; beginning with Rousseau's contractual sovereign, Schmitt argues, "the decisionistic and personalistic element in the concept of sovereignty was lost." With the popularization of sovereignty and the rule of law, he argues, immanent forms of authority promised liberation from both dogma and miracle, and an "organic" unity of the people replaced the "decisionist" character of a state unified by a personal sovereign. However, Schmitt also concedes that the replacement of transcendent political doctrines with doctrines of immanence was not absolute: "It is true, nevertheless, that for some time the aftereffects of the idea of God remained recognizable. In America this manifested itself in the reasonable and pragmatic belief that the voice of the people is the voice of God." Schmitt sees that U.S. democracy has not eradicated the *arcana imperii* of the personal sovereign, but has instead relocated sovereignty's powers of transcendence in the people.

Paraphrasing Tocqueville, Schmitt cites his remarks on the godlike position of the people as evidence of democracy's own peculiar political theology: "Tocqueville in his account of American democracy observed that in democratic thought the people hover above the entire political life of the state, just as God does above the world, as the cause and the end of all things, as the point from which everything emanated and to which everything returns." Although Schmitt invokes Tocqueville's definition of popular sovereignty to demonstrate the persistence of god in the democratic state, he understands this to be more an "aftereffect" of the representation of power than a reinvention of sovereignty.[20] The people may have assumed the transcendent position and they may speak with the voice of god, in Schmitt's account, but they lack the decisionist power of exception. Though democracy might require the name and the image of sovereignty, Schmitt sees the two as basically antithetical, in large part because he endorses a historical narrative that replaces a personal sovereign with a juridical, contractual notion of sovereignty that empties it of its exceptional power by seeking to formalize it in law.

This is precisely the narrative of modernity that Michel Foucault disputes, arguing that the problem of sovereignty after the eighteenth century is not its concealment or dissipation by constitutional governments but its persistence as "the right of life and death." Foucault argues that, while the bourgeois revolutions of the eighteenth and nineteenth centuries instituted the regime of normalization and regulation that he calls "discipline," the essentially dominative, absolutist character of sovereignty never disappeared.[21] Instead, he argues that sovereignty became rearticulated as "public right," and while this allowed something like its "democratization," public right, like earlier assertions of right, remained rooted in force, domination, and war. Foucault's basic definition of sovereignty is broader than Schmitt's strict interpretation of the exception as the suspension of all law, but it continues to be concerned with the boundaries of norm and exception, which Foucault translates into the boundaries of life and death. In Foucault's account of the fate of sovereignty in the nineteenth century, the regime of disciplinary normalization is gradually replaced by a power over life that he calls "biopower," but rather than recede with this new power "to make live and let die," sovereignty persists, maintaining its right of exception by instituting a "break between what must live and what must die." This "break" takes on the very specific form of a biological racism that is modeled on war, made internal to a population, and managed by the state. Foucault does not mention the particular case of U.S. slavery—indeed, he is studiously abstract in his 1976 lectures on state racism—but his account of how racism derives from sovereign right effectively counters the assumption that slavery and racism are antithetical to constitutional democracy and the abstract form of citizenship that it instates. Instead, Foucault's claim for the persistence of sovereignty explains how modern states became dependent upon racism—indeed, he calls it their "basic mechanism of power."[22] But as Foucault describes the translation of sovereignty into racism, he remains focused on the state as the chief agent of both. Hinting that "murderous power and sovereign power" might be "unleashed throughout the social body," he nonetheless suspends the question of whether popular sovereignty might demand the same "basic mechanism" as the sovereignty of states.[23]

In *Homer Sacer*, Giorgio Agamben invokes Foucault's concept of biopower to rewrite Schmitt's classic definition of sovereignty (under modern biopolitics, he quips, "sovereign is he who decides on the value or nonvalue of life as such"[24]), and with this, he offers one interpretation of what it might mean for democracy to "unleash" sovereignty throughout the social body. Agamben begins by disputing Foucault's timeline for the emergence of biopower, which he calls "absolutely ancient." Modern sovereignty, he argues, cannot be defined simply by "the fact that life as such becomes a principle object of the projections and calculations of State power." Power's concern with "bare life" is the origin of all politics; its exclusion "founds the city of men." What is new in the modern era is that "bare life . . . gradually begins to coincide with the political realm." The biological life that had been the decisive outside of politics—as well as its "hidden foundation"—becomes both the "subject and object" of politics. This is most evident, he argues, in modern democracy, "in which man as living being presents himself no longer as an *object*, but also as the *subject* of political power."[25]

Sovereignty's incorporation into modern democracy results in what Agamben calls its "specific aporia: it wants to put the freedom and happiness of men into play in the very place—bare life—that marked their subjection." Sovereignty, in his model, is thus integral to democracy, which internalized the structure of exception in the very constitution of the democratic subject as both a subject of natural right and a subject of law. As bearer of political right, the democratic subject is also a potential sovereign; as bearer of protected "natural" life, that subject is also liable to death. For Agamben, recognizing the "aporia" of democracy—in short, its dependence upon sovereignty's structure of exception—is not a means of denying its legacy of rights and protections, but of understanding how, at moments of crisis, democracy has "proved itself incapable of saving" the life to which it dedicated itself. Specifically, Agamben refers to the rise of totalitarian and fascist states in the twentieth century, but he alludes to an earlier crisis as well: "Modern democracy's decadence and gradual convergence with totalitarian states in post-democratic spectacular societies (which begins to become evident with Alexis de Tocqueville and finds its final sanction in the analyses of Guy Debord) may well be rooted in this aporia." Agamben calls upon Tocqueville's study of nineteenth-century America as evidence of both democracy's original and structuring contradiction and as a harbinger of a "decadence" to come. In this, he suggests that, more than a failure to save life, democracy's "complicity" may be marked by the same "murderous" tendencies that Foucault locates in nineteenth-century racism, without Foucault's assumption that racism is the mechanism of a monolithic state. As Agamben traces the migration of sovereignty's basic structure out of the state and into individual subjects under democracy, so he also offers an account of how sovereignty might implicate those who become the bearers of its right.[26]

In a 2002 lecture, Derrida directly addressed the problem that Agamben describes as democracy's "complicity with its most implacable enemies," describing a kind of autoimmune disorder peculiar to popular sovereignty. Like Agamben, Derrida begins by citing the history of fascist or totalitarian states that arose from "formally normal and formally democratic electoral processes"; calling such occurrences a kind of suicide—the democratic end of democracy—he then links them to what he terms an "autoimmune" response, also suicidal, but instituted by states acting to forestall the formally democratic processes that would effectively end democracy. From the perspective of the state, Derrida argues, the former look like the acts of undemocratic "rogues," while the latter are assertions of sovereign right under Schmitt's definition, but these two tendencies are really mirror images of each other, rooted in the basic inseparability and the inherent contradiction of democracy and sovereignty. If popular sovereignty can yield undemocratic results, it is because all sovereignty is suicidal to democracy. The problem, Derrida claims, is that it has also been fundamental to democracy: "Now democracy would be precisely this, a force, a force (*kratos*) in the form of sovereign authority . . . and thus the power and ipseity of the people (*demos*). This sovereignty is a circularity, indeed a sphericity. Sovereignty is round." To explain what he means by the roundness of sovereignty, Derrida follows Schmitt and Agamben and turns to Tocqueville: "Tocqueville himself, in

describing the sovereignty of the people, speaks of this circular identification of cause with the end." In Derrida's account, Tocqueville's sphere
becomes emblematic of the problem of democratic sovereignty by demonstrating its eradication of the division between what transcends the
social body and what is internal to it. In other words, Derrida argues,
democracy finds its "effective fulfillment" in its suicidal capacity to incorporate everything that should lie outside of it.[27]

The image of Tocqueville's sphere has implicitly returned theorists
of sovereignty—who explicitly invoke the history of twentieth-century
fascist and totalitarian states—to the nineteenth century, but their use
of Tocqueville remains somewhat ahistorical, borrowing from him
little more than a metaphor. In Derrida's biological trope, Tocqueville's
sphere accounts for both versions of an autoimmune response that seems
to characterize all democracies, in all times. Resisting occupation and
referring only to itself, Tocqueville's sphere marks off and contains the
empty place that Claude Lefort describes in his study of *Democracy in
America* as the similarly transhistoric space of democratic power.[28] Tocqueville's image of the sphere also takes Schmitt's claim that sovereignty
is "a borderline concept" to its extreme; it is nothing but borderline, with
no outside and nothing but emptiness contained within it (linking it, as
well, to Agamben's structure of the threshold). But whatever its metaphoric capacities, Tocqueville roots his image specifically in the context
of popular sovereignty as he finds it in the United States in the early decades of the nineteenth century.[29] Thus, it finds its most telling elaboration in a complementary figure from its own time—Frederick Douglass's
famous description of the "circle" of slavery. More than metaphoric,
Douglass's circle bears a metonymic relationship to Tocqueville's sphere,
associating and confronting popular sovereignty in antebellum America
with its most persistent violence.

Originally composed for the 1845 *Narrative*, and cited verbatim in
*My Bondage and My Freedom*, the "circles" passage narrates Douglass's
evolving comprehension of the work songs sung by slaves on allowance day, "the mere hearing of which would do more to impress truly
spiritual-minded people with the soul-killing and death-dealing character of slavery, than the reading of whole volumes of its mere physical
cruelties."[30] As a child, Douglass insists, he heard these songs but could
not comprehend them: "I was myself within the circle, so that I neither
saw nor heard as those without might see and hear." But who are "those
without," and where might they stand? Douglass describes no fewer than

six positions from which these songs might be considered—that of the slaves and that of the slaveowners; that of his own position as a child; the positions he assumes in writing about the songs in 1845 and 1855; and, finally, the seemingly impossible position of someone who might sneak into the woods on allowance day and "in silence, thoughtfully analyze the sounds that shall pass through the chambers of his soul." But each of these positions seems to mark a place within the ever-expanding circle: if the final position marks what it means to be "without" the circle, then to comprehend the meaning of the songs would require one to assume an impossible position similar to that of the quiet rider whom Douglass imagines passing by the spectacle of his abuse along the road to Easton. But even such a hypothetical position "without" cannot be sustained; as the sounds of the songs "pass through the chambers of his soul," so this impossible spectator would find himself carried inside the circle, involved through his exposure in the most quotidian horrors of slavery. The slave songs, like the scene at Easton, admit of no clear outside or transcendent position from which to be viewed comprehensively. Instead, they form a circle, associating everyone who approaches in a relation of seeing and hearing that allows for only partial knowledge but demands an intimate and penetrating involvement. With this, Douglass's circle suggests yet another form for Tocqueville's sphere: that of a spectacle that generates and sustains itself through all of those who see and hear. As the window on slavery's "death-dealing character," this spectacle is the mirror image of the normalization of death under a sovereignty, out of which every-thing rises and into which everything is absorbed.

## "The Sovereign People": State and Public in Antebellum America

While Tocqueville's sphere connects recent formulations of sover-eignty to a nineteenth-century interpretation of the term, the basic structure of the sovereign power invoked by thinkers like Agamben and Derrida remains, in many ways, a product of twentieth-century crises of the state. Such an understanding of sovereignty as a problem of state power has, in turn, shaped contemporary narratives of sovereignty's nineteenth-century history. While invoking Tocqueville's 1835 text, studies of sovereign power in the nineteenth-century United States have often focused on the assertions of executive power and emergency excep-tion enacted three decades later, during Abraham Lincoln's presidency, which William Novak describes as "awash in novel exertions of central-ized governmental power."[31] The narrative of the rise of the U.S. state typically begins with Lincoln's expansion of executive powers through a series of presidential proclamations that bypassed Congress to declare the war, expand the military, suspend the writ of *habeas corpus*, and, ultimately, to end slavery.[32] Agamben, in particular, refers to Lincoln's wartime proclamations in his comparative survey of state sovereignties, arguing that Lincoln effectively "generalized the state of exception" dur-ing the Civil War to establish a model emulated by later presidents (from Woodrow Wilson to George W. Bush), who invoke war in order to act continually under the sovereign powers that fall to the commander in chief.[33] In each of these accounts, sovereign exception is first invoked un-der the emergency of the Civil War, but rather than receding into latency (as it would by Schmitt's definition) after Emancipation and the end of the war, it gradually becomes part of the general operation of political power to drive a transformation in the state itself.

Although this narrative accounts for the considerable expansion of the U.S. state following the Civil War, it implies that something like a normal operation of law and right, without assertions of sovereign ex-ception, preceded the emergency brought on by the war. However, the operation of such a "norm" in the antebellum U.S. is very much in ques-tion, especially in the wake of another key interpretation of U.S. sover-eignty: the 1857 decision in *Dred Scott v. Sandford*. Largely known as the decision that both nationalized and generalized slavery—in Martin Delany's interpretation, it made "every free black in the county . . . li-able to enslavement by any white person"[34]—the *Dred Scott* decision also described a fairly limited view of the state's sovereign powers while in-voking another sovereignty as the basis for an explicitly exceptionalist political community. In Chief Justice Roger Taney's majority opinion in that case, he argues that, "although [the U.S. government] is sovereign and supreme in its appropriate sphere of action, yet it does not possess all the powers which usually belong to the sovereignty of a nation."[35] But even as Taney insists upon the relative weakness of national sovereignty in the U.S., he preserves both the concept and its operation, and in place of what he calls the "usual" sovereign, he opens his decision by defining "the sovereign people" as "the political body . . . who form the sovereign" under the Constitution.[36] Taney then exerts himself to prove that Dred and Harriet Scott and their children are not "constituent members of this sovereignty," neither persons nor citizens and thus not party to its rights and privileges. As Stephen Best deftly shows in his reading of the majority decision, Taney does this by "wresting" out of the Constitution's references to "free persons" and "other persons" the figures of "slave," "negro," and "property." Appealing to "intent," Taney must read through the text, citing everything from colonial laws to the "fixed opinion" of eighteenth-century Europeans in order to divine an intentional exclusion of all blacks, free and enslaved, from the political community of "the sovereign people."[37]

But it is not only the intent behind the Constitution that Taney's ruling fabricates; his figurations of the sovereign people throughout also burden this body with a similarly dissembled intent. Originally construing the people as the collective body of citizens at the moment of the nation's constitution, Taney gradually broadens the scope of this people, outlining the ways in which both personhood and citizenship have been understood to include subjects other than propertied white males. He does not confine citizenship to birth, for example; as citizens of "foreign" governments, he argues, both "Indians" and "aliens" might be naturalized. Nor does he confine it to members of the franchise, since "incapacitated" parties to "the political family," like white women and minors, can be counted as citizens with rights and yet "no share of the political power." Since Taney cannot prove exclusion through the citation of text that expressly withholds the rights and privileges of citizenship from enslaved or free African-Americans, he must instead perform exception.[38] Listing forms of natal belonging and processes of naturalization, he fashions through his ruling a "sovereign people" whose very existence is structured around the one class that, he insists, cannot be incorporated into it, making that class both necessary and internal to the sovereignty of the body it defines. Taney's political body is thus burdened by the sovereignty that created it, made to reiterate its constitutive exception, regardless of any changes one might find in "public opinion": "No one, we presume, supposes that any change in public opinion or feeling, in relation to this unfortunate race, in the civilized nations of Europe or in this country, should induce the court to give to the words of the Constitution a more liberal construction in their favor than they were intended to bear when the instrument was framed and adopted."[39] Taney argues that the sovereign people can only be amended through and along with the Constitution itself. This sovereign is neither responsive to the feelings or opinions of the public from which it is constituted, nor capable of changing its own character. Taney's ruling yokes the sovereign people to the Constitution as he reads it, making it static and placing it outside of history, while also burdening it with the task that the Constitution does not explicitly perform. In the absence of plainly exclusionary language in the text, Taney's ruling imputes to this sovereign the constant work of exception.[40]

While Taney strains throughout his majority decision to craft an image of the sovereign people that enables the expansion of slavery—giving to the ruling, Best argues, something like a *poesis*—the ruling does not so much invent as formalize an understanding of popular sovereignty that very much concerned critical observers of antebellum political culture. In particular, in the decades before the Civil War, antislavery writers and activists decried a model of citizenship that made exception part of its structure of belonging. In her 1833 *Appeal in Favor of That Class of Americans Called Africans*, Lydia Maria Child lamented the constitution of a national community that essentially made her party to a "crime": "If union cannot be preserved without crime, it is an eternal truth that nothing good can be preserved by crime."[41] Writing twenty-four years before *Dred Scott v. Sandford,* and seventeen years before the Fugitive Slave Law came into force with the Compromise of 1850, Child anticipates Martin Delany's assessment of both, fearing that a form of belonging structured around exception made every citizen personally complicit in sovereign violence, submitting every black, free or not, to every white in the community.[42] Two years later, Tocqueville's traveling companion, Gustave de Beaumont, compared the consequences of unjust power under monarchic and democratic governments in his novel, *Marie; or, Slavery in the United States*, arguing that the despotic acts by a monarch could be located and contained, "but in a land of equality all citizens are responsible for social injustices; each is a party to them. Not a white man exists in American who is not a barbarous, iniquitous persecutor of the black race."[43] What each of these writers sees is that the exceptionalism of political belonging generalizes the violence of sovereignty, but not only in the sense that Novak, Agamben, and others describe as its transformation into a normal function of state power. Instead, as slavery and mastery become latent in the public sphere—reducing everyone to potential slave or potential persecutor—so sovereignty comes to shape the lived experience of the public. In the interpretations offered by Child, Beaumont, and Delany, crime and guilt mark the citizen who is both created by and burdened with sovereignty, as they also mark those whose exception and enslavement give that sovereignty its force.

The legal and political battles that kept slavery at the center of U.S.

political culture in the decades before the Civil War gave shape to a public sphere that became a staging ground for enactments of sovereign force and exception that seemed to occur almost automatically. The body of citizens that resulted was not exactly passive, but neither was it self-directed or self-defining in the way that Tocqueville's formulation of popular sovereignty might suggest. Instead, it appeared to remain subject to the conditions that created it, forging association through a shared, involuntary complicity with a power that, at its root, claimed "the right of life and death." Emerson's "Fate" speaks of "complicity" in precisely these terms: "there is complicity—expensive races,—race living at the expense of race."[44] Neither an agency nor a passivity, complicity describes an intimate involvement of the lives of some with the deaths of others that appeared to many critics of antebellum America as a condition of the public sphere. Further, the complicity that made "every free black in the county . . . liable to enslavement by any white person," and turned every white into "a barbarous, iniquitous persecutor of the black race," also bled beyond the institution of slavery. Slavery stood as the most violent and visible—but certainly not the only—institution of sovereignty, around which the antebellum public took shape. Writers like Child, whose activism began with the antislavery movement, also saw that the migration of sovereign powers into the public sphere created forms of complicity in acts of violence that had once fallen under state monopoly: "What is the hangman but a servant of the law? And what is that law but an expression of public opinion? And if public opinion be brutal, and *thou* a component part thereof, art *thou* not the hangman's accomplice?"[45] Child's syllogism derives culpability from constituency, and though she regards public opinion from a very different vantage point than Frederick Douglass does as he sits in the Easton jail, she recognizes in it a similar power to undermine "the happy consolations of innocence." Judge Taney may deny public opinion the political force to alter the constitution of the "sovereign people," but it nonetheless speaks with a sovereign's voice. In *American Notes*, Charles Dickens finds in the pronouncements of the public the full force of sovereign violence, arguing that "public opinion has knotted the lash, heated the branding-iron, loaded the rifle, and shielded the murderer."[46]

But even as antislavery writers like Douglass, Beaumont, and Child regarded the public opinion that supported slavery as the power to be opposed and altered, they could not consider themselves as entirely separate from it. Instead, public opinion comes to represent a key term in an experience of public life as both intimate and alienating, the place where political power could be regarded as abstract, external, and yet also strangely personal, intimate, even familiar. As Douglass shows when he describes the withering effects of public opinion on his conviction of the justice of his acts, the sovereign power that is identified with public opinion uses mechanisms other than physical force. In Tocqueville's analysis, such changes in form follow from sovereignty's migration out of the control of princes and monarchs: "Princes made violence a physical thing, but our contemporary democratic republics have turned it into something as intellectual as the human will it is intended to constrain."[47] Without abandoning spectacular displays of physical violence—Douglass's "bloody gates"—this sovereignty also moves inward, operating with an intimacy that links spectacular sites of punishment, like the public scaffold and the auction block, to more secretive spaces of discipline, like the solitary prison cell.

The story of popular sovereignty in the nineteenth-century United States that I trace in *Democracy's Spectacle* both bears out and challenges what Foucault characterizes in *Discipline and Punish* as a transformation in power after the eighteenth century, as writers from Beaumont and Tocqueville to Dickens and Child all testify to a continuity between older forms of sovereign violence, the spectacular atrocities of slavery, and America's innovations in prison discipline (the U.S. penitentiary system was the primary thing Tocqueville and Beaumont had come to observe). In Foucault's well-known narrative, the symbolic and spectacular punishments of public torture and execution were gradually replaced over the course of the seventeenth and eighteenth centuries by the secretive, coercive, individuating model of solitary imprisonment, which he calls "the exact reverse of spectacle."[48] However, in the United States, these two tendencies remained tightly coupled, in part because the penal systems that were touted as modern, innovative, and humane existed alongside the most ancient practices of symbolic, corporal punishment under slavery.[49] In many ways, antebellum America revitalizes the punitive spectacle to perform both the popularization and the exclusions of democratic sovereignty through rituals of violence and exception that appear everywhere in public.[50] By following both the mutations and continuities of sovereignty, this book examines the ways in which intimate and interiorizing modes of power become yoked to spectacular forms in the public culture of nineteenth-century America. But more than simply describing the containment or domination of subjects in the public sphere, *Democracy's Spectacle* examines the problematic forms of empowerment and complicity that also followed from the popularization of sovereignty. From prisons to theaters, museums to marketplaces, democracy's spectacle appears everywhere in the antebellum United States because that entity known as the "sovereign people" entangles belonging with complicity.

## The Society of the Spectacle: New York City, 1849

With the residual forms of spectacular punishment evident in the daily practices of antebellum sovereignty, another model of spectacle also began to take shape during this period, to become a defining form of public life. Most discernible in the era's mania for theater, parades, exhibitions, and mass cultural phenomena, this other spectacle was closely identified with an image and idea of the public as it mediated relations between subjects and defined their common sphere as one of both cultural consumption and collective self-contemplation. Mass spectacle in the antebellum era took many forms—theatrical, reformist, commemorative, political. As Benjamin Reiss argues, popular spectacle both "engendered new social relations" and facilitated the creation of a "new mass politics."[51] But regardless of how novel these spectacular relations and mass politics appeared, they were never separable from the more archaic uses to which spectacular political power had traditionally been put. As Saidiya Hartman has powerfully shown, pleasure and terror converged in antebellum popular culture through scenes that linked the violent spectacles of slavery, such as the coffle and the auction block, to theatrical spectacles, such as melodrama and blackface minstrelsy.[52] Put another way, the middle decades of the nineteenth century might be said to mark that moment when the remnants of Foucault's epoch of public violence crossed paths with the earliest traces of Guy Debord's "society of the spectacle," and what emerges from this crossing is a surprising glimpse of the correlation between two seemingly distinct forms of spectacular power. Where Debord's spectacle refers to "a social relationship between people that is mediated by images" and appears in Western liberal democracies decades into the age of mechanical reproduction, and Foucault's refers to the punitive violence of monarchs in the seventeenth and eighteenth centuries, it is in the antebellum United States—as analyzed by two other Frenchmen, Tocqueville and Beaumont—where both forms of spectacle converge to shape the contours of the public sphere.

Writing in 1967, Guy Debord describes a formation of late capitalist states in which all social, political, and economic relations appear as a universal spectacle that is "the chief product" of society.[53] But despite the twentieth-century technologies that perfect it—film, television, the automobile—the basic effects of Debord's spectacle echo several of Tocqueville's key claims about democratic society in the nineteenth-century United States. Like Tocqueville's spherical model of popular sovereignty, Debord writes that "the spectacle is essentially tautological," uniting means and ends to "cover the entire globe." Like the post-enlightenment political theology that makes such sovereignty immanent rather than transcendent, "the spectacle is the material reconstruction of the religious illusion." Finally, like the democratic subjects whom Tocqueville describes as atomized and isolated from one another, Debord's "spectators are linked only by a one-way relationship to the very center that maintains their isolation."[54] Debord's spectacular society is one in which the separation of subjects from each other, and from their lives and labor, is achieved through a loss of distinction between politics and culture, public and private, "material life" and its "visible negation." Atomized and isolated by the purely visual relations in which they find themselves, subjects come to regard the "real" as only what appears to them, and material life as "a world beyond," over which they have no power to act. The spectacle thus negates life by asserting it as "mere appearance," at the same time it achieves what Debord characterizes as a "totalitarian" control over the conditions of existence. Echoing Tocqueville on the one hand, Debord looks forward to Foucault on the other, suggesting that the spectacle is the realization of a potent biopolitical regime: "By means of the spectacle, the ruling order discourses endlessly upon itself in an uninterrupted monologue of self-praise. The spectacle is the self-portrait of power in the age of power's totalitarian rule over the conditions of existence."[55]

Such an understanding of spectacle—as "the self-portrait of power"—offers a useful point of entry into the complex operation of spectacular forms and relations in antebellum America.[56] In addition to the ways in which Debord echoes Tocqueville's observations about the tautological and atomizing tendencies of U.S. democracy, Debord's emphasis on the self-producing and self-sustaining nature of the spectacle speaks to one key aspect of its antebellum incarnation—namely, as perpetual, collective self-contemplation. But where Debord and Foucault continue to invoke a "ruling order" or a "state," in whose service spectacular power operates, the spectacles that shaped social and political life in the United States of the 1830s, 1840s, and 1850s must be viewed in a much more ambiguous relationship to the state, and the power whose self-portrait is performed appears to be that of the public itself. Along with the concept of sovereignty, which came to refer to a basic feature of state power largely in the context of twentieth-century totalitarianism, that of spectacle has been shaped by its more recent associations with mass media, the centralized state, and the totalitarian crowd.[57] As sovereignty bore a less centralized shape in the decades leading up to the Civil War, so spectacle also took a different form before the emergence of a powerful U.S. state in the later 1800s. While the antebellum spectacle I describe may indicate an early formation of what Debord theorizes, it would oversimplify matters to view it as produced and mediated by a ruling class for the consumption of a public. Instead, spectacle may be best described as a primary form of the public itself in the context of sovereignty's popularization. In other words, spectacle is that circle, so evocatively described by both Tocqueville and Douglass, which constantly produces and incorporates its own outside, creating myriad forms of involuntary association, demanding intimate and penetrating involvement, while also endlessly performing exception.

Claims about the spectacularization of the U.S. public sphere have generally focused on its depoliticization as, in Donald Pease's words, citizens are reduced to "passive spectators" of a political process that is driven by leaders "who accrue power by 'staging.'"[58] By attending to the antebellum era's own complex interpretations of spectacle and spectatorship—rather than ones filtered through modernity's disconnected *flâneur*, or totalitarianism's swayed mass—I argue for another account of the spectacular public, one that is far from passive or apolitical and frustrates easy distinction from the state or ruling class. Spectatorship in the antebellum U.S. did not equate to the stance of an outside or distant observer; it was not a practice for the urbane *flâneur* alone, nor was it understood as a simply passive or receptive stance. Instead, it instituted forms of association and belonging that implicated spectators in what they watched, revealing the intimacy of their involvement with one another, while also exposing the contours of a collective power that was rooted in rituals of sovereignty. As a primary form of public life, evidence of such spectacle is everywhere. It is as operative in the punitive parading of Frederick Douglass and his companions along the Easton road in rural Maryland as it is in the Astor Place theater riots in New York City in 1849. Indeed, while I hesitate to privilege particular events as exemplary, the Astor Place Riots stand alongside Douglass's story in offering as succinct and powerful a case study as one could wish of the mutual implication of spectacle and sovereignty in the formation of the antebellum public. Beginning in a long-standing rivalry between two actors, whose disparate interpretations of Shakespeare were debated from Edinburgh to Philadelphia, the events of May 1849 indicate the ways in which popular theater produced mass-cultural phenomena as an incipient form of the Debordian spectacle. Culminating in a series of protests by thousands of fans of the American Edwin Forrest against the British Shakespearean William Charles Macready, that resulted in days of rioting and over twenty deaths, the riots further disclose the violence with which competing claims to the sovereignty of the "public" were fought in antebellum America.[59]

The epic rivalry that pitted Forrest against Macready was equal parts personal, aesthetic, nationalist, and classist. It dated at least to Forrest's tour of England and Scotland in 1846, during which the American came to believe that Macready was sabotaging him with a whisper campaign disparaging Forrest's loud, exuberant, and intensely physical acting style. Forrest responded with the infamous "Edinburgh hiss," made at a performance of the more subtle and staid Macready in Scotland, before Forrest's return to the United States.[60] When Macready then came to the U.S. in 1848–49, Forrest made a point of following his tour so that he could star in the same role at a rival theater in another part of the same town, showcasing their wildly divergent styles while denouncing Macready in the press as an elitist English aristocrat. By the time Macready returned to New York in May 1849 for his final U.S. engagement at the Astor Place Opera House, the feud was national news. Forrest was playing a run at the nearby Broadway Theater, and his base of fans was primed for a confrontation. On Macready's opening night in *Macbeth*, "the cheering, hissing, whistling, and other expressions of feeling began, and not a syllable was heard the remainder of the scene," until the star was finally driven from the stage by a shower of rotten eggs and vegetables.[61] After the disaster of his opening-night show, Macready decided to cancel the rest of his New York performances, but he was dissuaded by a petition published in the May 9 edition of the *New York Herald* that contained the signatures of many of the city's cultural elite, including Washington Irving, Evert Duyckinck, and Herman Melville. Reluctantly resuming his role of Macbeth at the Opera House on May 10, Macready found the theater filled with Forrest's fans inside and a crowd estimated at between ten and fifteen thousand people outside, along with a formidable show of police force. When the audience inside the theater again interrupted the show, police read the riot act and arrested half of the audience seated in the pit. When some in the crowd outside began to throw paving stones at the Opera House to protest the arrests, the police opened fire, killing twenty-three and wounding thirty-eight.

However astounding it seemed that the deadliest civil disturbance up to that time in New York had begun, as the *Tribune* put it, "all because two actors had quarreled," there was a great deal more at stake in what the editors of the *Herald* termed "theatrical human emotion."[62] Dennis Berthold locates "the ideology of Astor Place" in the ways the two actors "sharply demarcated" emerging distinctions of politics and social class, as Forrest and Macready almost literally personified the characteristics of Democratic Party populism, with its working-class nationalism, and those of Whig elitism, with its cosmopolitanism and concern for property.[63] The discourse of the controversy, up until the night of the massacre, mapped neatly into partisan rhetoric, and newspapers initially cast the rioting in competing terms of the right to expression or the protection of property. "Theatrical audiences in all countries," wrote the editors of the *Herald*, "have assumed the right of expressing their sovereign wrath and displeasure"; while the *Tribune* scolded Macready's May 7 audience for violating the rights of those who, they claimed, had "purchased" silence and peace along with their seats.[64] That the jeers of a theater audience could be regarded by a major newspaper as metonymic of popular voice and could be called sovereign testifies to the entanglement of political discourse with mass forms of entertainment. Clearly, there is something of Debord's spectacle already taking shape at Astor Place, as politics and class relations begin to erupt in and through spectacular cultural forms. At the same time, however, the fact that politics and material relations appeared as spectacle in no way impeded the audience's sense of their right and capacity to intercede.

Forrest's fans took the right to express their sovereign opinion of Macready both seriously and literally, and they interpreted it as the right to expel him, not only from the stage, but from the country as well. The objections to Macready were anti-aristocratic and Anglophobic, as the audience cried "Three groans for the codfish aristocracy!" and "Down with the English hog!" A flyer posted throughout the Bowery and other working-class neighborhoods by the leaders of the Native America Party (and signed by a group called the "American Committee") asked, "Shall Americans or English rule in this city?" Noting an apparently baseless threat by British sailors docked in the harbor, the flyer made its plea in explicitly nativist terms, calling on "Americans" and "working men" to "express their opinions at the English Aristocratic Opera House. We advocate no violence but a free expression of opinion to all public men." To be "public" and "American" was also to be both free and white, and the nativism of the rioters merged with the proslavery politics of the Democrats as well.[65] As the *Herald* reported, one spectator sarcastically linked Macready to Frederick Douglass and a well-known African-American minister: "Three cheers for Macready, Nigger Douglass, and Pete Williams."[66]

If the anti-Macready rioters cast their right to expression in "sovereign" terms that included the power to expel English aristocrats and define the category of the "public," Macready's apologists were no less ambitious. The petition signed by Irving, Duyckinck, Melville, and forty-three of the city's leading citizens also claimed to speak as a public in their promise to secure the rule of law and order: "The undersigned . . . take this public method of requesting you to reconsider your decision, and of assuring you that the good sense and respect for order prevailing in this community will sustain you on the subsequent nights of your performance."[67] What the petition did not mention was that what sustained "good sense and respect for order" was a heavily armed police force. On the day after the massacre, an estimated twenty thousand people gathered in City Hall Park to hear Bowery leaders condemn a use of force that they regarded as bloodsport to satisfy the elite. One speaker decried "the inhumanity of those who, dressed in a little authority, have shown a higher regard for the applause of those who courted a fatal issue than for the lives of their fellow citizens"; another claimed that the militia was called up purely "to please the aristocracy of the city at the expense of the lives of inoffending citizens."[68] In the face of these charges, many who supported Macready and, subsequently, the police remained utterly unapologetic, including the minister of Melville's church, Henry Bellows: "Let no weak and puling sentiments of humanity, no miserable sophistry about the will of the people, allow us to falter in our support of the public authorities, even though it be necessary to fall back upon the military."[69]

Despite what figures like Bellows might have insisted, the events of May 1849 did not unfold as the acts of a "crowd" or a "mob" against "the public."[70] Elias Canetti may provide a rich vocabulary in which to speak of the formation and agency of crowds, but none of his terms precisely applies to Astor Place, because both groups emphatically laid claim to the legitimizing name of "public."[71] Every bit as striking as the divisions exposed and deepened by these events are the common assumptions shared by all involved; in particular, petitioners and protesters alike assumed that they acted as a "public" whose claim to that name was sustained by violence. Together, the riot and massacre showcase how the very split between a massacre coded as the rule of law and a riot coded as populism rests not only on a common claim of public action, but also on a common assumption that the public is the form of association that maintains a sovereign right to violence. In arguing for such a continuity of assumptions underlying both the protesters' and the petitioners' acts, my intent is not to erase significant antagonisms by positing a monolithic public sphere that subsumes both parties, nor is it to discount the overwhelming use of force by that "public" which enjoyed the militia's support. Instead, my point is that, if such contests over the composition of the public were bitter and violent, this is because the public was understood less as a location or a field of action than as the form that grants that action legitimacy. The "public" was not simply conceived as a common space that preceded the riots and the massacre, nor as a shared stage on which events spectacularly unfolded. Rather, the public became the form of sovereignty to which heterogeneous groups in conflict with one another made claim. The public of Astor Place thus emerges in the spectacle of competing claims to sovereign right by groups who come to form themselves in and through that claim.[72] The elite, the rule of law, the crowd, the mob, even the people: each of these can speak and act as a public because all of them function as metonymies of a power that is defined as popular. Ultimately, my term, "democracy's spectacle," refers to those articulations and enactments of sovereign power which are made in the name of a public that can never be more than a metonymy, both because such exceptional associations are themselves only ever partial, and because sovereignty itself is peculiarly metonymic.

## Metonymies of Sovereignty: Theater and Prison in Antebellum Writing

There is a curious relationship between sovereignty and the poetic trope of metonymy; from the *OED*'s first recorded usage of metonymy, in 1547, to the most frequently cited examples of it still, illustrations of metonymy are often figures for sovereignty.[73] The ingestion of bread for the body of Christ in rituals of Communion, the use of the term "the Crown" to designate the monarchy, even allusion to the "White House" to indicate the power of the executive in the U.S. government: each of these convey metonymy's structure of reference by association while also suggesting something about the nature of sovereignty itself. If metonymy proceeds by contiguity, explicating a thing by means of its associations, then sovereignty (for all its pretense to the singularity of power) might also be understood to represent itself through a similar indirection, by its symbols and effects and the spaces in which it operates. In many ways, Schmitt's definition of the sovereign proceeds by metonymy, establishing its contiguity with the terms "decides" and "exception." Similarly, the structure of exception with which the concept has been so closely identified since Schmitt places the sovereign and the subjects of exception in a contiguous, symmetrical relationship with one another.[74] Although metonymy's close correlate, synecdoche, may appear to be representational democracy's particular figure of speech,[75] I want to claim a privileged place for metonymy as the rhetorical mode through which nineteenth-century Americans conceived and articulated the role of sovereignty in the shaping of public life and association. For while every claim made for a sovereign public is necessarily partial, in the manner of synecdoche, there is ultimately no whole (no "people") which is not itself made legible through metonymy—through the establishment of a defining relationship of association or exception.

In the following chapters, I draw on the structure of metonymy to examine the relations of exception that proceed from the popularization of sovereign power. Just as that sovereign form allows disparate groups to act metonymically as a public, so that form also produces a series of homologous subjects of exception, from the slave to the prisoner to that abstract exile whom Tocqueville calls simply the "stranger." Further, in tracking both those formations that go by the name of the public and the exceptional subjects of the public, I also show how antebellum writers consistently imagined the effects of popular sovereignty through a paired set of metonymic spaces—the theater and the prison—which recur with stunning frequency. It is no arbitrary thing that "the power of public opinion" becomes discernible to Frederick Douglass on that morning when he finds himself first at the center of a punitive, impromptu parade on a public throughway and then locked inside the Easton jail, for it is at just such junctures that the odd duality of physical force and intimate coercion emerges as a hallmark of sovereignty in the antebellum era. Douglass's experience of punitive theater is both exceptional and exemplary, but it is also one with parallels in a surprising variety of texts, most famously, perhaps, in Thoreau's "Civil Disobedience." When Thoreau spends a night in the town jail, he is suddenly made "an involuntary spectator and auditor" who is given a view of his "native village in light of the middle ages."[76] Though they stand on opposite sides of exceptional power, with Thoreau trying to exorcise his complicity in that violence which Douglass endures, both of them find expression for the oddly dispersed power of democratic sovereignty in the linked states of imprisonment and spectatorship. Beginning with Tocqueville's and Beaumont's appraisals of democratic culture in the United States in the 1830s, I trace a critique of sovereignty in public life through a group of writers who share a curious fascination with such pairings—a critique that continues in American writing into the 1850s. As metonymies of a public that has been transformed by sovereignty, theater and prison elaborate it by association, which is, indeed, the very thing that is at stake. By tracing their iterations of these metonymic sites, I argue that writers as diverse in their aesthetic and political investments as Lydia Maria Child, Nathaniel Hawthorne, and Herman Melville, all confront that dubious form of association that appears both involuntary and complicit with the power that structures it, each devising particular formal strategies through which to stage the intimacy of involvement with it.

Particularly significant for Beaumont, the spaces of prison and theater initially serve him as emblematic sites where the public might be contained and examined, but they quickly overtake their empirical function and become essential to the structure of his novel. In the 1840s, Child crafted her digressive portraits of civic life in New York by traversing between public spectacles and public institutions, only to arrive at the insight that these spaces are so closely associated with her experience of public belonging as to be almost interchangeable. Indeed, she feels more a prisoner to public opinion in the audience at P. T. Barnum's American Museum than she does during a visit to the penitentiary on Blackwell's Island. A decade later, Hawthorne's *The Blithedale Romance* portrays an intentional community that is alternately defined by its inhabitants as a theatrical illusion or as a reformed penitentiary, indicating how deeply these terms had come to be identified with the dilemmas of democratic association by mid-century. As Hawthorne's narrator, Miles Coverdale, shrinks from a performer, "accustomed to be spectacle of thousands," who is as isolated in her public display as the "blindfold prisoner" in solitary confinement at the notorious Eastern State Penitentiary, so the chief anxiety of the romance becomes the problem of complicity in a society organized as both democratic and sovereign. Finally, with a succinctness characteristic of the strange scenes comprising *The Confidence-Man*, Melville establishes a simple congruency between the public deliberations over character and authenticity on board the *Fidéle* and "the truly warning spectacle of a man hanged by his friends."

While theater and prison, in their diverse iterations, are not the only metonymic spaces I examine where conflicts over the role of sovereignty in the democratic public sphere come to the fore, they are the two that appear in some form in each of the texts in my study. This recurrence is perhaps due to the precision with which theater and prison stage the relationships of entertainment and punishment, pleasure and power, life and subjection, that lie at the heart of democratic sovereignty. In some sense, the spaces of democracy's spectacle are always both theaters and prisons at the same time, because, as Agamben argues, democracy is the form of politics that has "put the freedom and happiness of men into play in the very place . . . that marked their subjection." Agamben calls this democracy's "specific aporia"; Tocqueville calls it a new "thing" in political power that is both expansive and intimate: "Why should it not entirely relieve [citizens] from the trouble of thinking and all the cares of living?"[77] Theaters and prisons are so frequently, so relentlessly twinned in the antebellum imagination in part because democracy is the politics that locates life, pleasure, and subjection in the same place.

Finally, theater and prison also take on a privileged role in imagining and theorizing the forms of social and political association in this period because these metonymies derive from very material spaces that were both defining of and redefined by the antebellum era. The 1830s, 1840s, and 1850s were decades of profound material transformation in the United States, as the very infrastructure of a national culture was beginning to take shape through the construction of canals, railroads, and mail routes that connected remote localities together.[78] As part of this larger impetus toward public works construction, Americans also began to reimagine the prison. Beaumont and Tocqueville traveled to the United States in 1832 precisely to study the innovations in penitentiary reform that were believed to mark the republic's definitive break from the brutality of symbolic, corporal models of punishment. Their jointly published work, *On the Penitentiary System in the United States and Its Application in France*, offers a comparative study of the two novel theories of penitentiary discipline that were widely and intensely debated in the 1830s and '40s: New York's congregate model, organized around silent group labor, and Pennsylvania's infamous system of total solitary confinement. Beaumont and Tocqueville understood the innovations of these two models to represent, at once, democratic improvements aimed more at reforming than punishing the convict and responses to problems which they saw as peculiar to democracy, such as moral contagion among an expanding and leveling public sphere.[79] Other observers, however, saw in these innovations little more than refinements in ancient cruelty. Charles Dickens, in particular, argued that the methods of Pennsylvania's Eastern State Penitentiary engaged in a "slow and daily tampering with the mysteries of the brain" that amounted to torture.[80] For such critics of solitary confinement, the prison was, as Joan Dayan claims, the North's "unsettling counter to servitude," a metonymy for the sovereign power that shaped the public sphere of free and slave states alike, rendering explicit what it meant to be the exceptional subjects of such a power.[81]

A very different measure of the nationalization of public culture during these decades can be found in the emergence of theater as a primary form of popular experience and cultural consumption.[82] As the rioting and massacre at the Astor Place Opera House indicate, theater was no idle pursuit in antebellum America. The fact that a rivalry between actors could become a flashpoint for class antagonism, national identity, and the right to claim the name of the public shows how thoroughly the form of theater mediated relations between Americans, who identified themselves in and with what they watched. Writing about New York City in the 1830s and 1840s, Mary Ryan describes a city of spectators who attended plays, parades, concerts, lectures, and rallies in astonishing numbers. She notes that ten thousand people a night typically attended the New York theaters.[83] But the primacy of theater was not restricted to cosmopolitan centers like New York City alone. Itinerant performers toured the country, and celebrities like Edwin Forrest could draw fiercely loyal crowds in Pittsburgh as easily as they could in the Bowery. Further, as certain American-authored plays became national successes, characters like Forrest's "Metamora" or his "Gladiator" became iconic, with their famous lines peppering the national vernacular.[84] Beyond what might be termed the conventional theater (melodrama, endless revivals of Shakespeare), other forms of popular entertainment, like minstrelsy, traveling lecturers, or demonstrations of spiritualist phenomena, also helped to make the space of the theater and the experience of spectatorship primary ways in which the antebellum public was constituted and lived. Few figures exemplify the fundamental changes that popular entertainment worked in antebellum public life more vividly than P. T. Barnum, who is fairly credited with the creation of some of the earliest forms of mass culture in the United States. As Benjamin Reiss argues, P. T. Barnum's extravagant performances and exhibitions form a "template" for

Debord's society of the spectacle, mediating relations between citizens and linking them together in "the act of cultural consumption."[85] What I call "democracy's spectacle" was not confined to the space of the theater, any more than it was to the space of the prison, but together, these functioned as both evidence and engines of the transformations being wrought in the conception, the material forms, and the lived experience of the antebellum public.

* * *

*Democracy's Spectacle* begins with Tocqueville and Beaumont's writing on the United States in the mid-1830s and ends with Melville's final and most enigmatic novel-length work of prose, *The Confidence-Man*, published in the year of the *Dred Scott* decision. In the three decades before the start of the Civil War and the emancipation of the slaves, the burden of popular sovereignty identified by Tocqueville—which was explicitly linked to slavery, the penal system, and spectacular public culture by Beaumont and others—strained the public sphere, as the violence of force and exception in public life became increasingly apparent. While the stakes of my study lie with this history of popular sovereignty's transformation of public life in the United States, my methodology is emphatically comparative and cross-disciplinary, drawing almost equally on French and American writing, as well as on political theory, treatises on prison reform, dramatic works, journalistic sketches, and prose fiction. Central to my work is the insistence that American literature is a transnational literature, and the first half of the book is devoted to the voluminous studies of antebellum government, society, public institutions, and cultural life that Alexis de Tocqueville and Gustave de Beaumont completed after their 1831–32 tour of the U.S. Redressing a surprising gap in Americanist scholarship, I position the work of Tocqueville and Beaumont squarely within a tradition of writing about the United States that considers democracy as a social and cultural, as well as a political, form. In thus giving to Tocqueville and Beaumont the same level of analysis and close reading that I give to the other authors in my study, I wish to emphasize that "French theory" is by no means an imposition on U.S. literary history, but part of the antebellum era's conception of its own democratic culture.

To that end, in chapter 1 I outline Tocqueville's complex account of popular sovereignty—that strange spherical power with which he identifies both the very new and the very old manifestations of political right and force in the United States. On the one hand, popular sovereignty finds its clearest expression in the phenomenon of public opinion, which "leaves the body alone and goes straight for the soul," substituting an intimate and immaterial penalty for the ancient right of sovereigns to kill. On the other hand, popular sovereignty also operates through a structure of exception in the creation of what Tocqueville calls "strangers among us." What is most striking in this are the ways in which Tocqueville's account of the "stranger's" role in the sovereign public shapes his later discussion of the newly intimate tyrannies of U.S. slavery: "they have, if I may put it in this way, spiritualized despotism and violence." Working against long-standing assumptions of Tocqueville's antidemocratic monarchism, I argue that his apprehensions about democratic and popular forms of power—most famously expressed in the "tyranny of the majority" chapters—have more to do with their simultaneous expansion into the most intimate spaces of human life and their preservation of sovereign violence. A nineteenth-century analyst of something that looks very much like what Foucault terms "biopower," Tocqueville makes possible a critique of democracy's power over life and death that links the new frontiers of sovereignty to the newly intimate tyrannies of slavery.

However, the articulation of this link and a full account of its consequences falls to Beaumont, whose novel, *Marie; or, Slavery in the United States*, is an essential companion to *Democracy in America*. Examining Beaumont's novel, as well as the work on U.S. penitentiary systems that he co-authored with Tocqueville, I show in chapter 2 how he developed and expanded upon Tocqueville's key insights by interrogating the construction and function of race in the U.S. public sphere. *Marie* is primarily known as a foundational work in what becomes the tradition of the tragic mulatta narrative, but it is also remarkable for its unequivocal assertion that majority tyranny is racial tyranny. Focusing on male and female interracial characters, Beaumont describes the work of opinion as an explicitly racialized power through which ideas of difference are imagined and enacted by a potent consensus that he repeatedly represents as spectacle. From the theater to the voting booth to the streets of New York, the spectacle of racialized opinion introduces a violence into everyday life that exposes the incompletion of the American Revolution and invites comparisons to the French Revolution's ongoing nineteenth-century history. But as a revolutionary response to an authority that is contiguous with the public becomes harder for Beaumont to imagine, violence becomes pervasive and conventional as the novel climaxes in Beaumont's fictionalization of the 1834 New York City race riots, preventing the marriage of his protagonists and revealing the public sphere to be a site of terror from which private domestic life offers no retreat.

In the second half of the book, I show how three U.S. authors echoed and addressed the anxieties of democratic power outlined by Beaumont and Tocqueville, beginning with the work of the antislavery activist, Lydia Maria Child. While Child is best known for her novels and antislavery writings, I focus in chapter 3 on a series of sketches originally published in the *National Antislavery Standard*, which she edited from 1841 to 1843. Child's *Letters from New-York* offer an exemplary portrait of the antebellum public sphere, not simply because they treat "public" subjects in all their variety—street life, performance culture, prisons, asylums, even public works projects—but because she innovates in them an essentially public form of writing. Coining the term "vagrancies" to describe the style of the letters, Child invokes the literary tradition of the urban *flâneur*, only to undermine its twin premises of distanced spectatorship and aesthetic judgment. Instead, Child's vagrancies craft a public subject that is digressive, inconstant, and vulnerable; defying expectations of rational observation, Child discloses what might be termed the interior life of the public sphere, and practices a public spectatorship that she considers a foundation for progressive social reform. But rather than merging affectively with the victims of the public's crimes, she finds herself dissolved into the public she wishes to reform, fully complicit in its acts. Like Beaumont, Child roots this complicity in the public exercise of sovereignty, but she interprets that sovereignty broadly: not only does it involve her involuntarily in the literal exercise of lawful violence at a public execution, but it also implicates her in the apparently accidental deaths of two Native American women whom she sees exhibited as curiosities in Barnum's American Museum. Reading Child's letters alongside the work of her more-famous contemporaries, such as Poe and Emerson, I argue that her articulation of complicity as a condition of public life is both emblematic of antebellum anxieties and radical in its scope and expression.

In chapter 4, I examine those anxieties more closely through one of American literature's most ambivalent tales of life in association, Hawthorne's *Blithedale Romance*. From Miles Coverdale's fears of lost autonomy in an intimate community, to Hollingsworth's scheme to transform Blithedale into a prison of sympathetic influence, to the multiple public exhibitions of mesmerism and magnetism by the Veiled Lady, *The Blithedale Romance* repeatedly stages the dilemmas inherent in a community that is alternately defined as a theatrical illusion and a reformed penitentiary. Hawthorne's *Blithedale* has traditionally been read as an indictment of a community that is both impotent and stifling, and critics have extrapolated from this claims of Hawthorne's scathing views of a mass-market public culture composed of passive, politically inert subjects. I trace a new genealogy for the text by examining Hawthorne's relationship to contemporary debates over prison reform and solitary confinement, to propose a very different account of Hawthorne's public sphere. Rather than a public evacuated of political power and distracted by spectacular entertainment, *The Blithedale Romance* describes a public that has become deeply implicated in the various and intimate ways it can punish its members. Haunted by the image of "the blindfold prisoner" as a "spectacle of thousands," the nightmare of the text is a figure who is isolated in public, an exceptional subject of everyone else's "straining eyes." Further, such anxieties cannot be answered by a withdrawal into a remote and solitary privacy, as most critics have argued of *Blithedale*. Instead, I show how the text's fears are most pointedly addressed by a strategy that is first articulated in Hawthorne's prefatory definition of romance—theatricality. In the preface, Hawthorne calls the romance a "theatre, a little removed from the highway of ordinary travel"; eschewing realism, he privileges a stance of estrangement without withdrawal, and with this, I argue, he anticipates an ethos of collective life that finds fullest expression in Melville's *Confidence-Man*.

Throughout the book, I attend to the eccentric aesthetic and formal practices through which each of these writers elaborates the peculiar experiences of association in a democratic, sovereign public. But in my final two chapters I focus on the emergence of a single aesthetic strategy, which Hawthorne and Melville practice to differing degrees, and which both identify with theater. At once distinct from the material space of the theater and inspired by it, the aesthetic of theatricality is, at root, a gesture of representational opacity that addresses and contains the beholder within the aesthetic act. It introduces, I argue, something like a homeopathic response to the spectacle of a democracy whose sovereignty is marked by the exceptional production of strangers. Hawthorne imagines theatricality as an aesthetic and social relation that forces the subject—specifically, Coverdale—to confront his implication in what he watches, forbidding him that stance of remote isolation which Tocqueville describes as the defining feature of the democratic subject. Melville invokes a similar aesthetic of antirealist theatricality in *The Confidence-Man* when he demands that readers "sit down to a work of amusement tolerantly as they sit at a play, and with much the same expectations and feelings," but he takes its possibilities much further. While *The Confidence-Man* is often read as a dark satire of criminality and gullibility in antebellum culture, I argue in chapter 5 that Melville's enigmatic work also thematizes and performs an alternative vision of collective life through this aesthetic of theatricality. Comprising loosely linked scenes occurring among diverse passengers aboard the Mississippi riverboat, *Fidèle*, on the first of April, Melville's text frustrates all attempts to impose upon it any continuity of character or progression of plot. In place of continuity, the text proceeds by means of inexact repetitions which the narrator links to the aesthetics of theater and defines as "more reality than real life itself can show." Understood in this way, theatricality posits a form of mimesis in which an excess of sameness opens up both difference and a threat to self-identity. Through such excesses and inexact repetitions, the text insists on the basic strangeness of character—both individual and collective—ultimately revealing that the stakes of theatricality lie in its capacity to imagine the strangeness of everyone, both to others and themselves. By undermining faith in things like consistency and authenticity, Melville's theatricality demands a tolerance for strangeness that promises a far more mutual, more equitable basis for relations than confidence does. As I trace Melville's repetition of his peculiarly tautological syntax, from "more reality than real life itself" to the community of "strangers still more strange" who populate his floating theater, I show how the text turns Tocquevillean terms like "sameness," "confidence," and "the stranger" inside out to reimagine democratic belonging without the coercive dimensions of sovereignty. In short, the text imagines a world in which the stranger becomes, literally, unexceptional.

While these chapters follow a trajectory that begins with Tocqueville's critical assessment of popular sovereignty and public life and ends with Melville's subversive restaging of democracy's spectacle, I do not claim that theatricality promises either redemption or release from the conditions of complicity and coercion that these writers find in public life. What I do claim is that theatricality does something more than simply represent the effects and conditions that these writers trace. If "democracy's spectacle" is the term for the form through which nineteenth-century Americans came to experience collective sovereignty as a power in which they were implicated, to which they were vulnerable, and of which they were constituted, then "theatricality" describes one of the imaginative enterprises through which antebellum writers tried to envision a public sphere beyond the structures of sovereignty and exceptionalism. Such enterprises found expression in Melville's vision of a constantly shifting plurality of "strangers still more strange," in which all forms of consensus, sameness, and exception dissolve. They also found expression in Child's desire, after watching an enormous crowd gather to witness a public hanging, to "claim kindred with, and include all, without exception, in the circle of our kindly sympathies." Though their choice of terms may suggest otherwise, the same basic longing echoes through Melville's efforts to imagine an association of "strangers still more strange" and Child's call to "include all, without exception." That longing is for the possibility of a community whose only constitutive exception is exceptionalism itself.

# 1 /  "The thing is new": Sovereignty and Slavery in *Democracy in America*

In a long footnote appended to *Democracy in America*'s most famous chapter, "Tyranny of the Majority," Tocqueville offers two anecdotes whose relationship to each other appears, at first, to lie in the illustration of his claim that democratic government in the United States is by no means too weak, "as many Europeans make out," because the authority and operation of government are not necessarily limited to the state. In the first, "a striking example of the excess to which despotism of the majority may lead," an enraged Baltimore mob quashes the freedom of the press, seeking out the editors of a newspaper that had published criticism of the War of 1812. Tocqueville describes how, after first destroying the presses and offices of the newspaper, the mob hunted down the editors, who had taken refuge in the city jail, then broke into the jail and beat them: "one was killed on the spot and the others left for dead." In the second anecdote, Tocqueville relates a conversation between himself and a Philadelphia man: "I once said to a Pennsylvanian: 'Please explain to me why in a state founded by Quakers and renowned for its tolerance, freed negroes are not allowed to use their rights as citizens? They pay taxes; is it not right for them to vote?'" The man's response is exemplary of America's duplicitous articulation of citizenship: "'Do not insult us by supposing that our legislators would commit an act of such gross injustice and intolerance.'" The man goes on to explain that it is not for the state to enforce racial exclusion, because that work is reserved for the majority: "'Now, the majority is filled with the strongest prejudices against

Negroes, and the magistrates do not feel strong enough to guarantee the rights granted to them by the lawmakers.'"[1]

Democracy's autoimmune response appears to be in full operation in both of these stories, as ostensibly "popular" agents take power upon themselves, acting in place of—even against—the authority of the law and the state in order to prevent the exercise of rights specifically associated with democratic citizenship.[2] The Baltimore mob first determines the limits to press freedom and then assumes the work of enforcement, breaking open a prison in order to punish those whom the law would protect. The Pennsylvania majority claims the authority to regulate citizenship, denying the franchise to lawful citizens. The acts of both the "mob" and the "majority" described in Tocqueville's footnote amount to double claims of sovereign right with respect to both the state and its subjects. But as much as the pro-war mob and the racist majority enact an authority over and against the state, they also target with intimate precision the acts and opinions of fellow citizens. It is not merely the editors of the dissenting newspaper whom the angry Baltimore mob seeks to discipline, but also those who might read their paper and imbibe its opinions. Taking coercion even further, the Pennsylvania majority no longer requires physical force to ensure the racial exclusivity of the franchise, because, as the man brags to Tocqueville, it has so terrorized free blacks that they "voluntarily abstain from appearing." What Tocqueville seeks to illustrate with this footnote is how mechanisms that promised to liberate individuals from the tyranny of the state—the power of opinion, popular sovereignty—have become means of redeploying the most violent and intimate forms of domination and subjection.

Together, the two anecdotes also illustrate the ways in which *Democracy in America* resists and complicates two common, though somewhat conflicting, tendencies in the reception and interpretation of Tocqueville's work—the assumption of both its antidemocratic biases and its celebration of voluntary association in the U.S. public sphere.[3] On the one hand, while Tocqueville's anxieties about popular sovereignty are manifest throughout the text, the Pennsylvania anecdote suggests that it is not the expansion of the franchise that he fears, since his sympathies appear to lie with the freed blacks who are denied its exercise. On the other hand, while it is sometimes assumed, as Mary Ryan has written, that "Tocqueville's democracy was composed of associated people, of voluntary organizations,"[4] it is the primary claim of the chapter to which Tocqueville's footnote is appended that U.S. democracy is also one of

involuntary association. Though they appear in a footnote, these anecdotes are emblematic of a crucial strain in Tocqueville's wide-ranging
analysis of the nature and effects of popular sovereignty in the United
States, namely, a critique of the form of society that democracy has
yielded which cautions against its expansive powers and which cannot
simply be dismissed as aristocratic or antidemocratic. A more complete
account of this aspect of Tocqueville's thought begins with a consideration of the ways in which popular sovereignty—"the cause and the end
of all things"—structures association as both involuntary and explicitly
exceptional, creating subjects who are at once empowered and made vulnerable by their involvement with it. In this chapter, I turn sustained
attention on *Democracy in America* to recover his model of the U.S. public sphere as it is shaped by such a view of popular sovereignty, and to
recapture through this a conception of sovereignty in the first half of the
nineteenth century that has been eclipsed by twentieth-century preoccu-
pations with the power of a centralized state. In this, I read Tocqueville's
text in two distinct ways, finding in it a strategy that is expressly critical
of the new forms that sovereignty has assumed under U.S. democracy,
while attending to a blindspot that is symptomatic of the very model of
power which is his object.

Tocqueville's footnote serves to illustrate his thesis that political power has preserved and redeployed sovereignty by migrating out of state
monopoly, but it opens an unresolved question: Why does he require
two discrete stories in order to do this? If both stories speak to the same
basic "tyranny," why must he treat separately the attack on the white
Baltimore journalists and the de facto disenfranchisement of the freed
blacks of Pennsylvania? This footnote is emblematic of another feature of
Tocqueville's text that demands a fuller accounting: its formal, structural
performance of exception in its treatment of slavery and Native American
dispossession. Throughout *Democracy in America*, Tocqueville separates
his analysis of the vulnerabilities of white and non-white Americans to
the new powers of democracy, relegating his discussion of blacks and
Native Americans to the footnote quoted above and to a long chapter at
the end of volume 1. As Michael Denning notes, "Racial division . . . is
the exception on which Tocqueville as the first theorist of American exceptionalism founders," adding that "an adequate theory of American
exceptionalism must be able to unite 'democracy in America' with 'slavery in America' and 'Indian dispossession in America' in a persuasive
way."[5] In Tocqueville's insistent separation of racial tyranny from the
rest of his study, he does not escape the exceptionalist social and political

structures which he has made the object of his analysis. However, by replicating his model of popular sovereignty in his discussion of slavery, I argue, he implicitly forges the unified theory of American exceptionalism for which Denning calls. Tocqueville's minute accounting of the uneven effects of sovereignty on the subjects of American democracy—all of its subjects—outlines a power that has dispersed and popularized exception in the creation of the figure he calls the "stranger." First mentioned in the chapters on majority tyranny, as the internal exile of the public sphere, the stranger returns in the chapter on the "Three races that inhabit the territory of the United States," as the creation of slavery and racial ideology. To unite Tocqueville's theory of U.S. democracy with his ambivalent attempts to contend with racial exception and dispossession, I argue, one must simply follow the incarnations of his "stranger" as the peculiar offspring of democracy and sovereignty.

## Popular Sovereignty and the Politics of Life

I want to begin with the end of *Democracy in America* to highlight where Tocqueville imagined his own narrative might lead. Read for its narrative effect, as well as its anatomy of social and political forms, the text concludes tragically, with the death of the public sphere in a world of disassociation, withdrawal into private consumption, and expansive regulation. *Democracy in America* famously concludes with a warning that is addressed as much to "democracy" in the abstract as to "America." But in Tocqueville's attempt to articulate this warning, in trying to name the thing against which democratic societies must guard themselves, he confronts a peculiar inadequacy of language to his task. At the close of his second volume, Tocqueville arrives at the discussion of a form of society which he calls new, but which has hovered at the margins of the two volumes and nearly seven hundred pages of his study. It involves a power to which the United States "could lay itself peculiarly open," but which he finds difficult to name. He begins by calling it "despotism" but quickly dispenses with that term, seeing that this is a "despotism" without a despot: "In past ages there had never been a sovereign so absolute . . . that he could himself alone . . . administer every part of a great empire. No one had ever tried to subject all his people indiscriminately to the details of a uniform code, nor personally to prompt and lead every single one of his subjects" (*Democracy in America*, 690). This is despotism of a "different character," one which is broader and yet also "milder" than previous models, one which brings "all public power" into itself in order to "impinge deeper and more habitually into the sphere of private interests." Its tactics are those of "schoolmasters," not tyrants, but as yet, the existing terms of power and sovereignty fail to describe it (691). "I have myself vainly searched for a word which will exactly express the whole of the conception I have formed. Such old words as 'despotism' and 'tyranny' do not fit. The thing is new, and as I cannot find a word for it, I must try to define it" (691–92).

In order to define a thing that exceeds the limited language of political and social analysis, Tocqueville engages in a kind of distopic reverie through which he visualizes an entire world living under this new "thing." His loss of words is thus answered with a lengthy, speculative tableau that indicates how much Tocqueville's study owes to a kind of poetics:

> I am trying to imagine under what novel features despotism may appear in the world. In the first place, I see an innumerable multitude of men, alike and equal, constantly circling around in pursuit of the petty and banal pleasures with which they glut their souls. Each one of them, withdrawn into himself, is almost unaware of the fate of the rest. . . . Over this kind of men stands an immense, protective power which is alone responsible for securing their enjoyment and watching over their fate. That power is absolute, thoughtful of detail, orderly, provident, and gentle. It would resemble a parental authority if, fatherlike, it tried to prepare its charges for a man's life, but on the contrary, it only tries to keep them in perpetual childhood. It likes to see the citizens enjoy themselves, provided they think of nothing but enjoyment. It gladly works for their happiness but wants to be the sole agent and judge of it. It provides for their security, foresees and supplies their necessities, facilitates their pleasures, manages their principle concerns, directs their industry . . . Why should it not entirely relieve them from the trouble of thinking and all the cares of living? (*Democracy in America*, 692–93)[6]

The social space that Tocqueville imagines at the end of his study is a kind of anti-public, a network of personal relationships and private gratification, where individuals live in close proximity, "touch" one another, "but feel nothing" (693). Though he calls them "citizens," this "innumerable multitude" does not act with the legitimizing power of a public or a people; instead, these citizens seem to be subjects only, molded and shaped by a power that is over them, not of them.

As Tocqueville describes the world of this new "thing," he never says in what, precisely, its novelty lies.[7] Instead, as the portrait builds, he allows certain peculiarities to come into relief. "Freedom," for example, does not appear in these passages, evidently replaced by a form of regulated enjoyment, while "equality" seems to have been displaced by a perpetual, universal childhood. To maintain the viability of such distortions, the province of this "immense, protective power" must be both broad and deep, and throughout his portrait Tocqueville describes its operation on both masses of men and on individuals. "Thoughtful of detail," it attends to minute particularities across an "innumerable multitude." As the "sole agent and judge" of the happiness it produces, it also becomes intimate and individuated, incorporating into the sphere of public concern the necessities, securities, concerns, and pleasures of life: "Having thus taken each individual in turn in its powerful grasp and molded him in its manner, the sovereign then extends its embrace to include the whole of society. It covers the whole surface of it with a network of complicated little rules, minute and uniform."[8] To make the "whole of society" the province of power, Tocqueville says, "each individual" must be formed according to the manner ("*guise*") of that power. With this, Tocqueville grants this power a name for the first time: "*le souverain*" implies an agent invested with power, though as he uses it here, the term does not appear to coincide with any particular state or governing entity.[9]

Previously designated simply as "that power," the "sovereign" named here remains elusive. It possesses both the capacity to mold and a manner after which to mold, but its own shape is unclear. Forming individuals and covering social life with its blanket of petty rules, it fully regulates both the individual and the social, but it is not reducible to either. The novelty of this sovereign, it seems, is characterized neither by its form nor by its acts, but by its cumulative effects: "it is not at all tyrannical, but it hinders, restrains, enervates, stifles, and stultifies" (*Democracy in America*, 692). Emerging through the effects of hindrance and restraint, it is primarily known through the limits it imposes on "living"—the modes of existence it conditions for both individual and collective subjects. As individuals are "shaped" in the grasp of this power and configured into subjects of enjoyment, so the "whole of society" is also shaped, imagined as a sphere of comfort in which the habits, desires, and elements of life have become the province of politics. In this, it is not simply the case that the private sphere (what might be equated with property ownership and domestic space in a classic public-private division) has become politicized; instead, both the collective and individual subjects of Tocqueville's tableau take their shape through the politicization of the most intimate spaces of life—the assurance of comfort and enjoyment through the subtle networks of regulation which hinder, restrain, and enervate, without apparent prohibition.

With his portrait of the life of individual citizens and the whole of the social "shaped" by a power that is the bearer of a sophisticated network of regulation—a power which he never quite names, but which he passingly terms "the sovereign"—Tocqueville would seem to have wandered far in six hundred pages from his earliest discussion of the sovereignty of the people in chapter 4 of the first volume: "The people reign over the American political world as God reigns over the universe. It is the cause and the end of all things; everything rises out of it and is absorbed back into it" (*Democracy in America*, 60). At a glance, the popular "sovereign" that appears in the early chapters might resemble a classic Rousseauvian one, but unlike Rousseau, Tocqueville never imagines a moment of contract or constitution for this sovereign.[10] What characterizes "popular sovereignty" for him is that it seems to be always already there, in a relation of mutual constitution with the people (58–60). The people may give rise to power, but they must also be understood as already subject to the very power that ostensibly originates in them. They do not precede the constitution of the sovereign, either as individual subjects or as a collective, so they must come into being along with it. When Tocqueville begins to imagine the threat posed to democracy at the end of his study, it initially appears as if the people have been ousted from their position as cause and end to become little more than the effects of a power that now stands over them. But despite what appears to be a new form of subjection to something outside the people, Tocqueville does not abandon the concept of popular sovereignty as he struggles to name this new thing. Instead, he insistently preserves the term, suggesting that popular sovereignty remains operative within this thing he seeks to define:

> Centralization is combined with sovereignty of the people. That gives them a chance to relax. They console themselves for being under schoolmasters by thinking that they have chosen them themselves. Each individual lets them put the collar on, for he sees that it is not a person or class of persons, but society itself who hold the end of the chain. The citizens quit their state of dependence just long enough to choose their masters and then fall back into it. (693)

If "society itself . . . holds the chain," then the novelty that Tocqueville imagines lies less in the idea of power's centralization—its location in a state apparatus—than in the particular form of sovereignty that this pow-er takes—its modes of operation. In this reading, the questions begged by Tocqueville's warning have less to do with analyzing how "despotism" gradually emerges from "democracy" than with understanding the con-tinuity between the iterations of a single sovereignty whose location is as fluid as its reach is vast.[11] Sovereignty—popular or otherwise—conceived as the "cause and the end of all things" seems already to contain the elements of the broad politicization of social and individual life that Toc-queville conjures in his tableau, and despite the conceit of an imaginary world, Tocqueville may in fact be narrating the elements of this "new thing" throughout the whole of *Democracy in America*. In his attempt to define how an expansive power comes to shape both social life and indi-vidual life, Tocqueville outlines the emergence of a novel form of politics in 1835 that is echoed 140 years later in Foucault's efforts to name a simi-larly "new thing" in nineteenth-century political power. In the final lec-ture from his 1975–76 course at the Collége de France, Foucault invokes the term that marks the different form that political power took at the beginning of the nineteenth century: "The new nondisciplinary power is applied not to man-as-body but to the living man, man-as-living be-ing . . . After the anatomo-politics of the human body established in the course of the nineteenth century, we have . . . the emergence of . . . what I would call a 'biopolitics' of the human race."[12]

Foucault begins by defining biopolitical power in distinction from disciplinary power's attention to the individuated body. Unlike disciplin-ary power, biopolitics is characterized by its intervention in domains, such as birth control and public hygiene, which regulate and define an entire population, a "multiple body," as a problem for both political and scientific regulation. But rather than a total displacement of discipline or its replacement by a biopolitical focus on masses, what the nineteenth century witnesses, according to Foucault, is the coming together of these two forms—individuated discipline and mass regulation through the "norms" that circulate between them.

> To say that power took possession of life in the nineteenth centu-ry, or to say that power at least takes life under its care in the nine-teenth century, is to say that it has, thanks to the play of technolo-gies of discipline on the one hand and technologies of regulation on the other, succeeded in covering the whole surface that lies between the organic and the biological, between body and population.[13]

This "possession of life" that politics assumes requires both old and new technologies working together to cover the "whole surface" between the individual and the collective, and that "surface" designates both the individual body, subject to disciplinary power, and the space of collective life, politicized in new ways. Working in conjunction with traditional sovereignty, Foucault argues, new technologies complement the sovereign's exceptional right "to take life and let live," with the new power to "make live and let die," ultimately completing "one of the greatest transformations political right underwent in the nineteenth century."[14] The resonance of Foucault's language with Tocqueville's cautionary vision is striking: the "thing" that interests Tocqueville also "covers the whole surface," blanketing "each citizen" and "the whole of society" alike "with a network of complicated little rules, minute and uniform."[15] For Tocqueville, as for Foucault, normalizing regulations become blankets of power when they cover both individual and collective bodies, complementing models of disciplinary power with new technologies of mass regulation. Earlier forms of sovereignty are ostensibly displaced, only to reappear in conjunction with new techniques. Finally, both the citizen and the mass become subjects, shaped and molded through subtle forms of restraint, hindrance, and the regulation of enjoyment that condition the possibilities of life. "Why should it not entirely relieve them from the trouble of thinking and all the cares of living?" (*Democracy in America*, 692).

In reading Tocqueville alongside Foucault, my point is not to substitute Foucault's word for the "thing" that Tocqueville refuses to name, thereby resolving the studied ambiguity of Tocqueville's phrase. Emerging as it does from his long, imaginative tableau, Tocqueville's "thing" is by no means lacking for language to describe it. What Foucault supplies instead of a word is a fuller context for the newness that Tocqueville sees in it—a narrative of sorts for the reconfigurations of power and sovereignty in the midst of which Tocqueville finds himself, writing on the political and social transformations wrought by "democracy" in the United States in the 1830s.[16] Specifically, the intersection of discipline and biopolitics that Foucault describes, as well as the complementing of traditional sovereignty by the new power to "make live," helps to clarify a movement in *Democracy in America*, through which the forms of power Tocqueville describes appear both continuous and novel, both present and emerging. This is nowhere more apparent than in the persistence of the word "sovereign," from the early chapters of *Democracy in America* to Tocqueville's final warning. Foucault argues that the new power to regulate life marks a substantive transformation in political right, but all the while, he maintains, the most basic and ancient requirement of sovereignty—the exceptional right to kill—remains. "How can a power such as this kill, if it is true that its basic function is to improve life, to prolong its duration, to improve its chances, to avoid accidents, and to compensate for failings?" Foucault argues that this apparent contradiction is resolved by a sovereign state with the capacity to forge distinctions within and between populations, between those who are made to live and those who are allowed to die. Such divisions within the population become possible through the deployment of a very specific discourse— biological racism—which becomes "the basic mechanism of power as it is exercised by modern states."[17]

The appearance in Tocqueville's *Democracy in America* of a "thing" that echoes through Foucault's definition of biopower begs a similar question: if democracy institutes a political order that promises to take over "all the cares of living," how can it also institute a politics that kills, enslaves, dispossesses? Since the sovereignty which concerns Tocqueville is "popular," Foucault's concept of "State racism" does not offer a perfect analogy; nonetheless, the social and political order that Tocqueville describes is no less reliant on forms of division and distinction that preserve the "sovereign's" right of death. But who, precisely, is this "sovereign"? For Tocqueville to assert, in the opening pages of his study, that "equality of conditions" is the "novelty" that strikes him "more vividly" than any other during his travels through an expansionist slave society, that it is "the creative element from which each particular fact derived," he is obviously writing in the context of a potent caesura in the midst of social and political life. But if we are to take seriously and literally his claim that equality is the creative element ("*le fait générateur*") from which "each particular fact" of American life derives, we must come to see this break in the social as tied in essential ways to the mechanisms of popular sovereignty—and thus of "democracy" itself. Tocqueville does not ignore the material facts of slavery or Native American dispossession, however dazzled by the "creative element" of equality he is. These questions occupy a place in his text that is, in all senses of the word, exceptional. In order to understand the origin and ends of racial division in Tocqueville's study—indeed, in order to understand this "new thing" that America and democracy have introduced into the world—it is necessary to trace both this doubled-edged "sovereignty" and this generative "equality" that, together, drive the text.

## The Public and Its Strangers

In *The Structural Transformation of the Public Sphere*, Jürgen Habermas argues that Tocqueville's analysis of despotism and majority tyranny in the United States signals that, by the 1830s, "the original relationship of public and private sphere [have] in fact dissolved; the contours of the bourgeois public sphere eroded." With this, Habermas concedes the historical specificity of his own model, claiming that the transformation he traces—away from a state-governed public and toward a sphere of private citizens engaged in rational-critical debate—was essentially over by the mid-nineteenth century. The transformed public sphere of the eighteenth century had sought to create an order "in which domination itself was dissolved," in a medium of public opinion that "wanted to be neither a check on power nor power itself." However, Tocqueville's account of the "tyranny of public opinion" points to what Habermas sees as a series of "perversions" to that "original" public, which convert this sphere into a space of power, and opinion into an "agent of repression." For Habermas, what Tocqueville's analysis reveals is essentially the return of the state to the public through centralization and "the despotism of an increasingly bureaucratized" administrative apparatus. This, he argues, brought about the end of the public's critical function; no longer a discrete "sphere" of private property owners gathered together in rational debate, the "public" had "penetrated more spheres of society" and, at the same time, "lost its political function." The new public, which, Habermas claims, had radically altered European civil society in the eighteenth century, and along with it the forms of private and intimate life, had become obsolete in less than a hundred years.[18]

But even as Habermas invokes Tocqueville to narrate the decline of the sphere he theorizes, showing how Tocqueville's analysis reveals the obsolescence of his eighteenth-century European model, questions remain about whether that model was ever appropriate to the U.S. context. The status of Habermas's public sphere model in the U.S. has been heavily contested by critics and historians for more than two decades, and at stake in this debate is the question of whether the forms of coercion and domination that become so evident in the nineteenth century are later "perversions," as Habermas claims, or are endemic to the civil society and political culture of liberal democracy in the U.S. from the beginning. The earliest challenges to the Habermassian model questioned the usefulness to understanding the public sphere of the Early Republic exclusively through print mediation and circulation, given the centrality to

eighteenth-century American civic life of religious experience and oratorical performance. Focusing on alternative public spaces, these critics
also challenged Habermas's emphasis on rationality over affect, sympathy, and sentiment in public discourse, pointing to the ways in which
the Early American public relied on precisely those modes of affective
coercion which a "rational" sphere must expunge.[19]

More recent challenges have built on this critique, focusing on Habermas's assumptions of free association and voluntary communication
in a public sphere allegedly "free" of domination: whether this model is
understood as a historical precedent or an unrealized ideal, how is it possible to conceive of the freedom from domination which it presumes—
simply as an extension of the presumed independence of the public from
the state?[20] Even for theorists who have modified and updated Habermas's original model, the concept of the public sphere rests on such a
presumption—in Michael Warner's words, a public strictly understood
must be "organized by something other than the state" in order for it to
be "sovereign with respect to the state."[21] In Warner's revisions to the
Habermassian thesis, the public becomes a self-organized discourse
that creates a relation among strangers through "mere attention," and
this structure applies, regardless of whether that public is understood
as dominant or marginal, as congruent with the "people" or as a coun-
terpublic formed in explicit dissent from the state.[22] In this way, he argues, both publics and counterpublics participate in "the being of the
sovereign" without owing their existence to the state. On the one hand,
Warner's theorization of counterpublics indicates how reductive it is to
equate the idea of the public with yet another function or effect of an
expansive liberal state, or to understand it as little more than a mask
under which state power conceals itself. The public is, in some measure,
"sovereign," Warner argues, precisely because it is not reducible to the
state, suggesting that sovereignty lies outside of both. On the other hand,
what is less clear in his work is where that sovereignty intersects with
domination.[23] In other words, while it is possible to conceive a public as
separate and apart from the state, as long as it becomes a part of the "being of the sovereign," can such a public, even in the ideal, exist without
coercion, domination, and force?

Much of the ambiguity around the concept of the public sphere concerns the function of force, domination, and sovereignty in it, especially
as these connect the public to the state and the individual subject to the
public. At the same time the public is organized by something other
than the state, as theorists like Warner argue, it also depends upon it in

multiple ways, either by partaking of the same sovereignty or by becoming equivalent to a sphere of citizenship that is regulated by the state. The continued influence of the Habermassian model on American literary scholarship can be measured in the persistence of concepts like "emancipation," "abstraction," and "disembodiment" to describe the privileges of citizenship as both prerequisite and reward to participation in public life. Implicit in such terms is Habermas's contention that public life is contiguous with a certain formation of critical citizenship, so that the subject of the public is partly collapsed into the citizen, whose activities are imagined in separation from other "spheres," designated as private or intimate. While spheres such as the private, the intimate, and the interior are understood in Habermas's model to be effects of a public that privileges such separation, these categories seem to presume a subject already capable of orienting himself to the public. As Warner insists, "mere attention" can constitute a public, but who or what is the subject of that attention? Resisting the tendency to assume a subject that precedes the public, critics such as Lauren Berlant, Joan Dayan, Russ Castronovo, and Christopher Castiglia have turned instead to the ways that U.S. citizenship, rather than abstracting subjects from private and intimate life, regulates both of these. In this, they offer a fuller account of the public's role, alongside the state and in collaboration with it, in forming the subjects that comprise it.[24] An attentiveness to the formative dimension of the public, Castiglia argues, "requires that we recognize the institutions of the civil sphere, not simply as sites of popular criticism of the state . . . but as locations where subjectivity and state interest blend into affective hybrids that create both the possibilities for independent critique and forms of self-management that limit those very possibilities."[25]

Tocqueville's *Democracy in America* is an ideal text for such a critical task. Throughout both volumes of his study, Tocqueville describes the ways in which civil society in America acts in partial collaboration with the state, limning the possibilities of life for subjects who conceive of themselves as "free." Long before he arrives at his vision of the new thing, under which "citizens quit their state of dependence just long enough to choose their masters and then fall back into it" (*Democracy in America,* 693), Tocqueville grapples with the coexistence in the U.S. of unfreedom and popular sovereignty. "I know of no country in which, generally speaking, there is less independence of mind and true freedom than in America" (255). The problem that Tocqueville sees is not a repressive state, one that censors speech or writing; the problem is that "no one is tempted" to speak or write in ways critical of "the power which dominates in the United States"—the power of the majority which acts under the sovereignty of the people (256). More than simply noting the coincidence of this unfreedom with liberal democratic political forms, Tocqueville comes to see them as essentially linked, arguing that such a profound limitation of thought could only emerge in the context of popular sovereignty. In this, Tocqueville provides one of the earliest and most thorough narratives of the modes of subject-formation and the forms of domination to which the public, civil sphere in a liberal democracy can uniquely give rise. While a "king's power is physical only," Tocqueville writes, "the majority is invested with both physical and moral authority, which acts as much upon the will as upon behavior, and at the same moment prevents both the act and the desire to do it" (254).

Tocqueville traces the invisible and immaterial power of opinion, which he sees permeating public life in the United States, to the dispersal of sovereignty effected by the rejection of monarchy, and throughout, he repeatedly contrasts the sovereignty that invests a collective body with the sovereignty of kings. From nearly his first mention of popular sovereignty in *Democracy in America*, Tocqueville troubles the question of its precise location and source, first calling the people "the cause and the end of all things," then quickly renaming that "people" a "majority": "In the U.S., as in all countries where the people reign, the majority rules in the name of the people" (173). Tocqueville hints at a usurpation, as popular sovereignty gives way to "the absolute sovereignty of the will of the majority." But the reach of sovereignty does not diminish as it moves from "people" to "majority," which is at best a metonymy and at worst a usurper. Instead, the majority becomes, in his most infamous chapter, an agent of "tyranny," "for in democracies, there is nothing outside the majority capable of resisting it" (246). Even as the "sovereign" shrinks, transparently masquerading as the people, the majority's power becomes "not only predominant but irresistible," affecting "even the smallest habits of life" (247) and occluding everything that falls outside of it:

> Formerly tyranny used the clumsy weapons of chains and hangmen; nowadays even despotism, though it seemed to have nothing more to learn, has been perfected by civilization.
>
> Princes made violence a physical thing, but our contemporary democratic republics have turned it into something as intellectual as the human will it is intended to constrain. Under the absolute government of a single man, despotism, to reach the soul, clumsily

struck at the body . . . but in democratic republics that is not at all how tyranny behaves; it leaves the body alone and goes straight for the soul. (255)

It would seem that the body disappears twice in Tocqueville's account of the differences between monarchic and popular sovereignty: first, the monarch no longer serves as the embodiment of sovereign power who, in turn, gives a body to society;[26] and second, the king's power over the bodies of his subjects—in particular, his power to do violence to their bodies—is replaced by a power that "leaves the body alone and goes straight for the soul." With this line, Thomas Dumm notes, Tocqueville articulates an insight usually credited to Foucault: the "modern soul" has become the basic target of political power.[27]

In *Democracy and Punishment*, Dumm focuses on this apparent shift from "body" to "soul" to argue that Tocqueville's description of democratic tyranny anticipates Foucault's disciplinary society. "Liberal democratic discourse began," Dumm argues, "at the moment when the principle of sovereignty escaped from the prison of the king's body and began to invest itself in the procedures and techniques which would allow it to be reproduced in the 'least body of the condemned man.'"[28] Calling the penitentiary "the ideal democratic institution," Dumm argues that Tocqueville's most dire assessments of power in *Democracy in America*—the sections on "tyranny of the majority" in volume 1 and the warning against the new "thing" at the end of volume 2—"can be shown to have derived from Beaumont and Tocqueville's study of the penitentiary system."[29] This derivation is nearly direct for Dumm, who sees in both Tocqueville's analysis of democratic institutions and the study of penitentiary discipline a common interest in a concept of individual perfectibility and the production of good citizens—in short, "a struggle over the souls of men."[30] The transformation Tocqueville describes, from the embodied sovereign's violence on the bodies of his subjects to the invisible and immaterial power of thought, exemplifies the movement toward disciplinary power that makes the penitentiary such a tempting metaphor for Dumm. He sees Tocqueville's only error as the "misidentification" of a centralized state as the source of despotism: "'the network of petty, complicated rules' . . . originated not in a central government, but in the penal institutions scattered across the landscape of the various states."[31] However, insofar as Tocqueville suggests a disembodiment of power under democracy, he also suggests its dispersal and resistance to location in any central site, metaphoric or actual. In Tocqueville's analysis of the power, which he alternately calls "tyranny," "omnipotence," "despotism," "sovereignty," and sometimes simply "the thing," he makes it clear that it exists, in its countless effects, in the spheres and subjects which seem to come into being along with it and through it. In Claude Lefort's words: "The locus of power is an empty place. It cannot be occupied . . . and it cannot be represented. Only the mechanisms of the exercise of power are visible."[32]

In the narrative that Tocqueville proposes, the power that once invested the king with the exceptional right to commit physical violence also gave him a surplus of bodies, while this new tyranny seems at first to require no embodiment at all. Referring to this power most consistently by its tyrannical "nature," Tocqueville sees it acting over the immaterial regions of "thought," "soul," and "will," and he names its primary mechanism "opinion": "What is a majority, in its collective capacity, if not an individual with opinions, and usually with interests, contrary to that of another individual, called the minority?" (*Democracy in America*, 251). Although majority opinion initially appears innocuous enough—simply standing against the opinion of another, smaller "individual"—the power of the majority to occlude everything outside of it quickly converts majority opinion into a far more potent, coercive force. Throughout volume 1, opinion functions as the "invisible power . . . one almost impossible to lay hands on" (254). Tocqueville argues that opinion profoundly impacts the intellectual and cultural life of the United States; he claims that it "has enclosed thought within a formidable fence," leaving citizens fearful of alienation, isolation, or even exile should they diverge from its views (254–55). But more often than it punishes individuals for crimes committed, this tyranny restrains and hinders them, preventing "both the act and the desire to do it" (254). In this sense, the power Tocqueville describes is more formative than reformative; it does not presume a subject capable of transgression, because the subject's will and desire have been prepared for it.

But does such a power, whose mechanism is opinion and whose location is an "empty place," function without bodies? The tendency of two of Tocqueville's most attentive readers—Dumm and Lefort—has been to see in this internalization of power a "process of disincorporation." "Democratic society," Lefort argues, "is instituted as a society without a body, as a society which undermines the representation of an organic totality," not only because "popular sovereignty" deposes the monarch, but also because it requires that the citizen be "abstracted from all the networks in which his social life develops" to become a "mere statistic."[33]

Lefort refers here to the purported disembodiment that is the privilege of the enfranchised citizen, but in the eighteenth and nineteenth centuries, this disembodiment both presumed and concealed the corporeal conditions of U.S. citizenship. The rhetorical displacement of the body with the soul as the primary target of political power in readings of Tocqueville tends to reproduce the disembodiment of the abstract citizen who populates a public sphere of discourse. Countering such narratives of democracy's disincorporation, Paul Downes has suggested that the sovereign power that the American Revolution instituted might better be understood as a translation of the monarch's surplus bodies into democracy's own version of the same. Downes argues that the rhetoric of political discourse in the early republic is, in many ways, less "democratic" than it is anti-monarchic, resulting in a self-understanding that is fully entangled with monarchism through its attempts at negation—a rhetorical tendency that Tocqueville constantly replicates in trying to discern the features of democratic politics and culture in the United States. Because of this entanglement, republican discourse reproduces the very elements of monarchism that it seeks to repudiate, such as the "duplicitous ontology" of the king's two bodies. Specifically, Downes argues that American political ideology transformed the doctrine of the king's doubled, mortal and immortal, bodies into its own doctrine of the doubled democratic subject—a subject of natural right as well as civil right, the Bill of Rights as well as the Constitution, whose defining act is to "lose" his body in the moment of abstraction that is the magic of the voting booth.[34]

Although Tocqueville asserts that power "leaves the body alone and goes straight for the soul,"[35] his account of public opinion and majority tyranny also troubles claims of democracy's disincorporation. When Tocqueville uses the example of punishment to describe the transformation of power under a democracy—"formerly tyranny used the clumsy weapons of chains and hangmen . . . "—he invokes power in the specific sense of sovereign power, understood as the exceptional right to enact corporal punishment. In his example, Tocqueville emphasizes that this power is intimate and interiorizing, that it posits the "soul" as the deep site of subjectivity.[36] But if, by this, Tocqueville also suggests that the "body" has ceased to be a target of power, the question arises whether this new power can be conceived of as "sovereign" at all. In one sense, Tocqueville's phrase clearly suggests power's disembodiment, but in another sense, "leaving" the body suggests that the body has come to occupy a special case in this new politics, becoming something like a remainder, or an exception in its own right. Just as, in Downes's argument,

American political discourse reinvented the doctrine of the king's two bodies, so it might also be said that this discourse both reinvented and reproduced the sovereign right to violence, transforming the nature of that violence without losing its sovereign character. Parsing the question of sovereignty's persistence or transformation in Tocqueville's reading of U.S. democracy requires a more careful attention to the fate of this left-alone "body" under majority rule. In other words, by attending to the ways in which Tocqueville characterizes public opinion and majority tyranny as translations of sovereign power, I want to emphasize that the democratic subject he describes is an explicitly embodied one, and the power that acts over and through it is both material and corporeal. With this, a fuller account becomes possible of how democracy becomes a politics of "life" in his study—as well as one of enslavement, dispossession, and death.

As Tocqueville continues to describe the new function of political power in the passage on majority tyranny, he converts the "majority" into a single voice and then begins to speak as the "master" who has exacted democracy's penalty:

> The master no longer says: "Think like me or you die." He does say: "You are free not to think as I do; you can keep your life and property and all; but from this day you are a stranger among us. You can keep your privileges in the township, but they will be useless to you, for if you solicit your fellow citizens' votes, they will not give them to you, and if you only ask for their esteem, they will make excuses for refusing that. You will remain among men, but you will lose your rights to count as one. When you approach your fellows, they will shun you as an impure being, and even those who believe in your innocence will abandon you too, lest they in turn be shunned. Go in peace. I have given you your life, but it is a life worse than death." (*Democracy in America*, 255–56)

The "intellectual" violence that "goes straight for the soul" punishes with "a life worse than death." It makes its target into a "stranger," who nonetheless continues to live among his fellows with all the rights and privileges accorded by law. Tocqueville's stranger is not exactly an exile, nor is he a prisoner, despite the disciplinary power that acts upon him. This punishment by estrangement is enacted by and in the realm of the public. Indeed, such acts define the shifting contours of the public, as this stranger, who can be created only by his fellows, represents one frontier of the outside that remains inside of the democratic public sphere.

Once a fellow citizen, this stranger has now been made taboo, "impure," and contagious in that impurity. He is the victim of a "ban" in the sense that Agamben describes as "on the threshold" of politics: "He who has been banned is not, in fact, simply set outside the law and made indifferent to it but rather *abandoned* by it, that is, exposed and threatened on the threshold in which life and law, outside and inside, become indistinguishable." The capacity to enact such a ban, Agamben argues, indicates the power of the exception, the very "structure of sovereignty."[37]

Agamben amends Foucault's account of biopower somewhat to show that, more than the ability to kill, it is this regulation of the threshold of life and death that marks the ancient biopolitical "nucleus" of sovereignty.[38] The persistence of this capacity to arrange subjects on either side of a threshold between life and death in Tocqueville's analysis of majority tyranny suggests that something in the ancient structure of sovereignty remains basically intact, despite the transformations he narrates. Sovereign power—whether enacted by a monarch, or a "people," or a majority ruling in their name—is possible precisely because it deals in life and death. "I have given you your life," Tocqueville's master says, "but it is a life worse than death." In its capacity to define and regulate life and death, to place subjects on and around the threshold between these, and to make life into a kind of death, public opinion has not dispensed with the body, as Tocqueville's phrasing might suggest. Instead, in "leaving the body alone," this new sovereign "abandons" it like the stranger, holding it at the center of its concern through its continued interest in the regulation of life and death. Focusing on sovereignty's politicization of life, Agamben does not presume the disembodiment of either democratic power or the subjects over and through whom it acts; instead, he argues that the body comes to occupy a "new centrality" in modern democracy: "the root of modern democracy's secret biopolitical calling lies here: he who will appear later as the bearer of rights and, according to a curious oxymoron, as the new sovereign subject ... can only be constituted as such through the repetition of the sovereign exception and the isolation of *corpus*, bare life, in himself."[39] This "corpus" is not expelled from a democratic politics that believes it has left the body alone, because its discourse of natural right makes every citizen a possessor of that body.[40] Further, under this "curious oxymoron," both sovereign power and bare life are "shattered" and "disseminated," making it possible that every subject might occupy both sides of the sovereign exception.

Emphasizing the hidden centrality of the body to democratic sovereignty, the oxymoron that Agamben describes offers one account of the peculiar situation of the stranger in Tocqueville's anecdote. Without being exiled from them, the stranger is made to live as a dead man among his former fellows, any of whom might become a stranger as well. In one sense, this suggests that the relations of exception that emerge from *Democracy in America* have less to do with the relation of the state to its subjects than with the relations between subjects of the same public as strangers and fellows. But more than an allegory of the fate of a dissenting individual in a consensus-driven public, the story of Tocqueville's stranger might also be understood as the drama of the body's abandonment under such public acts of sovereignty. The fate of the stranger suggests that there is an internal relation of exception that develops in the context of a sovereign authority that "leaves the body alone"—the relation between the sovereign citizen of the public and the regulated life of every subject. Insofar as it stands for the abandoned body of the newly empowered citizen, this stranger also accounts for the curious vulnerability that Tocqueville identifies with the subjects of American democracy.

## "*L'esprit de tous*": Equality and Ideology

When Tocqueville introduces his "stranger" in the first volume of *Democracy in America*, he offers the first full view of a figure who becomes, in many ways, a kind of protagonist in the second volume. Rather than the expelled outside of the public sphere, this stranger reveals that the ideal subject of a civil society with ambivalent investments in the potency of collective opinion and the principle of individualism is at least a dual one. As he turns, in the second volume, to the social and cultural aspects of democracy, his efforts to depict the lives of Americans are increasingly characterized by a recurring trope of isolation among a crowd of uniform others. To a certain extent, he justifies his repeated recourse to the theme of isolation with his claims that this is a key attribute of U.S. civil life. But isolation is also a rhetorical figure of Tocqueville's writing, which accompanies his efforts to define the singular subject of the U.S. public sphere in the context of collective subjects like the majority, the public, and the "people" of popular sovereignty. Initially, the figure of the estranged, isolated man serves as an emblem of the ultimate punishment that the majority can inflict on its subjects. Gradually, however, that disciplinary isolation merges with another mode, the "calm and considered feeling which disposes each citizen to isolate himself from the mass of his fellows" (*Democracy in America,* 506). As punishment or self-seclusion, isolation becomes the defining feature of the singular subject in the text, at once the sovereign individual and the disciplined subject of the majority, whose separation from his fellows also marks his similarity to them.

From the opening chapter of volume 2, Tocqueville begins to draw the collective characteristics of Americans in far greater detail than he has in volume 1, describing surprisingly precise and wide-ranging attributes, from their philosophical approach to their religious beliefs, linguistic peculiarities, intellectual predilections, as well as their odd tastes for things like "bombastic" orators and "petty" monuments. He opens the second volume with the observation that Americans follow a Cartesian philosophy better than any other nation in the world (without bothering to read Descartes). He describes them as engaged in "continuous activity," always "looking to results without getting entangled in the means toward them and looking through forms to the basis of things" (*Democracy in America*, 429). Invested as he is in characterizing the philosophical habits of Americans in general, Tocqueville's subject throughout the chapter is a plural one. However, the irony of the chapter is how thoroughly the subject of democracy appears to frustrate identification with and as a collective, in large part because of this very passion for Cartesian empiricism. "Accustomed to rely on the witness of their own eyes," they "scorn forms" in order "to get the closest view they can in broad daylight" (430). Since private judgment and firsthand witnessing are the privileged means of knowing, Tocqueville continues, no philosopher can ever carry much weight over opinion: "When it comes to the influence of one man's mind over another's, that is necessarily restricted in a country where the citizens have become more or less similar, see each other at very close quarters, and . . . are continuously brought back to their own judgment." In such "close quarters," where "conditions have become more equal and men more like one another," everyone comes to trust himself more than any other individual. "So each man is narrowly shut up in himself," Tocqueville argues, "and from that basis makes the pretension to judge the world" (430).

Tocqueville's conceit of the American Cartesian, however, rapidly collapses as he turns from the influence of subjects on each other to the influence of public opinion on all of them. In the place of that self-reliant subject comes one who appears to be fully formed by a collective power:

In times of equality, men, being so like each other, have no confidence in others but this same likeness leads them to place almost unlimited confidence in the judgments of the public. . . .

The citizen of a democracy comparing himself with the others feels proud of his equality with each. But when he compares himself with all his fellows and measures himself against this vast entity, he is overwhelmed by a sense of his insignificance and weakness.

The same equality which makes him independent of each separate citizen leaves him isolated and defenseless in the face of the majority.

So in democracies public opinion has a strange power of which aristocratic nations can form no conception. It uses no persuasion to forward its beliefs, but by some mighty pressure of the mind [*l'esprit*] of all upon the intelligence of each it imposes ideas and makes them penetrate men's very souls. (435)

The distinction between "each" and "all" (*chacun* and *tous*) is a crucial one for Tocqueville. "Each" citizen is isolated both from and within "all," every member of which is so similar to him, he cannot seem to decide whether to be proud of his equality with them or to withhold all confidence from them. The sameness of each to the others is so excessive that Tocqueville resorts to a kind of tautology in order to describe it; "this same likeness" (*cette même similitude*) suggests that subjects are not only like one another, but also alike in all the same ways. More than that, as they become isolated and separated from each other, lacking confidence in anyone who appears as another version of themselves, they become strange to each other in precisely the same ways as well. Tocqueville introduces a double paradox of the public sphere in this passage. First, rather than producing community, this excess of sameness produces the strangeness that isolates each from each; like repels like and compels subjects to retreat into the "private judgment" that makes each one a stranger to the others. Then, just as this isolation might be expected to weaken the authority of the public, Tocqueville insists that it only makes the public stronger. With "no confidence" in any individual, Tocqueville argues, public opinion increases in power, acting with a "mighty pressure of the mind of all" that goes right for the "soul."[41] With this, Tocqueville again invokes the operation of power that defined majority tyranny—the "thing" to which democracies peculiarly give rise.

But if it is a collective of "each" that comprises the totality of "all," why is it that Tocqueville's individuals fail to recognize themselves in that collective? The resistance to collective identification that, according to his earlier claim, gives Americans their decidedly Cartesian bent no longer seems to be a consequence of "individualism"—the decision of a sovereign subject to withdraw into some sphere of private judgment. Instead, isolation and estrangement become the effects of a collective power that individuates—the "mighty pressure" of an "all" upon "each." The collective—whether it goes by the name of public, majority, or people—takes on the character of a "vast entity" wholly distinct from the individuals who become its estranged subjects, but at the same time, the immense pressure that penetrates them seems clearly to involve a process of consensus that makes these subjects more alike. The complexity of the models that Tocqueville offers to describe U.S. civil society and political life frequently lies in the impossibility of assigning priority to any of the elements within them. Every element seems to depend on and give rise to every other element at the same time. In volume 1, it was the "people," the agents of popular sovereignty, who appeared as both the origins and the ends of power. Here, the subjects of individualism (isolated from each other by virtue of their sameness) are made to resemble each other by the very power of opinion to which they turn because they have "no confidence" in their fellows. As the "majority" comes to resemble a "vast entity" that seems wholly other with respect to each subject, this also appears to be both the cause and the consequence of their sameness and equality.

The apparent difference of the majority—whose mind and spirit cow every single subject—fosters an illusion of sameness between individuals that comes to infect the very language that Tocqueville uses to describe it. Tocqueville slips without comment from "sameness" to "equality" in this passage; just as "this same likeness" leads each subject to place confidence in the public over any individual, so "this same equality leaves him isolated and defenseless in the face of the majority." Elsewhere, he suggests that there is an almost seamless movement from one to the other: where "conditions of life become more equal . . . men [become] more like each other" (430). Although, in the introduction to the second volume, Tocqueville expresses a certain self-consciousness about his tendency to attribute all peculiarities of political and social life in the United States to the "equality of condition," insisting that he does not consider it "the sole cause of everything that is happening now" (417), he certainly indicates that he does consider equality to be the "sole cause" of the similarity of men to each other. However, in this easy grammar of equation, where "sameness" substitutes for "equality," and both are presumed to be conditions of U.S. civil society, Tocqueville obscures the real function of these terms, which his own analysis throughout both volumes of the *Democracy* lays bare; sameness and equality are not "conditions" to be assumed, but engines of that powerful "thing" whose primary tools are thought, opinion, and consensus.[42]

In the very phrase, at the outset of his study, with which Tocqueville posits "equality of condition" as a kind of ground, declaring it to be "the creative element [*le fait générateur*] from which each particular fact derived" (*Democracy in America*, 9), he also insists that it is one of the most powerful forces acting in the public sphere. As a "creative" or "generative" element, equality can be understood less as a material fact for Tocqueville than as a potent and formative imaginary. Along these lines, the political theorist Morton Schoolman argues that "equality of condition" possesses a formidable "pedagogical" aspect: "The pedagogical consequences of the equality of condition . . . create in each individual an 'ardent, insatiable, incessant, invincible' feeling and conviction that the equality each possesses in principle is an equality that can be possessed in fact." Understood as a pedagogy, one which "'teaches,' 'inspires,' 'lodges,' 'reminds,' 'impresses,'" the idea of equality can be seen as central to the disciplinary processes that form the subjects whose "condition" it purports to describe. Schoolman argues that it does this by fostering "an unflagging determination to overcome any and every difference—material and otherwise—between oneself and others." Further, Schoolman claims, the subject of "equality" is the subject of a desire to overcome difference without necessarily becoming the "same" as those around him. Understanding the pedagogical function of equality, he argues, ultimately poses a challenge to a reading of *Democracy in America* that has become commonplace: "It would be inaccurate, then, to read Tocqueville, as he is so often read, as simply arguing that democratic society molds all its members in the same identical image so eventually there will be no difference among them." Instead, Schoolman claims, the idea of equality prompts individuals to create themselves in mimetic relation to "all others," so that "each individual in a democracy develops identities that are many identities."[43] In this, Tocqueville's subjects may be isolated, but they are never alone: "In democratic societies, where all are insignificant and very much alike, each man, as he looks at himself, sees all his fellows at the same time" (*Democracy in America*, 484). Containing multitudes that rival Whitman's poet, this subject is also endlessly changing, incorporating more and more fellows into itself through mimicry: "They are so close to each other that men of different classes are continually meeting. Every day, they mix and exchange ideas, imitating and emulating one another" (458).

Claude Lefort describes an "idol" that takes hold of the subjects of a democratic society in Tocqueville's analysis: "Democratic peoples do indeed have an instinctive taste for freedom, but they make only 'rapid and sudden efforts' to obtain it; equality, on the other hand, is their idol, and they would rather perish than lose it." Where freedom functions as a commodity in Tocqueville's text, something to pursue, possess, or exchange, equality takes on an almost ontological status, something "so deeply imprinted on life that considerable energy would have to be mobilized in order to extirpate it." Both an idol and a central aspect of life, equality becomes the spectacular center of the public, the thing on which all eyes seem to focus. Riveted in this way on the idol of equality, subjects are formed by the desire to become equal to all their fellows by appropriating and overcoming difference, as Schoolman suggests. However, under the spell of this idol, Tocqueville's subject also passes through a highly ambivalent relation to sameness and similarity; "proud" of equality, this figure nonetheless has no confidence in anyone who resembles his image of himself. Ultimately, this ambivalence drives the tendency toward isolation and seclusion that makes "the intelligence of each" into an object of power. Isolated and withdrawn into the position of the "stranger," Tocqueville's subject becomes complicit in the creation of the majority that, in turn, forms him through public opinion. "Public opinion," Lefort writes, "becomes detached from subjects, thinks and speaks for itself, and becomes an anonymous power standing over them."[44]

As the idol and spectacular center of democratic public life (as opposed to its material fact or condition), equality functions in Tocqueville's work in many ways like ideology.[45] Certainly, the power of public opinion that derives from equality, the "mighty pressure of the mind of all upon the intelligence of each," suggests the operation of ideology. But more than a reified illusion masking and concealing the truth of social relations, it is more accurate to describe the interplay of public opinion and the idol of equality in Democracy in America in terms of what Slavoj Žižek calls "ideological fantasy." Žižek's distinction hinges on knowledge: if the subjects of ideology are those who "do not know it, but they are doing it," the subjects of ideological fantasy "know very well . . . but still they are doing it as if they did not know."[46] Ideological fantasy continues to involve a powerful illusion, but rather than concealing a reality of social life or relations beneath it, this is an illusion that structures social life, an illusion that makes its "reality" possible. "Equality" is "generative" in *Democracy in America*: "it creates opinions, gives birth to feelings, suggests customs, and modifies whatever it does not create" (*Democracy in America*, 9). In short, equality generates the real of public and social life, and the subjects whose relations to each other it would seek to define. Equality also makes possible the strategic notions of sameness and strangeness through which subjects both relate to each other and define themselves as the vulnerable—and, consequently, innocent—subjects of an imaginary, monolithic "majority." But even as this "equality" structures the reality of social and political life in the United States, the sheer fantasy of it is perpetually in view. As spectacular center and generative power, equality is the thing on which all eyes focus, but this in no way distracts from or conceals its most persistent exceptions.

In describing the present and future conditions of enslaved African-Americans and displaced Native Americans in a long chapter that concludes the first volume, Tocqueville says that these populations "touch" the subject of his book without "entering" it.[47] Not surprisingly, Tocqueville's critics have made much of this phrase, often reading it as evidence of a mimetic fallacy, through which Tocqueville appropriates textually the great hypocrisy in his object of analysis. However, more than an oversight or a lapse, more even than an appropriation of hypocrisy, Tocqueville's belated treatment of slavery, dispossession, and racialization is structurally essential to his text and to its subject. It is not just ideology that is at work in racialization—the division of the population into citizen subjects and those who "touch" upon that subjecthood without entering it—but ideological fantasy. Rather than reading a blindness or a lapse in Tocqueville's belated and bracketed discussion of the condition of slaves and Native Americans in the United States, it is far more instructive to consider this chapter along the lines of the exception that makes political power—specifically sovereignty—possible. "Touching" without "entering" the subject of Tocqueville's study, the exceptional subjects of racialization and expulsion reveal that the politics which has made life its object is also dealing in death. If the subject of Tocqueville's *Democracy* is divided between the equality that makes it sovereign with respect to its fellows and the strange, isolated life that is the target of public opinion and political power, that division must, therefore, be understood in terms of American racial divisions. Ultimately, the vulnerability that Tocqueville's subjects internalize with this division enables the fantasy that they are innocent of the violence that their sovereignty enacts.

## "*Américaines sans être démocratiques*": Popular Sovereignty and Racism

> There are other things in America besides an immense and complete democracy, and the inhabitants of the new world may be considered from more than one point of view.
>
> In the course of this work I have been led to mention the Indians and the Negroes, but I have never had the time to stop and describe the position of these two races within the democratic nation I was bent on depicting . . . . These topics are like tangents to my subject, being American, but not democratic, and my main business is to describe democracy. So at first I had to leave them on one side, but now at the end I must return to them. (*Democracy in America*, 316)

Tocqueville opens the final chapter of volume 1 with a telling distinction: concerns that are "American without being democratic." In this, he is surprisingly explicit about the status of this chapter with respect to what has preceded it. From its placement at the end of volume 1, to its lengthy title—"Some Considerations Concerning the Present State and Probable Future of the Three Races that Inhabit the Territory of the United States"—to the opening distinction between American and democratic topics, he makes no pretense that the "inhabitants" of the "territory" of the United States are coextensive with the "people" of democracy. In the original, Tocqueville switches between "*ces objets*" (those things that have been left out of the study thus far) and "*mon sujet*" (the content of the study itself), as if to alert his reader that the organization of his book reflects a chilling distinction between those who inhabit a continent and those who become subjects of democracy.[48] In the transparency of these first paragraphs, in the deliberate division that Tocqueville makes between the American and the democratic, he openly admits his own strategy of exclusion. Although he attempted to "leave them on one side," the topic and subjects of "the three races" in the territory of the United States cannot be made to disappear any more than the body of the democratic subject can: "now at the end I must return to them."

Despite Tocqueville's uncharacteristic self-reflection here, he raises more questions than he answers about the implications of this textual decision for his wider theory. For one thing, it would be a mistake to assume that the transparency of his text on the subject of racial exclusion in American politics amounts to anything like an explicit critique of racial attitudes or expansionism by the United States. Indeed, Tocqueville's writings on slavery, imperialism, and race throughout the

1830s and 1840s leave an ambivalent record. While Tocqueville joined with other French liberals as a leading advocate for the (gradual) emancipation of slaves in the French colonies, he was also the key architect of France's policy of colonization through outright domination in Algeria.[49] Jennifer Pitts has made a strong case for the necessity of reading Tocqueville's Algeria writings alongside *Democracy in America* for a clearer picture of the intricate intertwining of democracy and imperialism in Tocqueville's thought—especially given that two of Tocqueville's official letters on Algeria were written in 1837, after the publication of volume 1 of *Democracy in America* and during the completion of volume 2. "Only in the writings on Algeria and slavery did Tocqueville develop the notion, implicit in the *Democracy*, that imperial expansion might be more than an arbitrary fact of democracy."[50] Pitts argues that it was the North American frontier, in particular, which convinced Tocqueville of a democratic nation's dependence upon territorial expansion, leading to his conclusion by 1841 that the future of a degenerating French nation relied on successful subjugation of its African colonies.[51] But if imperial expansion—and with it the subjugation and enslavement of non-Europeans—is more than an "arbitrary fact," Pitts hesitates to articulate its precise relationship to liberal democracy in Tocqueville's thought.

Both Jennifer Pitts and Dominick LaCapra, in reviewing Tocqueville's American and Algerian writings, caution against finding in the intersections between these texts clear evidence that racism and imperialism constitute something like a secret core of liberal democracy. LaCapra writes:

> One important current of liberalism could defend both liberal democracy in the West and imperialism and colonialism in non-Western areas of the world. . . . This current should perhaps be seen as neither anomalous nor as unmasking the true face of liberalism; it was one important form liberalism could and did take . . . . In Tocqueville, this orientation went against biologistic racism of the sort found in Gobineau, but it was compatible with a cultural or "moral" racism closely bound up with a theory of stages of civilization—a theory in which Tocqueville firmly believed.[52]

Several questions come together in LaCapra's remarks—about the nature of liberal democracy's investments in imperialism; about the relationship between imperialism and the specific discourse of biological racism; and tying the others together, about Tocqueville's personal notions of race in the context of his writing on the United States and Algeria. Reading across Tocqueville's work from the 1830s and 1840s, LaCapra suggests that Tocqueville's "stages of civilization" racism is closer to Rousseau than to the scientific racism of Gobineau, and in defending Tocqueville from the charge of "biologistic" racist, LaCapra seems to preserve some form of liberalism that subsists without a reliance on racial divisions. While the resistance that both Pitts and LaCapra demonstrate to any wholesale indictment of liberal democracy as essentially racist is a prudent caution against oversimplification, both leave unanswered the question of why racism is more than an arbitrary fact or an anomaly and how, precisely, Tocqueville's thought might be indispensable to unraveling the relationship between racism, liberalism, and democracy.

To begin addressing such questions, it is necessary to remember the historical specificity of Tocqueville's *Democracy*; rooted as it is in the United States of the 1830s, it resists any claims that treat "liberalism" or "democracy" or "racism" as transhistorical entities.[53] Far from revealing racism as the secret core of some transcendent liberal-democratic form, Tocqueville's work shows how racism and popular sovereignty became entwined with one another through very specific practices and articulations of political power three decades prior to the end of U.S. slavery and in the midst of tremendous territorial expansion. Ultimately, Tocqueville's writings on the United States, the international slave trade, and colonial expansion do disclose a vital, structuring relationship between democratic politics and racist, imperialist practices. But this does not expose the secret "face" of liberal democracy, largely because, for nineteenth-century Americans, these practices were not hidden.[54] They were the overt strategies of a politics that continued to define itself in sovereign terms by dividing populations between the subjects of democracy and the strangers who live "a life worse than death." What Tocqueville's belated discussion of "the three races" highlights is that, along with the popularization of sovereignty and the generative fantasy of equality, U.S. democracy also innovated a blanket of power that made citizens vulnerable to newly intimate forms of discipline, isolated them in the face of public opinion, and involved them in a devastating practice of racism that divided a continent's inhabitants into democratic subjects and American objects. Moreover, this chapter proves that these are all part of one and the same "thing."

Part of the challenge of deciphering the relationship of racism to democracy in Tocqueville's text surely arises from the peculiarity of the voice—or, more accurately, voices—that he adopts in the "Three Races" chapter. In this chapter, more than any other, he speaks dialogically and through anecdote, alternately romanticizing racial difference, justifying it, and fretting over its implications in baffled resignation.[55] Where the rest of the text dwells persistently on the prospect of homogeneity and the sameness of (white) men to each other, the chapter on the "Three Races" opens with a meditation on a form of difference that Tocqueville at first considers absolute: "It is obvious that there are three naturally distinct, one might almost say hostile, races . . . they have mixed without combining, and each follows a separate destiny" (*Democracy in America*, 317). Tocqueville is struck here, not by the "fact" of equality, but by what he calls an "obvious" and "natural" distinction between races, a distinction that he "almost" says is maintained by outright hostility. Hesitantly naming this relation hostile, Tocqueville is nonetheless vague about the origin and direction of racial animosity, suggesting a certain willing participation of all in the perpetuation of mutual hostilities, while also condemning the brutality of whites. He vacillates throughout this chapter between a view of race relations in America as one of all-out war and another view that insists upon a "bond of affection unit[ing] oppressor and oppressed" (320). Oddly enough, Tocqueville's confused vacillations produce one of his closer approximations of America's own deranged rationalization of slavery and dispossession: in one passage he offers a fairly clear-eyed view of the violence that maintains distinctions of race (317), and in another he imputes to the enslaved and the dispossessed all blame for their exclusion from democratic society (320). In a particularly bizarre moment, Tocqueville explains what he means by "mixing" without "combining" (or "touching" without "entering") by evoking a scene outside a log cabin in Alabama, in which an "Indian" woman and a "Negro" woman attend to a young girl "of the white race" (320). As he watches the three women, Tocqueville converts the scene into an allegory of affective domination and willing submission that supports the mythic account of racial subjugation in America. Despite the "weakness and age" of the child, Tocqueville writes, the "Negro" woman was "divided between almost maternal affection and servile fear," while the "Indian" woman maintained a distant reserve, ultimately removing herself from the scene altogether, as if to allow the drama of black and white affective subjugation to play itself out. Tocqueville's concluding remark on the scene repeats his opening assertions, but he conceals his own authorial contrivance under cover of "nature": "nature, bringing them close together, made the immense gap formed by prejudice and by laws yet more striking" (320).

The peculiarities of Tocqueville's rhetoric in this chapter compound as he adopts multiple voices throughout, moving between that of an incredulous European ("What could be more fictitious than a purely legal inferiority!") and that of a defensive American who articulates a view of human differences as biological and permanent ("His face appears to us hideous, his intelligence limited, and his tastes low; we almost take him for some immediate being between man and beast") (342). Mimicking a dialogue between European and American conceptions of race, he both relativizes and historicizes the attitude he ascribes to Americans, indicating that there is something novel in their understanding of race. However, what is less clear is whether Tocqueville understands this novelty as owing to peculiar theories of human difference in the United States, or to their attachment of slavery to what he agrees is "physical and permanent difference." In other words, in identifying the modernity of U.S. racial attitudes, it is unclear whether he is attributing to Americans the invention of biological human difference out of fictitious legal difference, or the attachment of legal difference to what he too accepts as "natural" permanent and physical difference in the racialization of slavery. "In the modern world, the insubstantial and ephemeral fact of servitude is most fatally combined with the physical and permanent fact of difference in race" (341). The stakes of the distinction that LaCapra notes—between a reading of Tocqueville's understanding of "race" as biological or cultural—are clearly high. But as Tocqueville's views disappear further and further into those he ventriloquizes, they become harder and harder to trace. Ultimately, in speaking through American voices, he begins to speak with one—and a very particular one at that:

> This opinion is moreover supported by authorities much more weighty than I. For instance, in Jefferson's *Memoirs*, one reads: "Nothing is more certainly written in the book of fate than that these people are to be free; nor is it less certain than that the two races, equally free, cannot live in the same government. Nature, habits, opinions have drawn indelible lines between them." (356n46)

Thomas Jefferson hovers over Tocqueville's chapter on the "Three Races" as both a "weighty" authority and a hazy specter.[56] From his division of the diverse inhabitants of North America into a mere "three races," to his reliance on hostility and war as the paradigms through which to analyze the relations of these inhabitants, Tocqueville repeatedly echoes Jeffersonian categories and metaphors. But it is primarily in Tocqueville's citation of physiognomy as the grounds for political exclusion that Jefferson's influence over this chapter appears strongest. As Tocqueville catalogs the rationalizations for the denial of citizenship to freed slaves, ostensibly translating for Europeans the peculiar views held by white Americans (341–42), he nearly reproduces Jefferson's own list in the infamous Query XIV from *Notes on the State of Virginia*: "Deep rooted prejudices entertained by the whites; ten thousand recollections, by the blacks, of the injuries they have sustained . . . the real distinctions which nature has made . . . will divide us into parties, and produce convulsions which will never end until the extermination of the one or the other race."[57] Jefferson's narrative trajectory—from historical conflict through "natural" difference to all-out race war—efficiently establishes the rationale for political exclusion as preemptive defense against "extermination." In a chapter on "Laws," Jefferson offers up the presumption of "war" as the grounds from which to establish civil society and determine its membership. (In doing so, he also gives a tidy illustration of Foucault's reversal of the famous aphorism: "Politics is the continuation of war by other means."[58]) Rather than an Enlightenment narrative of natural right, which might extend gradual and grudging legal protection to former slaves and their descendents, Jefferson assumes a war of races that precludes the possibility of both universal right and a multiracial citizenry. Where his political philosophy fails him, Jefferson turns first to a scientific and then to an aesthetic discourse of human difference ("The first difference that strikes us is that of colour"). He seeks out "greater or less share[s] of beauty" in the "skin" and the "scarf-skin," and then extrapolates from skin to sexual preference and ardor, positing the beauty of the human body and its reproduction as political concerns. The object of Jefferson's most monstrous speculations in this Query is fairly clear— the justification of an exception from the "universal" right that forms the basis of political belonging. In articulating this exception, however, Jefferson takes care to imply that racial exclusion originates anywhere and everywhere but in the law—in nature, in civil society, even in private aesthetic tastes and sexual morals—while simultaneously perfecting the rhetoric through which, in Foucault's words, "racism is inscribed as the basic mechanism" of political power.

But even as Tocqueville pays excessive homage to Jefferson, he remains ambivalent about the claims of inassimilability with which Jefferson is so strongly identified, sometimes accepting the language of hostility and war which precludes natural and universal right, sometimes appealing to that right. In quoting another source on Native American removals, for instance, he marvels at the total transparency of the arguments that the United States puts forth: "one is astonished at the facility and ease with which, from the very first words, the author [of a report for the Committee on Indian Affairs] disposes of arguments founded on natural right and reason" (*Democracy in America*, 339). Tocqueville regards the conception of hostile races as both novel and "modern," but as he begins to clarify this novelty, he also reveals its connection to the other innovations of American political and social life that he has analyzed in the earlier sections of volume 1. Speaking once again through the voice of a defensive American, Tocqueville gradually begins to translate the Jeffersonian model of racial difference into the idiom that he has developed throughout *Democracy in America*: "You can make the Negro free, but you cannot prevent him facing the European as a stranger. . . . [T]his man born in degradation, this stranger brought by slavery into our midst, is hardly recognized as sharing the common features of humanity" (341–42). In Tocqueville's translation, a freedman can take legal possession of liberty, but he will nonetheless remain a "stranger," forbidden from acceding to the "equality" that the public treats as an ontology and confounds with sameness.

The allegorical stranger, whom Tocqueville describes several chapters earlier as the outsider within the democratic public sphere, enters into history at the end of volume one as the former slave who is inassimilable to political and civil life—and liable even to estrangement from "human" life. When Tocqueville introduces the first stranger ("from this day, you are a stranger among us"), it is as the abstract victim of a ban that defines the majority as sovereign and "master." When, in volume 2, he develops the relationship of individual subjects to collective ones, that stranger comes to be internalized, harbored within each individual as the isolated and abandoned target of public opinion. This shift in focus from punishment and exception to the internalization of abandonment unfolds in volume 2 as if the "stranger" had remained an abstract figure, as if it had never been concretized and historicized in the first volume. But in tracing the vulnerabilities of the democratic subject and conferring with this a kind of innocence, volume 2 begs the question, To what are these subjects so vulnerable, and of what are they so innocent? The "stranger brought by slavery into our midst" is more than an instance of the first stranger, more even than an exemplary figure of estrangement and ban. For the moment in which Tocqueville is writing, the enslaved "stranger" is the most salient and defining limit-case of American popular sovereignty. To borrow a phrase from Melville, the slave is "a stranger in the extremest sense of the word."[59] In a chapter of exceptions and tangents that "touch" without "entering" the subject at hand, Tocqueville seems to establish something like a ground here. "Slavery" may have placed this "stranger" into the "midst" of democracy, but the work of maintaining the stranger at the center belongs to all, through a systematic practice of racialization that here comes to define the operation and practice of power in the sovereign public sphere. Biological racism is literally a matter of opinion in this chapter, and as such, it is almost intractable. Like Jefferson ("the first difference that strikes us is that of colour"), Tocqueville employs a particularly coercive third-person plural here, speaking through this voice and in it, and thereby performing the work of opinion in constituting a public voice through the creation of a stranger. However, if this stranger is indeed in the "midst" of the public, then Tocqueville also betrays how utterly untenable the distinction he makes at the outset of this chapter really is. Racialization cannot lie outside or even tangential to "democracy," because it operates through the very mechanisms with which democratic power in the United States has been defined.

Specifically, when Tocqueville elaborates on the novelty of American racial theories by describing the modernity of American slavery, he defines such innovations in enslavement in precisely the terms that he has already laid out as the mechanism of majority tyranny:

> The ancients only knew of fetters and death as a means to maintain slavery; the Americans of the South of the Union have found guarantees of a more intellectual nature to assure the permanence of their power. They have, if I may put it in this way, spiritualized despotism and violence. In antiquity men sought to prevent the slave from breaking his bonds; nowadays the attempt is made to stop him wishing to do so. (361)

Tocqueville manages to overlook the "fetters and death" that do in fact maintain slavery in the United States in order to identify the other forms of violence that slavery has enacted. Just as the majority has foregone physical violence alone, acting "as much upon the will" and preventing "both the act and the desire to do it" (254), so "Americans of the South" have "found guarantees of a more intellectual nature" (361). Tocqueville repeats his analysis of the intellectual violence of majority tyranny almost verbatim here, and given this, his attempt to regionalize this spiritual despotism rings false. If the intimate "moral" and "spiritual" power through which majority opinion disciplines its subjects is also the power that maintains a new and peculiarly American racial tyranny, then it cannot be localized as "southern" in that way. The "master" of the earlier chapter is every bit the "master" of this chapter, and through these parallel analyses, the majority becomes a holder of slaves. Moreover, as in the case of majority tyranny, a new power emerges to replace the power of kings and princes without abdicating the rights of sovereignty, so in the instance of slavery, the power that is ultimately at stake is the power over life and death. With "no intermediate state" between "the excessive inequality created by slavery and the complete equality which is the natural result of independence," the United States has "violated every right of humanity" by making slavery an eternal and inheritable condition (362). As the power invested in the majority, this sovereign power to kill spiritually, legally, and actually must also be understood as "popular"—disseminated throughout the population of those whose lives are both politicized and guaranteed by it.

Permanently expelled from political and civil life—while still being held at the center of its power—and "hardly recognized as sharing the common features of humanity," the enslaved and racialized stranger is Tocqueville's "extremest," but by no means his only one. Tocqueville repeatedly notes the ways in which new forms of death have become the hallmark of power in the United States. Focusing on Native American expulsion, Tocqueville registers an ambiguous tone of wonder as he describes the regularization of mass eliminations: "Nowadays the dispossession of the Indians is accomplished in a regular and, so to say quite legal manner" (324). Land deals, treaties, and legislation have accomplished far more destruction, he argues, than three centuries of genocidal colonial war, and he claims that the United States has achieved a precision in practices of extermination that Spanish colonists could only dream of: "It is impossible to destroy men with more respect for the laws of humanity" (339). Finally, this "legal" and "humane" destruction of life is not limited, for Tocqueville, to the treatment of racialized populations alone. In a chapter on industrialization, he notes that a division is developing between the social conditions of workers and their "masters," which has quickly become analogous to the racial divide he has already analyzed: "there is no resemblance between master and workman and daily they become more different," as "the industrial aristocracy of our day...has impoverished and brutalized the men it uses" (556–57). What Tocqueville reveals in these examples of the humane, regular, and perfectly legal destruction of populations is the creation of a break or divide, which brings both the projected threats to political and social life and the means of eradicating them "into our midst." Brought "into our midst," such powers of estrangement and eradication are no longer located in some centralized sovereign entity; instead, they reside among everyone, everywhere.

## Tocqueville's Spectacle

Tocqueville can visualize the increasing blanket of power that is covering political and social life in America, regulating the individual as well as the mass. He can also see that there is a new model of psychic tyranny operating in the racialization of slavery and the eradication of native peoples, which partake of the same techniques. But this is where the limitation of Tocqueville's vision becomes clear: he remains stubbornly incapable of perceiving that these are one and the same "thing." Tocqueville, it seems, cannot see what his text makes so visible. It is worth a brief return to Tocqueville's famously dire, but oddly circuitous, final warning to democratic societies to note what he does and does not articulate there. Or, to put it another way, it is worth noticing what Tocqueville does in these final pages instead of articulating or naming this new thing. By refraining from settling on a name for that powerful thing to which the United States finds itself peculiarly susceptible, Tocqueville insists that the scene he imagines and describes *be* his definition. "In the first place, I see ... " Tocqueville places seeing at the inception of the thing that is too new for any word, but he remains vague about whether he sees something already in front of him, or whether his seeing conjures this thing. Read as a seeing that conjures, Tocqueville's vision might take on an hallucinatory quality, as each of the elements of his portrait becomes a sign that brings this new thing into view. However, from the individual (the subject formed to be preoccupied with personal comforts and enjoyments), to the collective (the public enervated by this withdrawal into personal pleasure), to the administrative entities (agents of regulation that inhibit, bend, and soften), no one of these things is, in and of itself, "new." Each of them appears in previous sections of the *Democracy*, suggesting that it is not what Tocqueville sees that is new so much as how he sees. Tocqueville's seeing composes them, combining them into the conditions under which the whole of social and individual life becomes a concern of political power, but this seeing does not provide him a critical vantage on them. He remains, on some level, subject to his own seeing.

Both the conditions that Tocqueville imagines in these pages and the seeing that composes them into this new thing speak to Agamben's assertion that democracy's "decadence and its gradual convergence with . . . post-democratic spectacular societies . . . begin to become evident" in *Democracy in America*.[60] Agamben's claims for Tocqueville as an early theorist of Guy Debord's "society of the spectacle" not only resonate with the speculative manner in which Tocqueville presents his tableau of a spectral threat within democracy's mechanisms; they also give a name to one of the chief forms that this threat seems to take. Defined by Debord as "a social relationship . . . mediated by images," and "the self-portrait of power in the age of power's . . . rule over the conditions of existence," the concept of the spectacle is both capacious and precise.[61] Like Tocqueville's thing, Debord's spectacle captures both a social world constituted through the (specifically visual) relationships that develop between subjects, and the power that seems to stand over and regulate the lives of these subjects. If Tocqueville's thing lacks a specific placement or precise embodiment, in the manner of more ancient political modes, it does not lack a form. But insofar as Tocqueville's thing assumes the form of spectacle, it is not something to see so much as it describes a way of seeing.

Throughout *Democracy in America*, Tocqueville emphasizes the visual, as if in order to see Americans, he must first see them seeing: "Accustomed to rely on the witness of their own eyes," Americans "scorn forms . . . so as to get the closest view they can in broad daylight" (*Democracy in America*, 430). "In democratic societies, where all are insignificant and very much alike, each man, as he looks at himself, sees all his fellows at the same time" (484). Schoolman argues that, in Tocqueville's text, "democracy calls the senses into play," and "among the senses . . . democracies appear to privilege vision." Lefort calls Tocqueville's democracy a constant "theater" of change and movement, through which Tocqueville attempts to see the outlines and forms of the "social" itself.[62] Seeing provides a means of forming relations with others and forming the self in relation, and as a primary activity of Tocqueville's "democratic peoples," seeing also becomes a principle activity through which collective entities like the majority and the public are constituted. Seeing "all his fellows" as he looks at himself, the subject of *Democracy in America* is already a plural one, formed in the face of a public whose "mighty pressure" penetrates and isolates, as it gathers subjects together

(*Democracy in America*, 435). Such a seeing cannot be read simply as a subjection to an ideological spectacle imposed from outside (concealing some reified reality), any more than it signals a removal or distance from the public sphere. The seeing that concerns Tocqueville is that activity which structures the real of public and collective life. Recognizing fellows and also distinguishing strangers—"his face appears to us hideous" (343)—Tocqueville's intensely visual subjects actively engage in generating and perpetuating the spectacle of the democratic public. But as their seeing generates the public, it also produces "a strange melancholy" that leaves each one "disgusted with life":

> Among democratic peoples, men easily obtain a certain equality, but they will never get the sort of equality they long for. That is a quality that retreats before them without getting quite out of sight, and as it retreats it beckons them on to pursue. Every instant they think that they will catch it, and each time it slips through their fingers. They see it close enough to know its charms, but they do not get near enough to enjoy it, and they will be dead before they have fully relished its delights.
>
> That is the reason for the strange melancholy often haunting inhabitants of democracies in the midst of abundance, and of that disgust with life sometimes gripping them in calm and easy circumstances. (538)

Tocqueville's description of the "strange melancholy" that haunts subjects "in the midst of abundance" reads like democracy's hangover. But if Tocqueville's subjects are glutted with anything, it is unfulfilled desire at the almost compulsive pursuit of an equality that recedes before their eyes. The "creative element," the fantasy and idol of equality that generates "each fact" of democracy in America, is both a mirage and a projection that is maintained by the force of eyes riveted on it. The seeing that preserves this mirage also drives the desire and the movement that become confounded with "life." But death, like the "stranger," is in the midst of such a life ("they will be dead before they have fully relished its delights"). The melancholic disgust with life that plagues Tocqueville's democratic subject might be read as the residue of a politics that has made living its object, and thus the place where political power is experienced most intimately. But this melancholy disgust might also be explained as the affective response of subjects to a life that is entangled with the deaths of others, involving them intimately with the power to kill. Such a reading may take Tocqueville further than he was willing to go himself in connecting democracy and sovereignty in the United States to racialization, slavery, and expansionism, but it does not require a twenty-first-century perspective to see these links. In his novel, *Marie; or, Slavery in the United States*, Tocqueville's traveling companion, Gustave de Beaumont, proceeds from just this assumption—that the U.S. public sphere constitutes itself as sovereign through the spectacularization of racial differences. Tocqueville's tropes posit spectacle as formative of the democratic public sphere, but it is Beaumont's more calculated and deliberate association of spectacle, sovereignty, and racialization that will ground my studies of antebellum America in the chapters that follow. From a segregated Philadelphia theater to that city's Eastern State Penitentiary to the race riots that tore through New York City in 1834, Beaumont locates the U.S. public sphere in precisely those spaces and moments that Tocqueville relegates to footnotes and supplementary chapters, finding in Tocqueville's exceptions the rule of U.S. sovereignty.

# 2 / Color, Race, and the Spectacle of Opinion in Beaumont's *Marie*

If Tocqueville struggled to name the new thing that haunted him about U.S. political and social life, it would seem that his traveling companion had no such trouble. Gustave de Beaumont's novel, *Marie; or, Slavery in the United States*, opens with the frank admission that "a single idea dominates the work and forms the central point around which all the developments are arranged." He continues, "The reader is aware that there are still slaves in the United States; their number has grown to almost two million. Surely it is a strange thing that there is so much bondage amid so much liberty; but what is perhaps still more extraordinary is the violence of the prejudice which separates the race of slaves from that of the free men, that is, the Negroes from the whites."[1] Beaumont finds in the United States a "double element"—an institution of slavery created and maintained by the state, and ("still more extraordinary") a customary practice of racial exclusion and debasement which he finds to be ubiquitous in public life. Although he indicates that "slavery" will be the singular focus of his work, once he mentions this double element and separates the customary practices of racial prejudice from the institution of slavery, Beaumont finds his "thing." Beaumont's *Marie* is not the study of "slavery in the United States" that the title promises; indeed, this is one of only a few explicit references to slavery in the text. Instead, Beaumont focuses intently on the concept and the practice of "race," isolating the mechanisms of racialization and tracing "the violence of the prejudice" through those who both enforce and suffer it.

In part, the turn that Beaumont makes in his foreword from

institution to custom is dictated by his efforts to distance his project from Tocqueville's. As he claims, "It is solely the customs of the United States that I propose to describe," thus leaving "the most brilliant illumination upon democratic institutions" to his friend (*Marie*, 4). If Beaumont's text labors under the shadow of Tocqueville's, it is not entirely the fault of critics and historians, who for more than a half-century have regarded *Marie* as little more than a companion piece to the *Democracy*.[2] Beaumont himself inaugurates the tradition of relegating *Marie*—with its fictional form and singular focus—to secondary status. He mentions Tocqueville's book three times in his short foreword, repeatedly explaining the different aims of the two projects and directing his reader to Tocqueville for analysis of political forms and governing institutions. By choosing to examine the side of the "double element" that he does—the practice of racial prejudice—Beaumont makes an attempt to keep himself within the boundaries of custom that he designates as his concern. But, clearly, his isolation of custom in no way distinguishes his work from Tocqueville's—again and again, *Democracy in America* exposes how permeable the lines between law and custom, state and public, have become. Instead, it is Beaumont's singular focus on race and its centrality to life in the United States that marks his departure from Tocqueville, though he acknowledges this only obliquely. At the end of his foreword, Beaumont justifies the very different impressions of America that a reader might take away from *Marie* and the *Democracy* as follows: "Now, in the United States, political life is far finer, and more equitably shared than civil life . . . . Envisaging American society from such diverse viewpoints, we have not been constrained to use the same colors in order to paint it" (7). The difference between their texts is one of color. Without respecting the divide between "American" subjects and "democratic" ones that structures volume 1 of Tocqueville's *Democracy in America*, Beaumont's novel attempts to examine democratic culture exclusively through the lens of race, a concept which he first comes to understand when he witnesses the hallucinations and manipulations of color in the public sphere.

Beaumont's final justification of his work in relation to Tocqueville's—"we have not been constrained to use the same colors in order to paint it"—serves a double function. Overtly, it explains—for the fourth time, at least—his decision to write a novel in order to treat America's customs as distinct from its political institutions. But in apologizing for his own fictions, Beaumont ends up exposing Tocqueville's: the "political life" that is "far finer and more equitably shared" is clearly the more fictive life in light of Beaumont's concerns with civil society and its customary racism. Beaumont's anxieties about the form of his work, in particular his use of fiction, seem to stand in for other anxieties entirely—namely, the fictiveness of political equality amidst the lived reality of fictional racial categories. In this sense, the ambivalence that Beaumont expresses in the foreword about the form of his text maps onto the very concerns that motivate it, suggesting a much closer tie between the fictional "*forme*" and the serious "*fond*" of *Marie* than Beaumont will admit (1). Unquestionably, *Marie* is a bizarre text. The novel about an expatriate Frenchman's love for a beautiful American girl of mixed racial origins comprises only about one-half of the total work, the remainder of which contains copious notes and lengthy appendices on the social conditions of slaves, free blacks, and Native Americans, as well as essays on American religion, the theater, and Anglophobia, plus two detailed accounts (one fictional, one historical) of the July 1834 New York race riots. So unwieldy is its mixed form that the full text has never been published in English; both the 1845 translation serialized in the *National Anti-Slavery Standard* and Barbara Chapman's 1958 translation abridge the novel and cut most of the appendices. With all of the text's peculiarities, in both its heft (the original two volumes weigh in at over six hundred pages) and the ambition of its claims, *Marie* holds its own against *Democracy in America*. More than that—and because of the very mixing of rhetorical modes, cultural critique, and aesthetic investments that have troubled the critical reception of his text—Beaumont's work offers a formal, textual response to the unsettling spectacle of race and democracy in America that challenges even Tocqueville's most intricate analyses.

## "*Une éclatante blancheur*": The Spectacle of Invisible Color

For all of Beaumont's efforts to explain away the "work of imagination" in his foreword, he is almost incapable of articulating the thing that is the focus of his text without recourse to two specific aesthetic modes: theater and fiction. Early in the foreword, Beaumont elaborates on the "single idea" that motivates and dominates the text, not with the careful analysis that he so admires in Tocqueville, but with an account of a theatrical spectacle that marks the origin of the work:

> To give the reader an idea of the barriers placed between the two
> races, I believe I should cite an event which I myself witnessed.
> The first time I attended a theatre in the United States, I was

surprised at the careful distinction made between the white spectators and the audience whose faces were black. In the first balcony were whites; in the second, mulattos; in the third, Negroes. An
American beside whom I was sitting informed me that the dignity
of white blood demanded these classifications. However, my eyes
being drawn to the balcony where sat the mulattos, I perceived a
young woman of dazzling [*éclatante*] beauty, whose complexion, of
perfect whiteness, proclaimed the purest European blood. Entering into all the prejudices of my neighbor, I asked him how a woman of English origin could be so lacking in shame as to seat herself
among the Africans.

"That woman," he replied, "is colored."

"What? Colored? She is whiter than a lily!"

"She is colored," he repeated coldly; "local tradition has established her ancestry, and everyone knows that she has a mulatto
among her forebears."

He pronounced these words without further explanation, as one
who states a fact which needs only to be voiced to be understood.
(*Marie*, 4–5)

As Beaumont looks up and down the galleries and aisles of the theater, it becomes clear that the spectacle it offers is not the play but the
audience. Initially struck by the attempt to fix firm and visible barriers
between "two races," Beaumont's eyes are quickly drawn to the very spot
where those barriers—as well as the dualism they attempt to impose—
have clearly been crossed, the section where black and white intersect,
overlap, and blur together. More precisely, his eyes are drawn to a woman
of "*éclatante*"—dazzling, blinding, stunning, and he adds, lily-white—
beauty whom custom has "colored." Baffled by the way in which her
visible "color" seems to confound all of the divisions by "race" so apparent in the theater, Beaumont attempts to learn more about American
taxonomies of color and race by "entering" into his American companion's prejudices. With this, Beaumont also enters into the very spectacle
which conditions the way that Americans see one another. In a single
glance through the theater, Beaumont sees the prohibition against racial mixing, its violation in the figure of the stunningly white colored
woman, and its reinstatement through the force of opinion, for which
the "essence" of one's race, established by tradition, trumps the evidence
of color. He is astonished at both the visible force of a prejudice that demands rigid physical boundaries and the power of custom and opinion

to repudiate that very visibility. However, in trying to see with American eyes what French eyes have trouble discerning, he cannot long sustain his stance of baffled remoteness from it.

Initially, Beaumont's surprise at first realizing the power in America of the concept of race as a potentially invisible essence signals to him the abnormalities of American racial thinking, and that surprise is, in turn, registered through his use of the word "*éclatante*" to describe a shade of white that both dazzles and blinds.[3] The whiteness that blinds signals the disruption of the entire visible field of race which Beaumont initially began to examine in the theater. If the power of racial prejudice is first made manifest to him through the segregation of the audience, then the woman's white face plainly disrupts the logic that segregation attempts to impose and should, by extension, undermine the basis for prejudices of race and color by proving both categories to be indeterminate, fluid, and open to abuse and manipulation.[4] But Beaumont's theater companion proclaims the woman's "color" as a self-evident fact from which the pronouncement of her "race" follows, while for Beaumont, the testimony of her whiteness is the fact whose self-evidence is irrefutable against all racial stigmas established by tradition or imposed by custom. The color whose legibility is at stake in this scene is not black, but white, a color which proves transparent for the American, who sees right through it, and blinding for Beaumont, who cannot see past its incongruities.

In what will become a kind of primal scene in American literature—it happens to Melville's Ishmael and Poe's Pym, to name just two—Beaumont is struck by the blinding potential of whiteness, and he claims that this sight unravels the epistemology of race on which he had relied.[5] In response, Beaumont makes his appeal to the visible absence of one color by highlighting the excess of another—she cannot be "colored" black because she is "whiter than a lily" (*elle est plus blanche qu'un lis!*). Faced with the same incongruity of visible color and proclaimed race at a pivotal scene in the novel, Beaumont's narrator, Ludovic, echoes his author's own astonished appeal to whiteness when he is told that he cannot marry Marie because she carries a similarly invisible mark: "A strange situation! As Nelson spoke, there sat Marie whose complexion was even whiter than the swans of the Great Lakes" (*Marie*, 58). In both scenes, Beaumont shows the bafflement of a Frenchman who witnesses the exposure of something that cannot be seen, and both times the response is to assert an excess of the very quality that is at stake. As visible whiteness is trumped by its invisible counterpart, the whiteness of these women instead comes to signal the strange procedures of both law and custom, whereby the invisible fiction of "race" is forced into visibility, as well as the extraordinary manipulations of the visual field required to accomplish this.[6]

Although Beaumont's interest in the disruptive whiteness of this woman implicitly counters the prevailing notion of an "inward racial essentialism" (to borrow Werner Sollors's phrase) that stigmatizes her, his surprise in no way indicates that he had abandoned racial thinking. Indeed, the first thing that Beaumont's experience of *éclatante blancheur* blinds him to in his novel is blackness and all of its social meanings. Throughout his writing on America, in his letters as well as his novel, Beaumont grapples with the ways in which notions of race in the United States have been differently applied to Native Americans and African Americans, but he abandons neither the concept of race nor its supposed basis in visible and measurable physical features. In a letter written from Lake Superior in August 1831 to a friend, Beaumont indulges in some armchair ethnography and reveals that he does not have very far to go to "enter into" the racial prejudices of his American theater companion: "It seems certain to me that [Indians] do not at all form a race distinct from Europeans: the shape of their bodies, the silhouette [*coupe*] of their faces, the nature of their physiognomy, have no difference from ours. One could not say as much for the Negroes who, the more one examines them, appear to have received a particular organization."[7] Three months later, in an odd letter to his young niece sent from Philadelphia, he teases the girl with a kind of racial terror: "What would make you laugh above all are the large black faces of the negroes, which are so ugly, so ugly that each has the air of a devil." Tripping on his own prejudices, he quickly adds a double-edged qualification: "But these Blacks have a soul like ours and all their crime is to have a very evil color."[8]

Again and again in his writing, Beaumont participates in his era's relentless phenotyping, examining human colors and forms in search of anatomical bases for social distinctions.[9] He continues to attach the concept of race to features that can be examined and made subject to both moral and aesthetic judgment, and if one is tempted to take his remarks in the foreword as a narrative of his own burgeoning understanding of American racism, his letters belie any assumption that the experience in the theater was in some way transformative for him. His racist jokes to his niece follow by several weeks the letter describing the visit to the Philadelphia theater, which historians cite as the most likely site of the incident he describes in the foreword. What is more, that letter is written on the same day (8 November 1831) as the one to his brother in which he mentions for the first time his intention to write a novel about American slavery.[10] Clearly, Beaumont does not abandon the idea of race as an observable sign of difference, and his own prejudices prove fully compatible with his growing antipathy for slavery, and for those who perpetuate it. Given all of this, it would require no great leap to argue that his novel's treatment of an interracial and visibly white heroine stands as further evidence of such intractable prejudices. Like much of the white-authored interracial fiction that follows it, *Marie* evades the representation of slavery, shuffles dark-skinned characters into marginal roles, and explores northern racism through the experiences of characters who are socially but not visibly black, through a plot of forbidden marriage—a plot which, in many ways, focuses the novel's critique on how racism curtails the freedom of white men.[11] However, even as Beaumont's blindingly white heroine displaces the representation of American racism and slavery in its more ubiquitous and accurate forms, his focus on interracial characters also moves him away from the paralyzing questions of physiognomy that preoccupy him in his letters home, and turns him instead to the origins and the ends of the concept of race.

A basic argument motivates the novel and the numerous appendices marshaled in support of it: "Intermarriages are certainly the best, if not the unique, means of fusing the white and black races." Such a "fusion" would serve as the "most obvious index of equality" and, he argues, ultimately abolish all notions of racial difference through a blending of colors (*Marie*, 245).[12] But the persistence in the United States of racial stigma in the absence of visible signs confounds the argument that guides both the reform-minded plot of his novel and the apparatus of research on which it is based. As a result, throughout the text, Beaumont seems to stage, again and again, versions of this very scene in the theater, this confrontation with the paradox of invisible color that enables a racialized body to be hallucinated into existence. In many ways, the figure of the interracial subject comes to function for Beaumont like the "stranger" does for Tocqueville, exposing the abandoned corporeality that allows political power to function. Where Tocqueville's stranger marks the limits of democratic sovereignty, living as a dead man at the center of the public sphere, Beaumont's invisibly colored subject literalizes the collapse of that stranger into the allegedly abstract subject of democracy. Invisible color becomes Beaumont's emblem for the hidden body that is always the object of sovereignty, and the scene of its spectacular exposure—to which he returns again and again—serves as a reminder of that body's centrality to public life. Invisible color, he suggests, can become so real in the United States because it operates through the very mechanisms that define the citizen-subjects of popular sovereignty through and against the embodied strangers in their midst. As Ludovic and Marie are constantly besieged by a racism that seems ever present and totally vigilant, it becomes clear that their marriage is metonymic for an even more fundamental and transformative "fusion"—one that would expose the persistence of the estranged and abused body and reveal it at the center of democratic politics. But where Beaumont's marriage plot fails to bring about the transformative change he imagines, his text nonetheless explodes into a strange formal mixture, whose peculiarities—its multiple voices and genres, its constant return to scenes of blinding whiteness and exposed color—ultimately stage the political crises it addresses.

When Beaumont introduces the story of the woman in the theater, he does so explicitly to address the question of fiction and its credibility, and a certain code of fictionality attaches to it from its first mention. This incident, which Beaumont claims as the origin of his novel, has no documented historical origin of its own. While George Wilson Pierson and others trace it to the evening that Beaumont and Tocqueville spent at a French play in Philadelphia in October 1831, the details of the segregated audience and, in particular, the woman of "*éclatante*" beauty are not recorded in any of the copious notes, letters, or diary entries that Beaumont kept of their travels, suggesting that it stands at the threshold between the two forms of writing that Beaumont sees as comprising his text. Not only does this anecdote serve as Beaumont's major piece of evidence for the claim that the deployment of a fictive concept of race has come to define American public life; it also supports his recourse to fiction in order to pursue this claim by providing a model for his dazzling heroine. But at the same time that the story supports the novel to which it gives rise, it also poses a threat to Beaumont's plot. In a footnote, Beaumont reiterates how profoundly the incident he describes influenced his novel, as he defends his decision to include the anecdote against the advice of friends, who argued that it would reveal the central secret around which the plot turns: "The odious prejudice that I have taken for the principal subject of my book is so extraordinary and so foreign to our mœurs, that it seemed to me that the French would have difficulty believing in its reality if I confined myself to exposing it in a work in which imagination had some part."[13] Beaumont fears that the "veil of fiction" threatens to obscure the very subject which it has been crafted to "expose" (*exposer*), so he tells the story and potentially compromises the suspense of that fictional narrative, in order to show his readers "at once, in all its nakedness, the prejudice that I am going to describe and from which I have made follow, without exaggeration, such sad consequences."[14] In other words, Beaumont sacrifices the pleasures of plot—narrative's slow build to a shocking revelation—for the power of spectacle.

More than a conventional novel with a progressive narrative that moves forward in time, *Marie* reads like a continual return to a scene of disruption that is both blinding and revelatory.[15] The episode in the theater introduces into Beaumont's text the model for a public racial spectacle which exposes the reach of power precisely through the distortions it is able to accomplish. With it, "color" takes on the paradoxical status of an inward quality determined through public consensus; observation fails in this bizarre epistemology of "race"; and fiction enters as the sole means of exposing what he sees. The spectacle of the segregated audience introduces a series of disruptions (in the visible operation of social power and in Beaumont's own notions of the relationship of "color" and "race") that only an imaginative mixture of fiction, spectacle, and theatricality can adequately address. And this highly self-conscious amalgamation of forms emerges from his foreword as inextricable from the mixing that he takes as the subject of his work. By establishing the text's empirical "origins" in the theater, Beaumont highlights the convolution of perception, appearance, invention, and imposition that is fundamental to the very nature of his subject. But, though it is first identified in a space of enacted illusion, the fiction of this woman's color, established and reinforced by opinion, slides effortlessly into a place of irrefutable authority. Where the theatrical setting might invoke a fluidity of identity, mobility, or the de-essentialization of roles that can be adopted and shed at will, the scene in the theater reveals to Beaumont quite the opposite. What he sees instead is the naturalizing and essentializing power of public opinion, its manipulation of visual evidence through a voiced accusation backed by collective authority. The more arbitrarily invented and assigned the woman's "colored" role appears to be, the more firmly it is cemented in place.

Whiteness and blackness both emerge in this scene as rooted in fictions that are invented, imposed, and then performed according to social codes, but their performative status makes them no more fluid or changeable as categories. The space of the theater, which underscores racial categories as roles established by custom, should undermine the very concept of racial essence, but this is also the space of the audience, which metonymically represents the public empowered to impose the function of race as an "inward" essence. As Sollors argues, what Beaumont's hero ultimately realizes about race in America is that "there is no escape, as race is the only permanent social category" in a nation otherwise defined by mobility.[16] Given the traditional associations of fluidity and mobility that attach to theatricality, Beaumont's location of this scene in the theater is initially surprising.[17] When Beaumont invokes the space of the theater, he is exposing the fissures of a world in which invented qualities and abstract roles have achieved currency, but his critique focuses less on the instabilities of the resulting social roles than on their incredible rigidity. Beaumont's attention is drawn to the audience, not to the stage, and in linking the precarious position of the interracial figure to the image of the public as audience, Beaumont examines the idea of "race" in America as a fiction of consensus that becomes more real than any other quality. Rather than a fiction of law and letters, color and race become fictions of custom and opinion, and with this, spectacle and theatricality become Beaumont's privileged aesthetic modes.

The scene in the theater provides Beaumont with a basis for the critique of public opinion that runs through the entire text; it also introduces both a trope and a formal device rooted in the theater to which he repeatedly returns, as though to seek out sources of mobility, ways of unsettling the fixed category of "race," through a wide variety of textual "performances"—odd narrative devices, a virtual reenactment of the scene in the theater, and a highly public wedding ceremony. The visual disruptions that enter the text through the spectacle that Beaumont describes in the foreword return through echoes of the theater in the novel, and these moments comprise what I call the theatrics of the text. The theater serves Beaumont as a recurring site for exploring the relentless popular desire to expose racial origins and the fissures of racial power, as well as the model for a formal performance with which he periodically breaks the continuity of narration. At several key moments in *Marie*, the narrative is stripped to bare dialogue marked only by the name of the speaking character and a colon. By breaking the narrative into dramatic dialogue, Beaumont seems to turn the novel temporarily into a play. In the most prominent of these scenes, Beaumont places the characters' speech in relief and distances them from their situation within the scenes and settings of the novel. As if to mime formally the discontinuities of body, race, and national belonging that his "tragic mulatta" plot explores, Beaumont represents characters who were embedded in narrative descriptions of their faces or bodies as *dramatis personae*, disembodied, and momentarily serving as sites of substitution for other voices. In another scene, he returns to the theater, but he reassigns all of the roles, so that his narrator is the companion of the person whose origins are exposed, and that person is not a beautiful woman, but an angry young man, who resists and challenges the audience that stigmatizes him. Finally, in the climax of the novel Beaumont stages the wedding ceremony between an interracial couple that he argues is the surest means of unsettling the basis for racial inequality. But with each of these performances, the spectacular force of the public always returns—through an internalized racial stigma, exposure, and even through its most literal manifestation in an angry mob—with greater and greater force to combat the disruptions that Beaumont seems to seek. The repetition of these scenes and, in particular, the persistent return of an immobilizing racism, ultimately work on the reader much as the experience in the theater worked on the French traveler: as disruptive moments where the artifice of race becomes clear, only to be revealed as a powerfully intractable fiction into which the reader is obliged to "enter."

The critique of Jacksonian democracy that Beaumont launches in *Marie* focuses on a vision of the public sphere whose sovereign authority is explicitly racialized, whose chief mode is spectacle, and whose primary instrument is opinion. In the foreword, Beaumont calls this instrument "*l'opinion flétrissante*," an opinion which stigmatizes, brands, and punishes. Through the characters of Marie and George Nelson, Beaumont defines two very different subjective responses to the stigmatizing force of racialized opinion. Where Marie becomes the classic "tragic" mixed-race woman, who has internalized the stigma, George becomes a revolutionary, who initially confronts and later seeks to overturn the power that is always external to him, and through the gendered difference in how these two characters embody invisible color, Beaumont amends Tocqueville's model of opinion as a "mighty pressure of the mind" by rendering explicit its violent embodiments. At the same time that Beaumont explores the price of the body's estrangement in public life through those who live under opinion's punitive stigma, he also examines the intimate costs to those who impose this stigma. By defining "*l'opinion flétrissante*" through the episode in the theater, and by exploring the different applications of and responses to its power through the characters of George, Marie, Nelson, D'Alamanza, and Ludovic, Beaumont suggests—with far more direction than Tocqueville does—that racialization is not merely an effect of "*l'opinion flétrissante*," but that it actually defines the operation of opinion in the American public sphere as a chief manifestation of its sovereign right to punish.

## "*L'opinion flétrissante*": Crime and Penalty in *Marie* and *On the Penitentiary System*

Beaumont's phrase, "*l'opinion flétrissante*," succinctly conveys race's function as stigma, a hereditary punishment, he says, that is applied to "even those generations in which the color has disappeared" (*Marie,* 5). More than a social distinction, Beaumont argues, this stigma has formed an "abyss" within the population of the United States, which transcends time and pursues both whites and blacks "in every phase of social and political life." He continues: "It governs the mutual relations of the whites and the colored men, corrupting the habits of the first, whom it accustoms to domination and tyranny, and ruling the fate of the Negroes, whom it dooms to the persecution of the whites" (5). And, Beaumont adds with the kind of foresight usually associated with Tocqueville, "it generates between them hatreds so violent, resentments so lasting, clashes so dangerous, that one might rightly say it will influence the whole future of American society" (5). With its connotations of punishment and stigma, Beaumont's phrase captures the vast implications of systematic racialization: it has carved an "abyss" in the middle of the American population that has made all blacks the hereditary bearers of a crime and all whites their jailors and persecutors, thereby involving virtually all American lives with either criminality or punishment. "There is but one crime from which the guilty can nowhere escape punishment and infamy: it is that of belonging to a family reputed to be colored. The color may be blotted out; the stain remains" (78).

Beaumont shares with Tocqueville an understanding of public opinion that is articulated in the language of penalty, and their common idiom of punishment highlights how firmly rooted all of their writing on the United States—the two volumes of Tocqueville's *Democracy in America* and Beaumont's *Marie*—remains in their collaborative study of penal systems, *Du système pénitentiare aux États-Unis.* Critics have traditionally found something of an irony in this bibliography, to which Thomas Dumm has responded by demonstrating the continuity between the prison study and Tocqueville's *Democracy.* He concludes his reading of Tocqueville by arguing that "no irony need be made of this coincidence" at all, since the theories of majority tyranny and democratic despotism that Tocqueville develops in *Democracy in America* can be directly traced back to the prison study.[18] While concurring with Dumm's conclusions, I would add that some surprises remain in this textual genealogy; for

one thing, the complexities of collaboration suggest that the line linking the prison study to *Democracy in America* is not perfectly straight.
Although *On the Penitentiary System in the United States* is attributed to
both Tocqueville and Beaumont, it represents an unusual collaboration.
While they researched the project together throughout their travels in
the United States—visiting prisons, interviewing government officials,
prison administrators, guards, reformers, and inmates—on returning
to France, Tocqueville evidently gave the bulk of the writing over to
Beaumont, who composed the main text while Tocqueville contributed
only the notes and appendices.[19] In light of Beaumont's greater role in
the composition of the prison study, it may be more accurate to speak
of influence along with continuity in describing the relationship of the
earlier text to *Democracy in America*.

But beyond questions of authorship and collaboration, the greatest
surprise to be found in the relationship of the prison study to the later
works may lie in the critical assessments of public opinion and popular
sovereignty that both Beaumont and Tocqueville develop out of it. While
an analysis of prison systems and theories of punishment and rehabilitation would seem to lead them in the direction of law and the state,
this work instead leads them to the space of the public as the key site of
power in the United States. In Tocqueville's discussion of majority tyranny, he uses the example of punishment to define the transformation
of sovereignty that has taken place in American politics—"[I]t leaves the
body alone and goes straight for the soul." With this, political power
mimics disciplinary power, becoming more intimate and coercive as it
also alters the ancient relationship between the sovereign and the body
of its subjects. But rather than a disembodiment of political power, Tocqueville suggests that the body has been "left alone," abandoned to an
exceptional place as the regulation of life becomes the primary object
of power. The complexity of Tocqueville's analysis in these passages lies
in the fact that, in defining majority tyranny, he is describing the collapse of the sovereign into the subject. Under the sign of this collapse, he
suggests, a split occurs within the subjects of democracy who become,
at once, participants in sovereignty and bearers of that life on which it
acts most intimately. The violence of this split becomes evident when
Tocqueville nearly duplicates his description of the majority's disciplinary power in trying to define the novel cruelty of American slavery:
"[T]hey have, if I may put it in this way, spiritualized despotism and violence." The creation of the "stranger"—Tocqueville's overburdened term

for the democratic subject isolated from his fellows and for the racialized slave—marks the persistence of punishment at the heart of this newly sovereign public sphere.

Tocqueville comes as close as he ever does to making the link between slavery, race, and popular sovereignty that forms the basis of Beaumont's work when he arrives at the discussion of the "stranger brought by slavery into our midst," who endures an intimate penalty without partaking of sovereignty. By the same token, Beaumont sounds most like Tocqueville when he describes the operation of race through the disciplinary mechanisms of public opinion: "Public opinion, so charitable when it protects, is the cruelest of tyrants when it persecutes. Public opinion, all-powerful in the United States, desires the oppression of a detested race, and nothing can thwart its hatred" (*Marie*, 77). What they share is the basic assumption that popular sovereignty has not ended domination but reinvented it, both popularizing tyranny and transforming it into an intimate and coercive power that involves all subjects in it, however unevenly. The roots of this shared theory of power in the United States can be readily traced to their work on American penal reforms. The prison study emphasizes the isolation of inmates from society and from each other as the crucial innovation that radically alters the nature of punishment by aiming at reformation through the cultivation of reflection and remorse on the level of the individual conscience. But while the book examines the reform of inmates through their isolation and removal from society, what Tocqueville and Beaumont really describe in it is the intensification of a collective, public power and its concentration on the individual prisoner.

Beaumont and Tocqueville conducted their study of American prison reforms at a critical moment in the well-known transformation of penal systems, which Foucault traces in *Discipline and Punish,* from symbolic, collective, and spectacular public punishments to the secretive, coercive, individualizing model of the prison.[20] Their trip to the United States coincided with the period of heated debate over which model of penitentiary discipline best produced the results of rehabilitation: New York's congregate system, which forced inmates to labor together in absolute silence, or Pennsylvania's system of total solitary confinement. In studying this debate, and in comparing the New York and Pennsylvania systems, Beaumont and Tocqueville found the common assumptions of these models to be more striking than their differences. In particular, they argue that the practice of isolating and separating prisoners from each other had become a "popular truth" in the United States by 1831, with both systems presuming that any kind of reform required the atomization of prisoners, individualizing their punishment to prevent them from forming any sort of community inside the walls of the prison. Arguing in favor of the basic principle of isolation, Beaumont and Tocqueville fully endorse its underlying premise that moral contamination is the inevitable result of mixing prisoners together in large, undivided facilities. "Whoever has studied the interior of prisons . . . has become convinced that communication between these persons renders their moral reformation impossible, and becomes even for them the inevitable cause of an alarming corruption."[21]

If the new model of penitentiary discipline had abandoned some uses of corporeality in punishment—such as torture and attainder—it clearly retained others.[22] Beaumont's recourse to the language of contagion in the text signals the persistence of corporeality in the debates over penal reform: inmates are imagined as diseased subjects who bear their crimes in their bodies; thus, he argues, the prison is charged with the task of containing the spread of criminality both outside the prison and within it: "If this part of the social body on which the penitentiary system operates is but small, it is at all events the most diseased, and its disorder the most contagious and the most important to be remedied."[23] To cure the diseased part of the population and maintain its health, the penitentiary offers a double dose of isolation; isolating infectious criminals from one another, it also contains society's "diseased" part to prevent further spread. But alongside this corporeal rhetoric of contagion and disease, Beaumont and Tocqueville's study offers a narrative of the penitentiary's ostensible abandonment of the body as the crucial site of punishment, in a gradual movement of power "inward," which closely mirrors what Tocqueville describes as the key feature of majority tyranny. "Thrown into solitude, he reflects," Beaumont writes of the solitary inmate of Philadelphia's Eastern State Penitentiary. "Placed alone, in the presence of his crime, he learns to hate it, and if his soul is not yet jaded by evil, it is in solitude where remorse will come to assail him."[24] The principle of isolation is, at once, the mark of the allegedly humane abandonment of the body as the site of punishment, and the precise place where the body returns—both through the rhetoric of contagion invoked in the system's defense and in the language of "assault" that describes the inmate's relationship with his own sense of remorse.

In both Beaumont's text and in Tocqueville's notes of his interviews with inmates, they describe how punishment in these segregated prisons relies upon the "assault" of the conscience and the terrors of solitude.[25]

With nothing present to the inmate but his crime, he has no choice but to dwell in his guilt and feel the burden of his solitude. Responding to Beaumont and Tocqueville's image of the inmate "alone, in the presence of his crime," Foucault describes the intimate and deeply internalized penalty that is one of the results of the transformation that he traces. In isolation, no other influence can overthrow the power that guides an inmate's reform; the solitary prisoner is subject to "an intimate exchange [with] the power that is exercised over him," creating a totally individualized punishment that originates in the convict himself. "It is not, therefore, an external respect for the law or fear of punishment alone that will act upon the convict, but the workings of conscience itself."[26] In solitude, the inmate becomes the agent of his own penalty, containing in himself both the power that punishes and the disciplined subject of that power. As Beaumont and Tocqueville describe it, this results in a kind of insanity: "The solitary cell of the criminal is for some days full of terrible phantoms. Agitated and tormented by a thousand fears, he accuses society of injustice and cruelty, and in such a disposition of mind, it sometimes will happen that he disregards the orders and repels the consolations offered to him."[27] Where the punishment of isolation begins with an effort to protect the prisoner from the contagion of others, it succeeds by splitting him in two, turning him in on himself, and proliferating within his solitary cell a world of phantom others who torment him.

Foucault's assessment of how segregation operates on the individuals imprisoned within the two systems follows the analysis that Beaumont and Tocqueville offer closely; he makes precisely the same distinctions between the New York and Pennsylvania systems, while also noting the basic assumptions common to both of them.[28] But Foucault's account diverges from Beaumont and Tocqueville's in several key points: in what he describes as the disappearance of the body as the primary site of punishment; in his emphasis on secrecy over spectacle; and tied to both of these, in the role he describes for the public in the formation of disciplinary authority. The authority that functions "automatically" in Foucault's definition of the panoptic prison is produced by an architecture that controls visibility; the prisoner's subjection emerges from his belief that he is permanently visible to a guardian whom he can never see, whose presence he can never verify. These mechanisms of authority create a fictitious, vertical relation between subjects and disciplinary power, preventing any "lateral" relations from forming. Thus, "the crowd, a compact mass, a locus of multiple exchanges, individualities merging together, a collective effect, is abolished and replaced by a collection of separated individualities."[29] As the mechanisms of the panopticon "abolish" the crowd within the prison, so the public outside the prison also recedes, according to Foucault. The punishment of the prison is secret and totally individuated, and the public that once served crucially as "witnesses" and "guarantors" of earlier spectacular punishments disappears entirely from the process.[30] When Foucault extends this model of automatic authority to institutions outside the prison (hospitals, schools, factories), he also traces the abolition of the crowd of spectators in each of these sites: "We are neither in the amphitheater, nor on the stage, but in the panoptic machine, invested by its effects of power, which we bring to ourselves since we are part of its mechanism." The power that functions through the "trap" of visibility becomes more ubiquitous for Foucault the more deeply it recedes into individual subjects, ultimately "investing" them with the effects of their own subjection and "fabricating" them through this investment. Such a function of power is "the exact reverse of spectacle"; it counters the effects of the crowd and leaves no audience outside it to witness it.[31]

However, as Joan Dayan argues, Foucault's account of the decline of spectacular corporal punishments after the eighteenth century is somewhat hasty: "If Foucault's metropolitan world of public torture, what he described as the 'liturgy of physical punishment,' died out by the eighteenth and the beginning of the nineteenth century, the punitive spectacle and the requisite bodies were resurrected in the colonies."[32] This resurrection is most evident in the spectacular violence of North American slavery, with its extravagant displays of torture and suffering, but, Dayan argues, it is also evident in the law, which creates two artificial subjects out of human life: the civil body ("the artificial person who possesses both self and property") and the legal slave ("the artificial person who exists as both human and property").[33] Dayan traces the genealogy of the legal slave from the slave codes of the southern United States and West Indies to sixteenth-century common law principles, such as "tainted blood, bondage, and servility." These provide legal precedent for the invention of a class of persons who were, in essence, criminalized at birth and whose criminal status would be inherited by their children. With deep roots in common law, the slave code provided legal grounds for the creation of "disabled citizens," which, in turn, influenced innovations in penitentiary reform throughout the nineteenth and twentieth centuries, as the "shifting identity of the slave [is] reborn in the body of the prisoner." Dayan is not arguing for a chronology of the disabled citizen—in which the attainted criminal is supplanted by the slave, only to be transubstantiated in the body of the solitary inmate—so much as for an account of a capacious and constantly shifting legal form for the incapacitation of human life. It is no coincidence, she argues, that the system of solitary confinement was pioneered in a slave society, since it offers "an unsettling counter to servitude, an invention of criminality and prescriptions for treatment that turned humans into the living dead."[34] To Dayan's legal history, Beaumont and Tocqueville add a narrative of civil society's active engagement in the incapacitation of certain lives through the estranging and racializing work of "*l'opinion flétrissante.*"

When "metropolitan" reformers like Beaumont and Tocqueville looked to U.S. penal systems for innovation, what they found instead was the reinvention and redeployment of very old principles and practices for the incapacitation of human life. Where the effects of isolation, segregation, and visibility lead Foucault away from figures of the public like the crowd and the audience, these same effects lead Tocqueville and Beaumont right back to the figure of the public and the form of spectacle. For Beaumont and Tocqueville, the authority behind the prison's individuated and self-perpetuating penalty also appears ubiquitous, but not because its effects radiate outward from a central site like the state or the law. Rather, its ubiquity comes from the seemingly "panoptic" authority that they find at work in American public opinion itself. For them, the public's interest in and ultimate supervision over the prison system provides both a basis for the authority that operates within the prison and a model for its attentive surveillance: "Above [the prison authorities], there is an authority stronger than all others, not written in the laws, but all-powerful in a free country, that of public opinion."[35] Rather than prisons that are rigorously separated from public life, Beaumont and Tocqueville describe institutions that are integrated into the public through overlapping circles of surveillance. Despite the two systems' architecture of segregation and emphasis on isolation, which would seem to thwart publicity, the public attempts to peer into these fortresses at every opportunity.[36] When Tocqueville briefly describes in *Democracy in America* how the attention of the public has focused itself enthusiastically, if somewhat unevenly, on the reform of prisons, he is explicitly arguing that no energy or authority is exercised in America without the full force of opinion behind it, but his comment implicitly highlights that the innovations in punishment also mirror some of the more intimate operations of public opinion, specifically, its formation of an immaterial power through the fabrication of the thought, will, and desire of individual subjects (*Democracy in America*, 250, 255).

Just as the public retains its constitutive place in the system of punishment that Beaumont and Tocqueville describe, so it also maintains
a particular reliance on spectacle, though that, too, has undergone a
transformation. Foucault argues that the difference between a society
of spectacle and a society of surveillance might be summarized as a
near total reversal in how such a society observes itself, a shift from a
large number of people gazing on a small number of objects to a small
number of people observing the multitude, each atomized member of
which remains constantly seen but unseeing.[37] The emphasis that Beaumont and Tocqueville place on the public's engagement in prison reform
suggests that a different shift of punitive visibility has occurred under
American prison reforms, one in which the gaze of a collective public on
institutions of reform accompanies the constant vision—either actual or
imagined—of that public in the eyes of sharply individuated subjects.
Ultimately, it is not the sense of being seen that puts terror to work on the
conscience of the isolated inmate, but what he sees in that solitary cell
"full of terrible phantoms."[38] Part of the disciplinary function of solitude
is the creation within the inmate himself of the hallucinated specter of
the public that haunts Tocqueville's democratic subject: "Each man, as
he looks at himself, sees all his fellows at the same time" (*Democracy in
America*, 484).

The sense that penalty has migrated from the exclusive province of
the state to the public sphere, expressed tentatively in *On the Penitentiary System*, becomes so explicit in *Marie* that it approaches the point of
absurdity. Early in the novel, Beaumont's French narrator remarks with
surprise at the number of voluntary commitments that his American
hosts maintain, each of which reveals both how civil society has taken
on the work of the state and how good citizenship has become conflated
with efforts to reform and normalize one's fellows. Nelson, for instance,
had "obtained successively all the honorific titles to which an influential
citizen of the United States can aspire: he was a member of the Historical
Society, president of the Bible Society, the Temperance Society, the Colonization Society, Inspector of Prisons and Asylums, and he was, besides,
an anti-Mason" (*Marie*, 32). In Ludovic's catalog, Nelson's republican
commitment to countering the influence of secret political cabals and
strong drink is all of a piece with his work as a prison inspector and
advocate of African colonization, as civic duty collapses into the work of
policing the public and its borders. But Nelson is not the only character
thus engaged in the work of monitoring his fellow Americans. In an early
chapter, called "The Baltimore Alms-House," as Ludovic is beginning to

fall in love with Marie, he secretly follows her one day and tracks her to an almshouse, where she attends to "the poor, the ill, and the mad" by crying (literally) *on* them.[39] Marie's unusual method of giving comfort seems out of keeping with the mission of a public institution, but her sentimental labor at the almshouse turns out to be crucial to its purpose. Serving as Ludovic's "guide through the miseries of humanity," Marie participates in the work of the institution as she calms the most unruly of its inmates by her mere presence and helps to reconcile each of them to their incapacitation as public subjects.

During the guided tour of human misery that Marie gives him, Ludovic describes in detail three of the inmates confined for madness—"the poor people who have lost their reason"—and he struggles to impose some sort of meaning onto their shared condition. He notices the first two when "lamentable outcries reached my ear" (*des cris lamentables frappent mon oreille*); his interest is particularly piqued by the two because, he says, they "had reached madness by opposite paths"—one by crime and the other by innocence (44). Although Ludovic insists that the first inmate has gone mad from crime, as he tells the man's story it becomes clear that it was punishment that robbed him of reason: "the first, condemned to solitary confinement had gone mad in his cell." Ludovic recounts the man's insanity in terms that follow closely Beaumont's accounts of solitary confinement in the prison study. Isolated in his cell, the man begins to hallucinate; he is haunted by "bloody phantoms" all day and accosted at night by a voracious eagle who waits to tear out his heart. Driven insane by the "assault of conscience" in solitary confinement, the man has hardly faired better in the almshouse; he continues to see the same bloody phantoms in his jailors, and accuses them of killing a butterfly which had become his sole companion. The second, "innocent" inmate is a young girl who has gone mad through an extremity of religious enthusiasm; she had lost touch with the material world, Ludovic says, because "she was already an angel." Ludovic meditates on these two figures, pondering the "mysteries of humankind" that led two such different people to the same state, and he condemns the mainstream of society for its failure "to admit of extreme goodness or extreme evil." But just as Ludovic seems to wrap up the troubling mystery of the two inmates in a tidy condemnation of "society's" paradoxes, his meditations are disrupted by several "frightful shrieks" (*hurlements affreux*).

These shrieks introduce the only enslaved character in a novel subtitled

"Slavery in the United States," and the pairing of the story that follows with those of the convict and the enthusiast complicates Ludovic's initial attempts to make sense of insanity, innocence, crime, and penalty in America. Although Beaumont ends up pairing the ex-convict and the enthusiast, interrupting Ludovic's contemplation of the first two with the slave's cries, it is clear that the slave figures crucially into this grouping. In an early draft of this scene, Beaumont used the same phrase— "*hurlements affreux*"—to introduce both the convict and the slave (he changes the ex-convict's introduction to "*cris lamentables*" in the final version), and as those "frightful cries" echo through the corridors of the almshouse, it seems that something more than lamentation and pity is being demanded.[40] The man whose frightful shrieks disrupt Ludovic's reveries was once a slave in Virginia; he was purchased and transported to Maryland by "the foremost dealer in human flesh in the United States," a man named Wolfolk, in whom "all the vileness of slavery was personified" (46–47). If Wolfolk is the personification of slavery's crimes, the former slave is the personification of its suffering: "[He] was subject to such brutalities that his reason had snapped." Even after his escape from the slave trader, the man remains prey to terrifying visions: "[He] believed his mortal enemy was constantly at his side, awaiting the moment when he could cut out from his body strips of flesh for which he hungered" (46). Like the ex-convict, the former slave lives in terror of being devoured, and the voracious eagle—with all of its obvious nationalist iconicity—morphs into the slaver-trader hungering for human flesh.

The ex-slave is the figure who cannot be contained in Ludovic's moral calculations of guilt, innocence, and madness. Like the enthusiast, he is an innocent, but like the convict, his incapacitation is the result of a punishment that is both legal and publicly sanctioned, thus his madness is an accusation. As Ludovic and Marie enter the man's cell, Ludovic describes a tall, "manly," and "noble" figure who sees in every visitor (including Ludovic) another persecutor: "'Monster!' he cried, 'You thirst for my blood'." Only Marie can provide any comfort to the man, but her sympathy mostly serves to blunt the full effect of his wide-ranging indictment. "His madness presented a horrifying spectacle to me; however it was softened by the memory of Marie's compassion for him" (46). Marie's work of compassion in the almshouse ends up insulating Ludovic from realizing—for a time, anyway—the full implications of its "horrifying spectacle." Only later, after Marie's father has demanded that Ludovic tour America for many months to come to a truer sense of the nation and its prejudices, does Ludovic begin to comprehend what the spectacle of the former slave's madness and his universal accusation might mean.

> In a barbaric country, one has but one hate in the presence of the greatest misery—hate against the despot. To him alone belongs all the power; through him alone comes all the evil; against him alone are aimed all imprecations. But in a land of equality all citizens are responsible for social injustices; each is a party to them. Not a white man exists in America who is not a barbarous, iniquitous persecutor of the black race. (73)

Rather than a form of madness, the slave's "frightful shrieks" signal his response to an injustice for which "all citizens" are responsible, but his efforts to direct "imprecation" and hatred against the public which is party to his abuse only result in his incarceration and total incapacitation. There is no singular despot whose persecutions one can assail, because, as Ludovic comes to understand twenty years before the *Dred Scott* decision formalizes this into law, citizenship itself entails persecution.

The legacy of the American Revolution—for Beaumont, as for Tocqueville—does not lie in the eradication of despotism, but in the dissemination of responsibility for its persistence throughout the citizenry. Making explicit what Tocqueville merely implies, Beaumont reinterprets popular sovereignty as "the sovereignty of hatred and scorn" (77). Rather than a public sphere of deliberative debate, Beaumont finds one in which a sovereignty of malign sentiment directs everything from the punishment of the isolated prisoner, to the abuse of the slave, to the organization of the theater audience by visible and invisible "color" alike. Democracy's most brutal spectacle is repeated everywhere Ludovic travels, creating structures of punitive visibility in the theater, the prison, the almshouse—even within the Nelson family. Throughout *Marie*, Beaumont explores the different meanings of revolution that circulate in the United States and France, and as he strikes at a series of nested fantasies about the American Revolution—that it has ended tyranny and despotism, that it has decorporealized power and punishment—he is most critical of the conviction that the Revolution is complete. Beaumont recognizes that the discourse of the Revolution's completion—the insistent belief that it ended with the overthrow of a monarch—is essential to the constitution and preservation of the form of sovereignty that has taken the place of monarchy—"the sovereignty of hatred and scorn" that predicates citizenship on racial persecution. In the links that Beaumont's narrator repeatedly makes between the popularization of sovereignty and the virulence of racist persecution, he shows how racism emerges in the very gestures which call an end to revolution.[41] Thus, rather than the post-Revolutionary republic he expects to discover, Ludovic finds something closer to a restoration of hereditary despotism through an aristocracy of skin, an American Thermidor.

## America's French Revolution

A discourse of failed, incomplete, and deferred revolution runs throughout *Marie*, and with it, Beaumont interrogates Americans' investments in the completion of their own revolution without fully relinquishing the promise and the possibility of its continuation. The text's preoccupation with questions of revolution makes a certain historical sense, given the events that prompted Beaumont and Tocqueville to travel to the United States in the first place. Having sworn an oath of loyalty to the newly enthroned Louis-Philippe in the aftermath of the 1830 July Revolution—which deposed the last Bourbon king, Charles X, and marked the end of the restored aristocracy—the two young aristocrats had acted against the strong wishes of their families without fully dispelling the suspicions of the new government about their true allegiances. The opportunity to tour the United States to study prison systems provided an escape from an awkward political situation at the same time it offered them a chance to examine the social and political institutions of a nation whose revolution had ostensibly concluded.[42] Revolution, for Beaumont and Tocqueville, was thus an urgent present condition, not the monumental historical object that it was becoming in the United States, and in many ways the tension between these two understandings of revolution motivates and structures the text. Beaumont was struck both by the manifest failure of revolution-era politics in a nation whose identity was so indebted to its Revolutionary history, and by the persistent cycles of violence which indicated to him that the Revolution had by no means ended. In *Marie*, Beaumont portrays the persistence of violence in the United States—particularly racial violence—as evidence of the kind of counterrevolutionary struggle that had prolonged the French Revolution into the nineteenth century, re-reading America's recent history through the lens of France's.

Indeed, the link between the legacies of the French and American revolutions is embedded in the structure of Beaumont's novel. The July Revolution provided the impetus for Beaumont's own writing; the failures of the 1790s send his French narrator fleeing into the American wilderness; and both the American and the Saint-Domingue revolutions subtly emerge as models for George Nelson's plot to overthrow southern slavery and northern racism late in the novel. The narrative that Beaumont frames with the anecdote of the woman in the theater on one end and numerous appendices on the other begins with its own framing device: an unnamed French "Voyageur" arrives in the American wilderness in 1831, seeking an escape from the complications created for progressive young aristocrats by the July Revolution. Attracted to the idea of settling on the frontier, the traveler makes his way to a remote area of Michigan, virtually retracing the itinerary that Beaumont and Tocqueville followed on their western tour. The young man has come to America with wild illusions about the happiness that he can find living on the border of the wilderness with an American wife. There, he meets Ludovic, another Frenchman who fled to the United States to escape the recurrent failures of earlier revolutions, only to discover the violence of American racism when he attempts to wed Marie. The conceit of the narrative is thus a curiously doubled plot of flight from European revolution toward a hope for regeneration through expansionist settlement and marriage in America, which traces a path that also recalls the author's own westward movement, ambivalent relationship to Revolutionary France, and response to American racial attitudes specifically as they focus on an apparently "white" woman. In positing the strange, layered narration of the work as the product of both the cycles of French revolution, reaction, and counterrevolution and the violence of racialization in America, Beaumont forges a link between the unfinished work of the American and French revolutions, and he derives literary form from it. Ultimately, in the multiplication of narrators, the doubling of stories, and the interruptions to narrative, the text performs the dispersion of authority that the thematics of Beaumont's inquiry into revolution, race, and public opinion introduce.

This is nowhere more apparent than in Beaumont's peculiar use of dramatic dialogue in the middle of prose narration, which occurs for the first time when the young French traveler meets Ludovic, and again, crucially, at the revelation of Marie's origins. In the first instance, stripping away the voice of the unidentified third-person narrator and highlighting the voices of speaking characters serves to introduce Ludovic as the embedded narrator and protagonist of the novel. The dialogue begins as an exchange between equals, but it ends with Ludovic's seizure of the narrative, as he seeks to dispel the young man's illusions about the United States. Ludovic accuses the young man of a willful ignorance—"There are illusions that sometimes cost us many tears!"(13)—and he claims that his (Ludovic's) life is an example not to be imitated, as he attempts to impose on the young man a clearer view of the nation he has chosen as his home. When the traveler lists the attractions that have brought him to America (solitude, wilderness, the liberality of rights and political institutions), Ludovic counters them one by one, while the text mirrors his efforts to dispel the young man's illusions by purging the page of everything but dialogue. The appearance of dramatic dialogue plays with the visual register of the text in two ways: while it suppresses all descriptive narration, making the speakers themselves "invisible" to the reader, it lends a heightened visibility to that speech by allowing it to stand alone on the page. In this, it performs on the reader a version of the disillusionment that the traveler is experiencing, and it once again evokes Beaumont's story of the segregated theater. If the spectacle that Beaumont recounts in the foreword stands as a kind of primal scene for the text, it introduces, among other things, a pattern of punitive visibility that contains an enforced seeing (on the narrating Beaumont) and an imposed visibility (on the woman), both of which are backed by the authority of consensus uttered performatively by Beaumont's theater companion. As this mutual dependence of visibility and vocal agency makes spectacle the primary means through which Beaumont apprehends the public sphere in America, so it also directs his turn to the theater as the principle aesthetic form through which to interrogate and engage it.

With his periodic use of theatrical dialogue and chapter titles like "Le Drâme," it sometimes seems as if Beaumont conceived his novel as a play. (In a marginal note on a draft page of the chapter that introduces the Nelson family, he even described the chapter's mise-en-scène: "Nelson reading the Gazette, George in profound reflection and looking up often from his reverie to admire his sister."⁴³) In staging the Nelsons' domestic scene, Beaumont installs Ludovic first as an internal audience, and then as a participant to their tragedy once he learns the family's secret. This secret is, in truth, a fairly open one in the novel. If the anecdote in the foreword hasn't already given it away, Ludovic's description of Marie as a "stunning" (éclatante) beauty (32), oppressed by an inexplicable darkness certainly should: "Her glance was melancholy . . . yet one could see shining in her great dark eyes a flash of that ardent light which scorches the Antilles; her brow would bend, weighted by an indefinable sadness" (40–41). But the more intrigued Ludovic becomes by Marie's mysterious melancholy, the more confounded he is by the garbled signification of her gaze, melancholy and bright, somber and fiery. Ludovic regards

Marie simultaneously as an erotic object and a riddle to be solved, but despite the "mystery" that the chapter's title alludes to, the epistemological problems that Marie first presents him with are resolved quite quickly in a chapter titled (helpfully) "The Revelation."

As soon as Ludovic declares his love for Marie, Nelson gathers Marie, George, and Ludovic together and candidly tells him that his children are both legally considered "colored" through a distant relation of their mother's, and that a marriage between Ludovic and Marie would be illegal. Through the story that Nelson openly tells of his wife's origins, Beaumont presents another, more insidious, model of "revelation." Theresa Spencer was an orphan from Louisiana, "innocent and beautiful" (and also in possession of "*une éclatante blancheur*"), whom Nelson married in New Orleans. Just after the birth of their children, a jealous former suitor of Theresa's produced proof that her great-grandmother had been a slave. Theresa quickly died from the shock; the stigma ruined Nelson's business; and he and his children fled to Baltimore, where Ludovic meets them passing as a "white" family. The revelation of Theresa's past by the relentlessly (and pointlessly) villainous Fernando d'Almanza follows the model established by the audience in the foreword, the bearers of "*l'opinion flétrissante*" who impose racial stigma by establishing family origins. Despite his Spanish name and Caribbean provenance, D'Almanza is repeatedly referred to as "the American," and he serves primarily to condense the amorphous force of opinion into a single agency. D'Almanza's accusation slips fluidly into a kind of universal accusation; with a word from him, all of New Orleans is enlisted in a retroactive effort to "color" generations of Theresa's family. "At Fernando's voice, sleeping memories awoke . . . . Public opinion was in a turmoil; a sort of inquest was held; the oldest inhabitants were consulted, and it was found that a century before, Theresa Spencer's family had been soiled by a drop of black blood" (55).

As Nelson explains to Ludovic why he cannot legally marry Marie, Ludovic registers the same bafflement at the incongruities of color and race that his author does in the foreword, and it becomes clear with this repetition that the real enigma has only just begun to appear. Even though the "mystery" of Marie's burning melancholy eyes is apparently solved, Ludovic cannot see what has been revealed about her—he really sees nothing but her "*éclatante*" whiteness. The warring signs of burning eyes and blinding whiteness occlude the authority of visual evidence: that her eyes supposedly betray the "ardent" light of the Caribbean implies one color, which Nelson's revelation seeks to make clear to Ludovic, while the whiteness of her face (evoking the "swans" of northern regions) suggests another, blinding the baffled Frenchman with two illegible and overdetermined shades that will not be allowed to blend. *"Éclatante"* whiteness, as it appears throughout the text, is an excessive and illegible whiteness from which both the crime and penalty of color might be established by opinion. The term also functions as a kind of shorthand for the recurring revelation of the incongruities of an invisible color and a biologized, heritable concept of race, which unleashes a crisis of knowing that here alters the narrative texture of the novel. In this scene, Beaumont again brings together the trope of publicly established origins (through Theresa's story) and the figure of the interracial woman, whose very appearance dramatizes the paradox of racial thinking. But whereas in the earlier scene Beaumont stops at the unsettling, disruptive revelation of racial power and its slippage, in this scene he goes further. By shifting the focus from Marie to the character of George and shifting from narration into dramatic dialogue, Beaumont explores more deeply the roots of opinion's sovereignty and the various forms of corporeality it requires, from voice to color.

Ludovic insists that his intention to marry Marie has not been altered by the revelation, but Nelson tries to change his mind by describing to him the relations of whites and blacks and the severity of the prohibition against interracial marriage in America. At this point, Ludovic and Nelson engage in an argument that Ludovic describes as a kind of flashback. He presents it, he claims, exactly as his memory has preserved it: "[It] left traces on my memory which time cannot efface."[44] Ludovic's ostensibly oral narration—the voice that speaks to the traveler—gives way to a dialogue between Nelson and himself which can only be marked textually, and it signals his temporary shift out of the mediating position of spectator and narrator. The disappearance of Ludovic's narrative voice implies an abdication of authorial power; rather than controlling the representations of the characters through an overarching narrative voice, Ludovic allows them to speak for themselves. As the discussion turns on questions of citizenship and equality, so this formal device seems to mime the equal standing of the speakers. The representation of dialogue provides both the illusion of immediacy and a representation of equality, but it is worth reiterating that this formal illusion of perfectly remembered and immediately rendered dialogue also enters just as Ludovic has finished describing another crisis of seeing and knowing:

NELSON: The black race is despised in America because it is a race of slaves; it is hated because it aspires to liberty. Common practice and law say the Negro is not a man, he is a thing . . . . For the slave, there is neither birth, marriage, nor death. The child of the slave belongs to the slave's master, as the fruits of the soil belong to the owner of the land. The loves of a slave leave no more trace on society than does the breeding of plants in our gardens; and when he dies, the only thought is to replace him, as one replaces a fruitful tree destroyed by a storm.

LUDOVIC: Thus your laws forbid Negro slaves to have filial respect, paternal love, and conjugal tenderness, then what is left to them in common with mankind?

NELSON: The principle once admitted, these consequences follow: The child born in slavery knows no more of family life than does an animal. The maternal bosom nourishes him as the teat of the wild beast feeds her young. The touching relationship of mother with child, of child with father, of brother with sister, have neither sense nor moral value to him, and he does not marry because, belonging to someone else, he cannot give himself to anyone.

LUDOVIC: But why do not the American people, enlightened and religious, recoil in horror from an institution which offends the laws of nature, morality, and humanity? Are not all men created equal?

NELSON: No people are more attached than we to the principles of equality; but we will not allow a race inferior to ours to share in our rights. (58)

Initially, Nelson and Ludovic debate the outrages of slavery in an oddly impersonal way, as if rehearsing familiar and tired arguments, with Nelson defending slavery and Ludovic arguing for abolition. Briefly unanchored from their situation in the narrative, they leave behind the matter of Ludovic's love for Marie and articulate positions on the political question of slavery which are only obliquely related to the scene. But even as their dialogue seems to interrupt the climax of the scene with this somewhat general digression into the origins and consequences of slavery, the break into dialogue enacts textually a fascinating family drama of division and exclusion. Nelson gives his matter-of-fact explanation for slaveowners' denial of family ties to slaves just after he has described (and reiterated) the denials of marriage and birth rights that his own children must endure. But despite his earlier proclamations of love and grief for his children, Nelson will not renounce his patriotism, and as he continues to outline American notions of white supremacy, they appear to be his own. Nelson's "we" clearly refers not to his disenfranchised, stigmatized interracial family, but to the exclusive "we" of the "people" he describes, attached to an equality defined through slavery, racism, and division. In a passage that Beaumont eventually cut from this dialogue, Ludovic reacts to the stunning transparency with which egalitarianism cedes to nationalism and yields racism: "Thus you often say 'men,' but it is 'Americans' who are equal—you recognize nothing but a national equality."[45] Nationalism is the discourse that dictates Nelson's sentiments, and as he embraces this "we," he shows how intimately that feeling works on him. He clearly reveals the power of a consensus that links family life so seamlessly to state and public; his nationalism takes on an almost biological character, trumping even filial affection, as the good American patriot is shown to be a very bad father.

Immediately after Nelson most clearly articulates a racism which he now seems to own through his repeated invocations of a national, white "we," the narrator briefly interrupts the dialogue to remark on George's appearance: "At these words, I saw the color mount to George's features, and his lips trembled on the verge of uttering a cry of indignation, but he made a powerful effort and succeeded in restraining his wrath" (59). George's exclusion from this presumptuous dialogue is thus represented in the text by his appearance and subsequent disappearance as the speakers' names eclipse the description of him in the narration, and the reference to his heightened "color" seems to emphasize the reason why. Ludovic's narrative voice, which had ostensibly been suppressed to highlight the immediacy and purity of the represented speech, must return in order to account for the silent characters present in the scene. When the dialogue resumes, Nelson persists in his proslavery argument, claiming that slavery can only end slowly and that liberty is "dangerous" for those not accustomed to it. With this, George explodes, shouting "Stop!" and abruptly ending the closed dialogue between his father and Ludovic that he calls "iniquitous and cruel" (60). By first interrupting their conversation and then entering it, George challenges the authority that Nelson claims, both as his father and as the speaking representative of the dominant culture, and through George's silent rage, which quickly explodes in a vocal interjection, Beaumont exposes the flaws in his own formal conceit of self-representation and equality by revealing its exceptionalism.

With George's assertive entry into the dialogue, the scene might be said to stage a subtle allegory for the American Revolution and its failures.

To paraphrase two well-known narratives of Revolutionary America, George's shouted "Stop!" signals an oratorical revolution against patriarchal authority that, as the scene progresses, ultimately becomes a challenge to the legitimacy and completion of the American Revolution.[46] Rather than the patriarchal authority of a king, Nelson clearly stands as a figure for the Revolutionary father who is also the enslaver of his children. Nelson's naming of the American "we"—a people "attached to the principles of equality" who nonetheless "will not allow a race inferior to ours to share in our rights"—both cites and alters the opening of the Declaration of Independence, suggesting that the bad father whom he most resembles is drawn from the image of the slave-owning Jefferson. When George voices his opposition to the unjust and prejudiced authority that his father represents, he challenges the ambivalent results of the Revolution even as he initially follows its model. In *My Bondage and My Freedom*, Frederick Douglass describes just such a cycle of repetition and revolution as the undercurrent of any patriotic utterance in the context of slavery: the slave owner "never lisps a syllable in commendation of the fathers of this republic . . . without inviting the knife to his own throat and asserting the rights of his own slaves."[47] That George does not actually draw his knife in this scene (though he will) speaks even more clearly to his initial imitation of the Revolutionary fathers as he speaks out against their legacy; in performing his first act of rebellion vocally, forcefully entering into the dialogue, George also draws on what might be seen as a Jeffersonian model of declamatory revolution, with all of its ambivalence about the political relevance of the body.

By initially testifying to the injustice of his exclusion with a blush of rage—"I saw the color mount to George's features"—George gives a pointed answer to Jefferson's infamous rationale for the racial exclusivity of United States citizenship: "Are not the fine mixtures of red and white, the expressions of every passion by greater or less suffusions of colour in the one, preferable to that immovable veil of blackness which covers all the emotions of the other race?"[48] Jefferson's bizarre ruminations on "suffusions" of color and the highly charged "mixtures of red and white" serve as an oblique, digressive response to his own rhetorical question: "Why not retain and incorporate the blacks into the state?" Rooting citizenship directly in the skin—or, in the skin's alleged capacity to reveal a speaker's sentiments—Jefferson dispenses with the myth of abstraction and construes the citizen as explicitly embodied and resolutely biological. But whereas Tocqueville appropriates Jefferson's rhetoric throughout his chapter on the "Three Races Who Inhabit the Territory of the United

States," Beaumont's George offers barbed mockery of it, exposing the absurdity of the blush as political agent. Simply put, George cannot allow his skin to speak for him, because it automatically subjects him to representation by another—in this case, Ludovic, whose narration returns in order to describe George's physical response. The sign of George's full inclusion in the dialogue is the concealment of his body, as Ludovic's narration cedes once again to speaking voices. But this concealment does not deliver George a total abstraction from his body. Instead, with his entry into political speech, his body ceases to be mediated by other spectators and speakers, but his voice entails him in other forms of physical vulnerability.

In playing with the representation of speech and the appearance and concealment of characters' bodies as they debate the exclusions of citizenship, Beaumont employs a formal trope that locates George's vocal authority in his assumption of a role that can be adopted by other speakers. In the long dialogue that takes up most of this scene, the three men become *dramatis personae*, represented as parts on the page of a printed script where other voices might enter to speak their lines. In representing roles or parts, rather than particular individualities, the scene suggests that the men speak as dramatic personifications and this permits them two key kinds of mobility: they move out of the narrator's fixed physical descriptions of them, and they invite other voices to speak through their speech. As Nelson, George, and Ludovic are momentarily released from the narrative, their lines become sites of substitution, utterances that might be spoken by any reader. In thus inviting the substitution of other voices, the switch to dramatic dialogue signals a point of entry into the text for a plurality of voices.[49] The private discussion opens up to a public, which is made present throughout the dialogue by Nelson, who constantly speaks not as "I," but as "we." The dialogue initially seems to extend to George the possibility of speaking for just such a "we," while inviting it to speak through him; however, the first person plural has already been defined by his father as racially specific and violently exclusive, and it is Nelson's insistent adherence to this plural voice that reveals his domestic sympathies to be corrupted by consensus. Rather than emphasizing George's access to a position of equal standing with his father through his assumption of a similarly interchangeable role, this opening of the text to other voices instead signals the entry of the public, the social, the crowd that threatens George with a return to silence by "exposing" the color that cannot be seen.

At first, George's entry into the dialogue appears to offer a release from his invisibly raced body, a discursive "passing" that allows him to assume the position of an abstract role, from which he eloquently condemns his father's racism. But the problem of this scene becomes the viability of such a passing. When George first enters the dialogue, he reproaches his father for his iniquity, repudiating everything Nelson has said about the slave owner's refusal to recognize the slaves' filial ties and his attempt to define the slave as "chattel" outside of the "human" (60–61). George goes straight to the corporeal roots of the concept of race, attacking its construction through dubious sciences that seek to locate difference in the "measure [of] the Negro brain," and as he turns the discussion to the political uses of the body, he also exposes the hidden corporeality of vocal abstraction. While George speaks, he complicates his comments with an odd choice of pronouns, using the third person and distancing himself from the position of the slaves whom he has spoken up to defend. As he continues in his long monologue, he gradually claims pride in his African origins, and with this declaration George reveals his unwillingness to "pass." But even when George affirms his color, he does not switch to the first person plural in the more abstract discussion of slavery and racism; the plight of the slaves, the imminence of their revenge, not even the prejudices of color in the North are articulated as problems of a "we" in the way that Nelson speaks about the exclusionary consensus of the dominant white majority. The use of "we" is limited in this scene to Nelson—the only one speaking for a plural subject in possession of sovereign, majority status. To speak through the conceit of dramatic abstraction may permit George to confront his father, but it also threatens him with a certain corruption of his voice, either by distancing him from the identity he wishes to claim or by permeating his speech with the voice of consensus that seeks to annihilate his own. If dramatic abstraction stands for the prevailing forms of public discourse and political belonging in this scene, those forms are revealed as both raced and racializing, and as George's story will show, rebellion cannot come from speaking through them, but will require a more profound dismantling of them.[50]

The moment George returns to the question of skin color, he reaches the point where invisible color and the limitations of the dramatic voice collide. When he says, "a white skin is the mark of nobility" (62), the narrator instantly returns to lament the continual operation of all racial stigma, both seen and unseen. George's participation in the dialogue ends here (though the conversation between Ludovic and Nelson continues to be represented as dialogue) with this clear reminder that the privileges of abstraction, like certain colors, are subject to opinion. The only access George has to this position is through a performance that the text treats as subject to inevitable reversal: he cannot "pass" as white (even when he wants to), because the public hallucinates color and declares race. Nor can he affirm his color and speak with authority, because his utterance enacts his embodiment of that unseen color through which he is silenced. Racial exposure in the novel is not simply the visual uncovering that the word implies. Instead, it is an emphatic and anxious process of rendering embodied invisible notions of difference through an accusation that enacts something that cannot be seen. Made to embody color invisibly through public accusation, George reveals the ways in which the conditions of citizenship operate through a series of performances—abstraction, impersonality, invisibility—that keep the body at bay while regulating the most intimate spheres of life. And the more manipulable and subject to public opinion these performances become, the more Beaumont treats citizenship as a spectacular enactment of sovereign power.

Insofar as the theater is a form of visible movement, audible dialogue, and embodied abstractions that enact an imaginary scene, Beaumont's narrative device can be seen as formally mirroring his critique of a social power which functions through the manipulation of these terms. The hallucinated theater in the narrative evokes the spectacle of opinion, through which "race" is naturalized in the text's paradigmatic example of an enacted imaginary quality. Forging a kind of theater out of the text, Beaumont places the reader in the position of a spectator who witnesses the frustration of George's attempt to sustain resistance against both his father and the consensus of opinion, through the conceit of a dramatized persona. The scene exposes the fissures of a public sphere that guards its own embodied particularity through the anxious "revelation" of color in certain of its members, a public that offers George no access to positions of either consensus or defiance. Ultimately, if George is to overturn the American Revolution's legacy of enslavement and racialization, he must abandon its model altogether, looking instead to alternative figures of New World revolution, such as Nat Turner and Toussaint L'Ouverture.[51] Faced with the failure of abstractions like universal and natural right, George instead comes to imagine revolution as an uprising of the wronged. In response to Jefferson's predication of democratic citizenship on the expressive "mixture of red and white," he proposes a revolutionary alliance of "red and black"—an insurrectionary army of displaced Cherokee and enslaved blacks to overthrow white sovereignty.

"Courage, friend," George tells Ludovic, "we shall see better times—the dawn of liberty is not far off. The oppression weighing on our brothers in Virginia has reached full measure" (85). When George and Ludovic accidentally meet on a street in New York several months after Ludovic has parted from the Nelsons, George makes it clear that the revolution is coming. Ludovic is struck by George's mysterious looks, nervous gestures, and veiled allusions to the imminent "dawn" of southern liberty. But George refuses to say more of his mysterious errand in New York, so in a bizarre digression, they go to a play. With this return to the site of the theater, Beaumont once again invokes the figure of the audience as the bearers of stigmatizing opinion who enact the fictions and penalties of color. But in his third staging of spectacular racial exposure, it becomes clear that Beaumont's repetitions are not structured as circular returns to the same moment of blinding realization, but rather that they are structured as a spiral which, in its repeated confrontations with the outrages of racialized power, actually moves the narrative closer to an eruption of the violence that underscores each of these scenes. In the "Revelation" chapter, George first articulates his revolt against patriarchal racialism after Marie has been exposed by speaking through her silence, but the limitations imposed on his access to a position of speech quickly silence him. In the New York theater, Beaumont instead places George in the position of Marie and the Philadelphia woman when he is brutally exposed by an enraged crowd. If the failures of his father's revolution lead George into the plot murmured about in the beginning of this scene, the events at the play cement George's turn toward a violent and more absolute rejection of white authority.

As Ludovic and George walk through the city, "chance" leads their steps to a theater where a favorite play of Ludovic's is being performed, *Napoléon, ou Schoenbrunn et St-Hélène*.[52] "The name of Napoleon is great the world over!" Ludovic exclaims, and he urges George inside to watch Charles Dupeuty's nine-act portrayal of, essentially, a blunted revolution. Dupeuty's play traces Napoleon's occupation of Austria, a failed plot by a group of young Austrian revolutionaries to assassinate him, and the emperor's ultimate magnanimity and justice toward the would-be assailants when the plot is uncovered. In the play's climactic scene, the young revolutionary, Frédérich Staps, futilely lunges at Napoleon in the presence of the entire French army, but instead of executing him, Napoleon declares his admiration for the youth's bravery and spares him. Napoleon's apparent benevolence masks his call for an end to cycles of revolution. Remarking on Frédérich's resemblance to himself, Napoleon

is obviously invested in quashing any further revolt. Nonetheless, Frédérich persists, promising that if Napoleon frees him, he will only attempt the assassination again. The play's ambivalence about the repeat-
ability of revolution clearly sets the stage for the scene that unfolds in
the theater. Always susceptible to illusions of glory, Ludovic misses this
ambivalence and begins to feel himself swayed by the play into a patriotic
nostalgia for the "liberty" and "glory" of Napoleon's era (86). Suddenly,
however, his reveries of the Empire are interrupted when someone from
the audience yells, "Throw him out, he is a colored man!" The audience
quickly turns its attention from the glorious spectacle of "the Man of the
Century" to George:

> All eyes were fixed upon us. The shouting died away at times, but
> soon recommenced louder than before; the crowd was alternately
> calmed and aroused, as though what vexed them was sometimes in
> doubt, sometimes a certainty. I distinguished in the crowd a single
> man who seemed to be directing them and who made great efforts
> to communicate to everyone his real or feigned indignation. "Dis-
> graceful!" he cried, "There's a mulatto among us!" And he pointed
> to George. Then, the general cry arose, "Throw him out! He is a col-
> ored man!" (86–87)

Like all of the crowds in Beaumont's novel, this audience is peculiarly
eager to participate in the violent outing of a black man passing as white,
but when they see that the accusation has been made against the very
white-seeming George, they yield slightly, doubting the charge. But the
relentlessness of the man who leads the taunts arouses them, and they
redouble their shouts. This man turns out (of course) to be the malicious
d'Almanza, whose presence in every crowd lends both a face and a uniformity to this sometimes materialized, sometimes immaterial "opinion" that is ever vigilant in the novel. Confronted again with his family's
chief antagonist, George refuses to pass; he stands up, stares down the
crowd defiantly, and cries, "Yes! Yes—I am a colored man! . . . Cowards!
You are a thousand to one, and I defy you all! I demand satisfaction for
your affronts!" (87). If the play has horribly failed to do as Ludovic hoped
and awaken the audience to a truer sense of its own glorified dreams of
liberty, it clearly inspires George, whose fearless defiance of the hostile
crowd follows the unyielding assault of the young assassin against Napoleon and his army. But the audience has taken its own lessons from
the play's portrayal of Napoleon. When George challenges the crowd
to a fight, they laugh at him, refusing to recognize in him the slightest

threat. "What a fate—to have to bear insults and not avenge them!" (88). The audience's refusal to recognize George's defiance or to meet it with an appropriate response becomes its most devastating and hateful act. Mocking, belittling, silencing, and emasculating, the audience's laughter enrages George and provides the most immediate context for his insurrection, hinted at early in the chapter, though ultimately unrepresented in the novel.

Historians from C. L. R. James to David Brion Davis and Eric Sundquist remark upon the dialectics of New World slavery and French imperial expansion, through which the image of Napoleon necessarily conjures that of Toussaint L'Ouverture, the leader of the Saint-Domingue Revolution who ended Napoleon's "vision of an American empire."[53] Similarly, William Wells Brown, in his essay "St. Domingo: Its Revolutions and Its Patriots," describes an alternate history of the revolutionary period, arguing that Toussaint L'Ouverture ought not be read as a protégé of leaders like George Washington and Napoleon, but rather as their clear superior, the only general of the revolutionary era to free all his countrymen, enslaving no one and destroying no other nations in the process. "Toussaint liberated his countrymen; Washington enslaved a portion of his," Brown asserts. "Toussaint fought for liberty; Napoleon fought for himself."[54] As the crowd imposes a color and a body onto George, it takes on the sovereign character of the emperor; so supremely confident is this crowd in its power that it treats George's threats as, literally, laughable. When the crowd converges with Napoleon, though, George takes up the mantle of Toussaint. Certainly, his Virginia revolt delineates a revolutionary path that escapes from the failure of his father's revolution by seeking to overturn its legacy and vastly extend its liberatory project. However, unlike every other scene of racial strife and confrontation in the novel, this one goes largely unrepresented. When Beaumont details Ludovic's idealized dreams of participating in the "vast theatre" of 1790s Paris, he uses the language of theatrical spectacle to describe the young man's delusions, but in marked contrast, when George actually fulfills this fantasy, he does so in a decidedly un-theatrical way—his entire revolt happens off-stage (as it were) in a brief story related to Ludovic by a stranger at the very end of the narrative. The brevity of this scene seems purposeful: in an earlier draft of the chapter, when Ludovic hears of George's death, Beaumont devised an extended flashback in which George's comrade narrates the details of the final battle at great length.[55] In the published manuscript, however, Beaumont cut the description of George's death to a few sentences: "After these words he was kindled with new ardor; he had recognized a mortal enemy in the fray. I heard him cry out boldly, 'Fernando! Cowardly assassin of my mother, die—I am avenged!'" (165). Resurrecting D'Almanza once again, Beaumont stretches the boundaries of credulity, but he also achieves a certain economy in demonstrating what is at stake in this fight. As Toussaint stood against Napoleon, personifying the revolutionary challenge to New World empire, so George stands against D'Almanza, condensing into personal vendetta the battle over racialized sovereignty in the United States.

Throughout the novel, Beaumont uses the space of the theater, its imagery and variations on its form, to articulate a particular vision of racism and social power that always goes hand-in-hand with an indictment of the failures of Revolutionary projects, both French and American. In light of this view of the theater as a site of counterrevolution and the distortion of ideals of liberty and equality, the elision of George's revolt in the novel might be read, not as a dismissal of the possibility of a slave revolt or as an apprehension about representing black-on-white violence, but rather as Beaumont's acknowledgment that in showing this failed attempt at a truer revolution, he might risk its degeneration into disillusioning spectacle. While the story of George's failed rebellion and ultimate death are elided by Ludovic's narrative, the racial violence that appears to dissipate into the audience's mocking laughter does emerge, when Ludovic returns to New York to marry Marie and touches off a race riot. The violence that George's direct challenge fails to incite in the New York theater audience comes out instead in response to the specter of interracial marriage. Indeed, this story of Ludovic and Marie's disastrous attempt to marry during the riot at the novel's climax emerges in place of George's revolt. By backdating the New York race riots of July 1834 and folding this event into the fictional narrative instead of the 1831 Nat Turner rebellion (which George's Virginia revolt also invokes), Beaumont displaces Turner just as he does Toussaint. But in doing so, he also suggests a correlation between the two eruptions of racial violence, representing the riot as a kind of counterrevolt, a reactionary inversion of the slave rebellion that must happen off-stage if its imaginative power is to be preserved.

## The Wedding Rites: Sex and Violence in Public

Although historians refer to 1834 as the "year of the riots" in New York City, the April election riot, the May anti-abolitionist disturbances, and the August stonecutters' riots all paled next to the days of fighting, burning, looting, and demonstrating that began with anti-abolitionist protests on the Fourth of July and ended eight days—and nearly seventy destroyed homes and churches—later when the militia was called to restore order.[56] Spread over several days and throughout much of Manhattan, the July 1834 riots present a formidable complexity and frustrate easy summary. Unlike many anti-abolitionist actions in the 1830s, the riots were neither planned nor directed once they began, nor did they clearly target any particular institution or organization.[57] Indeed, so variable were the scenes of unrest—the Chatham Street Chapel, the Bowery Theatre, the Five Points neighborhood, the homes of wealthy antislavery activists and poor African-Americans—that historians do not even agree on what to call the events.[58] Disturbances began on the Fourth of July, when protesters gathered to shut down an abolitionist-sponsored Independence Day celebration at Charles Grandison Finney's Chatham Street Chapel. On 5 July, a story began to circulate that an English stage manager working at the Bowery Theatre had spoken ill of Americans (evidently calling them "a damn set of jack-asses"), which stoked anti-British feeling that was already intense in the wake of England's 1833 act to abolish slavery in its colonies.[59] On the 7th, the abolitionists whose Independence Day celebration had been shut down reconvened at the Chatham Street Chapel, but due to a scheduling error, they were interrupted by a music society, whose members became irate at being displaced by the mixed-race, antislavery group. A fight broke out between the two groups that was characterized in the newspapers as "a negro riot" and accompanied with calls for reprisal.[60]

These preliminary incidents provided a loose script for the seemingly incoherent sequence of events with which the rioting began in earnest on the night of 9 July. A huge crowd gathered early in the evening at the Chatham Street Chapel to break up another meeting of abolitionists, but when the police dispersed the crowd, they proceeded to the Bowery Theatre to disrupt a benefit performance for the English stage manager, George Farren, who had allegedly insulted Americans. Four thousand people arrived at the theater and hundreds broke inside to drive the actors from the stage.[61] When this was accomplished, a portion of the crowd then moved on to the home of the abolitionist Arthur Tappan, where they broke windows, looted the furniture, and set what they did not take on fire.[62] Burnings and lootings continued on the 10th and 11th, more explicitly targeting black-owned properties and churches. On the night of the 11th, groups of white men paraded through the Five Points, ordering everyone to light candles and stand in their windows. "Taking their cue from the Book of Exodus," Leonard Richards writes, they "passed over" the homes of whites and attacked every structure with no light or with black occupants visible through the windows.[63]

Though Richards describes the riots as unplanned and unorganized, he nevertheless argues that there was "rhyme," "reason," and "much purposefulness" in the selection and destruction of targets: black-owned homes, black churches, and meeting-houses known as gathering places for abolitionists.[64] Like Richards, both Sean Wilentz and Eric Lott read the rioting in terms of its "symbolic" logic and "narrative," finding in the riot—in Lott's words—"intentional, overlapping weaves of social codes and signifying systems whose larger, 'narrative' designs transcended the goals of single individuals."[65] In thus finding strategy, meaning, and intent in the acts of the disparate and converging crowds, the twentieth-century historians all follow one of the first and most comprehensive narrative accounts of the events of July 1834—Beaumont's final appendix to *Marie*. Cited by both Richards and Lott, Beaumont's appendix culled together multiple newspaper stories to present both a coherent narrative of the riots and a clear thesis about them.[66] For Beaumont, the accounts from which he drew his narrative confirmed the argument that he had established as the foundation of *Marie*: "All this proves that in the United States, under the rule of popular sovereignty, there is a majority whose actions are irresistible, which crushes, breaks, annihilates everything which opposes its power and impedes its passions" (251). The riots served for Beaumont as an exemplary case study in the centrality of both racism and slavery to the articulation of political power in the public sphere. Finding in them a formal consistency with other representations of the empowered public—from the theater to the prison to the alms-house— Beaumont presumed an almost total continuity between popular sovereignty and the actions of a disparate mob. For him, the riots were less an isolated local incident or an act of defiance by a marginalized group, than a symptom of national political culture and majority power. They stemmed, he argued, from a "sophism" often repeated in the press that tied the preservation of the Union to the perpetuation of slavery, characterized abolitionists as "traitors to their country," and ultimately excused the "noble sentiments" of "the factionists who abandoned themselves for three days to the most iniquitous and impious violence," for (he noted sarcastically) "every good citizen in the United States should keep the blacks in servitude" (250).

Even more profoundly, the riots appeared to validate Beaumont's focus on the politically explosive issue of interracial marriage in his novel and the crises of citizenship and political power, which his plot staged.[67] If the preservation of the Union required the endorsement of slavery, citizenship simultaneously compelled and empowered subjects to defend the nation in curiously direct and intimate ways. In the historical account of the rioting that he gives in the appendix, Beaumont suggests that one precipitating event was a personal ad placed in the *New York Commercial Advertiser* on 7 July 1834 by a white man seeking "to marry a young colored girl" (245). Given the ardent opposition of the *Advertiser*'s publisher, William Leete Stone, to the goals of the American Anti-Slavery Society, it is infinitely more likely that the ad was placed to raise paranoia over "amalgamation." Stone was among the powerful opponents of the AASS's goals of immediate abolition and the assimilation of freed populations, which he repeatedly cast as "amalgamationism" in his paper.[68] Indeed, nothing about the printed ad appears genuine. Alleging that the ad was taken from the *Liberator*, the editors "reprinted" it alongside a mocking rejoinder titled "A white wife wanted," which was written in a minstrelized slave dialect. Making an incendiary racist joke of the prospect of interracial desire, the *Advertiser* clearly undercut its own claims for the first ad's authenticity. In the ad, a man claiming to be "a friend of equal rights" writes in search of

> a young, respectable and intelligent Colored Woman (entirely or chiefly of African descent) who would be willing to endure the insults and reproaches that would be heaped upon her for being the partner of a white man, and who is either in low circumstances or would be willing to cede all she has or may have of this world's goods to the Anti-Slavery Society, that the mouths of gainsayers be stopped.[69]

Pointed in his designs, the purported suitor clearly intends that he and his bride shall stand as a testimony, and he specifies that she should be "entirely or chiefly of African descent," presumably so that their union would be all the more provocative a confrontation with the stigma. However, in the decidedly unromantic use to which the man means to put his intended, in his specific physical description of the ideal candidate, and in the demand that she relinquish all her property, the advertisement bears a discomforting resemblance to a request for the purchase of a slave. Nonetheless, in mentioning the ad in his account, Beaumont notes none of this and treats it as genuine, pronouncing its author "a friend to the Negroes" who openly "scorned" prejudice. If Beaumont misread the ad's authenticity, his error may be attributed to how closely its strategy mirrored his own. Indeed, a similarly doubled tactic of proving equality and provoking outrage lay at the very premise of his novel: "Intermarriages are certainly the best, if not the unique means of fusing the white and the black races. They are also the most obvious index of equality. For this twofold reason, unions of this sort arouse the rancor of the Americans above all else" (245).

Given his claim that the woman of "*éclatante*" beauty whom he spies in the Philadelphia theater prompted him to write *Marie*, Beaumont had little reluctance putting young women of color to political use as volatile and potentially explosive symbols of racial unity. Indeed, Marie is the figure in whom the most violent contradictions of American life inhere in his novel, but at the same time, she represent her author's hope for ultimate equality through a total union of races. The punitive visibility that in the prologue establishes the public's power to stigmatize, emerges in Beaumont's heroine as an immaterial and deeply internalized penalty that turns her character into a puzzle of self-negation. As a living figure of blinding paradox and visual disruption, Marie becomes a rather incoherent character. What little Marie does manage to say in the scene of the "Revelation," for example, is an attempt to repudiate the testimony of her white skin, which in turn repudiates the revelation of her hidden "color," essentially neutralizing her every expression, whether vocal or visual. When she tries to discourage Ludovic's affections, even her speech becomes confused: "[B]ecause my heart can love, you believe I am worthy of love; because my brow is white, you think that I am pure. But no! My blood contains a stain, which renders me unworthy of your esteem or affection. Yes! My birth condemned me to the contempt of men" (66). Vacillating between interjections of "Yes!" and "No!" Marie can only articulate the inherent contradictions of her status, troubling her father's testimony with her face as her speech meekly and confusedly affirms the "stain" he asserts. It is an imposed visibility that repeatedly silences her brother's public utterances, but it is Marie's actual appearance, beautiful but incoherent, that converts her every utterance into confused self-abnegation.

If Marie's situation resembles the typical bind of the tragic mulatta, caught between two races but belonging to neither, it is not in the traditional sense.[70] By accentuating her excessive whiteness while constantly reiterating the "color" imposed on her, Beaumont portrays her not as a victim of "warring blood" (torn between incommensurable racial stereotypes), but instead as the projection of an internally divided public ("discoursing on equality among three million slaves . . . uniting in itself, in a monstrous alliance, the most incompatible virtues and vices" [120]). In her inability to articulate any coherent expression of herself, Marie nonetheless expresses for Beaumont all the incongruities of the nation's false equality. But along with this, Marie also bears the weight of Beaumont's hope that full social equality will be achieved through interracial union. Beaumont's reliance on interracial marriage as "the best, if not the unique, means of fusing the white and black races" originates in the kind of transporting sexual desire that Ludovic evidences—a desire that is also palpable in his description of the woman in the theater. In his letters, Beaumont often dwells on the relative beauty of American women, but he reserves a particular ardor for women of mixed racial heritage. He writes in August 1831 about a population of women on the frontier who possess a strange beauty, and he attributes to them one of the few glimpses of social harmony that he witnesses in his travels: "Without ceasing to be as lively, they lose something of their primitive rudeness. . . . The Canadians call those who come from this double origin 'métiches' ('métis'). I saw some young métiches girls of a remarkable beauty."[71] Giving the feminine form (métiches) as the general term with the masculine form in parentheses, Beaumont implicitly genders this population as feminine and suggests that physical beauty might yield a balanced and peaceful social state. In light of what his novel reveals about the fate of interracial love in the United States, however, such sentimentalities appear grotesquely naïve. What happens between the romantic transports of Beaumont's letters on the métiches and the climax of Marie in an anti-amalgamation riot involves a total rethinking of marriage and its viability as a politically emancipatory act.

With the scene of the riot in Marie, Beaumont arrives at a particular impasse in the political strategy of interracial marriage, which Nancy Bentley has analyzed in postbellum writers like Charles Chesnutt. According to Bentley, interracial marriage in the postbellum era could not eradicate the stigma of race because that stigma is firmly "lodged in the domain of marriage," which recreates the "stigmatic body" of the former slave as a criminal. Interracial marriage presents a ruse of consent throughout the nineteenth century, Bentley argues, because rather than delivering on its apparent promise of uniting two contractually equal parties, it more often functions in public discourse as both a specter and a joke, "transform[ing] the emergence of a civil right for African Americans . . . into a ritual of public degradation."[72] Such a transformation is both so seamless and so relentless, I would add, because of marriage's doubled status as legal contract and public performance. As

Beaumont shows, the public's role as witness and guarantor of the wedding ceremony at the climax of *Marie* facilitates its conversion into a ritual of spectacular punishment. Initially, Ludovic's determination to marry Marie bears many of the transformative political imperatives that George's entry into the dialogue in chapter 8 does; it represents a drive to extend the reach of democratic political and social institutions without fundamentally altering them. However, when the lovers' disastrous attempt to marry emerges at precisely the place in the plot where George's insurrection might be expected (Marie's father alludes to the reasons for George's absence), the prospects for political reform have already been eclipsed. Instead of allowing the marriage of Ludovic and Marie to stand as "an index of equality," Beaumont stages the riot as a kind of counter-revolution that erupts for the explicit purpose of preventing the union of Ludovic and Marie, in a display of violence that Marie terms their "wedding rites" (125).

The events that theater historians call the "Farren Riots," for the Englishman whom the rioters sought to expel from the Bowery Theater, that historians of slavery call the "Tappan Riots," for the AASS leader whose home and business were destroyed by the mob, and that Beaumont frames in his appendix as complex and layered evidence of the irresistible power in the United States of the racial majority, clearly unfold within his novel as an "anti-amalgamation" riot. Beaumont claims that he added the fifteen-page appendix on the riots to "place beside the story, whose basis is entirely true, the exact account of all that happened," but what stands out in any comparative reading of his fictional and historical versions is the striking difference between them. In addition to backdating the riots, so that they serve as the climax of his novel in May 1827, he also condensed the events in time, space, and scope. While his historical account traces the rioting over several days and through its various and moveable scenes, the novel focuses on a single day and a single space— the Catholic church where Ludovic and Marie are to be wed. Instead of the multiple precipitating events that he traces in the appendix—from the conflict at the Chatham Street Chapel, to the insults attributed to Farren, to the advertisement in the *Commercial Advertiser*—Beaumont condenses the pretext and object of the riots to a single event: "Judge of our amazement on learning that the announcement of my union with Marie had been, if not the cause, at least the pretext of the insurrection!" (130).

Like all of the pivotal scenes in the novel, the riot scene plays off the aesthetic tensions between narrative and spectacle, but here, in the novel's most potent example of the violent return of "*l'opinion flétris-sante*," Beaumont preserves uninterrupted Ludovic's narration. If the disappearance of the narrator's voice in "The Revelation" allows the men's voices to emerge unmediated, performing a form of abstraction through public discourse that George exposes as impossible, then the preservation of conventional narration to describe the wedding riot expresses the impossibility of abstraction in a different way. Ludovic maintains control of the narrative throughout the chapter, but what he describes is the crowd's complete assumption of the plot. Abstraction becomes an absurd fantasy when Ludovic and Marie are targeted, personally and directly, by a violence that defines the public sphere. Against the performative fantasy of the wedding ceremony—the proclamation of equality with the enactment of the union—Beaumont stages the reactionary spectacle of the crowd, its violent attempt to stop the union in a paranoid repudiation of the sameness and equality that the marriage contract allegedly promises. Indeed, it is at the very moment when the priest prepares to consummate their vows that the angry crowd reaches the door of the cathedral: "The terrible shouts re-echoed from all about; terror seized the assembled faithful; the priest grew pale, his knees failed him, the ring that was to unite us fell from his hand!" (126). The "rite" of the riot interrupts the ceremony at its most performative moment—the conferral of the rings and pronouncement of Ludovic and Marie as husband and wife. When the rioting crowd bursts through the door of the church, it halts and supplants the wedding, just as the "wedding rites" scene itself supplants the representation of George's revolt. But even as the novel climaxes in a double evasion of two potentially transformative acts, the scene of the wedding literalizes the public's anxious and obsessive interest in maintaining boundaries of race by policing sexual relations.

By staging the wedding ceremony (as well as its interruption) that the advertisement in the *Commercial Advertiser* purportedly sought, Beaumont highlights the explosive function of interracial marriage—and its ritualistic prohibition—in public life. When Beaumont alters the appearance of the bride, from one "entirely or chiefly of African descent" to one of mixed racial heritage and white complexion, the effect is not to downplay the potential for provocation that Marie's marriage represents. Instead, what Beaumont's emphasis on Marie's white skin seems to do during the wedding riot is shift the entire burden of the political expression and explosive symbolism of the union onto her. As Marie is made to bear all of the paradoxes of race and color, as she is made into the object of both the public's racist opinion and Ludovic's antiracist fantasies, so Marie and her blinding, stunning, disruptive whiteness are made to be the site around which the public explodes in its violent rejection of interracial union. Just after the mob stalls the conclusion of her wedding, Marie faints under the weight of her insupportable over-signification, and Ludovic bizarrely marvels that Marie is "so beautiful in terror" that her limp and silent form only exacerbates the "confusion of our enemies" and the intensity of their violence (127). The success of the rioters' acts emerges on several levels: they disrupt the wedding, take over the plot, and convert Marie into an insensible reflection of a power that is both material and immaterial.

Beaumont's other significant revision to the historical record of the riot, his shift away from the Bowery Theater as one of the rioters' stops on their rampage through the city, is somewhat surprising given his constant recourse to theatrical tropes to stage exactly such moments of racial exposure and the violent interdictions of opinion. That the largest single crowd that gathered on the first night of rioting—four thousand people—formed outside the Bowery suggests something deeply spectacular about the riots, by which I mean something inconceivable without some relationship to an audience. And while Beaumont abandons the literal theater, in his shift from the Bowery to the church, he retains the language of performance and applause and ultimately does little to repress the staginess and spectacle of the riots. Instead, he converts the church into a theater, highlighting the self-conscious theatrics of the rioting crowd in its performance of reactionary violence against the legal performativity of the wedding ceremony. The riot becomes a movable theater in Beaumont's fictionalized account, and it carries democracy's spectacle with it. As Marie faints, Ludovic watches the crowd feed itself on its own applause, converting its violence into a terrible kind of entertainment that recalls the mocking laughter of the audience that expels George from *Napoléon, ou Schoenbrunn et St-Hélène*: "[T]he attackers cheered each other on to violence; each success was greeted with tumultuous applause." Beaumont describes a crowd that witnesses itself in the process of its own constitution as an arbiter of licit and illicit unions; empowered to designate and enforce an exception to the law, this crowd gleefully ascends to a position of "irresistible" sovereignty.

With the narrative's shift from George's revolt to Ludovic and Marie's prospective marriage, Beaumont's novel appears to abandon revolution and return to the public sphere and the questions of equality and civil right which it regulates. If George's path would overthrow and reconfigure the constituent sovereign power of the United States, then Ludovic's is the path of the reformer, seeking recognition by that power whose authority he, in turn, recognizes. However, when the wedding triggers a riot, Beaumont shows the public answering that appeal to recognition and reform with counterrevolutionary force. To the rioters, the sovereign constitution of the public *is* at stake in the question of interracial marriage, and they claim an authority that transcends both church and law to legitimize it. Interracial union is thus foreclosed as a politically transformative path in the novel, instead becoming an affirmation of national union and counterrevolutionary spectacle. Gone with it is also the image of the public as the sphere of rationalized inequity to which Nelson clings, as the public metonymically represented by the rioting crowd is one that forms itself through the spectacle of its own power and maintains that authority by its monopoly—however temporary—on force. By the time Beaumont sends Marie and Ludovic west into exile on the edge of the wilderness for the novel's denouement, their union is so overdetermined by public opinion that even domestic privacy has become unavailable to them, both within the boundaries of the United States and on its frontier. The only transformative, revolutionary prospect that remains at the end of the narrative is the one that goes unrepresented in it. However, if George's revolt defies representation in the novel, that may be because it can only be imagined as radically external to any constituted power whatsoever—that is, as absolutely outside the U.S. public sphere as Beaumont understands it.

# 3 / "The Hangman's Accomplice": Spectacle and Complicity in Lydia Maria Child's New York

In an 18 August 1842 column written for the *National Anti-Slavery Standard* during her two-year tenure as the paper's editor, Lydia Maria Child recalled the anti-abolitionist riots of the 1830s as a specter that had haunted the antislavery movement for nearly a decade. Child's reminiscences of the 1830s had been triggered, she explained, not by any signs of renewed violence against abolitionists, but by the sound of a katydid as she wandered one evening in Brooklyn: "Instantly it flashed upon my recollection, under what impressive circumstances I, for the first time in my life, heard the singular note of that most handsome insect." She goes on to describe George Thompson's harrowing 1834 visit to the United States, during which Thompson, his family, and their hosts were evicted from their lodgings, pelted with eggs and stones, and repeatedly assailed as "foreign agents" trying to foment disunion.[1] Child and several other members of the movement had accompanied the English abolitionist to New York on a steamboat that, she wrote, was "filled with our masters." Once Thompson was recognized by several passengers, he quickly became the subject of escalating threats, from angry looks to whispered insults to a drawn sword. "Never has it been my fortune to witness such fierce manifestations of hatred written on the human countenance," Child remembered. Though no violence had erupted, Child's writing portrays their antagonists as both "masters" and a latent mob, linking northern anti-abolitionists directly to southern slaveowners, while casting Thompson, herself, and their fellow abolitionists as fugitives, who are kept on the run. Upon learning that the news of Thompson's arrival had preceded them and that placards had appeared all over Manhattan calling for Thompson to be carried before "Judge Lynch," Child and the others fled the city to take refuge in Brooklyn, before beating a hasty retreat to Boston. "That night, I started at every sound, and when the harsh and unusual notes of that army of katydids met my ear, I was again and again deceived by the impression that they were the shouts of the mob in the distance . . . to my mind, the katydid will forever speak of mobs."

Like Beaumont, Child sees in the anti-abolitionist rioting of the 1830s "images of the French Revolution" with its alternating cycles of terror and reaction. As she describes the tense audience at one of Thompson's lectures, she indulges in some predictable fears about the working-class origins of the Revolutionary crowd, recalling one "ill-looking fellow, whose bloated countenance, so furious and so sensual, seemed a perfect embodiment" of the Parisian mob. However, she quickly added a complication, noting also the presence of a "genteel-looking young man, with nice gloves and white fur hat," who whispered furtively into the man's ear. Upon a closer examination of the audience around her, Child then offers a second reading of the forces that developed into anti-abolitionist violence, which now look less to her like a Paris mob than like an organized and widespread campaign. Catching "various nods and glances . . . exchanged between fine broadcloth and shirt sleeves," she concludes that the greatest threats to antislavery are not in local, isolated mob actions, but in the evident collaboration between the white elite and working classes, who act together in the name of "the glorious union." The danger Child sees is thus the capacity of such an unequal alliance to speak as a public and act as if in the interests of the entire nation. Child's "genteel young man," whispering riot to urban workers, clearly resonates with Beaumont's favored figure of malignant, aristocratic agency, Fernando D'Almanza. But where Beaumont's ubiquitous D'Almanza functions as a trigger, setting off mobs which appear to be latent in the public sphere because their power seems to Beaumont to be contiguous with popular sovereignty, Child finds a more complex relationship between "fine broadcloth and shirtsleeves," with more dire consequences for the public activities of the abolitionists. In Child's writings from the 1830s and 1840s, rioting represents just one of many instruments through which proslavery interests worked to curtail serious debate on abolition, most of them fully in keeping with what one might call the "legitimate," or "liberal," public sphere. The campaigns

against antislavery were wide-ranging and well financed, often by northern elites with ties to the southern economy, and their efforts to quash
any and all expression of abolition involved not only organized violence
but economic boycott and religious protest—key instruments of the antislavery movement as well.[2] Even print media—generally held to be the
hallmark of a liberal public sphere—became a central front for both antislavery and proslavery activism. Following the American Anti-Slavery
Society's broad pamphlet campaign in 1835, for example, what Carolyn
Karcher describes as an "American style" tactic of censorship emerged,
which sought to "discourage the publication and distribution of works
that [went] beyond the bounds of acceptable opinion, but the opinion
in question [was] attributed *to the public*."[3] Tracing the changing front
of the slavery debates, Karcher's analysis also reveals how the "public"
was coming to be understood less as the space in which the battles over
slavery were waged, less as the majority whose opinion was the prize to
win, and increasingly as the legitimizing political form through which
both sides must make themselves and their claims appear.[4]

Writing in 1842, Child stands at a distance from the violence of the
1830s: "Times have changed since 1835. Thanks to the despised agency
of anti-slavery societies, the abolition sentiment has now spread widely,
and taken a firm hold of the sympathies of the people." Her irony notwithstanding, Child is playfully sanguine about the "spread" of antislavery, but the fate of this essay—in which the sound of katydids recalls
to her more violent times—offers a qualification to her optimism. This
piece originally appeared in Child's "Letters from New-York" column,
which she began writing in regular installments when she assumed her
position as the *Standard*'s editor in 1841. Child imagined the "Letters"
as part of a larger program to broaden the paper's scope beyond its exclusive focus on antislavery activities, and they became a popular feature
(to the dismay of those who opposed the very premise that the mission of
the *Standard* or the Society ought to expand).[5] On leaving the *Standard*
in 1843, Child sought to return to her literary career, and to that end,
she decided to publish in bound form an edited collection of her "Letters
from New-York." The volume that was published in 1843 ended up sell-
ing out its first print run in a matter of months, and went on to sell out
ten more runs in seven years.[6] But Letter No. 33, on George Thompson's
thwarted trip to New York City, along with several other letters treating
antislavery topics, never made it into the book. In an exhaustive analysis of Child's process of editing the *Standard*'s letters for inclusion in
her book, Karcher argues that a tendency toward self-censorship guided

many of Child's decisions, suggesting that she had, to some degree, internalized the pressures of "acceptable opinion" which she assumed that her publishers would impose upon her. For Karcher, Child's overcautious editing represents a partial capitulation to what conservative publishers deemed consistent with "public opinion," and the price of wider public visibility was the toning down of the radicalism of the original "Letters."

The evidence of Child's aggressive editing and revision is significant to the evolving conception of the public that emerges from her *Letters from New-York*, but I would argue that it is significant in somewhat different ways than Karcher concludes. If Child's excision of overt antislavery sentiment tells us something about the coercive forces at work in public opinion, it is not only because it is symptomatic of her apprehensions over rejection or her internalization of opinion. These edits also yield a text that explicitly interrogates the forms, spaces, and instruments that comprise public life, providing an intimate and inside account of both the public and its subjects. Child's writing from the 1830s and 1840s is an index of her changing relationship to a public which she ceases to imagine in terms of sympathetic readers and hostile mobs and begins to identify with larger, more fundamental forms of American social and political power. In this, Child's 1833 *An Appeal in Favor of That Class of Americans Called Africans*, her 1841–43 columns in the *National Anti-Slavery Standard*, and her 1843 collection, *Letters from New-York*, offer an unusual archive of several movements that were indeed altering the shape of the U.S. public sphere in these decades. Child's early association with William Lloyd Garrison and the American Anti-Slavery Society links her to the efforts—and successes—of the Society in nationalizing the antislavery movement by nationalizing slavery itself. Articulating slavery as a federal sin sealed into the Constitution, the Garrisonians sought to tie citizenship to enslavement, fostering the very sense of complicity that animates Beaumont's critique throughout *Marie*, while also fueling the counterclaims of proslavery activists that abolition was a threat to the Union.[7] The nationalization of the slavery debate was both enabled by and a crucial part of a broad expansion in national culture, which was partly fueled by what Leonard Richards calls a "revolution" in new printing technologies.[8] However, the expansion of a national public culture in the 1830s and 1840s did not happen in print alone. It also involved changes in the relationship of the public to the government, as evidenced by the construction of public institutions and public works projects, as well as an explosion in other cultural media such as popular theatrical entertainment and traveling spectacles. While the "public" of prisons and aqueducts and the "public" of popular spectacle would seem to be sharply distinct, all of these things came to inform the antebellum understanding of the word, and it is precisely the locus of their intersection that inspired Child's weekly investigations of public opinion, public life, and public belonging. The New York City that Child so meticulously documented in her "Letters from New-York" column was, by the early 1840s, fast becoming the center of a national culture industry that indicated an early version of the Debordian spectacle, mediating social relations and providing both spaces and occasions for collective self-contemplation. But, as Child's writings also reveal with stunning clarity, public spectacle has more than one face and form, and many of its pleasures functioned as and merged with administrative powers and punitive terrors. One of the hallmarks of Child's letters is their capacity to illuminate in the parades, plays, and exhibitions that comprise the spectacles of public life in New York City the normal functioning of a power that mingles life and pleasure, domination and exception—the day-to-day experience, in other words, of Tocqueville's new "thing."

If Child's collected *Letters from New-York* indicates a suppression of overt abolitionism, this volume also performs a more wide-ranging interrogation of the capaciousness of sovereign power as it circulates through the antebellum public sphere. Child's attention unarguably shifts between the original letters and the edited volume, but without losing sight of the slave, she begins to take into view a public that is dangerously identified with the power to enforce its own limits in the designation of exceptional subjects, from the vagrant, to the prisoner, to the racialized "varieties" whom Americans loved to watch but refused to count among themselves. Beyond this, a key part of what changes with Child's *Letters* is her sense of her own position in and relationship to a public, which she formerly addressed somewhat pedantically in an effort to "correct" its opinion. The voice that speaks in *The Letters from New-York* is one that speaks from within the public, shaped by it and subject to it, and Child crafts in her edited text a peculiarly wandering, digressive style of writing that she terms her "vagrancies." "But you must pardon my vagrancies," she writes in the second series of the *Letters*, "I can seldom write a letter without making myself liable to the Vagrant Act."[9] More than the studied aimlessness of the *flâneur*, Child's "vagrancies" involve counterintuitive, often jarring, juxtapositions and connections that defy expectations of a rational observer of civic life. In this, she forges a distinctly "public" voice—one that is subject to instabilities and inconstancy, one that explicitly performs both its vulnerability and its complicity, and one that is markedly different from that of her earlier writings. Like the sound of katydids, which impressed Child with a sense of foreboding that is neither rational nor escapable, the experience of publicness that unites the disparate *Letters from New-York* is one that is both sensory and involuntary. Ultimately, the aesthetic and political challenge that she engages in this text involves the question of how to see and speak of a public sphere of which she feels increasingly "a component part"—both in it and of it.

## "The dreaded public": Antislavery Politics and Public Opinion in Child's *Appeal*

Writing of the night in 1835 that she spent hiding out in Brooklyn, hearing mobs in the notes of katydids, Child remembered feeling a rather different sense of her relation to the public around her: "It seemed to me that antislavery had cut me off from all the sympathies of my kind" ("Letters from New-York" No. 33). In many ways, this remark could be taken as a reflection on her career over the two years prior to Thompson's visit. From the height of her popularity in 1833 as a novelist, author of domestic guides, and editor of an influential children's magazine, Child had seen her *Mother's Book* go out of print and her *Juvenile Miscellany* close down. Beyond that, she had lost the privileges she had earlier enjoyed as one of only two women granted access to the collections of the Boston Athenaeum; her former friends and associates publicly renounced her; and her family members had cut all ties with her. All of this had followed from the publication of *An Appeal in Favor of That Class of Americans Called Africans*, Child's studied analysis of the institution of slavery, which cemented her allegiance to Garrisonian abolitionism and became a key text of the American antislavery movement.[10] According to Karcher, the damage done to Child's reputation was so lasting, it was not until the 1843 publication of the *Letters from New-York* that she regained her prior status as a popular author. For Karcher, the relationship between the *Appeal* and the *Letters* offers a case study in Child's difficulties with the vagaries of public opinion, but these texts also provide an index of her changing conception of the public sphere itself. Specifically, reading in and across these works, a transformation can be mapped in Child's thinking, from an understanding of the public as a discrete sphere of readers whose opinions might be changed through reasoned appeal, toward a vision of a broader, agonistic power that both punishes those whose views it rejects and that proves infinitely more difficult to transcend. In other words, departing from the classic model of a critical public sphere of readers, Child arrives at one much closer to Tocqueville's and Beaumont's vision of a capacious realm, inseparable from private and intimate life, and characterized by a coercive, intimate, and estranging power.[11]

In one sense, the most palpable change between the public of Child's *Appeal* and that of her *Letters* can be measured in spatial terms—in Child's growing understanding of herself as a "component part" of the public, rather than one whose opinions cast her outside of it, for better or worse. Throughout the *Appeal*, Child describes an inside-outside relationship to a variety of publics—the readers she addresses, the "world" whose mockery she disdains, and the "dreaded" agent of coercive convention whom she calls upon her readers to resist. Even her recollection years later of feeling "cut off from the sympathies of my kind" expresses a belief in a space that lies outside of the public, its opinion, and, to an extent, its power. However, at the same time that Child describes the public as a space with boundaries and an outside, her *Appeal* explicitly engages in the strategy of the AASS to eradicate the conceptual geography that isolated slavery and abolitionism into problems of sectional politics. As Trish Loughran demonstrates in a superb materialist account of the early abolitionist movement, two of its key tactics and greatest successes lay in its articulation of slavery as a federal—not a sectional—institution and in its construction of abolitionism as a national movement that functioned "through the circulation of actual material objects and persons." With the 1835 mass mailings of antislavery periodicals and the 1839 campaign to distribute Theodore Weld's *American Slavery As It Is* nationally, Loughran argues, abolitionism achieved the status of a "national culture industry," whose power was measurable in the ferocity and ubiquity of the reaction against it. Although such campaigns relied heavily on the tools of a classic, Habermassian public sphere—newspapers, pamphlets, and innovations in print technology—Loughran argues that the vision of the public that they represented was far from Habermas's ideal of communicative relation. Indeed, her study shows that the model of the public that emerges from the AASS's national campaigns was one predicated on the subject's relationship of complicity in federal institutions and acts, not its critical distance.[12] But even as the movement succeeded in constructing a clear, national geography of antislavery

political action, which centralized tactics that could be widely disseminated and enacted locally, the space of the "public" imagined by the
antislavery movement became increasingly ambivalent, as its claims of
complicity also eroded that public's borders.

Child's *Appeal* is, in many ways, emblematic of the AASS's strategy
of erasing sectional boundaries to posit what Loughran calls "a sense of
material simultaneity" between the North and South.[13] It is also a work
of calculated polemicism addressed to a public that it figures as, at once,
amenable to reasoned debate and culpable in a national crime. Child
was sufficiently attuned to the scandal the work would create to open
it with a plea to her reader "not to throw down this volume as soon as
you have glanced at the title," though the text inside contains little that
would palliate a reader who paused at the cover.[14] Child's polemic does
nothing to minimize the extent of slavery's crimes or to mitigate collective, national guilt for them. In it, she gives a history of American slavery
that emphasizes the ways in which slave law has fractured and discred-
ited the institutions of white America, from Christianity to the family;
she defends slave insurrections, from the Saint-Domingue Revolution to
the Nat Turner uprising, arguing that only immediate emancipation can
prevent further violence; and she analyzes how deeply entangled the entire American political system, from the Constitution to the expansion
of U.S. territories, is in the perpetuation of slavery. In her chapter on
American political institutions, for example, she describes the Constitution as the nation's foundational "wedge," which forged the nation out
of a schism, enshrining slavery, disproportionately empowering smaller
slave-owning states, and creating a warped mode of representation that
forced slaves to "vote" phantasmatically for their own enslavement.[15]
Such a tainted foundational act, she argues, produced a nation and a citizenry constantly forced to sanction and repeat these original crimes. Revealing the institution to be internal to the union, she locates no outside
to slavery within it: "[I]f the union cannot be preserved without crime,
it is an eternal truth that nothing good can ever be preserved by crime"
(*Appeal*, 100).[16]

All the while Child refuses northern states the comfort of occupying a geographical space outside of slavery, she also particularizes her
critique, targeting especially sensitive local and regional prejudices.
The most controversial of Child's arguments in the *Appeal* involved her
claim that racism in the north could only be eradicated with the repeal
of anti-miscegenation laws. Where Beaumont's invocation of interracial
marriage carried with it the utopic goal of a fully mixed citizenry, Child's

derived from the pragmatic view that such laws served more to perpetuate prejudice than to prevent interracial unions.[17] Child's introduction
of interracial marriage is remarkable both for this libertarian pragma-
tism—its call to leave matters of affection and desire outside the reach
of law—and for the shift that it marks in her articulation of a shared,
national space of responsibility. Conscious of the scandal likely to erupt
around such a claim, Child introduces the topic of interracial marriage
by declaring herself unafraid of public censure: "I am perfectly aware
of the gross ridicule to which I may subject myself by alluding to this
particular; but I have lived too long, and observed too much, to be dis-
turbed by the world's mockery" (187). In her stated disregard for opinion
on this matter, she links herself to the poor white women, "those whose
condition in life is too low to be affected by public opinion" (187), who,
she says, already form interracial alliances in spite of the laws. Reading
this statement, Karen Sánchez-Eppler has argued that Child is only able
to defend interracial desire "when she has placed the sturdy barrier of
class between herself and the women who enact it."[18] But while Child
is, without doubt, too quick to point out that such women "differ from
us in matters of taste," she also claims an indifference to opinion that is
similar to what she imputes to them, and it is in part this position just
outside the reach of opinion that permits these radical, extralegal unions
to take place. The barrier that Child's appeal to "taste" erects is mutable,
personal, and far from absolute, and throughout this passage, she makes
it clear that she longs for freedom in such matters. Refusing to recognize
the authority of an opinion that makes desire a public matter marks a
privilege for Child, who must first be able to claim public recognition
in order to disdain it. But in imagining a position either outside or "beneath" public opinion for both these women and for herself, Child suggests a conception of the "public" that equates to a particular class which
controls the dissemination of opinion and the reach of law. Identifying
this public as relatively narrow, she challenges its capacity to represent
the general populace, at the same time she presumes its receptiveness to
reason by addressing it. Finally, in claiming the ability to transcend—or
rather, the desire to descend beneath—the reach of public opinion, Child
also suggests the possibility that a reform-minded individual might separate herself from that public and thereby absolve herself of culpability
in the constant reenactment of its crimes.

   In short, Child suggests that there is one national public responsible
for slavery, to which all citizens belong, and another, just outside its
reach, to which one might aspire. With this, the *Appeal* shares many of

the assumptions about the subject's capacity to secede from the public and the nation that lay at the foundation of William Lloyd Garrison's doctrine of "disunion," which the AASS officially adopted in the early 1840s. Robert Fanuzzi argues that Garrison held to an "anachronistic" notion of the public sphere that, rightly conceived, should be separable from the state, critical of it, and protected from its influence.[19] For Garrison, the structural flaw that prevented such separation was the mechanism of representation, which yoked the citizenry too tightly to the state, permitting regional factions of slave owners to represent their interests as those of the whole nation, while in turn entailing all citizens to the acts of a government that claimed to represent them. By reimagining the relationship between the people and the state, Garrison argued, the "tyranny" of a representative government beholden to proslavery interests could be eradicated. The doctrine of disunion grew directly out of this belief in the flawed nature of representation and the presumed right of a sovereign individual to remove himself from it, thereby freeing himself from complicity in its crimes. But, Fanuzzi asks, "who or what was the subject declaring disunion?" Rather than resolving the corrupted relationship between the people and the state, Garrison's disunion doctrine relied on an assumption of sovereign individuality that seemed to bypass altogether both an analysis of that individual's relationship to the general public, and the public's relationship to the state.[20]

In its premise and its execution, Child's *Appeal* echoes many of Garrison's beliefs about national culpability in the preservation of slavery and the necessity of unflinching polemic as a political instrument. Certainly, her work shares his understanding of how a small class of slave owners had come to represent its own interests as those of the whole nation, and she, too, longs for the possibility of individual "disunion" from the crimes enacted with its sanction. But where Garrison's focus remains on the tainted mechanism of representation that ties citizens to a criminal state through the franchise,[21] Child tends to linger on the question of the public, showing how proslavery interests have come to be confounded with "majority" opinion, while laying bare the problem of conceiving a "public" to counter it:

> A cautious vigilance against improvement, a keen-eyed jealousy of all freedom of opinion, has characterized their movements. There *can* be no doubt that the *majority* wish to perpetuate slavery. They support it with loud bravado, or insidious sophistry, or pretended regret; but they never abandon the point. Their great desire is

to keep the public mind turned in another direction. They are well aware that the ugly edifice is built of rotten timbers, and stands on slippery sands—if the loud voice of public opinion could be made to reverberate through its dreary chambers, the unsightly frame would fall. (*Appeal*, 95; Child's italics)

Child articulates both a phenomenon and an impasse of U.S. political culture. Initially, she identifies the tactics employed by extra-legal, non-statist forces in the shaping of public discourse and the directing of the "public mind." Elaborating the metaphor of a structure ("the ugly edifice . . . built of rotten timbers") that bears a glancing resemblance to a theater, she imagines a "them" who control the public's mind by controlling its gaze, keeping it "turned in another direction." But when Child concedes that the "public mind" is at least partly a creature of influences that range from the state to a particularly influential class, she has already implicated the very agent on whom she calls for a corrective—the "public opinion" whose voice will "reverberate through its dreary chambers." Given the susceptibility of public opinion to manipulation and distortion, it is more than a little unclear how she conceives that such a public can either cleanse or disunite from itself. At the point where Child turns from the state to the public, she reaches the limits of Garrisonian disunion. Representation and enfranchisement are the mechanisms that bind the subject to the state and suggest the means by which one may separate from it, but what binds the subject to the public?

The rhetorical tactic through which Child's *Appeal* sought to instill a sense of national responsibility by eradicating a belief that there was a geographic or political outside to slavery begins to erode the borders that mark the inside and outside of the public as well. As Child comes to define a political sphere that is increasingly reliant on coercion and obfuscation to create the illusion of a proslavery consensus, so her sense of what constitutes politics shifts, and along with it, the scale and scope of what she terms the public. In concluding the *Appeal* with a consideration of "Prejudices against People of Color and Our Duties in Relation to this Subject," Child identifies prejudice not with the acts of the state, but (like Beaumont) with the customary practices of public life, from attending the theater to riding the stagecoach. Throughout the *Appeal*, Child is wary of gestures that attribute to a "public" the opinions of a specific class and race, and even as her use of the term grows broader, she continues to chide those who cloak their views in "public opinion." But at the end of her text, she also openly mocks the desire to separate oneself from this public—the very desire that she expresses, only pages earlier, in her discussion of interracial marriage—as she comes to recognize in such gestures an attempt to avoid the political implications of one's most quotidian activities.

> Stage-drivers are very much perplexed when they attempt to vindicate the present tyrannical customs; and they usually give up the point, by saying they themselves have no prejudice . . . they are merely afraid of the public. But stage drivers should remember that in a popular government, they, in common with every other citizen, form a part and portion of the dreaded public. (198)

Child suggests that popular sovereignty forms the public and constitutes subjects as members almost involuntarily. The "dreaded public" is everyone, and the form of belonging that it entails is not easily evaded. In the final chapter of her *Appeal*, Child gestures to the view of the public that makes her *Letters from New-York* so complex an account of collective political life in the antebellum United States. The public that becomes both the subject and motivating force behind the letters that she writes, publishes, and rewrites between 1841 and 1843 cannot be transcended or escaped, because it has no clear borders and no outside. No longer conceived as a closed circle of readers whose relation to her is largely mediated by her books, nor as a mob or a class whose opinion she can escape, the public that she finds in New York City assumes another form altogether—that of permanent, pervasive spectacle.

## Public Works, Public Spectacle: Child's *Letters from New-York*

Arriving in New York City in the summer of 1841 to take her post as editor of the *National Anti-Slavery Standard*, Child entered a city in which the political and cultural meanings of the "public," as well as the material practices of its daily life, were rapidly transforming. Mary Ryan argues that the public of antebellum New York was more an ongoing invention than a given, and she traces its development through a wide range of civic projects and performances, from celebrations of infrastructure (like the opening of the Erie Canal), to parades of associations (like trade groups, ethnic societies, and reform organizations), to outbreaks of violence (like the anti-abolitionist riots of 1830s or the Astor Place Riot of 1849), even to what she calls the general "sensual bounty" of everyday life on city streets.[22] Child's letters bear out Ryan's litany of public activities, recounting an eclectic set of travels—through parks, markets, prisons, asylums, parades, and civic and religious celebrations—that amounts to an investigation into the stuff and spaces of urban public life. Child does not address a public in her letters, as she had in her earlier works, so much as she pursues one which was being literally constructed and conceptually reconstructed during this era. A measure of the transformations in what was coming to be defined with and as the public can be found in two seemingly disparate events that occurred within a year of Child's arrival: the completion of the Croton Aqueduct, which delivered Hudson River water to Manhattan, and the opening of P. T. Barnum's permanent exhibit space, the American Museum.[23] If a public works project and an entertainment venue seem to involve very different definitions of public interest and public life, both nevertheless put Child in mind of the peculiarities of this form of association, while giving evidence of a productive and expansive entity that was as much a motivating agent as an object and target of politics and culture.

Ryan describes the Croton Aqueduct as the "crowning achievement of antebellum public works projects," adding that its completion was either "a miracle or an accident." For a city governed by a chartered private corporation until 1846, whose services—water included—had always been managed by "profit-taking interests," the construction of a $20 million aqueduct, conceived "for the general good" and financed by the city was, Ryan argues, an unprecedented indication of the democratization of civic government.[24] The public which was served by the aqueduct was also understood to be its proprietor. That public could be said to stand, in Tocquevillean fashion, as both "cause" and "end" of a project, whose origin was a petition campaign and whose end was its own health. Further, like the sovereign public which Tocqueville named as a new thing in politics, the one that emerges from the Croton project as both agent and beneficiary does so in a specifically biopolitical context, in the protection and management of the biological life and health of its subjects: "It provides for their security, foresees and supplies their necessities, facilitates their pleasures, manages their principle concerns, directs their industry" (*Democracy in America*, 692). Substantiating Tocqueville's abstractions about a society that "acts by and for itself" (60), the aqueduct is also emblematic of a growing antebellum understanding of the public as a politically empowered agent of government, acting for its own good by administering to the barest needs of its subjects.

But no less indicative of the transformations in the practical meaning of public life in New York City in 1842 was the wholly private, speculative venture with which P. T. Barnum parlayed a worthless piece of

Connecticut swampland into one of the largest and most profitable per-manent spectacles in the city.[25] Indeed, the success of Barnum's venture relied upon a related set of assumptions about the agency of the public in the facilitation of its own "pleasures." To the collection of oddities and curiosities already housed in the former Peale Museum, Barnum added a wide array of performances and traveling exhibitions, from "Industrious fleas," to "Live Yankees," to "American Indians," as well as a "questionable dead mermaid." But Barnum's most lucrative "stock in trade" was what he called his "humbugs" or "clap-trap"—the vast public-ity campaigns that hyped his exhibitions for weeks and ultimately bore little resemblance to them. For Barnum, the public was not simply the audience or consumer of spectacle, but an essential component part of it. Eager to be caught up in a humbug, Barnum's spectators were less dupes than willing participants; they were drawn in by the "exaggerated pictures and puffing advertisements," but they paid the price of admis-sion fully aware that that they were part of what it delivered.[26] Like the public of the aqueduct, the public of the American Museum served both its origins and its ends, motivating and fulfilling performances to which it was essential.

The aqueduct and the museum thus shared a good deal more than the coincidence of their openings; both were creations of a public which they, in turn, helped to define and construct, and both defined that public, in part, through spectacle. Croton water quite literally fueled Barnum's spectacle, as spectacle ushered the arrival of Croton water. The first big show that Barnum mounted at the American Museum was billed as "The Great Model of Niagara Falls With Real Water!" With puffing advertise-ments posted throughout the city and in the papers, Barnum's exhibit drew the attention of the Croton Water commissioners, who summoned him to appear before them. Demanding compensation for what they pre-sumed to be the vast amount of water consumed by an operating model of Niagara Falls, the commissioners were amused to learn that his "Falls" were no more than eighteen inches high and, through a rusted and creak-ing pump that recycled water over them, required less than a barrel of water to operate.[27] Barnum's drain on the public water supply may have been minimal, but the city's debt to showmen like Barnum was signifi-cant. The opening celebration for the aqueduct in the fall of 1842 was a citywide holiday that included a massive parade (between five and seven miles long) and an extravagant pageant at the aqueduct's termination in a dancing fountain at Lower Manhattan's Bowling Green.[28] In Letter XXX, Child marvels at both the fountain and its opening extravaganza:

"Well might they bring it thirty miles under-ground, and usher it into the city with roaring cannon, sonorous bells, waving flags, floral canopies, and a loud chorus of song!" (*Letters,* 132). For Child, the arrival of "clean, sweet, abundant water" in "the great prison-cell of a city" is fitly marked by the spectacular display of public power and culture—flags, cannons, bells, and song.

Writing on the Croton spectacle for the *Standard,* Child finds in it the very material of public life, as well as an occasion to reflect upon both the forms of association and the powers that it entailed. She begins by describing the fountain and the shapes the waters could be made to assume—vases, domes, weeping willows, sheaves of wheat—but she quickly converts the fountain into an extended metaphor for the public, which serves as both performer and audience in this celebration of its own project to sate its thirst. "Water will rise to its level, as surely as the morality of a nation . . . rises to its idea of God," she writes, but in her elaboration of the metaphor, "*lateral pressure* overpowers the leaping waters, and sends them downwards in tears" (*Letters,* 133; Child's italics). The very pressure that allows the water to rise also forces it into artificial shapes and makes it dance. For Child, the fountain offers an image of the reformer under the "pressure of public opinion" (134), submerged and drawn downward by the very element of which she is a member and equal part. In the end, the spectacular celebration of public works is also a performance of the power—the "lateral pressure"—lodged in this entity called the public. "Under this despotic influence, men and women check their best influences, suppress their noblest feelings, conceal their highest thoughts" (134). In seeming to digress from the scene at hand in the pursuit of her metaphor ("Strange material this for a reformer!" [134]), Child instead gives an intimate account of the subject of all these publics at once—audience and performer, subject and object of administration, origin and end of political power. This letter is exemplary of both what Child accomplishes in the collected *Letters from New-York*—the portrait of a public that spans government, entertainment, and commerce—and *how* she accomplishes it through her "vagrancies"—her digressive and almost compulsive collection of material, which she almost compulsively converts into metaphors for political and social conditions.

Child portrays herself engaging in virtually all of the activities that Ryan describes as characteristic of public life in mid-century United States cities:[29] she wanders incessantly, through parks, streets, prisons, and institutions; she attends countless gatherings, including a Washington Society parade, a Scottish festival, and a Rosh Hashanah service;

and she details the daily lives and customs of the city's inhabitants with the exhaustive intensity of a foreign traveler. But through all of Child's wide-ranging forays into the public life of New York City, her letters convey an abiding sense that, lying latent within all of these spaces and performances, is a formidable power. Sometimes that power takes the form of "pressure," as in her reflections at the opening of the aqueduct; sometimes she finds outright violence. In Letter II in the book, for example, after celebrating the "beautiful pageant" of a Washingtonian temperance parade, she concludes the letter with surprising remarks on the "dog killers," whose brutal "Reign of Terror" over the city's strays has claimed 1,500 canine victims (15). Although the change in subject and tone seems bizarre and abrupt, what she published in the book as Letter II is actually the merging of two letters originally printed four months apart in the *Standard*, so the effect of digressiveness is strategic, not accidental.[30] Indeed, as the letter turns from what Child sees as the edifying pageantry of a reformist parade to the "frightful sight" of the blood-spattered dog killers, it follows a coherent path of meditation on the primacy of spectacle as a public form, as well as spectacle's double operation through pleasure and terror.

Letter II traces through its wanderings and juxtapositions the persistence into the "Age of Reform" of almost Gothic, feudal rites of spectacular terror, drawing a startlingly literal connection between nineteenth-century urban biopolitics and ancient rights of sovereign violence. Noting the "military character" of the Temperance pageant and wondering that such sights as the dog killers "do not prepare the minds of the young to take part in bloody riots and revolutions" (15), Child implies that there is more continuity than dissonance between these two scenes seemingly picked at random from the street life of New York. For one thing, the twinned spectacles of temperance and dog-killing are clearly united by a "spirit of reform" that is rooted in ideologies of purification—the cleansing of both civic and individual bodies—and Child accepts to a degree that "the safety of the city" requires the expulsion of both drink and strays. But Child also suggests that what animates this reforming spirit is far from modern, and here her peculiar manner of linking these two scenes is instructive. Between her tales of parades and dog massacres, she ruminates on the faulty appropriation of Gothic architecture in New York City. The problem, as she sees it, is not that a New World city so eagerly appropriates Old World aesthetics in its buildings; the problem is that the Gothic is misinterpreted in light-colored stones: "applied to the Gothic, they become like tragic thoughts uttered in mirthful tones"

(15). Like the reinterpreted Gothic, the persistence of spectacle as a mode of public representation and experience belies the liberal, modern self-conception of what she calls "the thinking, toiling Age of Reform" (11), while dissembling its tragedies and terrors in the "mirthful tones" of progress and purification.

As Child's vagrant and digressive voice forges a link between celebrations of temperance and the slaughter of stray dogs, so it also finds in the opening of an aqueduct evidence of the "lateral pressure" that characterizes public opinion and—as I'll discuss below—in Barnum's American Museum a deadly performance of exception. In each of these examples, the effect is the same: the interrogation of spectacle as the public mode through which the protection of life and the pursuit of pleasure are discovered intersecting with forms of domination and violence. In this, Child's portrait of the transforming antebellum public sphere offers up an archive for Tocqueville's new "thing," and what Giorgio Agamben calls the "aporia" of modern democracy: evidence of the intersection of sovereignty and democracy in those spectacular spaces and events where power concerns itself with life and pleasure. But in pursuing the public through such spectacles, Child's letters also stage the paradoxical condition of the subject of this public. Turning her gaze on events like the opening of the aqueduct and spaces like Barnum's Museum, Child submits herself to them. To admire the dancing fountains at the termination of the Croton Aqueduct, she must feel the lateral pressure of the waters in which she is immersed. Ultimately, her letters suggest that the most profound transformation is not what she sees in public, but how she sees—more precisely, how a public of spectacle is inaugurating a new way of seeing and forging a new kind of spectator.

## The Public Spectator: Child, Irving, Poe

If Child's vagrant and digressive voice suggests a carefully crafted and strategic literary response to the pleasures and terrors of a public of spectacles, it also reveals the struggles of a spectator who cannot always evade the ways of seeing that such spectacles produce. Ways of seeing thus become just as central a concern and preoccupation of the letters as the public life of the city is. In the letter that opens both her weekly column and her collection,[31] Child describes her acculturation to New York specifically in terms of how she sees it, and she begins by outlining two distinct visual registers that define the parameters of how she lives in the city:

> There *was* a time when all these things would have passed by me
> like the flitting figures of the magic lantern, or the changing scen-
> ery of a theatre, sufficient for the amusement of an hour. But now
> I have lost the power of looking merely at the surface. Everything
> seems to come from the Infinite, to be filled with the Infinite, to
> be tending toward the Infinite. Do I see crowds of men hastening
> to extinguish a fire? I see not merely uncouth garbs, and fantastic
> flickering lights of lurid hue, like a tramping troop of gnomes,—but
> straightaway my mind is filled with thoughts about mutual helpful-
> ness, human sympathy, the common bond of brotherhood, and the
> mysteriously deep foundations on which society rests; or rather, on
> which it now reels and totters. (*Letters,* 10; Child's italics)

Child attributes her newfound affinity for New York to her lost powers
of superficiality; no longer a detached spectator, taking in the city as she
would a play, Child insists that she now sees through the surfaces into
the "infinite."[32] But with this claim, Child does not tout her own penetrating gaze or powers of deep discernment so much as she suggests that
the "Infinite" comes to her, filling her mind with unwonted thoughts
and sensations, revealing invisible connections and relations. The new
way of seeing that opens her letters is one that happens to her, one that
almost bypasses her eyes to fill her mind without conscious effort on her
part, and it introduces the subject of the letters as a surprisingly passive,
surprisingly vulnerable spectator.

But even as Child's new way of seeing presumes the vulnerability of
the subject who receives it, this seeing does not evacuate that subject of
ethical and political capacity or obligation. The "Infinite" that comes at
Child is, after all, a strikingly material one. Like some kind of secular,
reform-minded typology, it allows Child to read hidden material relations back into the visible world; these "mysteriously deep foundations"
are hardly transcendent, as they lead her to link the "blind negro beggar" to the "stately mansion of the slave trader," and to see the "war, pes-
tilence, and famine" behind the "cool calculations" of Wall Street (9).
While perhaps less "mysterious" than she implies, the social conditions
and relations on which Child now gazes also involve her in the public
sphere in new ways. When Child claims that she has dispensed with
her former, superficial way of seeing the city, "like the flitting figures
of the magic lantern," she rejects along with it a particular relationship
to the public, which she often describes in theatrical terms. What Child
rejects she calls "the outward" public, and she allies it with "a seeming

and a show" (56) that creates a "false necessity" out of shifting, external standards; "public opinion expresses what men will do, not their inward perceptions" (101). In Letter XIII, she voices her fears about the influence of public opinion in relatively conventional antitheatrical rhetoric; she compares it to a French comedy of manners, whose title she sees erroneously printed on a billboard as "Valley de Sham." Punning on the error, she asks, "Is not that comedy New York? Nay, is not the whole world a Valley of Sham? Are not you, and I, and every other mortal the 'valet' of some 'sham' or another?" (57). Where Child's call to shun this outward "show" of a public might seem to demand a removal from it, she instead describes a more intimate, "deep," and "inward" relationship to it, and she continues to rely on the visual in order to define that relation. In a sense, Child describes with her new way of seeing a kind of homeopathic response to a public that presents itself as spectacle. If seeing superficially alienates her, placing her in a false relationship with the public, seeing inwardly the "deep foundations" on which it "reels and totters" involves her in public life with an unsettling intimacy, and it is that intimacy of involvement which her vagrant and digressive writing mimics and performs on her reader.

In Child's writing, turning from outward show to inward perception maintains a connection to the public and the social because, she insists, these "inward perceptions" are not private; they arrive at her from the "Infinite" through the medium of the material conflicts and conditions that she witnesses each day. In the difference that emerges in Child's writing between the "inward" and the "private," the mode of vagrant spectatorship that Child begins to develop in her letters can be distinguished somewhat from its obvious literary models—the wandering sketcher and the urban *flâneur*. When Child describes her shifting ways of seeing and invokes the metaphor of a walk in her opening letter to define her perspective as mobile and her voice as digressive, the gesture is hardly novel. Washington Irving opens *The Sketch-Book* (1819–20) with the assertion that he will not examine "the shifting scenes of life . . . with the eyes of a philosopher, but rather with the sauntering gaze with which humble lovers of the picturesque stroll from the window of one print-shop to another."[33] In "The Author's Account of Himself," Irving claims to survey shifting scenes with a view that wanders from object to object, but also with a deliberation and a pleasure that suggest a fundamental constancy within the looking subject, what Kristie Hamilton describes as a posture of "urbane detachment" that filters experience through a stable private judgment.[34] Throughout *The Sketch-Book*,

Irving's sauntering gazers often encounter moments of uncertainty that register as visual instability—dreams merging with waking reality, as in "The Art of Book-Making," reality transformed after a twenty-year nap, as in "Rip Van Winkle"—but what most characterizes these moments is how little they ultimately alter their viewers. Although Rip Van Winkle can hardly be called a figure of "urbane detachment," he does suggest a model of constancy bordering on imperviousness: on waking from two decades of sleep to a post-Revolutionary America, Rip rubs his eyes in confusion and finds himself duly baffled when he meets the "precise counterpart of himself" in the form of his now-grown son. But once all is made clear to him, Rip simply takes "his place once more on the bench at the inn-door," since "the changes of states and empires made but little impression on him."[35] As Hamilton argues, the voice and gaze of Irving's sketches derive authority from just such stability in the face of disorienting change, producing privacy as a space of authenticity and security from which the public can be reflectively and meaningfully judged.[36]

Closer to Child's darker, more vulnerable and unsettled mode of spectatorship may be that of Edgar Allan Poe's narrator in "The Man of the Crowd," whom Dana Brand describes as a kind of meta-*flâneur*, since this figure lays bare the strategies and limitations of what by 1840 had become a conventional literary type.[37] Like the wandering, watching subjects in both Child's letters and Irving's sketches, Poe's narrator portrays the experience of urban spectatorship through the introduction of two distinct practices of seeing. The first is an "abstract and generalizing" gaze through which he surveys the crowd and orders it into a taxonomy of types, while the second "arrests" and "absorbs" all his attentions in a single, illegible figure who draws him out of the café and into a night of manic, aimless wandering.[38] In Poe's story, the second mode of seeing thoroughly undermines the first. By literally dragging the narrator out of abstract observation and assured judgment, hurling him into the crowd which he had been content simply to watch, and binding him to the spectacle of a man who will not be read (as the opening and closing lines of the story attest: "Es laßt sich nicht lesen"), this absorbed and obsessive mode of seeing undoes the assumptions of transparency and distance that permitted the narrator to pass his earlier judgments on the "aggregate relations" of the city. The one-time *flâneur*, who "assumes a posture of receptive passivity,"[39] quickly becomes the subject of a seeing that happens to him, his spectatorship both mimetic and involuntary as it leads him through twenty-four hours of frantic wandering. The vertiginous shifts and digressions in Child's letters resonate with the sense of abandonment that takes over the second part of Poe's story, especially given that Child's self-titled "vagrancies" root that style in the many homeless, itinerant, and impoverished figures about whom she writes.[40] But where Poe's narrator returns to a posture of rational judgment at the end, ceasing to follow the old man when he realizes that there is nothing to learn of him, Child never detaches herself in this way. Instead, in her vagrancies, she suggests that the three subjects of Poe's tale—the watching narrator, the vagrant old man, and the crowd—are inseparable, mutually dependent, and internal to each other, and in this, her vagrancies reveal very different aesthetic and political investments.

Two scholars have recently examined Child's relationship to the tradition of the *flâneur*, comparing the wandering style of her letters to Poe's narrator and other mid-century specimens, but the two draw nearly opposite conclusions about Child's political and aesthetic practice from the comparison. In her essay, "The Public Heart: Urban Life and the Politics of Sympathy in Lydia Maria Child's *Letters from New York*," Heather Roberts argues that Child "implicitly rejects the defining principles and methods of flanerie" in three ways: by raising the political and spiritual stakes of the urban spectator form, by being "acutely aware of the ways in which her gender shapes" her relationship to the city, and by rejecting the "predominantly scopic quality" of the *flâneur* in favor of the heart as her primary organ of perception. Roberts notes the ways in which Child's assertions of affective intimacy with those around her prevent her from acceding to the freedom of the *flâneur*'s more "consumerist" and "aesthetic" stance. But even as she argues that Child's radical notion of sympathy renders her vulnerable to the violence and tragedy on which her letters dwell, Roberts sees limits to that vulnerability, since for her, the political viability of sympathy depends upon Child's ability to recover herself from it. While Child never divorces herself from the objects of her sympathy in the manner of Poe's narrator, Roberts understands the subject of Child's letters to be capable of a certain self-protective distancing, and she ultimately reads the letters autobiographically as "a narrative of trauma, healing, and recovery."[41] In contrast to Roberts's emphasis on the rootedness of Child's political sense in a personal exercise of sympathy, Mary Esteve argues that Child is intent in her letters on "separating out the personal from the political," making her—in Esteve's estimation—an emblematic liberal subject. "She does not attempt to legitimize her political commitments through sentiment or particular attachments," Esteve argues, relegating such attachments to an aesthetic realm, which she defines as a "matter of personal, sentimental preference." In Esteve's comparison of Child's *Letters* and Poe's "Man of the Crowd," she links Child to the narrator of Poe's story, who abandons the old man once he comes to the conclusion that the man is unreadable, incapable of reflective judgment, and thus inassimilable to liberal democracy. This, for Esteve, amounts to a rejection of the crowd, whose coercive tendencies mark "the end of the political."[42]

Although Esteve and Roberts make nearly opposite claims for the relationship of the personal to the political in Child's letters, they share many of the same assumptions about both the subject of the letters and the aesthetic practice of them. While Roberts describes the collapse of the personal into the political, and Esteve insists on their separation, both argue for a self-reflective capacity (one sentimental, the other rational) which assumes that a stable, private, personal Child remains the subject of the letters. Clearly, Child invites this autobiographical reading through her epistolary form, but the letters undercut the constancy and integrity of a conventional subject of autobiography because, she insists, their voice does not originate in a reflective private subject: "But you will pardon my vagrancies. In good truth, I can seldom write a letter without making myself liable to the Vagrant Act." Claiming a writing style that will subject her to the Vagrant Act, Child invokes a specifically *public* transgression—one that penalizes the lack of private space and property and can, by definition, only happen in a public place. As Celeste Langan argues, the vagrant is a figure who is trapped by compulsive mobility, who has "being only in the public sphere."[43] But unlike the Romantics whose appropriations of vagrancy Langan examines, Child does not appeal to the vagrant as an emblem of negative freedom; instead, she is explicit in figuring the vagrant as the image of a subject construed as essentially public and criminal in that publicity, one closer to the fugitive slave than the Romantic bard. Finally, even as she names her aesthetic practice for a condition that is utterly lacking in "privacy" and wholly confined within the public, Child continues to ally it with an "inward" state, though it is an inward that is not exactly personal.[44] "Whence came all this digression? . . . What a strange thing is the mind! How marvelously is the infinite embodied in the smallest fragment of the finite!" (*Letters*, 16). The inward state of mind finds the "infinite" in the "smallest fragments" of material life and spins of these an aesthetics that, however vagrant and digressive, remains firmly attached to the world from which it came. Neither the reflections of a private consciousness, nor the revelation of a transcendent infinite, Child's vagrancies disclose the interior life of the public sphere through aesthetics of indirection and vulnerability, which perform new, often incongruous, and politically charged ways of seeing it.

## Spectacular Varieties and Vanishing Identity: Child at the American Museum

Part of reading a political and aesthetic strategy in Child's *Letters from New-York* involves attention to the paradoxes of a text which often performs the loss or abandonment of the very subject and voice one would credit with that strategy. The opening letter may turn decisively away from one way of seeing the city toward another, seeming to posit a mode of spectatorship that will remain continuous throughout the text, but the distinguishing feature of this second mode is precisely its insistent denial that it originates in a stable, private subject, and in many ways, it remains unintelligible without the first. Indeed, in letter after letter, Child invokes the supposedly discarded way of seeing ("like the flitting figures of the magic lantern"), so that she can repeatedly perform its abandonment in favor of the second, more receptive and "inward" spectatorship. Though she insists on this inward way of seeing as a corrective to the "outward" public and the magic-lantern view, she continues to depend for its elaboration on the recurring performance of relinquishing the first mode of seeing. Seeing deeply, affectively, and inwardly thus offers no more an escape from the conditions of public spectatorship than seeing superficially does, but it nevertheless produces those sensations of vulnerability and receptivity that, Child claims, allow her to perceive "the mysteriously deep foundations on which society . . . reels and totters" (*Letters,* 10). Together, these two ways of seeing allow Child to interrogate the complexities of belonging to a public that she increasingly identifies with a formidable social and political power. Further, her efforts to achieve an inward seeing that renders her receptive and vulnerable to that power also speaks to her desire to be innocent of it. Child's language of seeing and feeling registers her attempts to define for herself what it is to belong to a public sphere that makes her both a subject and an object of sovereign power. The subject of spectacle finds herself moving, sometimes manically, between vantage points, because to be the spectator of the public is to be a spectator within it, one whose seeing is not separated from it but conditioned by it.

This pattern of toggling between superficial, magic-lantern visuality and inward seeing is most pronounced—and most fraught—when

Child alternately succumbs to and resists an ethnological impulse to see what she calls "infinite varieties of character"—when, in other words, her spectatorship explicitly raises the question of public belonging and exclusion. Describing a visit to Barnum's American Museum, Child succinctly performs this maneuver. She derides the desire to gaze upon people as curiosities and supplants it with another iteration of seeing inwardly: "I do not care to travel to Rome, or St. Petersburg, because I can look *at* people . . . I want to look *into* them and *through* them; to know how things appear to *their* spiritual eyes" (185; Child's italics). She must first invoke and reject the desire to "look *at*," so that she may then posit her preferred way of seeing as a form of intersubjectivity that would allow her to merge with those she sees. However, in one instance when she attempts to do just this, to see through the "spiritual eyes" of others by attending a Rosh Hashanah service, she finds herself stuck in that first way of seeing: "The effect produced on my mind by witnessing the ceremonies of the Jewish Synagogue was strange and bewildering; spectral and flitting; with a sort of vanishing resemblance to reality, the magic lantern of the Past" (24). Trying to see "through the spectacles" of another faith, Child instead falls prey to a spectacle of her own invention: "I had turned away from the tumult of the Present, to gaze quietly for a while on the grandeur of the past; and the representatives of the Past walked before me, not in the graceful Oriental turban, but the useful European hat" (25). Child's peevish disenchantment at the modernity and cosmopolitanism—not to mention the blond hair and blues eyes (28)—of the German Jewish immigrants marks her need for their difference, her need for them to be outside and inassimilable to her present world. Her capacity to see into and through the worshippers is not blocked by difference, but by sameness. In and of the very world in which she finds herself, the synagogue fails to offer her the experience of spectatorship that she desires, one which would let her abandon not only that "spectral and flitting" view, but also herself, by allowing her pass into and through those she watches.

The spectacle of difference appeals to Child because it invites her to imagine herself into and as everyone else, enabling the performance of abandonment that drives the text. She elaborates on the attractions—and terrors—of losing herself in the spectacle of others in Letter X, which opens with a view of a crowded marketplace that reproduces the "abstract and generalizing" gaze of Poe's narrator in the "Man of the Crowd." "Variety" itself is the abstraction that becomes her focus, initially devoid of any content: "In a great metropolis like this, nothing is more observable than the infinite varieties of character" (43). But Child's grammar here is slippery, since "nothing" may indeed be easier to observe than what she chooses to substantiate this "variety"—the peculiarly invisible diversity of religious faith. "Almost without effort," Child insists, "one may happen to find himself . . . beside the Catholic kneeling before the Cross, the Mohammedan bowing to the East . . . and the Mormon quoting from the Golden Book which he has never seen." Child's assertion of effortlessness assumes both the receptivity of the spectator and the transparency of the crowd, which she initially regards as a pageant of "mute actors, who tramp across the stage."[45] But the longer she holds this view in her sight, the more it changes before her, as the "rapid fluctuation and never-ceasing change" of urban life fade to images of death. Where people are so numerous that they can only be comprehended through abstractions like populations and varieties, "life is a reckless game and death is a business transaction."

> There is something impressive, even to painfulness, in this dense crowding of human existence, this mercantile familiarity with death. It has sometimes forced upon me, for a few moments, an appalling night-mare sensation of vanishing identity; as if I were but an unknown, unnoticed, and unseparated drop in a great ocean of human existence . . . . But such ideas I expel at once, like phantasms of evil, which indeed they are. Unprofitable to all, they have a peculiarly bewildering and oppressive power over a mind constituted like my own; so prone to eager questioning of the infinite, and curious search into the invisible. (44)

Despite her attempts to see these varieties abstractly, Child comes to feel this "dense crowding" as physical pressure, "impressive even to painfulness." Like the "lateral pressure" she feels at the opening of the Croton Aqueduct, like the "mighty pressure of the mind of all upon the intelligence of each" that cows Tocqueville's democratic subject "in the face of the majority" of which she is a part (*Democracy in America*, 435), this is the sensation of a subject's location inside the crowd on which she so intently looks. So forceful is this feeling of pressure that Child does not even claim the vanishing identity as her own. It is identity in general that is vanishing, as if the very possibility of naming, grounding, and owning oneself could be washed away in a human "ocean."

Child is, she says, appalled by this "night-mare sensation," and the one "effort" she makes in this passage is the gesture of expelling it "at once." But to take Child at her word and read this expulsion as decisive does little to account for the strangeness of what follows it. Although Child claims to reject and recover herself from the feeling that she has vanished into a crowd of infinite variety, the remainder of the letter performs the vagrancies of a subject longing to vanish once again. She apologizes at one point for her digression—"Flibbertigibbit himself never moved with more unexpected and incoherent variety" (*Letters,* 44)—but it becomes clear that, instead of a mode of escape from the urban crowd, her wandering prose might best be described as another path to that vanishing. Child's "vagrancies" do not "expel" or flee this vision of annihilating abstraction and lost individuality, so much as they allow her to repeat (twice) the vanishing of a subject into a community of strangers. Forgetting her promise to return to the subject of New York's varieties, she goes on to digress wildly into a sentimental, secondhand story of an unnamed English immigrant who dies alone on a Mississippi steamboat. In its surreal sentimentality and its blurring of compassion and compulsion, Child's anecdote of the dying stranger almost reads like one of the interpolated narratives from *The Confidence-Man.* The story begins with the melancholy tale of an immigrant who finds, on his death, a sympathetic community of strangers to perform his last rites in the "silent solitude of the primeval forest" (45). The relation of the stranger's death quickly becomes secondary, though, to the story of its narrator, "Captain T.," who walks off to reflect on the sad events and becomes lost on a "widely devious and circuitous route." But Captain T. loses himself only to return to the scene he's just departed as a lost stranger himself. Wandering aimlessly, losing oneself on winding paths, only to find oneself looking once again on one's point of departure: the tale reads like a template for Child's letters. Beyond its structural echoes, Child's compulsively digressive account of compulsive digression also hints at the attractions of losing oneself. For the dying man, the captain, and for Child, the possibility of being lost becomes the promise of finding a community of sympathetic strangers into which one might be received.

The prospect of "vanishing identity" is less a nightmare to be expelled than the prerequisite for an affective experience that Child tries to imagine as a counter to the spectacular anonymity of the public sphere. Modeled, in many ways, on the example of Macdonald Clarke—the homeless "mad-poet" of Letter XV whom Child describes as having a "nerve protruding from every pore" (64)[46]—this affect is a reinterpretation of sympathy as involuntary intersubjectivity and near-fatal selflessness. Rather than an act of identification that reifies the self, this is a sympathy that would dissolve the boundaries between its subjects and objects, making each transparent and permeable to all. In this sense, it suggests an expressly public affect that, in its resistance to volition and direction, is also key to her definition of vagrancy. Child elaborates on her vision of this intersubjectivity after a visit to Barnum's American Museum leaves her troubled, and she proposes in Letter XXXVI that a sympathetic imperative to "look into . . . and through" people might serve as an escape from the violence that she locates in such spectacularizations of human life. However, as an affect that opens her to all, it refuses her attempts to direct it and reveals her intimate entanglement with the very scene she wishes to flee. Ultimately, in the American Museum, Child's two ways of seeing—abstractly and deeply—collapse into one another, producing the same deadly effect and revealing the violence at the root of the identity which Child would have vanish away.

As one of the most overwrought spectacles in antebellum New York, the American Museum seems both an inevitable and a surprising stop for Child.[47] The Museum embodied in structural form the strategies of hyperbolic promotion and complicated hoax that defined what Neil Harris has termed Barnum's "operational aesthetic."[48] By definition, Barnum's humbugs invited their viewers to examine and inquire into their modes of operation and display, making the mode of exhibition very much a part of the Museum, and Child takes this invitation quite seriously. On attending Barnum's exhibit of fifteen Native Americans from several Midwestern tribes in 1843, Child turns her attention to all of the conditions that have made this spectacle possible, from expansionist wars to the violent categorizations of racial science: "We who have robbed the Indians of their lands, and worse still, of themselves, are very fond of proving their inferiority" (162). But for all of her disapproval, the letter maps Child's alternating seduction by and rejection of the view the Museum establishes. In one breath, for example, she seems to mock the findings of racial science, listing on the page the reduction of human lives to the bare abstraction of cranial measurements. But in the next breath, she indulges in a little comparative ethnography herself, disputing the findings of "inferiority" but drawing racialist conclusions of her own. ("This merely proves that the Caucasian race, through a succession of ages, has been exposed to influences eminently more calculated to develop the moral and intellectual faculties.") In reply to Barnum's invitation to examine his mechanisms of exhibition and display, Child indeed finds the ideology that displaces, dehumanizes, and eradicates populations. But, as with looking at Romans and Russians, to look at this ideology, she must also look into it and through it. As Sam Otter argues, the letter itself becomes a "synecdoche for the United States' treatment of its native inhabitants, in which a fatal gaze objectifies, exposes, and contaminates."[49]

P. T. Barnum spectacularized racial varieties more extravagantly than almost any entertainer in antebellum America; from Joice Heth to the Feejee Mermaid to Cheng and Eng, Barnum's blockbuster humbugs played to antebellum fantasies about seeing and measuring difference empirically.[50] But Child's letter suggests that such exhibits were as much about the spectators as about the men and women on display. Drawn in by humbugs and curiosities, the crowd at the Museum was also called upon to reflect on the spectacle of themselves, as they enacted the privilege of looking, measuring, and inhabiting a norm. Initially, Child takes the bait, dwelling on the admirable "brow" of what she calls the "Caucasian race" and imaging herself as part of an "us" which claims for itself the inheritance of both "the Jews" and "the Greeks" (162). But the consolations of racial science only take her so far, and she gradually arrives at a feeling of "deep sadness" in being a part of such a crowd. Gazing on men and women "set up for a two-shilling show with monkeys flamingoes, dancers, and buffoons" (164), she tries to invert, or at least to make symmetrical, the terms of display and judgment. First, she argues that this implicit demand for racial comparison reflects more favorably on the men and women on the stage than on their spectators, and then she imagines how things look from where they sit, detecting in their faces "a slight expression of scorn at the eager curiosity of the crowd." But true to the imperative of her own form, Child cannot help being taken by the intense desire for what Otter calls "inside knowledge." As soon as Child begins to imagine what things look like to their eyes, "to know their thoughts," she begins to long for even more intimate understanding:

> I would suffer almost anything, if my soul could be transmigrated into the She-Wolf or Productive Pumpkin, and their souls pass consciously into mine, for a few days, that I might experience the fashion of their thoughts and feelings. Was there ever such a foolish wish! The soul *is* Me and *is* Thee. I might as well put on their blankets as their bodies for purposes of spiritual insight . . . . I do not care to travel to Rome or St. Petersburg, because I can only look *at* people; and I want to look *into* them and *through* them; to know how things appear to *their* spiritual eyes, and sound to *their* spiritual ears. (164–65; Child's italics)

Such a desire to see into and through the eyes and spirits of racial others is both intense and pervasive in antebellum writing. "Agonies are one of my changes of garments," Whitman writes. "I do not ask the wounded person how he feels, I myself become the wounded person."[51] But where Whitman's "changes of garments" offers a seamless metonym for donning another identity, Child's passage from looking to becoming is blocked by this very gesture. "I might as well put on their blankets as their bodies for purposes of spiritual insight." Child wrestles here with one of the more insidious paradoxes of the very form of sympathy to which she turns: If "the soul *is* me and *is* Thee," then the imaginative act of projecting herself into the soul of another cannot give access to the "fashion of their thoughts and feeling," because she can only know and feel her own. Child cannot inhabit the minds of these women and know what they experience without losing both herself and this coveted knowledge in the process.

In her dream of "pass[ing] consciously" into the souls of She-Wolf and Productive Pumpkin, obtaining that inward view of their thoughts and feelings without either supplanting them or losing her own ability to perceive them, Child imagines a model of identification that avoids displacing its object, and this is a measure of Child's unusual conceptions of spectatorship and sympathy. Saidya Hartman lays bare the dubious model of empathic identification frequently employed in abolitionist writing to forge ties of sentiment between white readers and black slaves—an identification that largely serves to reify the white reader's humanity specifically by evading the slave's own sentience and displacing the slave's own voice.[52] Such efforts to put white readers into the position of a slave, whose suffering is staged again and again for the sole purpose of such imaginative transports, ultimately emphasize the fungibility of the slave's body and suggest that his or her pain exists only insofar as it is confirmed by white readers who feel it for themselves. Child is emphatic in this letter about resisting such a form of empathy by making the sentience and voice of the women the unapproachable object of sympathetic inquiry. By focusing on the impossibility of such a transport, Child refuses to experience the display of these women and men as a self-reifying exercise in sympathetic displacement, but with this admission, she also bumps up against the limits of her own imaginative enterprise. Child's "soul" is its own obstacle, interposing a "me" and a "thee" between the subjects that she wishes to conjoin. Where she experienced the sensation of "vanishing identity" in the crowded marketplace as a nightmare, "identity" remains stubbornly present in Barnum's Museum, despite the intensity of her desire to be rid of it. But even so, the persistence in this letter of what she alternately calls the "soul," "me," and "thee," is not exactly a measure of identity's inviolability; instead its persistence becomes the mark of her utter confinement in public spectacle. The hopeless passage into the minds and souls of She-Wolf and Productive Pumpkin must be preceded by an equally impossible transport out of the crowd from which she watches them.

In the end, Child's daydream of a transmigration into She-Wolf and Productive Pumpkin cannot escape from the scene and conditions in which she views them, for this fantasy emerges from a spectacle that exposes them, demeans them, and as Child reveals in a stunning postscript, kills two of them:

> P.S. Alas, poor Do-Hum-Me is dead! So is No-See, Black Hawk's niece, and several of the chiefs are indisposed. . . . [O]ne hour half stifled in the close atmosphere of theatres and crowded saloons, and the next driving through snowy streets; this is a process which kills civilized people by inches, but savages at a few strokes. (166)

Stage lights, stifling air, and the contagion of the crowd: the very means of spectacle prove deadly for two of the women and gravely sicken the others.[53] Child notes the inclement weather, but she makes it clear that it is the "close atmosphere of theatres"—filled with crowds from "the pestilential city"—that is the real culprit. Because it is also within the confines of this fatal venue that Child's own daydream of transmigration becomes possible, her dream is less an inversion of that spectacle than it is an extension of the same scene of viewing into far more intimate, far more deadly realms. The obstacle of "me" and "thee"—the "soul" and the self that block Child's desire for intersubjective knowledge—is mirrored in the deadly presence of the watching crowd at the Museum. Child's gaze, too, comes from the pestilential crowd that surrounds them in the close theater, and the publicity that enables her fantasy is the publicity that kills them. In Barnum's exhibit, the "operational aesthetic" takes a deadly turn, and Child's perception of the conditions and mechanisms that make the show possible can do nothing to reduce the power of its noxious spectacle. Child finds herself in precisely that place where Debord's spectacle collapses into Foucault's, as her seeing involves her against her better wishes in a deadly performance of exception that is coextensive with the sovereign self-constitution of this democratic public.

Carolyn Porter describes a crisis of spectatorship in nineteenth-century American writing, through which an observer recognizes her participation in the world she has "presumed to observe" only, producing a startling view of a real that is neither objective nor given but made, a world which not only includes but also constitutes a subject who both determines and is determined by the scene of viewing.[54] Such, in many ways, is the crisis that reveals Child's implication in the spectacle at Barnum's Museum. Child never assumes the stable stance of detachment that, Porter argues, is undermined by this crisis, privileging as Child does a sympathetic seeing that constantly asserts its own vulnerability. However, when she fantasizes an extreme form of sympathy, one that would permit her to see deeply into and as the women in the Museum, she confronts the impossibility of suppressing the self's involvement, all the same. The stubborn necessity of preserving intact the identifying self renders her incapable of passing into others, while also revealing that this self is not hers. Rather than a private soul or a personal me or thee, the identity that blocks Child's dream of passage into the women's thoughts is a condition of her very location in public. In the end, Child does succumb to the "vanishing identity" that she both longs for and fears, but rather than a sympathetic bond that allows her to abandon herself and merge with others, it yields only complicity with a public of fellow spectators—a public whose desire to see and measure itself is predicated on its power to exclude.

## "The hangman's accomplice": Sovereignty and Complicity

"There is complicity," Emerson wrote in 1860, and his grammar echoes an impression that Child leaves in her letter on the American Museum: complicity is less an act or a decision than it is a condition, a kind of fate. Emerson's "Fate" pairs suggestively with many of Child's letters (she often describes the polarity of necessity and free will in Emersonian terms[55]), but a particularly strong resonance exists between the essay and this letter. For one thing, both Child's Letter XXXVI and Emerson's "Fate" open by rehearsing the most outrageous claims of ethnology in a manner that both mocks them and recognizes the power of a discourse to accede to the level of fatality. "We are told," Child writes, "that the facial angle in the Caucasian race is 85 degrees, Asiatic 78 degrees, American Indian 73 degrees," and so on (162), but though she scorns the absurdity of these precisions, Child is unsure what to make of them. In this, she follows Emerson: "A dome of brow denotes one thing; a pot-belly another; a squint, a pug-nose, mats of hair, the pigment of the epidermis, betray character."[56] Fate, for both of them, is a tyranny of necessity and limitation, and neither treats it in transcendent or prophetic terms.

Instead, what appears as fate arises from the most mundane of practices and beliefs; it is a creature of consensus that evolves from, shapes, and limits what is thinkable. Writing of what constrains the thinkable, both Child and Emerson also show themselves to be subject to the limits they describe, often making it nearly impossible to distinguish between what Sam Otter, in another context, calls "ambivalence" and "strategy."[57] In a reading of "Fate," Eduardo Cadava insists that such uncertain ventriloquism is Emerson's strategy, describing the essay as a "secret genealogy of what makes racism and slavery possible."[58] Cadava argues that this strategy emerges in the very "practice of Emerson's writing"; by staging conventional discourse rather than speaking it, Emerson refuses its tendency to conceal the connections and consequences that allow conditions to appear as "fate": "You have just dined, and, however scrupulously the slaughter-house is concealed in the graceful distance of miles, there is complicity,—expensive races,—race living at the expense of race."[59]

Clearly, Child sees the slaughterhouse at the end of her fork, and as with Emerson, the peculiarities of her writing often work explicitly to hold that bloody view up to her reader. Nowhere is this more apparent than in her letter on Barnum's Museum, which she edits to include the shocking postscript on the women's deaths (a dangerous supplement if ever there was). But the problem she encounters in the American Museum is that her capacity to see the long chain of actions and beliefs that leads to the spectacle of fifteen men and women on Barnum's stage, to see even her own complicity in these acts and beliefs, is insufficient to save them. Child's letter stages a complex and devastating recognition that even sympathy is complicity, but it also stages the limits of that recognition. If one was tempted to impose on Child's *Letters from New-York* something like a narrative, the letter on Barnum's Museum would serve as a fit climax for the text, so decisively does it arrive at an impasse that she approaches again and again. Certainly, the four letters that follow Letter XXXVI lack its power and complexity, slipping into a troubled denouement that treat nothing more substantial than a snowstorm and moving day in New York City. But in the series of letters that culminates in the American Museum, Child teases out a genealogy of complicity that rivals Emerson's, detailing the means by which consensus becomes fate—"necessity" in her words—in fairly concrete terms. Her focus in Letters XXIX through XXXII is specifically on the institutions of correction and a planned execution in New York City, but in considering how "society makes and cherishes the very crimes it so fiercely punishes" (60), she roots that complicity directly in the very power that constitutes the public sphere—in the exercise of sovereignty through the public's right to punish.

Child's letters on her visit to the prison at Blackwell's Island offer a near inversion of Beaumont and Tocqueville's penitentiary study, in that she shows little interest in debating the theories and methods of reforming inmates.[60] Instead, Child is preoccupied with how criminals are made in the first place, both by economic and social inequities and by the performative power of law. Noticing several magazine editors jailed for printing materials deemed pornographic, she leaps to their defense: "[T]hey dared to *publish* what nine-tenths of all around them *lived* un-reproved. . . . Why should *The Weekly Rake* be shut up while daily rakes walk Broadway in fine broadcloth and silk velvet!" (126). No prudish moralist, Child also defends the women imprisoned on the island for prostitution and becomes livid thinking of the equal partners in their "crime" who still walk free: "These men live in the ceiled houses of Broadway, and sit at city hall, and pass 'regulations' that clear the streets they have filled" (126). She is repeatedly struck by the arbitrariness of law, and she lists several examples of how the same act elevates some while criminalizing others. Reflecting on the primacy of violence in American life, for example, Child imagines a comparison between two known murderers: the first (a thinly disguised Andrew Jackson) "enters the army, kills a hundred Indians . . . and is considered a fitting candidate for the presidency." The second man, guilty of a far less calculated crime of passion, "fights, kills his adversary, is tried by the laws of the land, and is hung" (127).[61] Reflecting on the power of law to fabricate both crimes and criminals, Child converts the island itself into a metonym for the corrupting power of the state. A wilderness of thick trees and "verdant beauty" with a "loveliness of scenery unsurpassed by anything I have ever witnessed," she laments that the island now "belongs to government." As in Hawthorne's Salem, the settlement and ultimate corruption of Blackwell's Island begins with the erection of a prison.

But while the island "belongs to government," Child does not stop there with her critique. Reaching a dead-end in blaming the state alone, Child considers the ways in which the public forms and reforms citizens and criminals alike, but what is remarkable about her reflections is the place she imagines for herself in these processes. Child's politics are rooted in her belief in the inseparability of individual and collective life, and when she seeks out the "mysteriously deep foundations on which society . . . reels and totters," she presumes an intricate connection between intimate life and the public sphere. In her letters on Blackwell's

Island, this leads her to a keen sense of her own implication in both the reforming of the inmates and in the fabrication of their crimes: "How much have I done toward it by yielding to popular prejudices, obeying false customs, and suppressing vital truths, I know not" (126). The sense of collective responsibility that she describes seems both passive and inevitable, a simple yielding to a false social order. This is complicity as condition, a fatal consequence of her location in this public, which no amount of reforming spirit can dispel:

> I have not been happy since that visit to Blackwell's Island. There is something painful, yea, terrific, in feeling myself involved in the great wheel of society, which goes whirling on, crushing thousands at every turn. This relation of the individual to the mass is the sternest and most frightful of all the conflicts between necessity and free will. (130)

Child's pain and unhappiness stem not from suffering but from surviving the crushing wheel; there is "race living at the expense of race" and, by any material measure, she thrives. With this, Child articulates what Tocqueville calls the "strange melancholy often haunting inhabitants of democracies" (*Democracy in America*, 538). "In the midst of abundance," he writes, "disgust with life sometimes grip[s] them in calm and easy circumstances."

For Child, there is neither calm nor ease to be had in circumstances such as there. If what she describes—surviving the crushing wheel—is "necessity," it is also culpability, and such a life cannot be passive, even if it is nearly impossible for her to pin down any one act that implicates her: "Every jealous thought I cherish, every angry word I utter, every repulsive tone, is helping to build penitentiaries and prisons and to fill them with those who carry the same passions and feelings further than I do" (*Letters*, 144).[62] Child begins her meditations on collective culpability by linking herself to the inmates of Blackwell's Island, whose acts are nothing more than an intensification of her own, and yet the public imagines "a difference so great" between them, that they "are scarcely regarded as belonging to the same species" (144). Here, Child arrives at the name of the power she has been describing throughout, one with the arbitrary yet absolute capacity to divide lives along such biological lines, and she calls it "the ban of human laws." When Child invokes the term "ban," she means it in precisely the way that Agamben defines it—the "threshold" where law refers to, regulates, and includes life in its hold, the basic structure of sovereignty.[63] The ban, which appears to be a dividing line, is actually a chain that links all lives together, and as Child cautions, "you who now walk abroad in the sunshine of respectability, might have come under the ban of human laws" (144). This is a threshold which anyone might cross, but Child is clear that those who do are not the accidental or inevitable victims of society's "great wheel"—they are its deliberate and calculated exceptions. As she turns from the penitentiary to the gallows in her reflections on law's ban, Child also approaches more nearly the nature of her complicity through the "cool, deliberate calculation to take life":

> [W]hat is this hangman but a servant of the law? And what is that law but an expression of public opinion? And if public opinion be brutal, and *thou* a component part thereof, art *thou* not the hangman's accomplice? (145)

Child's pronouns shift curiously in this letter from "I" to "thou," as if she is more willing to identify herself with the convict than the executioner, but her implication is clear. In the terrible intimacy of a democratic public sphere constituted by a sovereignty that is ostensibly popular, everyone becomes both the hangman and the condemned.

It is little wonder that Child finds herself "unhappy" after her visit to Blackwell's Island, still less so that this unhappiness culminates in the mournful letter on the deaths of Do-Hum-Me and No-No-See after Barnum's lethal show. Like Tocqueville, Child roots the melancholy of the democratic subject in an experience of spectacle that exposes the entanglement of life and death in the public sphere. But where Tocqueville holds up "equality" as the receding object on which all eyes fix, generating the constant movement that keeps democracy's show on the road, Child insists on a different view. Rather than an "equality" understood in formal political terms, one predicated on the abstract sameness of subjects which continues to operate through the logic of exception, Child calls for an affective equality in kinship: "And so I return, as the old preachers used to say, to my first propositions; that we should think gently of all, and claim kindred with, and include all, without exception, in the circle of our kindly sympathies" (145). If Child's dream of a sympathetic transmigration of souls proves fatal in the American Museum, it is because the affect that she imagines is still structured by the long chain of exceptions that ends with her implication in the deaths of the Native women. A kinship "without exception" cannot be realized in a space likes Barnum's Museum—where American exceptionalism, in its most sensational and transparent varieties, is on permanent exhibition—any more than it can be realized at the gallows. To "claim kindred with all . . . without exception" is to imagine a radically reconfigured public where citizenship and sovereignty do not require either ban or death. It is to predicate public belonging on an affective bond whose only constitutive exclusion is the requirement of exception itself.

# 4 / The Spectacle of Reform: Theater and Prison in Hawthorne's *Blithedale Romance*

Pursued by a "deep sadness" from Blackwell's Island to Barnum's Museum—from prison to theater, as it were—Lydia Maria Child offers one of her era's more haunting accounts of democracy's melancholy. As she dissects the affective consequences of participating in public enactments of exception, Child exposes the continuity of punishment and entertainment in antebellum public life, locating a basic violence in what Saidiya Hartman has ironically termed the era's "innocent amusements." Hartman argues specifically that "antebellum formations of pleasure, even those of the North, need to be considered in relation to the affective dimensions of chattel slavery." For Hartman, this involves a reinterpretation of two of antebellum America's most popular theatrical forms, blackface minstrelsy and racial melodrama, forms which rely simultaneously on sentiment and violence, terror and pleasure, to reveal the spectacular atrocities of the auction block within the popular spectacles of the stage.[1] What writers like Tocqueville, Beaumont, and Child—as well as Nathaniel Hawthorne and Herman Melville—add to Hartman's account of the violence that inheres in melodrama and minstrelsy is a broader interpretation of public spectacle and its entanglements with political power, as well as an account of the psychic costs of complicity with it. These authors find the dynamic of pleasure and terror at the very foundation of public life because it is intrinsic to U.S. formations of a democratic sovereignty which "gladly works for the happiness" of its subjects (*Democracy in America*, 692), while creating of a chain of homologous exceptions and limits to that public.

Chattel slavery provided a model of lawful violence, against which other forms of exceptional penalty—capital punishment, solitary confinement—operated in the United States in the early decades of the nineteenth century. As the penal system learned from slavery, so reform movements in general began to partake of the rhetoric and practices of penitentiary reform, particularly insofar as sentiment and sympathy produced a kind of *lingua franca* for reform, shaping debates about technologies of punishment along with those on abolition, temperance, public education, and any number of reformist efforts.[2] Such a fluidity of connection between sentiment and punishment, reform, violation, and entertainment, in many ways, accounts for the crisis that begins to unravel the communitarian experiment in Hawthorne's 1852 "novel," *The Blithedale Romance*.[3] It is not accidental that the community, which first appears to Hawthorne's narrator as "a masquerade, a pastoral, a counterfeit Arcadia" (52), reveals itself to be an incipient penitentiary. When Hollingsworth the philanthropist admits his intention to "obtain possession of the very ground on which we had planted our Community" in order to realize his "scheme for the reformation of the wicked by methods moral, intellectual, and industrial" (134), Miles Coverdale's theater becomes a prison, and he finds himself occupying two metonymic sites of democratic sovereignty at once. With this, the most voluntary of associations—an intentional community created by reformers who "give up whatever [they] had heretofore attained, for the sake of showing mankind the example of a life governed by other than the false and cruel principles"—betrays its involuntary dimensions. But what is both surprising and significant about Coverdale's aversion to Hollingsworth's scheme is that it does not arise simply from the fear that the philanthropist intends to become a solitary, autocratic leader ruling over the community. Coverdale feels the greatest horror at the intended mobilization of "the sympathy of pure, humble, and yet exalted minds" in the service of punishment. In short, Coverdale most fears the community's engagement of a power which demands his involvement in it.

By reading Hawthorne's satire of mid-century socialist experimentation as linked to the same continuity that Hartman traces between "innocent amusements" and chattel slavery, I do not mean to imply that Blithedale's institution of involuntary association is analogous to the violations of slavery. Indeed, my interest in Coverdale's experience of the involuntary has less to do with his fears of coercion or compulsion by his fellows than with a corresponding anxiety of complicity in the violation of others. Coverdale's dilemma may be best summed up as "that strange melancholy often haunting the inhabitants of democracies" (*Democracy in America*, 538)—that self-serving sense of isolation and vulnerability that Tocqueville finds in those subjects who have become intimately involved with sovereign power. The condition staged in *The Blithedale Romance*, I argue, is a crisis of empowerment in a society organized as both democratic and sovereign. No matter how firmly its participants reject the "old system" (*Blithedale*, 83), no matter how remote they imagine themselves to be from conventional society (103), Blithedale is a creation of the antebellum imagination that replicates in miniature the public from which it flees. Structured largely around a complex form of mimicry (what I call "mimetic reform"), through which the members seek to influence and alter each other while serving as an example to the world outside, Blithedale turns Tocqueville's anxieties about the tyranny of democratic sameness into its guiding principle. And as in Tocqueville's analysis of the antebellum public sphere, mimetic relations may create a spectacular image of equality for the residents of Blithedale, but only at the price of isolation from one another and the community they seek to create. Furthermore, the mimetic relations instituted at Blithedale involve them in enactments of sovereignty that produce what Tocqueville calls "a stranger among us." That such acts are the ultimate achievement of the community becomes clear in a fleeting image that Miles Coverdale sees near the end of his narrative: a performer "accustomed to be the spectacle to thousands" suddenly morphs into "a blindfold prisoner."

Bridging the community's double function as a theater and a prison, the image of the "spectacle to thousands" as "a blindfold prisoner" hints at the exceptionalism on which the community founds itself. From Eastern State Penitentiary to Abu Ghraib, the hooded, blindfolded prisoner has stood alongside the slave as an exceptional object of U.S. sovereignty. But rather than being hidden away, Coverdale's prisoner remains "a spectacle to thousands," located in the most public of spaces to reveal the contours of political power even within the "innocent amusements" of popular entertainment. Beginning with an image that comes late in Coverdale's narrative, I will trace the development of the spectacle/prisoner figure both in the text and beyond it as a sign of the persistence of politics throughout the public sphere and into the separatist community at Blithedale. Though she is introduced as Coverdale's interpretation of the Veiled Lady, who is—ostensibly—Priscilla in disguise, this figure stands as the creature of a community that can only imagine itself in terms of spectacle and imprisonment. She is, like Tocqueville's stranger, the counterpart to the melancholy democratic subject, and in telling the story of one, *The Blithedale Romance*, of necessity, tells the story of both. Many scholars have examined Hawthorne's engagement with antebellum performance culture and the spectacularization of reform in *The Blithedale Romance*, suggesting various historical antecedents to the Veiled Lady.[4] Linking her to famous spiritualists like the Fox sisters, as well as popular entertainers like Jenny Lind and Fanny Elssler, these critics have generally regarded her as evidence of Hawthorne's critique of a mass-market performance culture that creates passive, remote, politically inert subjects.[5] By tracing another genealogy for *The Blithedale Romance*, through the career of the educator and prison reformer, Samuel Gridley Howe, and his prodigy, Laura Bridgman, I propose a somewhat different account of the fate of politics in both Hawthorne's romance and the spectacular public sphere, one that considers not the passivity of subjects, but their complicity in the creation of such figures as the "blindfold prisoner." There is nothing immaterial or apolitical about the Veiled Lady once she is figured as a "blindfold prisoner." Rooted as this image is in the mid-century's debates about the sovereign authority of the public to isolate, except, and alter subjects deemed criminal, it may be one of the era's most essentially "political" images.

## "Creating Laura Bridgman": Aesthetic Labor and the Blindfold Prisoner

"Sweetest wife, thou hast not written me," Nathaniel Hawthorne complained to Sophia Peabody in a letter dated from Brook Farm on the 22nd and 23rd of September, 1841. "Nevertheless, I do not conclude thee to be sick, but will believe that thou hast been busy in creating Laura Bridgman."[6] While enduring his last months at Brook Farm, the experimental community that would become the model for Blithedale, Hawthorne wrote to his fiancée about her involvement with the phenomenon of Laura Bridgman. A deaf, blind, and mute child, Bridgman was a celebrated prodigy, whose education and mastery of writing and "finger language" would make her, according to the claims of the *Boston Evening Transcript*, the most famous female in the world next to Queen Victoria.[7] By the end of 1841, the child was already known throughout the United States, and on the verge of transatlantic celebrity, as well, following her meeting with Charles Dickens in January 1842 and the account of her story that he would include in the *American Notes* later that year. However, when Hawthorne made reference to Bridgman in two letters to Sophia Peabody, he did so dismissively, in the midst of a series of complaints about his inability to write and Peabody's neglect of him, which he attributes to her work on a bust that she has been asked to sculpt of the girl:

> Dearest, do not thou wear thyself out upon that bust. If it causes thee so much as a single head-ache, I shall wish that Laura Bridgman were at Jericho. Even if thou shouldst not feel thyself wearied at the time, I fear that the whole burthen of toil will fall upon thee when all is accomplished. It is no matter if Laura should go home without being sculptured—no matter if she goes to her grave without it. I dread to have thee feel an outward necessity for such a task; for this intrusion of an outward necessity into labors of the imagination and intellect is, to me, very painful. (*The Letters*, 578–79)

Hawthorne's advice to Peabody not to exhaust herself on the sculpture of Bridgman rings somewhat false after two letters preoccupied with his own frustrated writing: "I doubt whether I shall succeed in writing another volume of Grandfather's Library. . . . I have not . . . perfect seclusion" (575). While Hawthorne admits that "nobody intrudes" into his writing at the farm, he nonetheless understands the obstacle to be external to him: "Nothing here is settled. . . . My mind will not be abstracted." The "ferment" of the farm and the continuing "labor of the body" thwart the "perfect seclusion" which Hawthorne cites as his ideal state for writing. Given such complaints throughout his letters to Peabody, his expression of "dread" at the intrusion of necessity into imaginative labor ("to me, very painful") clearly has more to do with his own anxieties than with any fears of hers. Noting the many echoes between Hawthorne's letters from Brook Farm and *The Blithedale Romance*, critics often cite Miles Coverdale's assertion of the total incompatibility of physical and intellectual exercise (*Blithedale*, 85) as evidence of Hawthorne's own conception of aesthetics as radically dematerialized, allied with privacy and spirituality, and opposed to all physical forms of labor.[8] Certainly, the language of "intrusion" and "necessity," which he projects onto Peabody's sculpting, echoes Coverdale's peevish excuses, but it seems a mistake to conflate Hawthorne so fully with his narrator, especially given that the romance itself thoroughly complicates this relationship between the physical and the imaginative, the material and the aesthetic. Instead, I would suggest that Hawthorne's expression of discomfort at the intersection of physical and imaginative labor in his letter to Sophia Peabody is masking another set of anxieties, which Laura Bridgman's strange career—and Peabody's brief, but specifically aesthetic, involvement with it—render clear. More precisely, in Laura Bridgman's spectacular fame can be found many of the questions of imprisonment and spectacle that surround the enigma of the mesmeric Veiled Lady in Hawthorne's romance. Through the story of the Veiled Lady, Hawthorne reaches the limits of the perfect, aesthetic "seclusion" for which he longs in his plaintive letter, and in doing so, he offers an oblique and belated—but also an extensive and damning— response to the conditions and culture that fostered Laura Bridgman's celebrity.

Although Hawthorne was dismissive of the celebrated Laura—wishing her "at Jericho" (*The Letters*, 578)—his phrasing, "creating Laura Bridgman," neatly captures the essence of her fame. Bridgman was widely considered to be an emblematic creation of antebellum reform movements, particularly the theories of pedagogy and discipline being developed by her mentor, whom Dickens calls "the man who has made her what she is."[9] Having lost her eyesight, hearing, and most of her senses of taste and smell after a near-fatal case of scarlet fever as a toddler, Bridgman received almost no education in the first several years of her life. At age seven, however, she was enrolled at Boston's Perkin's Institute for the Blind, where she came under the tutelage of the educator and reformer, Samuel Gridley Howe. With very little knowledge of the world outside what she could touch with her hands, Bridgman became for Howe a controlled and seemingly controllable site for his experiments in educating the blind. More than a test of his pedagogy, Howe described his work with Bridgman in terms that collapse Pygmalion with Dr. Frankenstein. Imagining himself faced with a wall of stone, "her poor white hand peeping through a chink," he saw his task as the creation of a human girl out of "a dog, a parrot." Early in their relationship, Howe devised a means to replace the language of signs that Bridgman had developed on her own to designate objects and people with a method for teaching her arbitrary language, "a knowledge of letters by combination of which she might express her idea of the existence, and the mode and condition of existence, of any thing." By first teaching her to draw letters with her hands and to feel others' hands as they spelled words out to her, Howe then led Bridgman to develop her expression of abstract thought and self-reflection. Although the finger language he devised was meant to bring Bridgman into relations with others, Howe notes a particular triumph in seeing her use it "in lonely self-communion . . . to reason, reflect, and argue." Beyond teaching her expression, Howe describes the finger language as giving Bridgman an ontology: the capacity for self-reflective solitude combined with the knowledge of "the mode and condition of existence."[10]

If the single best measure of Bridgman's transformation lay in the image of her "talking" to herself ("if she spell a word wrong with the fingers of her right hand, she instantly strikes it with her left, as her teachers do, in a sign of disapprobation"[11]), the best means of publicizing her story was to have her "perform" her solitude for visitors. Howe taught Bridgman to read books printed with raised type, to write, to sew, and to knit, and then he arranged for her to perform these skills routinely for the enormous audiences who flocked to the institute to see her. On a single day in July, 1844, Elizabeth Gitter notes in her history of Bridgman and Howe, the institute received eleven hundred visitors who came to watch Bridgman's studies, numbers that place her alongside Barnum's most successful exhibits. Bridgman was the center of Howe's spectacle of triumphant pedagogy, but her role in this spectacle was a form of oblivion to it. Bridgman went about her lessons and labors as if no one were watching, but she always "performed" in a kind of costume, wearing a green silk blindfold tied discreetly around her eyes. Such tensions between images of solitude and socialization in Bridgman's story were common. Although her education enabled her to develop social relations, Gitter argues that Bridgman's condition was continually characterized as her "imprisonment." Howe's first image of her is a small hand, pushing through a stone wall; Thomas Carlyle called her "a true Angel-soul and breath of Heaven, imprisoned as none such ever was before"; and a poem addressed "To Laura Bridgman" called on Howe "to guide / The imprisoned guest, through Nature's ample fields."[12] By continuing to figure Bridgman as a prisoner, Howe could be, at once, her creator and her liberator, but as long as her "prison" was her body, she could never be fully emancipated, making him also her warden. What people watched when they came to Perkins to see Bridgman was the spectacle of her ongoing reform—a form of public solitude in which she would discipline herself, smacking her own hand for misspelling a word.

Beyond describing her isolation, the metaphor of Bridgman's "imprisonment" reveals presumptions of her guilt, which follow automatically from her imperviousness to education as a young child. When Dickens pictures to himself the young Laura on her arrival at the Perkins Institute, he does not describe a sickly daughter of sentimental fiction; instead, he pictures a kind of Kaspar Hauser figure, likening her situation to that of an animal: "The moral effects of her wretched state soon began to appear. Those who cannot be enlightened by reason, can only be controlled by force; and this, coupled with her great privations, must soon have reduced her to a worse condition than that of the beasts that perish but for timely and unhoped-for aid."[13] Dickens imagines Bridgman's childhood as a Foucauldian history of punishment, from corporeal to disciplinary, which ends with her achievement of a self-regulating and social character. But, Gitter argues, Howe did not see the same success in Bridgman's growing independence from him that others did. Bridgman's incredible gifts at imitation and the intimate relations with teachers and other students which had promised to "enlighten" her began to appear to Howe as sources of contamination. Having "made her what she is," Howe came to believe that he must continue to make her, over and over again. In order to reverse what he regarded as the influence of unsuitable society over her, Howe began to mandate a strict control over Laura's companions, imposing a modified solitude on her that was broken only by occasional visits from teachers and friends whom he deemed suitable as models for her to imitate. In thus releasing Bridgman from her "prison" only to confine her to a kind of solitary reformatory, Howe imposed his own form of sensory deprivation on her, revealing his educational theories to be thoroughly entangled with the theories of punishment and prison reform that he was also advocating during the years of her education.[14]

Specifically, in the 1840s, Howe became an outspoken defender of Philadelphia's Eastern State Penitentiary and its model of (in Dicken's words) "rigid, strict, and hopeless solitary confinement."[15] Indeed, so total was the solitude enforced at Eastern State that prisoners were blindfolded and hooded whenever they were not locked alone in their cells. It was argued that this practice protected the identities of inmates, but the hooded inmate became the iconic image of the system's cruelty for critics like Dickens.[16] In Howe's *Essay on Separate and Congregate Systems of Prison Discipline*, he takes up the difficult task of advocating for the greater humanity of Eastern State, over the congregate model of rehabilitation pursued in New York. To make this claim, Howe aims to convert the blindfold and the hood into assets by specifically asserting the moral benefits of isolation and sensory impairment. Howe's defense of solitary confinement hinges on what he describes as a natural, almost magnetic, impulse toward mimicry: "The tendency to imitate, and the desire of approbation by excelling in what others think excellent, are in society what attraction is among the particles of matter; and they act, too, in the same way, inversely as the square of the distance." Because mimicry may also become a source of moral contamination, he emphasizes the presence of "good companionship" and "the society of virtuous people" among the isolated prisoners. Anticipating Hollingsworth's scheme for the reformation of inmates through "the sympathy of pure, humble, and yet exalted minds" (*Blithedale*, 134), Howe argues that "cutting [the inmate] off from companionship with his guilty companions . . . [and] giving him the companionship of good men" forces each prisoner "to love and imitate" the "virtuous" wardens, guards, and attendants who were to become each man's sole society.[17] In Howe's defense of Eastern State, solitary confinement functions as a tightly controlled theater. Imitation serves as the basic disciplinary tool, as the virtuous exert an irresistible, magnetic, and sensuous influence over the inmates by determining both how and what they see. Howe filters theorists of sensation and cognition from Locke to Smith to Diderot, but he finally reveals his primary influence to be his work with the students of the Perkins Institute:

> It is not sight, but speech, that is the organ of social communication; it is not through the eye, but through the ear that our social intercourse is carried on; and though a man have as many eyes as Argus, it were better to have them all put out than to seal up his ears, if his object in life be intimate social communion and sympathy with those about him.[18]

Earlier in the essay, Howe describes the faculty of vision as an obstacle to reform, arguing that "three or four hundred convicts present to the eye" of each prisoner "shut out from him the great public beyond" and literally eclipse the model according to which each prisoner's reform should be guided.[19] In the passage above, he claims that while sight creates a powerful illusion of community, it cannot produce social communication or intimacy. Eager to discredit the congregate system, which permitted prisoners to work and dine together in total silence, as a violation of the basic faculties of human relation, Howe claims that hearing and speaking are the primary paths by which true social feelings travel. Essentially, Howe answers one of the major criticisms of the Eastern State Penitentiary's model of solitude—its imposition of sensory deprivation—by attempting to convert it into a benefit of the system. If the eye is the site of "mutual contamination" between prisoners, while the voice and the ear are organs of sympathy, then Howe can insist that the blindfolded prisoner of Eastern State remains a living, social being rather than one whose total isolation amounts to a form of exile or even execution. But Howe's reliance on manipulated sensation to make his argument reveals that solitary confinement remains, at root, a corporeal punishment, marking a point along what Joan Dayan calls "the continuum between unnatural (civil or spiritual) death and natural (actual and physical) death."[20] In Howe's account, Eastern State creates socially blind subjects, trapped in a sphere of total isolation, whom he holds up as spectacles and examples to that "great public," which is both their model for imitation and the ultimate agent of their punishment.

Laura Bridgman's appearance in Hawthorne's letters from Brook Farm would be sufficiently remarkable for the link that she provides between Hawthorne and Howe, whose *Essay on Separate and Congregate Systems of Prison Discipline* resonates not only with the theories of prison reform espoused by Hollingsworth but also with the anxieties of imitative sympathy articulated by Coverdale.[21] But Bridgman serves as more than a mediating figure who connects Howe to Hawthorne. Laura Bridgman's theater—the institute where she studied and worked before thousands of visitors—was her prison. Standing at precisely the point where Eastern State's strategies of punitive isolation and incapacitation intersect with central features of spectacular public life, she already occupied the imaginative terrain that Hawthorne would later mark out for *Blithedale*. As Gitter argues, Bridgman was for her contemporaries a "metaphor" for "isolation and enclosure, transformation and redemption . . . surveillance, imprisonment and loneliness"[22]—a fairly complete list of the obsessions of *Blithedale*'s narrator. *Blithedale* offers a sustained, critical reflection on the fantasies and anxieties of reform that Bridgman represented as clearly as any other public figure of her time: the possibility of making and remaking character through the staging of a controlled, isolated, and ideal community; the potentially transformative effects of mimicry, as well as the corresponding fears of its intrusive, corrupting influence; and finally the spectacularization of all these in models of reform that merge activist discipline with theatrical entertainment.

Sophia Peabody's sister, Elizabeth, apparently recognized the potential links between Hawthorne's enterprise at Brook Farm and Laura Bridgman's celebrated education: after Hawthorne's return, she tried to convince her brother-in-law to write Bridgman's biography. Mary Peabody Mann mentioned this plan in a letter to Sophia in October 1842: "E[lizabeth] thinks Dr. Howe will be most happy to render up any documents he has about Laura for the sake of having Mr. Hawthorne write a memoir of her."[23] There is no evidence that Howe ever passed on any materials to Hawthorne, nor is there any sign that Hawthorne was inclined to pursue such a project. Nonetheless, it is tempting to imagine that, with the publication of *The Blithedale Romance* in 1852, Hawthorne pursued, however obliquely, Elizabeth Peabody's plan. Equally tempting is the suggestion that Sophia Peabody sculpted *The Blithedale Romance* a decade before her husband wrote it. In Sophia's small bust of the young girl, her head tilted slightly downward, her mouth closed, a ribbon tied firmly around her eyes, she offered her own vision of the image that haunts Miles Coverdale at the end of *Blithedale*:

> [T]he movement of the Veiled Lady was graceful, free, and unembarrassed, like that of a person accustomed to be the spectacle of thousands. Or, possibly, a blindfold prisoner, within the sphere with which this dark, earthly magician had surrounded her, she was wholly unconscious of being the central object to all those straining eyes. (*Blithedale*, 185)

A spectacle to thousands or a blindfold prisoner? On this question rests a great deal more than Miles Coverdale's interpretation of the Veiled Lady's performance in the village hall outside of Boston at the end of his narrative. For one thing, this image destroys any illusion of the "innocent amusements" of spectacle. The public who gazes with its "straining eyes" does as much to convert the Veiled Lady into a prisoner as her "dark, earthly magician" does. For another thing, in suggesting that the performance of seclusion from the scene of public spectacle is actually a means of punitive isolation, the Veiled Lady undermines the strategy of remote spectatorship that Coverdale frequently adopts over the course of his narrative. Finally, this association of remote privacy with isolation and violation also compromises the aesthetic condition of "perfect seclusion" for which Hawthorne longs in his letters to Sophia, as he advises her to suspend work on her sculpture. Standing alongside the Veiled Lady on the threshold of *The Blithedale Romance*,[24] Laura Bridgman indicates what will become of the community of Blithedale just as clearly as that mesmeric clairvoyant does (one of whose predictions "certainly accorded with the event"). Given her specific role in the letters, Bridgman also points to the ways in which Hawthorne's aesthetic concerns negotiate the social and political anxieties that drive his text. If Hawthorne's initial response to the phenomenon of Bridgman's spectacular isolation is to resent "this intrusion of an outward necessity into labors of the imagination and intellect," his eventual reaction is a performance of "removal" and "remoteness" which serves to indict precisely that impulse. In other words, in *The Blithedale Romance*, Hawthorne implicates the separatist community and the form of romance itself—both of which he likens to "a theatre, a little removed from the highway of ordinary travel"—in the spectacular public culture that leads to the violation of figures such as Bridgman and the blindfold prisoner. In doing so, however, he also suggests that the political stakes of romance lie not in its flight from the material realities of public life, but in its efforts to restage and reflect critically on the dynamics of power that sustain it.

## Mimetic Reform: Spectatorship and Politics

The last twenty years have witnessed something like a *Blithedale* renaissance in American literary studies, with nearly seventy articles and book chapters on Hawthorne's romance appearing since the mid-1980s. In the last few years alone—since the beginning of the twenty-first century—*The Blithedale Romance* has been the subject of nearly two dozen scholarly pieces, as well as essays in mainstream publications, such as John Updike's 2001 essay for the *New York Review of Books* on Hawthorne's unlikely residence at Brook Farm, and Megan Marshall's 2005 *New Yorker* article, speculating on Hawthorne's romance with Elizabeth Peabody. Through the lens of this most recent wave of critical attention, *Blithedale* proves to be both an elastic text and a conflicted one. It lends itself to Foucauldian readings (Brand, Bumas) and psychoanalytic ones (Gable, Greven), and it has become a seminal text for recent studies in nineteenth-century sexuality (Grossberg, Tanner, Mills).[25] With its panoramic account of antebellum urban life, popular culture, and reformist fads, *Blithedale* has served as something like an archive in itself of the United States public sphere in the 1840s and 1850s and, as such, it has become a particularly important text for work in both the cultural history and political culture of the period. Beginning with influential readings by Gordon Hutner, Richard Brodhead, and Lauren Berlant in the 1980s, scholarship in this vein has read *Blithedale* primarily as a meditation on a diseased public sphere, for which Miles Coverdale serves as the telling symptom. In Hutner's reading, Coverdale's repeated failure to sustain intimate social relations is a cultural malady, and the undisclosed "secret" of the text is "the general social, political, and cultural nature of his delusion" that intimacy is no more than a desire for desire. Berlant argues that Coverdale's sexual failings serve as the text's framework for the death of national utopian fantasies, while for Richard Brodhead, Coverdale signals the "passive, nonperforming *watching*" that is "constituted by the Veiled Lady's version of spectacle" and confounded with public activity. The form of spectacle that Brodhead traces in his cultural history of the Veiled Lady results from a new relationship between entertainment and mass markets, but it functions like a public sphere, producing two gendered forms of passivity: the nonperforming male spectator and the nonproductive woman, "publicly created as a creature of private space."[26]

In his 2001 book, *Necro Citizenship*, Russ Castronovo follows this tradition of criticism on Hawthorne's text fairly closely, offering the most sustained account yet of what it means to "diagnose" a diseased public sphere through *The Blithedale Romance*. Castronovo reads Hawthorne alongside Habermas, as comparable theorists of a publicly created interior life. For both of them, he argues, private life and intimacy are the twin effects of a historically specific configuration of the public sphere, which equates subjectivity with interiority and yet presumes that interiority is already directed outward, toward a public. In reading Hawthorne's vision of U.S. public life in 1852 through Habermas, Castronovo presumes that the eighteenth-century European model translates rather seamlessly, but he does not consider the liberal, rational-critical sphere to be in any way ideal (as Habermas does). Castronovo argues that Hawthorne's view of such a public is "much more conflicted than Habermas's," in part because "interiority" and "intimacy" in the text are never sealed off from the public and never yield the rational, abstract subjects crucial to its functioning. Castronovo goes further than this familiar criticism of Habermas, though, arguing along with theorists like Berlant that the liberal sphere's location of intimacy at the core of public life has also "privatized politics": "Hawthorne's novel reveals the interplay of public sphere and private affair as the ascendancy of privatization as a political mode." The ultimate effect of this, he argues, is "the death of political life."[27] Castronovo coins the phrase "the occult public sphere" to demonstrate how the era's obsession with spiritualist phenomena, such as mesmerism and spirit rapping, stand as evidence of the valuing of "(un) consciousness over sociopolitical awareness." He continues, "The occult represses material conditions and national divisions" and produces only "political passivity."[28]

But if—as Castronovo, Brodhead, and others assert—passivity is the result of a spectacularized public sphere that overvalues privacy and interiority in *The Blithedale Romance*, that passivity does not account for the nearly sadistic power relations that erupt almost immediately within the community. Even as the residents of Blithedale substitute sexual conquest for active social change during their experiment, these relations are never simply private or intimate, if such terms are meant to imply either insulation or remoteness from the material conditions of the public sphere. On the first night of his residence at the farm, for example, Coverdale describes overt assertions of class privilege and gendered power, as well as more subtle exertions of the involuntary, sympathetic influence that becomes the community's hallmark. From Zenobia's imperious reception of Priscilla (*Blithedale*, 57) to Hollingsworth's chastening reproach ("it was with that inauspicious meaning in his glance that Hollingsworth first met Zenobia's eyes and began his influence upon her life" [58]), social power conditions desire among the three principle characters. Whether rooted in sexuality, gender, class, or all of these, forms of power sustain each one of the central characters at some moment. Where Zenobia claims class privilege over Priscilla, Priscilla undermines Zenobia with the force of her sexually charged infirmity (not to mention her covert manipulation of their father's inheritance). Where Hollingsworth unabashedly threatens all women with "the unmistakable . . . sovereignty" of physical violence, he is reduced to total physical, emotional, and financial dependence on Priscilla in the end. Even Coverdale, who constantly bemoans his exclusion from the central love triangle, finds himself deeply involved in the group's dynamics of power. His poetry exerts a subtle form of influence over Zenobia, who responds with a decidedly backhanded compliment: "it has stolen into my memory without my exercising any choice or volition about the matter" (47). Conversely, he finds himself on the receiving end of a similar influence when he is nearly "penetrated" by what he calls "Hollingsworth's magnetism" (136). While it is certainly true that the movements of influence and power at Blithedale are often involuntary, it does not necessarily follow that the subjects of Blithedale are simply passive or nonperforming. A more complete account of how spectacular culture and a diseased or disordered public sphere condition relations at Blithedale must consider the problem of coercive, involuntary empowerment as one of the central *political* dilemmas that Hawthorne stages.

Such a reading itself begins with a reconsideration of spectatorship in Hawthorne's romance. Spectatorship in *The Blithedale Romance* is a layered and complex pursuit, and it does not automatically yield the passive, remote, private subjects that have so frequently been cited as symptoms of a deadened, mass public sphere in the text. Though it initially promises removal, remoteness, and disinterestedness, spectatorship instead delivers surprising degrees of vulnerability and entanglement.[29] Beginning with Hawthorne's insistence in the preface that "his present concern with the Socialist Community is merely to establish a theatre, a little removed from the highway of ordinary travel" (38), spectatorship is allied with removal, but it is removal of an odd sort. The romance and the community stand as metonyms for each other because both of them are, in turn, linked metonymically to the theater, which becomes the emblematic site for the unusual type of removal that Hawthorne imagines. Theatrical removal, as he defines it here, is not the distancing of an audience from a staged performance, but the preservation of distance between that performance and reality, which is designed to enhance the spectator's involvement. By keeping "the creatures of [the author's] brain" from "too close a comparison with the actual events of real lives," removal prevents "the paint and pasteboard of their composition" from being "too painfully discernible" (38) and, thus, from appearing false to the history from which it springs. In other words, romance practices a paradoxical mimesis: it finds its closest approximations of "real lives" by locating "a suitable remoteness" from them. The gap that remoteness secures is less an abandonment of history and the real than it is a restaging of these, addressed explicitly to those spectators (or readers) whom it seeks to draw closer.

The effects of this tension between remoteness and proximity on a spectator become clearest, not in Hawthorne's preface, but in the opening of Coverdale's narrative on the following page, when he describes attending a performance of the Veiled Lady the night before his departure for Blithedale. Coverdale compares the Lady's exhibition favorably with those of her successors, defining her superior attractions in the precise aesthetic terms that Hawthorne has given for the romance.[30] Through "skillfully contrived circumstances of stage-effect," which set "the apparent miracle in the strongest attitude of opposition to ordinary facts," the Veiled Lady has both illuminated her own "remarkable performance" and "further wrought up" the interest of her spectators in the "enigma of her identity" (40). Speaking as one of those overwrought spectators, Coverdale finds himself enthralled by the Veiled Lady's performance, in large part because it does not tax his credulity with appeals to science or natural law. Bypassing belief, the Veiled Lady draws her audience in theatrically, that is, through a "skillfully contrived" stagecraft that implicitly acknowledges that audience as the occasion for her performance. Rather than allowing her spectators to stand in distanced judgment, she reveals that they are already inside the performance, as its constitutive presence, and with this, she changes the way that they see. Indeed, Coverdale is so enamored of this show that he carries the experience of it with him to Blithedale. Although he believes that he has traveled "a world-wide distance" from Boston (46), on arriving at the farm, he finds himself once again in attendance at "an illusion, a masquerade, a pastoral, a counter-feit Arcadia" (52). In this context, Coverdale's remark on the community's theatricality is not derisive but descriptive; illusion and masquerade form the "knot" which holds these "dreamers" together in their position of estrangement from "the rest of mankind" (52). Coverdale's sense of the community's theatricality is, however, fleeting, and he spends the early part of his narrative trying to locate a position that will deliver the perfect balance of remoteness and proximity that once revealed to him his defining presence within the Veiled Lady's performance.

From "The Supper-Table" to "The Sick-Chamber," "The Wood-Path," "The Hermitage," and "Eliot's Pulpit," half of the opening chapters are titled for the spaces to which Coverdale removes himself within a community that is "itself characterized by a remoteness from the world" (103). Coverdale is fairly self-conscious about his proclivity for remov-als, but the interpretations he gives of them are as shifting and seem-ingly conflicted as his alternating sense of his alienation from and total obsession with the community. Describing the impulse that sends him into the apparent solitude of the wood-path, for example, Coverdale acknowledges the absurdity of retreating from a space of retreat, and he confesses himself to be highly vulnerable to the influence of others: "Unless renewed by a yet further withdrawal toward the inner circle of self-communion, I lost the better part of my individuality" (103). But for all of Coverdale's equation of removal and retreat with solitude and self-communion, each of his retreats clearly provides him with the opportu-nity to observe, contemplate, and further involve himself with the cen-tral figures of the community—Hollingsworth, Zenobia, Priscilla, and Westervelt. If "Coverdale's Sick-Chamber" is a chapter of retirement and convalescence, for instance, it is also a chapter of intimacy, in which he enjoys a period of great affection with Hollingsworth, for whom he per-forms manly infirmity and from whom he receives "more than brotherly attendance" in return (67). Similarly, in "The Wood-Path," Coverdale's stated aim of seeking "self-communion" is belied by the metaphors of predatory social intimacy that he uses to describe the retreat: "I abated my pace and looked about me for some side-aisle, that should admit me into the innermost sanctum of this green cathedral; just as, in human ac-quaintanceship, a casual opening sometimes lets us, all of a sudden, into the long-sought intimacy of a mysterious heart" (103). In every one of his removals, Coverdale manages to find another opportunity to become entangled, a paradox that is perfectly expressed in the twisted, knotted, strangling vines that make up his "hermitage."

Coverdale's hermitage is an overdetermined tree-house—"a hollow chamber, of rare seclusion . . . formed by the decay of some of the pine-branches, which the vine had lovingly strangled with its embrace" (110)—and much is read into it, both by Coverdale and his critics. Far and away the text's most frequently analyzed image, the hermitage is an ambivalent space, which has stood as a key emblem of identity as, alternately, inviolate, vulnerable, and cannibalistic.[31] To a large extent, Coverdale shares this ambivalence: "[o]ff the track" of the forest path, and "yet not so remote" that he cannot speedily return to the farm if he is suddenly needed (109), the hermitage initially represents Coverdale's best attempt yet to obtain for himself that "suitable remoteness" which he continues to imagine in terms of theater and spectatorship. Before introducing his hideout, Coverdale indulges in an extended analogy, in which the experiment becomes a classical play and he becomes the chorus "set aloof from personal concernment" in it. As chorus, Coverdale claims a role that is "singularly subordinate," unique in its secondariness to the central actors and yet sharing the stage with them. Mediating between the staged world and that of the audience, the chorus performs a model form of spectatorship that "bestows the whole measure of its hope or fear, its exultation or sorrow, on the fortunes of others, between whom and itself this sympathy is the only bond" (109). The fantasy of spectatorship that Coverdale lodges in the hermitage promises emotional fullness without any "personal concernment," and to some extent it delivers on this promise, since its twin assets are the vine that conceals him inside it and the "open loop-holes in the verdant walls," which (with some adjustments) give him a full view of the farm and everyone in it (110). However, if Coverdale seeks to reproduce the "suitable remoteness" of a classic stage in the treetops, he forgets that theater is a form of multiple sensations, and woefully miscalculates its architecture. Though he can "discern" Hollingsworth with his oxen in the distance, and almost make out Priscilla sewing in the farmhouse, when Zenobia and Westervelt pass directly under his tree, he cannot hear a single word either one of them is saying. As Samuel Gridley Howe remarks in his *Essay on Separate and Congregate Systems of Prison Discipline*, "though a man have as many eyes as Argus, it were better to have them all put out than to seal up his ears, if his object in life be intimate social communion and sympathy with those about him."[32]

In the impairment and isolation it yields, Coverdale's hermitage ends up resembling a prison every bit as much as it does the theater he hoped to make of it. Though as a prison, it is clearly no panopticon; if anyone

becomes subject to the form of spectatorship that Coverdale practices
in his tree, it is Coverdale alone.[33] Nonetheless, this scene makes it clear
that Hollingsworth is not the only descendent of Howe in this text, as
the modes of spectatorship that Coverdale engages here owe a debt to the
competing theories of penitentiary reform that were debated throughout
the 1830s and 1840s. Though partisans in the penal debates disagreed
on precise tactics, they tended to share a conviction that social isolation
combated the contagion of bad influence, facilitating controlled forms of
mimicry through the manipulation of the senses.[34] "Now," Howe asserts,
"the ordinary inmates of our prisons are like children and peasants; they
imitate only those immediately about them, and regard only the public
opinion of the little society in which they move."[35] Hollingsworth may
dream of instituting a penitentiary based on such assumptions, install-
ing a society of "pure, humble, and yet exalted minds" as models for imitation, but only Coverdale actually achieves anything like such a space in
the text. The hermitage becomes an emblematic site of mimetic reform
largely because of the limited isolation it constructs. While he can see
everything from his hermitage, Coverdale can "hardly make out an in-
telligible sentence" (114), and in this partial limitation of his senses, he
becomes extremely vulnerable to the coercive effects of mimicry. In his
tree, straining to decipher the scenes that play out before his eyes, he is
utterly captivated by what he watches—and, he believes, utterly excluded
from it. He imagines dialogue for Hollingsworth and tries to address
Priscilla through a passing bird: "say, that, if any mortal really cares for
her, it is myself, and not even I, for her realities" (112). "Suddenly," he
finds himself "possessed by a mood of disbelief in moral beauty or hero-
ism," and he feels the urge to "to laugh out loud" at the whole endeavor of
Blithedale. However, he quickly discovers that this "skeptical and sneer-
ing view" does not originate in him, but in Westervelt, who just that moment has passed under his tree and—quite literally—changed his mind.
In an odd, involuntary sort of mimicry, Coverdale absorbs the beliefs of
a man he loathes, whom he does not even know is present.

Though much might be made of Professor Westervelt's career here,
it cannot be said that the mesmerist has actively sought to influence
Coverdale. Westervelt simply becomes, for a fleeting moment, "the little
society" that is "immediately about," whose opinion Coverdale cannot
help but imbibe. Indeed, the view that Westervelt unknowingly imparts
to Coverdale is not even really his own:

There are some spheres, the contact with which inevitably degrades the high, debases the pure, deforms the beautiful. It must be a mind of uncommon strength and little impressibility, that can permit itself the habit of such intercourse, and not be permanently deteriorated; and yet the Professor's tone represented that of worldly society at large, where a cold skepticism smothers what it can of our spiritual aspirations, and makes the rest ridiculous. (112)

In a series of nested disavowals, Coverdale finally concedes that Westervelt is really no more than a representative—a medium himself—of a much more general opinion, and his mind turns out to be of no more "uncommon strength" than Coverdale's own. Isolated in his tree, believing himself excluded from the scenes that totally absorb him, Coverdale becomes permeable to every "sphere" with which he comes in contact. Tocqueville has his own name for "such intercourse": public opinion, which "by some mighty pressure of the mind of all upon the intelligence of each . . . imposes ideas and makes them penetrate men's very souls" (*Democracy in America*, 435). So does Lydia Maria Child: the "lateral pressure" of public opinion becomes "impressive even to painfulness," forcing upon one that "appalling night-mare sensation of vanishing identity" (*Letters*, 44). But while Tocqueville, Child, and Hawthorne all describe a threat of permeable identity in the democratic subject's perceived isolation from the public—one which allows them to posit that subject as coerced, disciplined, even imprisoned—the truth of this pressure that changes one's mind and makes one's identity seem to "vanish" is that it confers and conceals a considerable degree of power. Both Westervelt and Coverdale prove equally vulnerable to the mesmeric sway of worldly opinion, but rather than affirming their passivity, this is a vulnerability that confers on them a form of political belonging, however involuntarily. The power that impresses itself upon him, prompting this unwitting imitation of worldly opinion, gives Coverdale all the authority he needs to assume a stance of scoffing superiority over his companions at Blithedale. And this "cold skepticism" cannot be described as simply passive, an idle judgment, because it actively "smothers what it can of our spiritual aspirations." Coverdale may not adopt this set of opinions with any intention, but when mimicry of them happens to him, it allows him to stand in judgment of his community by incorporating him into the consensus of "worldly society at large."

In the isolation of his hermitage, Coverdale experiences one of Tocqueville's paradoxes of democratic belonging: "the same equality which makes him independent of each separate citizen leaves him isolated and defenseless in the face of the majority" (*Democracy in America*, 435). An excess of sameness delivers feelings of alienation and isolation that characterize both the perceived vulnerability of the democratic subject and that subject's intimate involvement with power. In Coverdale's case, the more he feels himself alienated from his companions at Blithedale, the more closely he approximates that much larger, more powerful collective which seems to be already inside him but which feels alien to him, as well. Coverdale's crisis comes when he fails to recognize himself as a part of either the small community of Blithedale or the monolithic bearer of worldly opinion, and in this, he exemplifies a characteristic of Tocqueville's melancholy American democrat that is equal parts symptomatic and strategic. Coverdale's failure to recognize himself as internal to his various publics helps foster that sense of isolation and vulnerability that implicitly absolves him of the acts done in the name and under the authority of the public or the majority. At the same time, however, in casting himself as the excluded, isolated, and yet also coerced object of these entities, Coverdale also lays bare the tactics of mimetic reform and coercive spectatorship on which they rely, refusing these tactics the transparency that facilitates their power. Read in this light, *The Blithedale Romance* does more than simply mark the ascendance of spectacular public culture as the death of politics. Instead, Hawthorne's *Blithedale* finds in relations of spectatorship a key index of political power and association in antebellum public life, and it accompanies Tocqueville's *Democracy in America* in tracking the central tactics, crises, and paradoxes of a politicized, sovereign public sphere.

## Penitentiary Aesthetics: Bender, Fried, Hollingsworth

Coverdale's hermitage does not start out as a theater and then become a prison. It is always both of these because it is, however paradoxically, an emblematic public space in the text. It is a space, in other words, that assumes a specific relationship to a public that is equally invested in punishment and entertainment and that confounds isolation with privacy. Thus, Coverdale's achievement of the coveted aesthetic stance of remoteness is also the mark of his liability to coercive influences like opinion and the very thing that, I argue, links his hermitage to Hollingsworth's edifice, and both of these structures to Howe's idealized portrait of Eastern State Penitentiary. Indeed, Hollingsworth's edifice, Coverdale's hermitage, and pretty much every other pivotal space and scene in the romance require both an aesthetic discourse and a historical discourse of power and reform in order to be legible. Like Child's term, "vagrancies," which invokes the formal practice and the social and ethical imperative of her *Letters* simultaneously, Hawthorne's key tropes of spectatorship, mimicry, and, especially, remoteness require one to attend to the aesthetic, ethical, and social dimensions that each of them registers at once. The "suitable remoteness" of romance is echoed in the Veiled Lady's theatrical performance of removal, which in turn both inspires Coverdale's efforts to seek belonging through spectatorship and fails him by producing isolation and vulnerability. Similarly, the mimetic relations that develop among the residents at Blithedale register both the anxieties of social contagion voiced by contemporary prison reformers, like Howe, and the peculiar mimesis of romance that Hawthorne theorizes in the preface. The relationship between the aesthetic and the historical resonances of Hawthorne's terms is never stable or predictable: the aesthetic discourse of romance promises neither redemption nor release from the history of coercive power that it invokes, but neither does it simply repeat the imprisoning effects of that history. What is does, however, is ensure that more than one outcome is always possible. Remoteness, for instance, does not lead only to isolation and violation in *The Blithedale Romance*, and if Coverdale's hermitage gives him a taste of what it would be to live in Hollingsworth's penitentiary, it also provides the impetus for his ultimate rejection of Hollingsworth's plan. Though both Coverdale and Hollingsworth practice the forms of sensory deprivation, coercive spectatorship, and mimetic reform that Howe praises as the benefits of solitary confinement, Coverdale's eventual critique of Hollingsworth reveals an essential difference between them that is as much aesthetic as it is ethical and political.

In his influential work, *Imagining the Penitentiary*, John Bender offers an account of how the history of the penitentiary system in eighteenth-century Britain informed a central aesthetic practice, the development of the realist novel, and his work provides a point of departure for thinking about the aesthetics of the prison in *Blithedale*. Reading the novel and the penitentiary as mutually constituting "cultural systems," Bender shows how transformations in philosophies of knowledge and reform in the penal system corresponded to emerging strategies of narration in the novel, in particular, the techniques of third-person omniscience and free indirect discourse. For Bender, the prison and the realist novel are twin "systems of knowledge," both of which imagine character as mutable and materially constructed through sensory experience over a period of time by placing it in isolation from everything but the influence of form—the architecture of the penitentiary and the model of anonymous, omni-scient supervision that it innovates. Isolation is, for Bender, a product of the formalization of impersonal supervision, and as such, it is as much an aesthetic convention as it is a disciplinary principle: "isolation, the penitentiary, and the transparency that attends them are productions of a culture in which experience is structured by a constitutive impersonal-ity that locates the beholding subject in a private world of response and that penetrates the very essence of consciousness." In Bender's analysis, a shared tactic of isolation links the novel to the prison through an as-sumption of transparency—essentially, the conviction that "both author and beholder are absent from a representation"—and with this, the novel achieves aesthetically a penetration of consciousness that corresponds to the prison, repeating and disseminating the effects of a power that has no clear origin or location, but simply appears to be.[36]

As E. Shaskan Bumas has noted, Bender's theory of the novel trans-lates somewhat unevenly to the American romance in general, and to Hawthorne's romances in particular.[37] This is certainly due, at least in part, to the quite different history of prison reform in the United States, where innovations in penitentiary design were not conceived solely along the panoptic model. Though Eastern State was the most infamous prison in the United States, it represented only one, very controversial model of "isolation" in the mid-century debates. Further, the aesthetic conven-tion of transparency that serves for Bender as a constitutive link between novel and penitentiary was not the privileged aesthetic mode in U.S. lit-erature that he claims for it in the British context. Bender derives an "aesthetic of isolation" and its convention of transparency directly from Michael Fried's model of absorption.[38] Fried himself draws on Diderot's writings on painting and theater, as well as the work of French painters like Jean-Baptiste Greuze, to identify what he calls the primacy of ab-sorption—the representation within a work of unconscious activity and obliviousness to everything outside the world represented. Absorption depends upon the convention of the beholder's absence from the scene of the painting, which in its representation of an engrossed and captivated consciousness, has the capacity to produce a mimetic response of rapt attention in its spectators. "What is called for . . . is at one and the same time, the creation of a new sort of object—the fully realized tableau—and the constitution of a new sort of beholder—a new 'subject'—whose innermost nature would consist precisely in the conviction of his absence from the scene of representation." For Fried and Bender, absorption pro-duces one of the key effects of realism in eighteenth-century aesthetics:

a transparency to the activity of representation that depends upon the "de-theatricalization" of art.[39] To Fried, this means that the beholder is purged from the representational world of the painting; to Bender, that novelistic consciousness becomes "an unenactable kind of drama that has shed every trace of the histrionic."[40]

The terms that Fried and Bender elaborate in their studies resonate in many ways with forms of imprisonment that appear in Hawthorne's *Blithedale*, from Coverdale's rapt attention in the treetops, to Priscilla's captivity under Zenobia's silvery veil, to the actual edifice that Hollingsworth intends to build on the farm. However, while instances of imprisonment in the text evoke both Bender's aesthetic of transparency and Fried's convention of absorption, none of these scenes is "de-theatricalized" in the ways that these scholars describe. Instead, the text constantly plays on the tensions between obliviousness and engagement, transparency and opacity, absorption and theatricality that Fried and Bender treat as oppositions—so much so, that it often seems as if Hawthorne is exploring the realist effects of absorption within the "theatre, a little removed" of romance. For example, Coverdale's trip to the hermitage could be read as a near allegory of absorption; certainly, nothing about that scene is more disturbing to him than its demonstration of his own absence from what he watches, and as he pathetically tries to imagine himself into these scenes—passing messages to Priscilla by way of birds, etc.—he becomes wholly oblivious to his own situation and surroundings. In thus imitating the obliviousness of his friends, Coverdale is shown to be vulnerable to "penetration" by Westervelt and "worldly society at large." However, when a version of this scene is restaged in Boston, with Coverdale staring out the window of his hotel at Zenobia and Westervelt across the courtyard, it is as an allegory of theatricality. Though the scene begins with Coverdale bemoaning the isolation of absorption—"there seemed something fatal in the coincidence that had borne me to this spot . . . and transfixed me there, and compelled me again to waste my already wearied sympathies on affairs which were none of mine" (153)—it ends with Zenobia's reminder of theater's opacity. With a gesture "comprising at once a salutation and a dismissal," she draws her drapes, which "fell like the drop-curtain of a theatre, in the interval between the acts" (154).

Even in its treatment of Hollingsworth's penitentiary scheme, the text vacillates between images of absorption and theatricality, in part because of Hollingsworth's own changing relationship to the plan and his alternating openness and secrecy about his designs. From the beginning, Coverdale makes it clear that Hollingsworth's "edifice" is not simply an exercise in philanthropy, but an aesthetic enterprise, as well. Hollingsworth betrays his aesthetic investment almost immediately with his insatiable impulse to materialize the plan, "sketching the façade . . . planning the internal arrangements . . . begin[ning] a model of the building with little stones" (78). The project he intends as "a spectacle to the world" is so well known, even in its unrealized state, that discussion of it precedes his arrival at the farm. Speaking with Coverdale, Zenobia calls it "a grimy, unbeautiful, and positively hopeless object," but she also confesses herself moved by Hollingsworth's performance in his lectures—"What a voice he has!" (53). Zenobia's capacity to separate her admiration for Hollingsworth's performance from her distaste for his actual theory indicates that his various representations of it (vocal and material) have not yet become transparent to it. In other words, it appears from Zenobia's reaction that Hollingsworth's efforts to represent his project are addressed to an audience, not yet to potential objects of reform. However, as Coverdale watches Hollingsworth "fast going mad" (78), he narrates the philanthropist's increasing identification with his theory, a system of coercive sympathy that begins to efface the edifice and the processes of representing and constructing it. As the edifice becomes transparent to its scheme of reform, so Hollingsworth becomes its first inmate, and the goal of making others "proselyte to his views"— more than the piling up of rocks—becomes its realization.

"[A] scheme for the reformation of the wicked by means moral, intellectual, and industrial, by the sympathy of pure, humble, and yet exalted minds" (134), Hollingsworth's is a prison of mimicry, through which character is molded by the powerful exercise of a subtle, yet dubious, sympathy. Gradually, its basic mechanism of reform—this coercive, sympathetic pressure that slowly transforms—becomes indistinguishable from Hollingsworth's efforts to implement the scheme on the land occupied by the community: "Our beginnings might readily be adapted to his great end. The arrangements, already completed, would work quietly into his system" (134). Like Howe, whose pedagogy collides with his theories of solitary punishment in the display of Laura Bridgman disciplining herself before an audience of which she is unaware, when Hollingsworth's project to build the edifice becomes transparent to the disciplinary theory that it would enact, he makes his former audience unwitting participants in his system. In other words, when Hollingsworth conceals the plan and process of constructing the edifice, allowing the community to "work quietly into his system," he no longer addresses his plan to an audience but enacts it upon potential proselytes and prisoners. As Fried and Bender predict, Coverdale experiences this transformation in Hollingsworth's tactics as an almost mesmeric penetration of his consciousness—"had I but touched his extended hand, Hollingsworth's magnetism would have penetrated me" (136). Hollingsworth's "magnetism" treats power as formless and without content, beyond both thought and debate. In response, Coverdale pleads for all of these: "If you meditate to overthrow this establishment, state your designs, support it with all your evidence, but allow them the opportunity of defending themselves" (135). More than a rejection of Hollingsworth's "rigid and unconquerable" philanthropy, Coverdale's response is a repudiation of the form it has taken, a repudiation, in a sense, of Hollingsworth's aesthetics. If Hollingsworth's dishonesty arises from his secrecy, that secrecy is enabled by the transparent relationship that develops between the scheme and the process of its implementation. "State your design" is no simple call for greater disclosure. It is Coverdale's demand for a new relationship to process and form, one that involves, paradoxically, a greater opacity that would render the scheme visible, material, and contestable.

Coverdale's ultimate rejection of Hollingsworth and his penitentiary project does not appear in the chapter of the "Crisis" when Hollingsworth nearly "penetrates" him, but in a previous chapter when the narrating Coverdale employs precisely the opacity he demands, making his own "design" quite clear:

> Of course I am aware that the above statement is exaggerated, in the attempt to make it adequate. Professed philanthropists have gone far; but no originally good man, I presume, ever went quite so far as this. Let the reader abate whatever he deems fit. The paragraph may remain, however, both for its truth and its exaggeration, as strongly expressive of the tendencies which were really operative in Hollingsworth, and as exemplifying the kind of error into which my mode of observation was calculated to lead me. (89)

Coverdale's remarks to his reader follow a paragraph of fairly damning judgment of Hollingsworth's "all-devouring egotism," which already highlights the gap between the narrating Coverdale and the Coverdale who, he admits, once loved the philanthropist intensely (88). Pausing to address the reader, Coverdale calls attention to his belated narration even more emphatically. He points out the previous paragraph as a paragraph, as writing composed after the fact, which he could have redacted or altered. He performs not only the process of writing, but also the process of editing and choosing not to edit what he's written. With this, he renders the activity of narration opaque and incorporates the reader into it. Coverdale insists both that his reader be present within his text and that the reader actively engage in it: "Let the reader abate whatever he deems fit." Basically, Coverdale refuses what Fried calls the "supreme fiction" of absorption that is key to realism's transparency—the formal convention that readers and beholders are "absent from the scene of representation." Instead, he theatricalizes his text, interposing it between the reader and the object of representation and estranging that reader from the sentiments he has expressed. The goal of Coverdale's writing is not that readers should experience the narrated sentiments mimetically but that they should recognize them as narrated and, thus, mediating. By calling attention to his own impulse both to condemn and to retract his condemnation of Hollingsworth, Coverdale does not negate the truth of those sentiments. He insists that "exaggeration" and "error" involve their own kinds of truth, exposing the mediating layers of design and accident through which both Hollingsworth and Coverdale appear.

As Coverdale's demand that Hollingsworth "state [his] design" repudiates both Hollingsworth's efforts to overthrow the community secretly and the system of penetrating sympathy that his penitentiary would institutionalize, so it might be tempting to read in Coverdale's response something like his liberation from the coercive transparency that characterizes all the philanthropist's acts. Hollingsworth's scheme conceals its origins and its form, acting out a power that appears to be without any precise location or content and fostering a sense of its inevitability. Certainly, Coverdale seeks to restore both an origin and a form to such designs, but it is important to note that his direct appeal to Hollingsworth has little effect. Though Coverdale introduces theatricality as a repudiation of transparency relatively early in his narrative, in what follows, he shows himself repeatedly failing to engage in it. In his constant recourse to the stance of the absorbed beholder, he perpetually feels the isolation of Tocqueville's melancholy democratic subject. Convinced of his own isolation, failing to recognize himself as internal to the community he watches, he becomes vulnerable to penetration and susceptible to mimicry of others (Westervelt, Hollingsworth, "worldly society at large"). Theatricality, it seems, is not a stance that can be so easily adopted, because it depends upon a relationship of mutual engagement, a mutual acknowledgment of the defining presence of others. Ultimately, the theatricality that Coverdale introduces is a textual strategy, one that is only available to Coverdale's narrative. In this sense, Coverdale does not behave theatrically so much as he and his peculiar narration become its sign. Coverdale is the opacity of the text, what Fried calls the "medium of dislocation and estrangement" that prevents readers and spectators from that absorptive and isolating sense of their absence from the scene of representation. But however limited it may seem, theatricality nonetheless suggests an alternative to the problem of isolation that Tocqueville associates with the subject of equality and that Coverdale confronts in his hermitage. Against the spectacle of a democratic public sphere that posits a subject who fails to recognize his participation in the collective acts and scenes on which he gazes, one who fails to recognize himself as a part of that power which "imposes ideas and makes them penetrate men's very souls," theatricality proposes that a performance of opacity might reveal that spectator to be constitutive and internal to what he sees, confronting him with his inclusion and engagement in the power to which he feels subject only.

## Veiled Theatricality

From Coverdale's opening sentence, praising the Veiled Lady's "carefully contrived circumstances of stage-effect" and "strongest opposition to ordinary facts," the celebrated clairvoyant stands as the most overtly theatrical figure in *The Blithedale Romance*. At the same time, the Veiled Lady is also the figure most frequently and most literally associated with imprisonment in the text. In "Zenobia's Legend," the Veiled Lady is a "sad and lonely prisoner in a bondage, which is worse . . . than death" (120). In the "Village Hall," she is the "blindfold prisoner" who is also "the spectacle to thousands" (185). But as the text designates theatricality and imprisonment as principle models of aesthetic and social relation, the veil emerges as something more than another iteration of this defining tension. Exploring theatricality and imprisonment from the perspective of the stage, the Veiled Lady offers an alternative to Coverdale's obsession with spectatorship. As the center of the text's spectatorial fantasies, the veil is clearly the Lady's prison, and in many ways, it condenses all the risks of a spectacular democratic culture that the text explores—isolation, remoteness, vulnerability to a formless and magnetic power. But in marking these as the ends of spectacle, the veil also takes the critical possibilities of theatricality further than Coverdale can. At the point where the Veiled Lady appears most to be "a victim of her display," "only exploited" by spectacle,[41] the text reasserts the basic theatricality of the veil itself, deploying it against the very isolation with which it has become identified. In this, the veil both exposes the politics of the remote, private interiority that the Lady has so effectively performed and posits an alternative to it—a mode of being in public that privileges externalization, opacity, and mutuality.

When Coverdale first describes the performance of the Veiled Lady, it is quite literally an opacity that captures his attention: "it was white, with somewhat of subdued silvery sheen, like the sunny side of a cloud" (40). Pausing to admire the veil itself—what would seem to be no more than a prop or a costume—Coverdale indicates his appreciation for the basic theatricality that the veil expresses, the "arts of mysterious arrangement" that become both visible and material in the veil. Indeed, according to Coverdale, the visibility of this contrivance is what is best about the performance. The Lady and her handler have created an "apparent miracle"—one that is all the more miraculous for the visible artistry that has gone into setting it "in the strongest opposition to ordinary facts" (40). They invoke neither "scientific experiment" nor the "laws of our actual life," resisting the temptations of realism, but they nevertheless remain firmly rooted in the materiality of stagecraft and performance. Though the veil purports to "insulate her from the material world," giving the Lady "the privileges of a disembodied spirit," Coverdale experiences the veil as a thing, and at first, he shows surprisingly little temptation to look for something beyond, inside, or beneath it.

A similar emphasis on the materiality of the veil appears in Zenobia's recitation of the legend of the "Silvery Veil" one night at Blithedale. Though Zenobia relates to the veil as a performer rather than a spectator, she shares Coverdale's sense that its greatest power lies in the connection it forges with its audience rather than its capacity to conceal, disguise, or insulate. When Zenobia takes it up (literally holding a piece of gauzy fabric) to tell her story, she does so as a way of mediating between her tale and her audience. Coverdale quickly begins to sense a rival, and he responds by damning Zenobia's version of the Veiled Lady legend through faint praise of its most sensational, spontaneous, and theatrical elements.[42] Zenobia tells the story extravagantly, he concedes, "giving it the varied emphasis of her inimitable voice, and the pictorial illustration of her mobile face, while, through it all, we caught the freshest aroma of the thoughts, as they came bubbling out of her mind" (116). But, Coverdale fusses, this performance was "greatly more effective than it was usually found to be when she afterwards elaborated the same production with her pen." Coverdale chooses to admire precisely those aspects of Zenobia's performance that cannot be conveyed on the page—the sound of her

voice, the expression of her face, even (oddly) the smell of her thoughts—
while also revealing a preoccupation with what is most corporeal in it.
By focusing on Zenobia's talents of improvisation, he denies her the skill-
ful contrivance and artfulness that he praises in the performed enigma
of the Veiled Lady. At the same time, though, he indicates how both the
Veiled Lady and Zenobia use the veil as a medium, calling attention to
the relational nature of performance: "Zenobia, all the while, had been
holding the piece of gauze, and so managed it as greatly to increase the
dramatic effect of the legend" (123). As Zenobia reaches the end of her
story, she handles the veil as she has throughout, dramatically flinging
the gauzy fabric over Priscilla's head to bring the tale to its showy climax.
But while Zenobia's audience is thrilled ("[W]e thought it a very bright
idea of Zenobia's, to bring her legend to so effective a conclusion"), Priscilla droops and nearly faints under the metaphorical weight that has ac-
crued to the otherwise light and airy gauze. Over the course of Zenobia's
story the veil retains its materiality, but the function of that materiality
changes markedly. For the first time in the narrative, the veil begins to
appear as a means of imprisonment.

Where Coverdale declares himself satisfied with the opacity of the
veil, Zenobia insists that the Lady's fans are far more intrigued by the
enigma of what lies beneath it, though what they find is rarely more than
a reflection of their own desires: "Again, it was affirmed, that there was no
single and unchanging set of features beneath the veil, but that whoever
should be bold enough to lift it would behold the features of that person
in the world who was destined to be his fate" (118). The veil may be the
most material of stage effects, but it designates a vacancy—a space of interiority that invites speculation, penetration, and projection, yet yields
nothing in return. Zenobia stages the story of the Veiled Lady as a series
of incursions, culminating in a sexually charged confrontation between
the Lady and her most skeptical spectator in her "private withdrawing-
room." Theodore pursues the Lady into these recesses with the dubious
purpose of removing her "veil," and the Lady responds with a marriage
proposal: if he kisses the veil, she pledges, "thou shalt be mine and I
thine with never more a veil between us" (120). Fearing the probability
of her bad teeth, among other things, Theodore refuses the kiss, lifts the
veil, and is punished with the sight of a face that he will always pine for
but never see again. Although Theodore is often read as Zenobia's sly
commentary on Coverdale, the two men adopt quite different stances
toward the veil. By regarding the veil as an obstacle to be overcome,
Theodore transgresses the artfully achieved distance from "actual life"

that, Coverdale contends, so attracted him to the Lady's performance. In his skepticism, Theodore breaks through the remoteness that sustains the Lady's carefully crafted illusion, insisting that her reality lies not in the veil but beneath it; once there, however, he finds only emptiness. In the punishment that Zenobia metes out to her hero—"to pine, forever and ever" after a "dim and mournful face" (121)—she almost endorses Coverdale's alternative, his declared satisfaction with the Lady's opacities. Certainly, Zenobia's legend derides the demand for interior "realities" that are false to manifest, external materiality.

But Zenobia's legend is no morality tale, and Theodore's ill-fated insistence that realism resides within does not end in his punishment alone. Though the Lady calls herself "a sad and lonely prisoner" beneath the veil, it becomes clear that her prison is less the veil itself than the fantasy of interiority that it fosters. Interiority appears in the tale as a site of mesmeric penetration, isolation, and absorption; it exists, Zenobia suggests, in order to be violated. Viewed as a container for violable interiority, Zenobia's veil becomes a transferable prison that adapts itself to everyone it captures. For the Lady, the veil is a public contrivance that effaces the very boundaries between public and private, functioning with greatest efficacy in the Lady's "private withdrawing-room"—in the absence of both the magician and the audience—to keep her defined as an emblem of unfathomable interiority. For Theodore, the veil transforms skepticism into a withering desire for an object that withdraws perpetually from him. But the most perfect and bitter prison that the veil fashions may be the one it creates for the female philanthropist at the end of Zenobia's narrative, who believes that her own freedom depends upon the Lady's imprisonment. "A woman of some nerve" who is "seeking for the better life," the philanthropist finds herself yoked to a stultifying image of feminine dependence and weakness in the form of the young women who suddenly appears "amid the knot of visionary transcendentalists" (122). To preserve her own "better life," the woman must impose the penalty of the veil herself, relegating the girl to the prison of interiority and (largely male) projection that it creates: "As the slight, ethereal texture sank inevitably down over her figure, the poor girl strove to raise it, and met her dear friend's eyes with one glance of mortal terror, and deep, deep reproach. It could not change her purpose."

Zenobia performs the role of Priscilla's jailor, both in her own narrative and in Coverdale's when she hands the girl over to Westervelt, but she is hardly freed by the act. Though Zenobia tells her story while wielding the veil theatrically, playing off its materiality to seduce her audience, she also performs her own subjection to its logic by requiring Priscilla as her victim. In this, Zenobia theatricalizes her own implication in the politics of the veil. The veil both is and stands for a material reality—the public creation of life as a private interiority to be contained and penetrated. Confining the Lady to a prison of interiority and expelling her from the "better life," the female philanthropist finds that her own freedom is negative, tied to an act that makes the girl a "bond-slave, forever more" (123). Rather than concealing the dependence of her freedom on another's captivity, though, Zenobia uses the veil to make this painfully clear. Tossing the fabric over Priscilla's head at the climax of her tale, she renders her own involvement in the coming sacrifice both visible and palpable. Though "it could not change her purpose," Zenobia's theatricality clearly marks her confrontation with what the "better life" has given her—the power and the authority to expel others from it. Furthermore, Zenobia's legend does not only foreshadow her own complicity; it lays out the ways in which each of the central figures—Priscilla included—also becomes implicated in such acts. In particular, it offers a glimpse of Coverdale's changing awareness of his involvement in the community, the gradual dissolution of his belief in remoteness and removal. His quibbles notwithstanding, Coverdale takes a great deal away from Zenobia's legend. He draws both points of plot and aesthetic insight from her, but most profoundly, Zenobia forces him to see something terrible in the performed remoteness that he so admires in the Veiled Lady's act.

Coverdale gets a second look at the Veiled Lady late in the narrative, after he has allegedly departed Blithedale and severed himself from Hollingsworth. Before the show begins, he eavesdrops on two members of the audience discussing the wizardry of a mesmerist, for whom "human character" (specifically female) "is but soft wax in his hands" (182). This, of course, conjures for Coverdale the very specter of transparent, coercive influence that sent him clambering up trees at Blithedale. To assuage his fears and calm his "unutterable" disgust, Coverdale reasserts his skepticism: "I would have perished sooner than believe it" (183). As if to fortify all of his faith in the efficacy of remoteness, Coverdale insists on relating to such spectacles as theater, viewing them solely as humbugs in which no credence should be placed. Unfortunately, as the mesmerist and the Veiled Lady take the stage, Coverdale begins to notice several differences in their overall presentation, specifically "the absence of many ingenious contrivances of stage-effect, with which the exhibition had heretofore been set off" (184). Where the earlier performance had struck Coverdale with its total opposition to actuality and fact, he finds in this second show a problematic plausibility: "It was eloquent, ingenious, plausible, with a delusive show of spirituality, yet imbued throughout with a cold and dead materialism." Speaking "as if it were a matter of chemical discovery," the mesmerist posits a continuity of past, present, and future, "a great mutually conscious brotherhood of epochs" linked in a "universally pervasive fluid." Coverdale recoils at the introduction of science, finding that it forces him to adopt a new relationship with the performance. Rather than an artful display of contrived enigma, clearly performed for the crowd, Coverdale sees this second exhibit as a cloying play for the faith of a credulous audience, whose minds the mesmerist seeks to change.

The difference that Coverdale perceives between the first and second performances of the Veiled Lady is both subtle and profound, and on it hinges the ultimate dilemma that she poses: "the movement of the Veiled Lady was graceful, free, and unembarrassed, like that of a person accustomed to be the spectacle of thousands. Or, possibly, a blindfold prisoner . . . wholly unconscious of being the central object to all those straining eyes" (185). The Professor clearly intends to prove the latter, inviting several members of the audience onstage to test the Lady's purported insensibility to their presence. "Accordingly, several deep-lunged country fellows" ascended the stage, shouting "so close to her ear, that the veil stirred like the wreath of a vanishing mist." But, "with a composure that was hardly less awful, because implying so immeasurable a distance betwixt her and these rude persecutors" (186), the Lady remained oblivious. Where Coverdale had once admired the Lady for her studied, artful remoteness, he now begins to see in it something grotesque, and he bumps up against Diderot's paradox of acting. Coverdale's earlier praise for the Lady echoes Diderot's celebration of the great actress whose indifference to her audience defines her artistry when its contrivance is subtly apparent: performing for an audience her seclusion from it, the great actress acts as if the audience is not there. But when such seclusion is taken too far, when the actress becomes so identified with her role that she is utterly oblivious to her display, all pleasure is destroyed and watching her becomes an awful violation.[43] The Veiled Lady's obliviousness here poses nothing but problems for Coverdale: her apparent freedom and lack of embarrassment might signify the shamelessness of a woman accustomed to public exposure, or these might suggest an insensibility so total that her display is involuntary and invasive. Either way, his "straining eyes" implicate him, and he begins to sense that his own relationship to the Veiled Lady's performance depends first upon hers.

With Westervelt's assertions of the Lady's total imperviousness to those who watch her, the romance all but names the scene of Laura Bridgman's public display, in which her insensibility to her audience marked both the authenticity and the violence of her involuntary performance. What Hawthorne reveals in thus restaging Laura's spectacular isolation is that, when the performer has no distance from her role—when that role is a transparency rather than an opacity—there can be no distance for the spectator, either. Coverdale's brief glimpse of a blindfold prisoner through the folds of the veil reveals how ineffectual his efforts at distancing himself from the construction of a prison have been. His removals amount to no more than a ruse of withdrawal, allowing him to indulge a fiction of his non-involvement, unconcern, and innocence. All the while he bemoans what he believes is his fate—forced to waste his attention and sympathies on "affairs which were none of mine" (153)—he is confronted with signs that remoteness has fostered his greater entanglement, while facilitating the violation of those he watches. Casting himself as isolated, cut off from the sympathies of his fellows, he has become complicit in the creation of the figure who represents the true limit case of inclusion in the community. This proves so problematic that his second response to the Lady's spectacularized insensibility amounts to a total contradiction of his first: "She had kept, as I religiously believe, her virgin reserve and sanctity of soul, throughout it all" (186). Clearly, a "spectacle to thousands" has no more access to a "virgin reserve" than a "blindfold prisoner" has "sanctity of soul," but in his desperation, Coverdale tries to invoke the very notion of a private self, construed as absorbed insensibility to public display, that has been explicitly undermined. With this, Coverdale also refers for the first time in his narrative to the existence of someone beneath the veil, someone other than the Veiled Lady herself. But whomever it is he means by this, he never says.

In one of the text's greatest (and most overlooked) feints, the reader is repeatedly invited to identify Priscilla as the enigmatic Veiled Lady. Beginning with Priscilla's entrance as a creature more spiritual than physical through Zenobia's overt attempt to unveil her by tossing the piece of silvery gauze over her head, the text makes an open secret of Priscilla's night-job. However, in the moment when Priscilla's long-awaited unveiling supposedly occurs, it doesn't. In the climactic scene in "A Village-Hall," while Coverdale frets over the Lady's apparent insensibility and his own straining eyes, Hollingsworth walks up to the stage on which the Lady is performing and beckons to her. Coverdale dutifully reports that "she threw off the veil and stood before that multitude of people," but he never mentions Priscilla's name. As the chapter concludes, Coverdale speaks of the "poor maiden" and the "forsaken girl," and he continues to insist on her seclusion, virginity, and sanctity beneath the veil, but he stubbornly withholds a name. In this, Coverdale might be understood as rescuing Priscilla from the scene of her exposure, refusing to repeat it for the reader. But in refusing to unveil the Lady himself, he also makes a powerful point: it may be that Priscilla fled the village hall with Hollingsworth that night, but it does not necessarily follow that she and the Veiled Lady are one and the same. Coverdale maintains a clear distinction between Priscilla and the Veiled Lady, refusing to allow one to collapse into the other, and in this, he reasserts the opacity of the veil. If the veil is opaque, a stage-effect and a theatrical contrivance, there is nothing behind or beneath it, no blindfold prisoner or spectacular interior. If Priscilla is distinct from the Veiled Lady, no one is so totally identified with the role of public insensibility that her display becomes a violation. Indeed, if the gap is maintained between Priscilla and the Veiled Lady, identity with the isolating interior designated by the veil becomes impossible, because the location of identity itself migrates outward, becoming a matter of opaque exteriors rather than transparent and penetrable interiors.

In insisting on the separation between Priscilla and the Veiled Lady, Coverdale repudiates the remoteness of absorbed insensibility, but he also signals the text's return to "a theatre, a little removed." Coverdale's coyness is theatrical; he interposes himself as narrator and mediator between the reader and the underside of the veil, effecting the reader's removal from the interiority to which the veil points, that space of isolated privacy totally constituted within the field of a public gaze. Coverdale thereby spares his reader the experience ("hardly less than awful") of participating in a gaze that isolates, incarcerates, and penetrates, and he institutes in its stead another, more mutual aesthetic relation. The Veiled Lady may "behold the Absolute," remaining blind and deaf to her audience, but Coverdale looks back at his reader with intent. The theatricality with which Coverdale addresses himself to his reader is most evident in the much-derided final line of the narrative, his purported "confession" of love for Priscilla, which is generally taken for the text's reification of interiority and privatization.[44] Certainly, in its rather too emphatic reassertion of heterosexual desire, Coverdale's declaration falls flat. But read for its form, as well as its content, the final lines of the narrative suggest how radically Coverdale seeks to depart from the vision of identity as private and interior. Coverdale carefully stages his confession, asking that his reader "charitably suppose me to blush and turn away my face," and then he stumbles ornately over his line: "I—I myself—was in love—with—Priscilla!" With every dash and fumble, Coverdale's confession reads less like an attempt at disclosure and transparency than as an exercise in opacity. The sentence is opaque as writing, for its typographical peculiarities, and opaque as sentiment, an utter *non sequitur* that has laughably little to do with the narrative that precedes it.

Formally, Coverdale's final lines forge a theater out of the text, placing the reader face-to-face with a narrator whose act of turning away his face only reinforces the reader's constituting, defining presence. Rather than an absorbed beholder, straining after a glimpse of intimate truth within an oblivious object, Coverdale's reader becomes the occasion for a performance of withdrawal that ultimately asserts physicality and presence. In this, Coverdale counters the removal *from* the world that converts the Veiled Lady into a blindfold prisoner with an aesthetic of removal *for* the world—that "theatre, a little removed from the highway of ordinary travel" that turns outward, toward relationship and toward the materiality of form.[45] In *The Blithedale Romance,* Hawthorne gives a hint of what this aesthetic might mean for both identity and collectivity: bringing identity to the surface, asserting its opacity, Coverdale also insists upon its essential relationality. Under such a relation, the blindfold prisoner would no longer stand as the consequence and constitutive other of the melancholy, isolated democratic subject, because theatricality forbids that exceptional distance that renders the one insensible to the straining, violating eyes of the other, insisting instead upon their mutual engagement and exposing their utter necessity to one another.

# 5 / Theatricality, Strangeness, and Democracy in Melville's *Confidence-Man*

In an unpublished manuscript fragment composed sometime in 1856, which may or may not have been intended as a chapter for *The Confidence-Man*, Melville offers a brief sketch of a shifting, discontinuous, and very strange subject that, whatever the fragment's original relationship to the larger work, almost literally maps out the text's basic concern with the multiplicity and inconsistency of character.[1] At the top of the fragment, one title, "The Mississippi," has been scribbled over and replaced with another, "The River," already hinting at the difficulties of identification and the obfuscations of naming that follow. The piece begins as an elaborate panegyric on "Mississippee": "As the word Abraham means the father of a great multitude of men, so the word Mississippee means the father of a great multitude of waters" (497). But from this first sentence, a question arises: Is the Mississippi to be understood as one thing or many, as the singular father it names or as the multitude of waters that comprise it? Though Melville employs the singular personal pronoun "he" throughout, the conceit of the fragment is that the river behaves in ways neither singular nor personal. Tracing the river from its source to the Gulf of Mexico, the piece narrates the constant accumulations and radical changes that defy assumptions of the river's continuity. "Above the Falls of St. Anthony," the river "winds evenly" with clear waters and "man . . . remote," but, largely wild and "undisturbed," this upper segment of the river does not represent it. "By his Fall, though he rise not again," Melville puns, the Mississippi "first forms his character."

Ennobled, deepened, and populated, the river truly becomes 'itself' after the Falls of St. Anthony, taking on the character of patriarchal majesty first invoked by its name only after it becomes something other than what it was. From this point, both in the fragment and along the river's course, the Mississippi accumulates attributes like silt; simile piles on top of simile as the river becomes "like a Larger Susquehannah like a long-drawn bison herd . . . fissured & verdant, a long China Wall." Such accumulations, however, do not effect another transformation in the river until the entry of the Missouri:

> At St. Louis the course of this dream is run. Down on it like a Paw-nee from ambush foams the yellow-jacked Missouri. The calmness is gone, the grouped isles disappear, the shores are jagged & rent, the hue of the water is clayed, the before moderate current is rapid & vexed. The peace of the Upper River seems broken in the Lower, nor is it ever renewed. The Missouri sends rather a hostile element than a filial flow. Longer, stronger than the father of waters like Ju-piter he dethrones his sire & reigns in his stead. Under the benign name Mississippi it is in short the Missouri that now rolls to the Gulf.

As the river takes on at least three distinct characters in this brief frag-ment, all the while accumulating new qualities, so it begins to echo (or, perhaps, anticipate) the warning of Melville's narrator in *The Confidence-Man*: "a consistent character is a *rara avis*" (69). The name "Mississippi," like the singular pronoun "he," operates like a confidence trick; it in-vites faith that it is what it names by fostering an illusion of continuity and consistency amid constant accumulation and change. In this, the fragment of "The River" gives a hint of the operation of character in the text—innumerable attributes and features, inhabiting several bodies, moving and changing ceaselessly, all the while masquerading under the name of a singular, continuous thing. The confidence man: is he one or many? This is the question around which criticism on Melville's last pub-lished work of long fiction has traditionally divided, but it posits a false opposition.[2] As "The River" makes clear, multitudes are present within the appearance of the singular, and names—like Abraham and Missis-sippee—are merely the words that gather them together. In "The River," Melville suggests that what is at stake in the problem of character is ulti-mately a question of "a great multitude of men," of "tribes," a "continent" and "nations," and the inconsistency that the fragment explores involves the capacity of such multitudes to masquerade under the sign of singular, and often misleading, names. "Under the benign name Mississippi it is in short the Missouri that now rolls to the Gulf."

"In the United States," Tocqueville writes in the first volume of *Democracy in America*, "as in all countries where the people reign, the majority rules in the name of the people."[3] Even less sanguine than Tocqueville about the capacity of majorities to make manifest the needs of a people, Melville proposes an image of majoritarian democracy in "The River" as usurpation. When the Missouri meets the Mississippi, the latter's "dream is run"; the word Mississippi becomes a lie as the ostensibly subordinate tributary "dethrones his sire & reigns in his stead." As the smaller body clouds and disrupts the course of the larger one, Melville finds in the movement of rivers a process congruent with the power of a faction to rule a democracy.[4] It is no accident that, at the entry of the Misssouri, the Mississippi crosses a sectional border. The first river that flows into the Mississippi from a slave state, the Missouri may ambush "like a Pawnee," but it usurps power like a rival god. The hostile strength of the Missouri's waters, the claying and cloudiness that it brings, draws on the power of the slave states, and as with the addition of slave territories to the nation under the Missouri Compromise, so the addition of the Missouri River is transformative. With its entry, the Mississippi assumes a radically different character, and the persistence of this name imparts nothing more than a false notion of continuity, a false sense of the river's identity with itself. No longer a mark of identity, the name "Mississippi" is now the mark of the river's strangeness.

It would not be difficult to imagine other names, as false and misleading as that of "Mississippi"; certainly "democracy" and "America" suggest themselves. But neither *The Confidence-Man*, nor this perhaps discarded fragment of it, permits anything so simple as an allegorical reading. Instead, in this final chapter, I want to show how Melville's most enigmatic prose work stages and performs processes that are congruent with public life in the United States, processes that both mimic and belie the movements of democracy. Massing, dissolution, deliberation, consensus, exception: these provide a fit summary of what happens in the first three chapters alone, from the appearance of the mute on board the *Fidèle* to the expulsion of Black Guinea from the charity of his fellow passengers. Throughout *The Confidence-Man*, Melville turns Tocquevillean concepts like sameness, confidence, and the stranger inside out. Theatricalizing the everyday exchanges of public life and making them strange, I argue, Melville both interrogates what collective political life in the antebellum United States is, and hints at what it might be. Comprised of largely unlinked scenes—connected only by the fact that they occur on the same day, 1 April, on the same riverboat, traveling south from St. Louis along a river masquerading as the Mississippi—the text lacks anything that could be termed a "plot." It opens in a place (or so "The River" suggests) of usurpation and assault, but the majority of passengers aboard the *Fidèle* live under conditions of "confidence," believing in the coherence of the river, of themselves, of the nation and the public sphere. Over and over, the text presents the persistence of confidence as a kind of consensus that ignores manifest evidence of dissolution, inconsistency, and strangeness. But, again and again, the text also warns its reader against the seductiveness of such beliefs, both implicitly and directly ("a consistent character is a *rara avis*").

Rather than expressions of cynicism, I argue, the text's warnings against confidence ultimately signal its radicalism. In *The Confidence-Man*, Melville subversively restages the spectacle of U.S. democracy, laying bare the costs of consensus and sovereignty to both collective and individual life. The opening chapters of the book present a sequence of two nearly identical scenes of collective deliberation; ostensibly inquests into the authenticity of the character of a stranger (first the mute in cream colors, then Black Guinea), the narrator exposes these scenes as democratic instances of public execution ("the truly warning spectacle of a man hanged by his friends"). From this point, the text quickly begins to erode everything that supports such a destructive faith in the "authenticity" of character—consistency, coherence, transparency—replacing it instead with a logic of theatricality. In theatricality, I argue, the text finds an aesthetic practice of estrangement that undermines the consistency and authenticity of identity and demands instead a tolerance for strangeness. In the work's feints and frustrations, in the games of confidence that it turns back on its readers, a powerful critique emerges of the forms of consensus that confidence makes possible (from identity to the market to the state). But more than that, in its refusal of consistency, coherence, and transparency, the text posits strangeness as an alternative foundation for the public sphere, a means of imagining democracy without the coercions of consensus or the exceptionalism of sovereign power.

## Democracy's Strangers

"Have men, by joining together, changed their characters?" Tocqueville asks rhetorically (*Democracy in America*, 251). In its first three chapters, Melville's *Confidence-Man* provides a pointed reply to Tocqueville's claim that, singly and collectively, Americans are basically the same. Melville's text opens with an image of the public as a multitude that is as shifting, inconsistent, and difficult to name as the Mississippi in the fragment of "The River." From a "crowd" to a "miscellaneous company" to "a variety of characters," the string of names that the narrator applies to the passengers who board the riverboat *Fidèle* indicates a wariness of misleading labels that falsely personify. Though this "traveling public" may behave as a "crowd" in one moment (*Confidence-Man*, 3), it is likely in the next to "break up from a concourse into various clusters or squads" (9). To impose a singular name, pronoun, or even a metaphor would amount to the kind of usurpation that permits the Missouri to hide itself under "the benign name Mississippi." But all the while the text refuses any kind of continuous grammatical subject that would unify and personify this shifting multitude, the first three chapters nonetheless make of it a kind of protagonist, tracing its activities as it gathers, deliberates, forms consensus, and disintegrates once again. In this, the opening chapters of *The Confidence-Man* both stage and perform the activities of democracy in ways that suggest Melville's interests are closer to Tocqueville's than might first appear. Without assuming a subject, without positing an agent, the text narrates the formation of a miscellaneous company into a deliberative body, an empowered crowd, a sovereign "justiciary," as well as its disintegration into mere parts, "quartettes, trios, and couples." Just as the text never assumes a singular name, so it also refuses to assign an agent behind such transformations. Instead, Melville leaves it an open question what constitutes such a crowd, what empowers it, and what sustains it, and he generates from this problem the scenes that launch the text. Though Melville's sense of the discontinuity of collective character clearly departs from Tocqueville's assertions of democratic sameness, he shares with Tocqueville a fascination with the character and acts of a disparate multitude "joined together." In both *The Confidence-Man* and *Democracy in America*, such a multitude is self-originating and self-defining, both the beginning and the end of everything that happens: "everything rises out of it and is absorbed back into it" (*Democracy in America*, 60).

As Tocqueville might have predicted, the first thing to "rise out of" the multitude of passengers on the *Fidèle* is a stranger. In *Democracy in America*, the appearance of such a stranger marks the ascendancy of the public to the position of sovereign—"from this day," public opinion declares, "you are a stranger among us." For Melville, the advent of the deaf and mute stranger in cream colors inaugurates a scene of deliberation which shapes all of the exchanges that follow, setting off a game of confidence that the text never resolves. "Stared at, but unsaluted," the extremely white man in the cream-colored suit arrives "unaccompanied by friends" and unencumbered by either suitcase or valise (*Confidence-Man*, 3). Instead of companions, this solitary traveler meets a "crowd," which quickly forms into an audience, and ultimately into a judging, evaluating, opining body. "From the shrugged shoulders, titters, whispers, wonderings of the crowd, it was plain that he was, in the extremest sense of the word, a stranger." The crowd's gestures and mutterings, its titters and whispers, are jumbled and seemingly incoherent, but its pronouncement is nonetheless clear: the man is a stranger in the "extremest sense," absolutely unknown, wholly remote. Under the crowd's close scrutiny, what is unfamiliar and unknowable about the mute only grows. Observation and speculation serve to distance the man further from the crowd, even as he occupies its center. "Whispers, wonderings" yield nothing in the way of knowledge; instead, these serve to intensify the very solitude and singularity that draw this crowd around the man in the first place. But while the crowd forms the man as increasingly, extremely strange, the strangeness of the man, in turn, forms the crowd, and the stranger and more singular he becomes under its scrutiny, the more the crowd itself comes to behave as a singular agent.

Melville's stranger, like Tocqueville's, signals the agency of a crowd that has gathered together around a shared opinion. But where Tocqueville assumes that such a crowd ("majority" is his word) and its authority exist prior to its pronouncement of the stranger's ban, Melville imagines a far more intricate temporality. No "crowd" appears in the text before the mute's arrival. His "advent" occurs in what Peggy Kamuf describes as the text's "collapsing of narrative time," a simultaneity the text labels as "in the same moment with" (3), in which neither succession nor causality organizes events.[5] The mute is not a stranger before he meets the crowd, but neither are the passengers a crowd before they recognize a stranger. Instead, Melville places the man and the crowd in a dynamic relationship of definition and constitution, which, if not exactly "mutual," is clearly dependent and simultaneous. "Plant[ing] himself just beside the placard"—a wanted poster around which a number of people have clustered "as if it had been a theater-bill"—the man assumes a double position in relation to the other passengers, first as the center of a spectacle as unanticipated as his "advent," then as a text to be read. This doubleness is matched by the crowd's similarly dual use of him. As he traces and retraces verses of Corinthians on his slate, carefully preserving the word "Charity" with each new line, so the crowd preserves the man's "strangeness" even as it offers up a proliferation of interpretations of him. The crowd both perpetuates the man's strangeness and resents it: "Illy pleased with his pertinacity, as they thought it, the crowd a second time thrust him aside, and not without epithets and some buffets" (4). Its hostility grows along with its efforts to interpret him, but though his strangeness annoys and begs interpretation, knowledge would thwart the constitutive effect that the man has on the crowd.[6] Rather than seeking knowledge, the crowd uses him as an occasion for the endless speculation that keeps it intact:

"Odd fish!"
"Poor fellow!"
"Who can he be?"
"Caspar Hauser."
"Bless my soul!"
"Uncommon countenance."
"Green prophet from Utah."
"Humbug!"
"Singular innocence."
"Means something . . ."

"Conflictingly spoken or thought" by "many men with many minds," this endless speculation is the text's joke; the apparent variety of opinion does little more than sustain consensus about the man's strangeness, thereby sustaining the "crowd" at his expense. In the end, the crowd's energetic curiosity and noisy debate are little more than exercises in self-perpetuation.[7]

Just as no crowd precedes the advent of the stranger, so no crowd remains behind once he disappears. As soon as the man falls asleep—or moves to another part of the boat, or disembarks, the narrator cannot say for sure (8–9)—he ceases to hold the crowd's attention and it disintegrates, "involuntarily submitting to that natural law which ordains dissolution equally to the mass, as in time to the member" (9). The crowd's deliberations have yielded no certain knowledge, and the mute in cream colors departs with no explanation of his origins or his purpose. All that really "happens" in these two chapters is the massing and subsequent dissolution of a crowd "in the same moment with" the advent of a stranger. With this, though, Melville proposes that such collective agents are contingent and temporary. Staging both the making and unmaking of a crowd, the text suggests that neither crowd, nor majority, nor public stands as a monolithic embodiment of power. Indeed, once the mute exits the scene, the narrator ceases referring to the passengers with collective identifiers altogether, and he begins to imagine a string of possibilities for the "miscellaneous company" that remains. In the second chapter, the narrator marshals a chain of metonymy and synecdoche to describe—or at least contain—the shifting, plural multitude that appears in the absence of the spectacle of a stranger. What is striking, however, is that as the narrator moves through images of the riverboat and river, trying to find an appropriate illustration of this multitude, it is precisely the figure of the stranger that he cannot shake:

> Though her voyage of twelve hundred miles extends from apple to orange, from clime to clime, yet, like any small ferry-boat, to right and left, at every landing, the huge *Fidèle* still receives additional passengers in exchange for those that disembark; so that, though always full of strangers, she continually, in some degree, adds to, or replaces them with strangers still more strange; like Rio Janeiro fountain, fed from the Corcovado mountains, which is ever overflowing with strange waters, but never with the same strange particles in every part. (8)

Constantly fed by strange parts that are never diluted or dissolved, the riverboat always contains strangers "still more strange." Such a strangeness is more than that of some "particles" measured in relation to others, more than the strangeness of the mute in relation to the crowd. In this passage, Melville suggests that the river, riverboat, and crowd are simply containers, metonymic spaces that fill with "still more" strangeness, making them strange to past, present, and subsequent versions of what they, at any given moment, appear to be.

Though Melville repeats the word "stranger" at least eight times in the opening pages of the text, the strangers he introduces in this passage are as distinct from the mute as the "crowd" of chapter 1 is from the "miscellaneous company" of chapter 2. Rather than abandoning the concept of the stranger, Melville begins to reimagine it, introducing into the text a second kind of strangeness that functions in an entirely different way. Where Melville's first stranger might be said to echo the plight of Tocqueville's, even as Melville revises the temporality of its relation to the public, the second stranger hints at another conception of the public altogether. As a stranger "in the extremest sense of the word," the mute is necessarily a "stranger among us"—one who "can keep [his] life and property," who "can keep [his] privileges in the township," but who has been spectacularly "shunned" by his fellows (*Democracy in America*, 255–56). This is the stranger whose abandonment does not entail expulsion from the public, because his continued presence is a necessary representation of the sovereignty that has mandated it. Thrust aside while occupying the center of everyone's attention, the stranger in the "extremest sense" is the internal outside that makes such collective formations as a "crowd" or a "majority" visible and viable. However, when the strange mute falls asleep and the crowd loses its visual center, Melville's narrator begins to pluralize and disseminate the man's strangeness. Rather than a singular stranger, Melville imagines "still more" of them, flowing into the *Fidèle* like waters feed the Rio Janeiro fountain. A multitude of strangers can never reach the "extremest sense of the word," nor can they find themselves surrounded by a mass or a crowd. Instead, like the "particles" of a tributary meeting "strange waters," these strangers only meet with others. Strangeness is no longer the thing against which a crowd fabricates its sameness, because it has become the only quality that these disparate, particulate passengers share. So what would it mean to imagine a society of such strangers? What would it do to entities such as crowd, majority, even public or nation?

Unfortunately, Melville does not pause to entertain such questions, because, almost as soon as he invokes the riverboat as a figure for the strangeness of men in multitudes, the Mississippi enters with its relentless flow and misleading name: "Here reigned the dashing and all-fusing spirit of the West, whose type is the Mississippi itself, which, uniting the streams of the most distant and opposite zones, pours them along, helter-skelter, in one cosmopolitan and confident tide" (*Confidence-Man*, 9). The final piece of Melville's extended chain of simile, metonymy, and synecdoche links the passengers aboard the *Fidèle* (themselves a metonymy for the broader "traveling public") to the Mississippi. All the passengers' activities of massing and dissolution, estrangement and judgment, accompany their relentless flow in a single direction. As "cosmopolitan," the tide may preserve its various composition from all parts, belonging to no nation or region alone, but as "confident," the disparate tide moves relentlessly in a single direction.[8] Confidence is reasserted as an "all-fusing" force at the end of a chapter that has narrated the dissolution of a crowd into "quartettes, trios, and couples, or even solitaires." Given the lessons of the unpublished "River" fragment, such a fusion can only result in a misnaming and a misrecognition ("under the benign name

Mississippi . . . "). The image of a river "overflowing with strange waters, but never with the same strange particles in every part," thus yields
to the figure of a river as overwhelming power and singular purpose,
and a confidently fused body—both singular and sovereign—seems to
move on from this chapter, masquerading as a democratic multitude of
strangers.

## "The Truly Warning Spectacle of a Man Hanged by His Friends"

While the opening chapters of *The Confidence-Man* stage the massing
and dissolution of crowds, demonstrating their unmaking and exposing
their contingency, the text never forgets the latency of the power with
which they may compose themselves. Though popular and apparently
self-generating, such confident formations are both unrelenting and so
contiguous with the conditions of the public sphere as to seem both inevitable and almost imperceptible. But even as the text suspends the possibility of alternatives—at least for a time—it works to combat this im-
perceptibility by minutely staging, again and again, the movements and
acts of collected peoples and crowds, even to the point of redundancy.
The effect of such constant, though inexact, repetitions begins to become
apparent in the scene that immediately follows the text's announcement
of "one cosmopolitan and confident tide"—a near reenactment of the
opening scene in which another crowd composes itself to deliberate the
character of the Black Guinea. Clearly an iteration of the mute's arrival,
chapter 3 more closely anatomizes the process of forming a consensus
around a strange and "curious object." Proposing another ending to an
almost identical scene of deliberation, the text also hints that what is at
stake in such scrutiny into the character of an individual is an assertion
of sovereignty as a popular, even "democratic," prerogative.

Responding to the many images that link Guinea to the man in cream
colors—their physical disabilities, their "fleece," their neatly contrast-
ing shades—critics have often treated these figures to the very scrutiny
that the respective crowds do, unmasking both of them as confidence
men, or presuming that one (generally the mute) serves as a warning of
the duplicity of the other.[9] More compelling, however, than the questions of identity posed to and about Guinea is the behavior of the crowd
that gathers around him. When Guinea first appears, it is as an object
of charity, "at once target and purse," catching the coins for which he is

named in his mouth with a grin. As Susan Ryan argues, Guinea exposes public charity not only as spectacular entertainment, but also as a form of prostitution, his routine and stature strongly suggestive of fellatio.[10] Already a target of white projection, Guinea becomes subject to an even more intimate and intense scrutiny—nearly to a stripping—when a fellow passenger voices doubt in his authenticity, "croak[ing] out something about his deformity being a sham, got up for financial purposes" (*Confidence-Man*, 12). Rather than joining in the crowd's scrutiny of Guinea, Melville's narrator shifts focus to the behavior of the crowd itself, scrutinizing its deliberations in response to the claims of the one-legged man in what becomes a painstaking dissection of a quintessential activity of democratic public life. Though Carl Schmitt considered the deliberative character of constitutional democracy inimical to the "decisionist" imperative of sovereignty, Melville suggests otherwise, finding in the prolonged scrutiny of and debate over Guinea's body, character, and life an assertion of violent right that he compares to a public hanging.[11]

Initially, the narrator suggests that the crowd responds to the suggestion of doubt by submitting "instinct" to "reason," but in the contortions of deliberation that follow, it is clear that neither reason nor instinct alone is governing the scene. "Yes, they began to scrutinize the negro curiously enough," on hearing the man's accusation (12). But, none too eager to see the one-legged man vindicated, they quickly change course and take "the part of the poor fellow, against one who had just before turned nearly all minds the other way." Torn between placing confidence in Guinea or the one-legged man, the onlookers begin to behave like Tocqueville's democratic subjects, who, "being so like each other, have no confidence in others," even as they place an "almost unlimited confidence in the judgment of the public" (*Democracy in America,* 435). As soon as the man leaves in frustration, the crowd finds "themselves left sole judges in the case," and they gleefully assume the authority of that confident public. If the crowd takes pleasure in this, the narrator insists that it is no mere *schadenfreude*, no "human weakness to take pleasure in sitting in judgment upon one in a box." Instead, he claims that this is the pleasure of indulging in a peculiarly democratic exercise: "it strangely sharpens human perceptions, when, instead of standing by and having their fellow-feeling touched by the sight of an alleged culprit severely handled by some one judiciary, a crowd suddenly come to be all justiciaries in the same case themselves" (*Confidence-Man,* 13). The pleasure of exercising their faculties of rational judgment trumps the relative pleasures of giving charity or witnessing suffering, as the public's critical function overtakes its sentimental proclivities. But even this is nothing compared with the glee with which it takes the power of judgment away from a singular authority, like a judge or a cranky old man. To elaborate his point, the narrator appends an anecdote to serve as a simile for such popular assertions of sovereign right:

> . . . as in Arkansas once, a man proved guilty, by law, of murder, but whose condemnation was deemed unjust by the people, so that they rescued him to try him themselves; whereupon, they, as it turned out, found him even guiltier than the court had done, and forthwith proceeded to execution; so that the gallows presented the truly warning spectacle of a man hanged by his friends. (13)

Though the narrator hastens to retreat from his simile—"but not to such extremities, or anything like them, did the present crowd come"—he has succinctly allegorized that transfer of power from singular to popular agents that sometimes goes by the name of "revolution," even as the rights of sovereignty remain unchanged. He has also established a congruency between the case of the crowd judging Guinea and the Arkansas lynch mob, offering nothing more than a semicolon by way of separation. Thus, when the crowd's scrutiny moves from Guinea's legs to his skin on the next page, picking his body apart piece by piece for evidence of some internal truth, the narrator makes it clear that he is on trial for his life. Indeed, this trial proves so compelling that, in one of the text's few examples of narrative continuity, several of the characters debating Guinea's authenticity return three chapters later to take up the question again: "Tell me, sir, do you really think that a white could look the negro so? For one, I should call it pretty good acting" (31). There is no need for this crowd or any other to arrive at a final judgment on Guinea's "case," since the power to prolong such scrutiny effectively demonstrates a sovereign right. Like Jefferson speculating on the ontological implications of a blush, or Tocqueville ruminating on the face and features of "the stranger brought by slavery into our midst," such power lies in the endless suspension of the question.[12] And, as with Tocqueville's stranger, Guinea is "hung" by his "friends."

This scene establishes what the later one confirms: Guinea's identity and every element of it have become matters of opinion, though they do not necessarily require consensus. In the absence of a charismatic figure, like Ahab, consensus is fleeting on the *Fidèle*, shifting with the vicissitudes of confidence and the fusing and dissolution of crowds.[13] Ultimately, the measure of the crowd's power does not lie in an answer to the question posed to it about Guinea's authenticity, but in the authority that the onlookers claim as a crowd to debate it. To assume a position of judgment over the authenticity of character is to presume that something lies beneath or behind the qualities, the story, or even the body that a character puts forth. It is, in short, to designate an interior as the space of authentic life and assume the authority to define that life. In this, Melville's inquisitive crowds engage in something like the penetrating spectatorship that both horrifies and implicates Hawthorne's Coverdale, or even the "spiritualized despotism and violence" that mark the new frontier of sovereignty for Tocqueville. On first glance, Melville's public sphere looks quite different from Hawthorne's; rather than a sphere of subjects, whose privacy and interiority are created in order to be spectacularly violated, Melville's is largely a public sphere of multitudes and crowds. Nonetheless, Melville shares with Hawthorne the view that public projections of interiority amount to acts of violence. What is more, as the deliberations over Guinea continue, Melville also follows Hawthorne in the introduction of theatricality as a response.

The debates about Guinea's body and character begin with the one-legged man's insistence that Guinea is playacting: "He's some white operator, betwisted and painted up for a decoy. He and his friends are all humbugs!" (14). His accusations depend upon the capacity of what he later calls the "discerning eye" to perceive both the "overdone" ebony and the "hoisted up" limbs of a "hypocritical beggar," against the presumed subtleties of an "authentic" one. But when later pressed by the man in gray—"For one, I should call it pretty good acting"—the one-legged man responds by eroding the very distinction between performed and authentic character that he has assumed: "Not much better than any other man acts . . . don't you both perform acts? To do, is to act, so all doers are actors" (31). With this, the one-legged man concedes the basic theatricality of agency—"all doers are actors"—and he turns the same question posed of Guinea back onto the men debating him. Under the man's proclamation, "acting" is universalized as a condition of character, confining judgment of it to gradations of artifice, the overdoing of ebony or the visible hoisting of limbs. Both his invocation of "humbug" and appeal to the "discerning eyes" of others channel P. T. Barnum's operational aesthetic, which turned on just such an invitation to scrutinize. Under the presumption of a humbug, an act, or a confidence game, judgment settles on the material and conditions of performance, and authenticity becomes nothing more than a figment of spectators' imaginations, the negative projection of "discerning eyes" that fail to see an excess of performance. Construed as humbug, theatricality may erode authenticity, but it authorizes scrutiny and deliberation, and as Lydia Maria Child discovers in Barnum's museum, no amount of care on the part of the curious spectator can prevent the operational aesthetic from turning deadly.

Karen Halttunen describes the 1850s as a period which saw at least a temporary decline in the sentimental culture which had privileged authenticity and transparency of character. As authenticity became indistinguishable from the outward signs that marked it, she argues, mainstream middle-class culture in the United States gradually embraced theatricality in dress, manner, and social ritual. With this, activities once associated with figures such as the confidence man—the sentimental villain, *par excellence*, in her study—eventually came to be normalized.[14] When Melville's one-legged man asserts that "all doers are actors," he articulates just such a normalization of theatricality, and he defeats his own efforts to expose a confidence game. But his assertion also accomplishes something else: establishing theatricality as key to the erosion of authenticity, and with it, identity and interiority, he turns that erosion back on those who would scrutinize ("don't you both perform acts?"). First introduced as a species of humbug, theatricality in *The Confidence-Man* quickly becomes more than a middle-class fashion, more than another indulgence in the operational aesthetic. With it, spectators also become actors, their seeing no less a role or an act than those whom they watch. In short, Melville begins with this scene to redefine theatricality, proposing through it another response to the "extremest" strangeness to which the mute and Guinea become subject in the opening chapters of the text. But the further possibilities of theatricality are not fully explored until the text's third iteration of those first two scenes—the pleas for charity made by the theatrical former prisoner, Thomas Fry.[15]

If Guinea's near-hanging by his "friends" exposes the violence latent in the crowd that gathers around the mute in cream colors, proposing a "truly warning" denouement to the first scene, then Thomas Fry suggests another ending still. The character whose overt theatricality comes out of his imprisonment in the Tombs, Thomas Fry preemptively makes himself strange, theatricalizing his own body and character as a means of repudiating the right of any crowd to do so. But this is only the beginning of what Fry's theatricality accomplishes. Traditionally associated with opacity and self-referentiality, theatricality is said to be a mode of estrangement, reminding its beholder of its status as aesthetic work and heightening the constitutive distances between beholder, actor, and role.

As Fry himself does, theatricality insists upon two or more things residing simultaneously in one space, one body, one name, one temporality.
In chapter 33, Melville comes to define theatricality through just such
excesses, calling it an aesthetics of "more reality than real life itself." Estranging even reality from itself, theatricality, I will argue, ultimately
proposes an aesthetic and material form for that community of "strangers still more strange."

## Wantonness or Sugaring? Thomas Fry's Critical Theatricality

Chapter 19 of *The Confidence-Man* ("A Soldier of Fortune") contains
the text's only instance of a character who introduces himself by explicitly exposing himself as a fraud. "A singular character in a grimy old regi-
mental coat, a countenance at once grim and wizened" with "interwoven
paralyzed legs" and a "rigid body" suspended between "rude crutches"
(93), Thomas Fry gives every appearance of a wounded veteran of the
Mexican War, and as he solicits donations from passengers, he requires
few additional details to complete the story: "Sir, a shilling for Happy
Tom, who fought at Buena Vista. Lady, something for General Scott's soldier, crippled in both pins at glorious Contreras" (97). So convincing is
the combination of his wrecked body and grimy regimentals that, before
Fry has uttered a single word, the herb-doctor greets him in anticipation
of a war story: "Mexico? Molina del Rey? Resaca de la Palma?" Unlike
the mute and Black Guinea (to whom he seems clear counterpart[16]), Fry
is not immediately subject to the doubt of those he solicits; indeed the
only reason that anyone becomes skeptical of his story at all is because
Fry himself loudly disowns it. In reply to the herb-doctor's greeting, Fry
promptly offers an alternate story, ostensibly his actual one, though the
doctor finds it harder to believe than the first, "it so jars with all, is so
incompatible with all" (97). But despite his initial doubt, by the time the
herb-doctor watches Fry solicit the other passengers, he knows that he is
watching both a performance and a confidence game.

The Thomas Fry episode is an unusual one in *The Confidence-Man*:
Fry never asks for the herb-doctor's "confidence"; he makes no claims
about his own authenticity, nor does he insist on his identity with the
role that he plays. Yet he plays that role eagerly and "with glee," prompting the following exchange between a "prim-looking" man (the first
speaker) and the herb-doctor, who watch as Fry begs:

" . . . I never heard more wanton lies. In one breath he tells you what appears to be his true story, and, in the next, away and falsify it."

"For all that, I repeat he lies not out of wantonness. A ripe philosopher, turned out of the great Sorbonne of hard times, he thinks that woes, when told to strangers for money, are best sugared. Though the inglorious lock-jaw of his knee-pans in a wet dungeon is a far more pitiable ill than to have been crippled at glorious Contreras, yet he is of the opinion that this lighter and falser ill shall attract, while the heavier and real one might repel." (97)

"Wantonness" or "sugaring": which explains Thomas Fry's blatantly fabricated performance? With his admission, Fry has forestalled the question that dominates the exchanges over Guinea—Is he or isn't he what he claims to be?—leaving the two men to debate the causes and consequences of his theatricality. Fry frankly admits that the character he performs is not himself, that the story he tells is a fabrication, all for the sake of an audience who pays: this is theatricality in its simplest, most bare form. For the prim man who sees Fry's performance as "wantonness," such acting is lying; "authenticity" belongs to the character whose history Fry confesses to the herb-doctor, the former inmate of the Tombs, imprisoned for lack of bail. For the herb-doctor, Fry's acting remains a kind of lie, but rather than a "wanton" lie, it is one fabricated for the sake of "sugaring." In the herb-doctor's fine distinction, Fry's lie is justified because it is strategically aesthetic—instrumental and ornamental. It pleases those he solicits by telling them the story they anticipate, the one that they most want to hear. With obvious sympathy for Fry, the herb-doctor appears also to be an apologist for theatricality, against the prim antitheatricalism of the other man, but as Fry returns from his successful performance, it becomes clear that the doctor only partially understands the "philosophy" with which he credits Fry. The herb-doctor's view of theatricality as "sugaring" values authenticity less than effective panhandling, but the view continues to rest on a distinction between a "lighter and falser ill" and a "heavier and real one" that has become untenable. Full comprehension of Fry's theatricality requires an abandonment of both authenticity and consistency, but it is precisely this abandonment that permits another reality—a lived truth of what Fry calls "free Ameriky"—to become visible.

The problem that theatricality first poses for the interlocutors is that, in Fry's displacement of one identity to reveal another only to reassume the first, neither identity can completely disappear or be forgotten. For the spectator who knows both stories—that of Fry's imprisonment in the Tombs and "Happy Tom's" crippling at Contreras—two men now inhabit the same ruined body at the same time and place. Tolerance for that particular kind of inconsistency and multiplicity is part of what theatricality demands. But it isn't only the addition of the fictional war veteran that multiplies Fry's identity. In the story he "confesses" to the herb-doctor, he essentially describes how both his body and his life became unrecognizable to him, forcing him to abandon the name and identity of his youth: "Until my twenty-third year I went by the nickname of Happy Tom—happy— ha, ha! They called me Happy Tom, d'ye see?" (95). What happens in his twenty-third year is this: "Happy Tom" witnesses a fight between a pavior and a gentlemen at a political rally ("I was in those days a great patriot"). A material witness in the case, though unable to afford bail, he ends up in "the wet and the damp" of the New York Tombs, where his legs become rigid and twisted, leaving him unable to work and "drifting down stream like any other bit of wreck" (97). Rather than implying the continuity of a single identity, Fry's decision to take the name of his youth as the name of the veteran he impersonates while he begs highlights these violent transformations with bitter irony ("under the benign name Mississippi . . ."). The sameness of the name makes that earlier self even more a stranger, and he tells his biography to the herb-doctor as the story of successive selves with discrete names, rather than as the gradual deterioration of the "real" Happy Tom to his current state. None of these names designates a version of the man that could be considered more authentic than any of the others; "Happy Tom" names both the benighted youth and the fictional veteran, while "Thomas Fry" designates the ruined former inmate whose story, according to the herb-doctor, is unbelievable "in the light of a commentary on what I believe to be the system of things" (97).

Like most everyone Fry encounters, the herb-doctor is far more willing to accept the "sugared" version of his misfortune, even when he understands it to be, strictly speaking, false, because that story accords with a "system" he accepts. This episode exposes the uneasy alliance of authenticity and credibility, as it reduces credibility to the consistency of a story with established systems. Against authenticity, consistency, and credibility, however, stands a truth that Fry's stories and fabrications make visible, tying them together into a coherence that is distinct from all of these. As a prisoner of the Tombs and Blackwell's Island, Fry's body is ruined by the state, no less than it would have been had he fought in

Mexico. As Fry tells it, his crime ("a worse crime than murder") lay in lacking the money and friends to free him from a judicial system that punishes guilty and innocent alike. Charged with nothing and held only as a witness, Fry nevertheless finds himself in the position of the solitary prisoner, made to live while his body and character are destroyed by confinement. Guinea may have been metaphorically "hanged by his friends" in a space of judgment outside of legal institutions, but the absence of such "friends" does nothing to save Fry from a similar fate at the hands of the state.[17] Fry has essentially survived his own execution, or at least that of "Happy Tom," so it comes as no surprise when Fry begins to speak "unhandsome notions . . . about 'free Ameriky,' as he sarcastically called his country." On expressing these notions, however, he promptly loses the sympathetic audience of the herb-doctor. The herb-doctor's tolerance for theatricality extends only so far as his own pleasure and comfort, which Fry's "sugaring" is designed to satisfy. For Fry, however, performing a more acceptably sugared version of the state's role in his corporeal ruin is all of a piece with his understanding of the state's own fabrications. More precisely, theatricality is born with Fry's knowledge of the fictiveness of justice. As much as he is a former inmate of the Tombs and Blackwell's Island, Fry is an escapee from Plato's cave: no longer a prisoner to shadows he believes are real, Fry "wantonly" theatricalizes his own actually destroyed body as a means of disuniting realities from others' expectations of authenticity and consistency with "systems."

Neither the prim-looking man nor the herb-doctor is exactly wrong about Fry's lies; theatricality begins in an act of wantonness, sugared to appeal, but as an act in both senses of the word ("to do is to act," says the one-legged man), it is one that renders all of their expectations about identity irrelevant. Contending with Thomas Fry's theatricality—and the tolerance for inconsistency and inauthenticity it demands—would make it possible to see both the former inmate and the Mexican War veteran at once, as well as the nationalist fiction that makes one body and name more profitable than the other. Such a theatrical view is necessary to gain any sense of the conditions under which Fry's body and story take shape, and with this view, both stories also emerge as parallel, congruent realities. In chapter 33, Melville describes this way of seeing in terms of a receptivity to "more reality than real life itself can show" (183). Theatricality begins as a humbug or a strategy of wanton ingratiation, but it comes to function in *The Confidence-Man* as something closer to what Leo Bersani and Ulysse Dutoit call "a special type of cognition." Writing on a similar formulation of Proust's—"art, as Proust claimed, is more real than life"—Bersani and Dutoit describe this cognition as a thinking that supplements life, making material and concrete "the principles or conditions that support and make possible the existent."[18] Understood in this way, Fry's theatricality materializes the conditions that both make possible and limit life, wantonly turning his body back on the state as a reproach. Beyond the critique of the state it performs, Fry's "wanton" theatricality also challenges the expectations of his public by playing to them. He forces his audience into a confrontation with the ways in which its own expectations of authenticity, consistency, and identity project character into subjects, as something private, continuous, and interior.

With theatricality, Melville introduces into prose fiction a strange and estranging aesthetic form. He first defines the estranging effects of theatricality within the Black Guinea and Thomas Fry episodes as an act that holds open the distance between beholder, actor, and role, but he suggests its most subversive possibilities through the performances of the text itself—for example, in the relationship that emerges between such scenes. The advent of the mute, the deliberations over Guinea, and the encounter with Thomas Fry's unapologetic theatricality: none of these scenes stands alone. They are linked theatrically, but not in the sense that a singular character "masquerades" through all of them for the "discerning" reader to identify (the title, in its promise of such a masquerade, is the text's first and most enduring confidence trick). Instead, their theatricality lies in their relationship of repetition and succession, which Samuel Weber argues is central to an understanding of theatricality as a "medium" that transcends any particular form: "Out of the dislocations of its repetitions emerges nothing more or less than the *singularity of the theatrical event*. Such theatrical singularity haunts and taunts the Western dream of self-identity." Theatricality is a "singular" aesthetic mode, Weber insists, because of its irreducible plurality, its indefinite and (as Bersani and Dutoit would say) "inexact" repetitions.[19] Converted by Melville into an aesthetic of estrangement and inexact repetition—from one of wantonness, sugaring, or humbug—theatricality promises both a critical engagement and an ethics that imagines another form for democratic belonging. Because it insists upon two or more things residing in one place, one body, one temporality, theatricality's strangeness may also be what allows the singular to be, at the same time, the plural.

## Shooting Othello: Theatricality and Estrangement

Wantonness or sugaring? The debate between Thomas Fry's two spectators is a fairly concise summation of several centuries of aesthetic and moral philosophy on the "problem" of theatricality. As Jonas Barish makes clear in his 1981 work, *The Antitheatrical Prejudice,* one of the peculiarities of theatricality is that it has been most frequently and most explicitly defined by its detractors. To its Puritan critics in the seventeenth century, Barish argues, theatricality signaled impurity, contamination, and mixture; actors onstage crossed and blended identities conceived as absolute boundaries, divinely ordained. To its eighteenth-century Enlightenment critics (in particular, Rousseau), theatricality became the mark of a secular fall "from primitive 'transparency' to civilized 'opacity,'" which was born of the desire to please, to be admired and applauded. Barish argues that, compared with the voluminous attacks on the stage, as well as on the aesthetic and social forms which partake of it, explicit defenses of theatricality in European writing are rare and relatively "feeble," sharing (as the herb-doctor does) in many of the same assumptions about "authenticity" and "constancy" invoked by its critics. Although Barish would clearly count among theatricality's apologists, his work reflects the history it tells; in nearly five hundred pages, he comes closest to defining theatricality when he summarizes the claims of its opponents: The antitheatrical prejudice "belongs to a conservative ethical emphasis in which the key terms are those of order, stability, constancy, and integrity, as against a more existentialist emphasis that prizes growth, process, exploration, flexibility, variety, and versatility of response." Without naming it, Barish allies theatricality with "an ideal of movement" and "an ideal of plenitude," and in this, he offers an implicit explanation for theatricality's resistance to positive definition. More than a stable form literally identified with the stage, theatricality designates an "existentialist emphasis," an ethos or disposition which privileges terms like inconsistency and variety, terms which suggest a fundamental hostility to definition and identification in general.[20]

The theatricality that emerges from Barish's work—the "existentialist emphasis" on "flexibility, variety, versatility"—is much less recognizable in contemporary criticism than the beholder-centered aesthetic that Michael Fried defines in *Theatricality and Absorption.* Published in the year before Barish's book, Fried's study of the transformation in representational strategies in eighteenth-century French painting could easily provide a postscript to Barish's study of antitheatricalism. In Fried's account of theatricality's rejection by French painters and critics, he articulates an aesthetic antitheatricalism that complements the religious and moral traditions detailed by Barish; instead of charging theatricality with the production of inconstant or dangerously mixed identities, Fried describes an aesthetic tradition that rejected it as mannered, "ingratiating and mediocre." The privileged aesthetic of absorption creates the effect of realism precisely by purging the beholder from the scene of representation, and with the beholder's absence, painting becomes "once again a mode of access to truth and conviction." In this, Fried's formulation of the distinction between theatricality and absorption turns on a paradox; by incorporating a space for the beholder into the painting, theatricality becomes a "medium of dislocation and estrangement," while the fiction of the beholder's elimination and absence from the painting produces "absorption, sympathy, self-transcendence." Theatricality "estranges" through inclusion, while absorption fosters identification through an exclusion that relies on a partial forgetting of representation, mediation, and the relationship that aesthetics demands.[21]

There is an infamous—though likely apocryphal—anecdote of the nineteenth-century American stage, which suggests that what is at stake in this question of absorption and theatricality is a very material social relation. Described by Stendahl in his 1823 essay, "Racine et Shakespeare," and cited by Gérard Genette, Timothy J. Reiss, and Stanley Cavell (to name just a few),[22] the story goes something like this: a white American man (in Stendahl's version, a soldier; in Cavell's, a "Southern yokel") walks into a theater during a climactic scene in a production of *Othello*. Seeing that "Othello" is about to "kill" "Desdemona," the man pulls out a gun and shoots the lead actor, screaming (according to Stendahl), "It will never be said that in my presence a cursed nigger killed a white woman."[23] For Stendahl, this incident illustrates that the result of forgetting one's relationship to aesthetics is a far more powerful and destructive illusion, a kind of mystification that admits of no distance between actor and act: "The soldier had an *illusion*, believing in the truth of what was happening in the scene."[24] Misrecognizing theater, the man becomes absorbed in the actions and emotions portrayed onstage. But rather than experiencing these aesthetically, the man falls prey to what Stendahl calls a "perfect illusion"—something that, Genette notes, "one never goes to the theater looking for."[25] Genette cites Stendahl's story to ask how one measures the distance and level of concern that mark a relationship as aesthetic. He argues that theater demands neither distanced disinterest nor "underdistanced" overconcern with the scene, but "a *different* way of being concerned." For Genette, theater is exemplary of the kind of "imperfect illusion" which allows one to focus attention equally on multiple levels at once—"on the fictional action" represented as well as on the "missing tooth" of the actress performing. Both forms of attention are relevant to the "concern" demanded by theater, and both occur at once.[26] The act of beholding that Genette describes involves a kind of plural, divided attention that allows for multiple relations between spectator and scene to exist simultaneously—all without discomfort or conflict.

But discomfort may be too quickly dismissed in Genette's reading of Stendahl's anecdote. In a meditation on this story, Stanley Cavell argues that it is insufficient to call what happens onstage mere playacting or pretending, nor is it enough to rely on the stability of the distinction between actors and the characters they portray: "Othello is not pretending. Garrick is not pretending." And yet the condition of theater is the expectation that the spectator will sit and watch the tragedy complete itself with the knowledge that there is "nothing to be done" to change the outcome of the play. Cavell shifts the stakes of this anecdote away from questions of interestedness and credibility to questions of acknowledgment and agency, arguing that the "yokel" errs not because he can't tell theater from reality, but because he attempts to *do* something to theater. What Cavell highlights is that the theatrical introduces a potentially destabilizing relationship between two worlds which exist in parallel but without any clear, causal links between them. Theater puts the audience in the present of the characters, not in their presence. For Cavell, to be "concerned" with theater involves the recognition that "there is nothing to do . . . I have given over the time and space in which action is mine." Theater thus demands not simply a recognition of artifice or fiction, but a state of mind in which spectators understand that they are not in the presence of the characters who are present to them, at least not in the same way. They have entered into a time and space which is not their "own." In this, theater would force the beholder to recognize the end of an act that can be owned.[27] The power of theater thus lies in its pluralization of the present, in the introduction of two simultaneous present tenses running in parallel to each other—a simultaneity which Melville invokes in the opening lines of *The Confidence-Man*, as the man in cream colors steps onto the *Fidèle* "in the same moment with his advent" (3).[28]

In positing a "time and space" where one's actions are not appropriately one's own, Cavell forces the question of whether there is any space in which one's actions are. In other words, if the racist "yokel's" mistake lies in acting out of himself when he should have recognized that, in the theater, such action does not belong to him, do we then assume that any attempt to kill "Othello" outside of the theater would be somehow based in an authentic understanding of his relationship to them, theirs to each other, and all of their relationships to codes of racial and sexual difference? This story clearly poses much bigger problems than a misunderstanding of "theater," and in reading it, it may be most instructive to turn back to *The Confidence-Man*, a world in which everywhere is the place where "I have given over the space and the time in which action is mine." The consequences of this become explicit in chapter 6, when the one-legged man attempts to discredit the Black Guinea by convincing the other passengers that he is a fraud, while insisting at the same time that "to do is to act, so all doers are actors" (31). Working at cross-purposes (trying to have his authenticity and his humbug, too), the man turns the tables on Guinea's judges, himself included, undermining authenticity in general and subjecting them all to the very uncertainty to which their "discerning eyes" have exposed Guinea. If "to do is to act," then every deed is already overdone, neither reducible to any singular act nor owned by any singular agent. He who "performs acts" does something that is repeated and repeatable, thus for the doer who is also an actor, one's actions are never one's own, inside the theater or out.

For Stendahl, believing in the reality of theater is the far more dangerous illusion because it allows Othello's assailant to act out of a set of illusions that he has come to believe are authentic grounds for an action which he can own. The man doesn't fall prey to one "perfect illusion," but several: he folds the illusion of theater's reality into those which he has brought into the theater with him—specifically, a view of sexual relations violently conditioned by racism—and he acts out of all of these at once. What this suggests is that the risk of absorption lies less in an overidentification with a work of art, than in an overidentification with social roles, especially those conditioned by violence. Robert Pippin makes a similar point in a recent essay on Fried's influential concept. Where a "mannered" and "theatrical" way of living "depends upon being confirmed by others," an absorptive ontology involves a near complete identification, not with another person, but with the social roles one takes on: "This genuineness and authenticity is manifested . . . in a kind of absorption in (identification with) a social role, a nonalienated sense of my deeds as my own."[29] By emphasizing the alternative—that in or out of the theater, the man's acts are not fully his "own," or that as a "doer" he is just another "actor"—I in no way mean to evacuate responsibility for racial violence.

Instead, I want to highlight the potentially catastrophic stakes of absorption (Fried's word) or confidence (Melville's) in the truth of what one sees. Derrida, too, has a term for this nonalienated sense of ownership over one's acts; he calls this "ipseity," the "power, potency, sovereignty, or possibility implied in every 'I can.'" "Before any sovereignty of the state, of the nation-state, of the monarch, or, in democracy, of the people," he argues, lies "ipseity's" presumption of a self-identical and self-motivating power.[30] If absorption and confidence foster a belief in a nonalienated self-identity, these also enable the presumption of sovereignty that underlies everything from the shooting of Othello, to Guinea's near-hanging, even to the massacre and the riot at the Astor Place Opera House. Clearly, the problem of theater is not all that is at stake in instances where illusions of race and class difference are so violently reified. However, in theatricality's capacity to undermine the illusion of authenticity as a ground for self-identity, thereby eroding what Derrida calls "the power that *gives itself* its own law," there may nonetheless be found a remedy.[31]

As an aesthetic of estrangement, theatricality can certainly be read as coinciding to some degree with the formalist concepts of "making things strange," "defamiliarization," and "alienation." The strangeness of theatricality in *The Confidence-Man* does share with these the effects of revivifying life, restoring sensation, and combating the hegemony of habit that Victor Shklovsky outlines in his definition of "*ostranenie.*"[32] However, in Melville's text, theatricality and estrangement do these and more. For one thing, the estranging effects of theatricality are not tied to any singular point of view that detaches from the world and renders what it sees critically unfamiliar, as has sometimes been assumed by interpreters of Shklovsky.[33] Instead, *The Confidence-Man* deploys theatricality to make the entire world strange. This becomes clearest in the three chapters usually described as metafictional digressions or asides—chapters 14, 33, and 44—each of which addresses an invisible reader's demand for aesthetic realism by specifically undermining its key assumptions, from the transparency of character to its continuity over time, even, as Sharon Cameron argues, to the confinement of character within the bounds of what is called the personal.[34]

In the opacity and insistent textuality of these chapters, they perform the theatricality that they advocate. They point to each other and themselves and the other chapters of the text as writing that takes place on the page to produce effects for a reader.[35] As their titles indicate—"Worth the consideration of those to whom it may prove worth considering," "Which may pass for whatever it may prove to be worth"—these chapters are also structured as tautologies, whose repetitions yield dislocation and strangeness. Addressed to imaginary critics of the text's inconsistency and unreality, these chapters turn the alleged peculiarities of the text back on the world, ultimately asserting that the conventions of realism are the greatest fictions of all. The duck-billed beaver and the flying squirrel may perplex both naturalists and novelists, the narrator says in chapter 14, but there they are in the world. In chapter 33, the narrator makes the case that the value of fiction and theater does not lie in any "severe fidelity to real life," but in their capacity to produce "more reality," to "present another world but one to which we feel the tie" (*Confidence-Man*, 183). Read through these chapters, the theatrical estrangement that Melville theorizes, thematizes, and performs in *The Confidence-Man* is closer to what Svetlana Boym has outlined in her corrective reading of Shklovsky. Boym distinguishes between an estrangement *from* the world (which she compares to "Marxist world alienation" and "romantic introspection") and estrangement "for the sake of the world's renewal." Citing Hannah Arendt, Boym argues that an estrangement for the world entails "an acknowledgment of the integral human plurality that we must recognize within us and within others."[36] To put this in Melville's terms, theatricality confronts us with "more reality than real life itself" in order that we can live in a world of "strangers still more strange."

## More Real, More Strange: Theatricality and Democracy

Chapter 33, the second of the text's three "digressive" metafictional chapters, opens with a gesture of inclusion to which Fried's charges of "dislocation" and "estrangement" would undoubtedly apply: "But ere be given the rather grave story of Charlemont, a reply must in civility be made to a certain voice which methinks I hear, that, in view of past chapters . . . exclaims: How unreal all this is!" (*Confidence-Man*, 182). In many ways, this conjuring by the narrator of a reader's voice suggests the beginning of a confidence trick. Projecting doubt onto the reader, implicitly charging that reader with a want of confidence, the narrator creates an occasion to perform his own credibility and make a play for the reader's faith. After all, "distrust is a stage to confidence," according to the herb-doctor (83). But the chapter does not follow the established pattern for a confidence game, and instead of supporting his plea for confidence with an assertion of authenticity verifiable through reference to reality, the narrator proceeds to erode the distinction between real and unreal altogether. First, he reminds this reader that the entry into fiction is a deliberate attempt to enter into another, stranger world. ("Strange," he says, "that in a work of amusement, this severe fidelity to real life should be exacted by any one, who, by taking up such a work, sufficiently shows that he is willing to drop real life, and turn, for a time, to something different.") Then, he invokes the example of theater to insist that the contours of such a world can only take shape with an acknowledgment of its reciprocity. Hearing the voice of one who has expressed an intention to attend to the text, the narrator concedes the constituting presence of the reader within it. By allowing that voice to speak through the text, the narrator further signals that presence as bodily, sensory, and theatrical.

Theatricality begins with a work's assurance that its audience—whether beholder or reader—occupies a constitutive place within it, and as Melville's theatrical chapter develops its defense of fiction, the posited reader takes that place as deliberately as if seating herself before a stage: "There is another class, and with this class we side, who sit down to a work of amusement tolerantly as they sit at a play, and with much the same expectations and feelings." With this, the narrator converts the conceit of the chapter into the foundation of his argument, but within the narrator's apparently simple structure of simile—one reads in the manner that one watches—there is also a hint of simultaneity—one reads at the same time, "in the same moment" one watches, and one does not watch alone because the narrative "we" now sits by the reader-beholder's side. Initially, the narrator's claims rest heavily on ideas of expectation. If skepticism, disbelief, and doubt are the products of a demand for a "severe fidelity to real life," which the text can only fail to deliver, then shifting the expectations and pleasures of fiction alters the currency of exchange between reader and text. This shift begins with the narrator's reassurance that, instead of faith to real life, this "other class" has turned to theater in search of "scenes different," looking explicitly for something other than the "same old" public through which life itself has been so confidently defined:

> They look that fancy shall invoke scenes different from those of the same old crowd round the custom-house counter, and same old dishes on the boarding-house table, with characters unlike those of the same old acquaintances they meet in the same old way every day in the same old street. (182)

Same old, same old. The narrator derides the taste for realism, as the opening tone of reassurance yields to the tedious cant of the everyday, repeated *ad nauseam*. However, with this quintuple repetition of the "same," things begin to turn somewhat strange—especially given that the repetitions of this paragraph negatively echo the repetitions of the previous one: "*Strange*, that in a work of amusement, this severe fidelity to real life should be exacted . . . *strange* that any one should clamor for the thing he is weary of" (my italics). Meeting that excess of "strangeness" with even more of the "same," the third paragraph of this chapter begins to locate something more in theatricality than what might be expected. Although the defense of theatricality and fiction begins in an assurance that these offer their spectators and readers a satisfying, reciprocal exchange—provided they make no demands for realism—the excessiveness of the language in this passage gradually undermines the premise that anyone who looks to theater or fiction finds exactly what they seek:

> And as, in real life, the proprieties will not allow people to act out themselves with that unreserve permitted to the stage; so, in books of fiction, they look not only for more entertainment, but, at bottom, even for more reality than real life itself can show. Thus, though they want novelty, they want nature, too; but nature unfettered, exhilarated, in effect transformed. In this way of thinking, the people in a fiction, like the people in a play, must dress as nobody exactly dresses, talk as nobody exactly talks, act as nobody exactly acts. It is with fiction as with religion: it should present another world, but one to which we feel the tie. (183)

The "class" with which the narrator sides looks for "scenes different" from "real life" and the "same old," but the difference that they seek can only be found in an excess of the real—in "more reality than real life itself can show." "More reality" is not exactly the "same old," nor is it "real life itself"; instead, this surplus reality becomes something else entirely by opening up a gap between two things that continue to go by very similar names. Melville's language makes it difficult to paraphrase, but what he does here is to alter so fundamentally the relations of representation that "representation" may no longer be the word for it. "More reality" cannot simply be read as another name for a representation of the "real life itself" to which it points. The distinction that the text is making emerges from an excess of the defining quality of "real life," the very thing from which the theater-going class has sought to distance itself. What this "more real" describes is not simply the difference or "unreserve" of representation, but a growing separation of the real from itself that becomes visible only when one turns to the page as—in the manner of and at the same time as—one looks at theater.

As "more reality" detaches real life from itself, so it also opens a division within the subjects who turn to it, those who are forbidden by "proprieties" from acting out themselves with "that unreserved permitted to the stage." The effects of this estranging excess most implicate the very audience whose expectations it allegedly meets, first dividing them into acting selves and the selves out of whom they act, and then proffering that doubled, unreserved self as "more real." Theater thus confronts this class with a world where the "selves" that they do "act out" in "real life" are insufficient, less than a performance, less than the "nobody exactly" whom they watch on stage. While continuing to use the language of expectation, entertainment, and exchange, chapter 33 slowly erodes the grounds on which the identity of the self to itself rests.[37] Beyond "wantonness" and "sugaring," "humbug" and "amusement," theatricality exposes faith in the authenticity of the self as the ultimate confidence game. "Nobody exactly"—the odd inhabitant of the stage of whom the narrator speaks here—articulates the problem with unsettling exaction: Is "nobody exactly" the precise replication of no one? Or is it the inexact replication of someone? Either way, the search for an original to "nobody exactly" becomes fruitless, as Melville's language throughout this chapter turns precision into ambiguity. Bersani and Dutoit describe a similar tendency in Samuel Becket's prose. What they call "minutely inexact replications" send the reader in an endless search for originals that are, themselves, little more than "inaccurate replications" of something else. Thwarting referentiality through the strangeness of repetition, such a use of language does not "make sense" so much as it "makes us do." For one thing, it impedes the progress of narrative by forcing the reader to backtrack and reverse course; for another, this hunting for originals that aren't produces a model of reading through misrecognition that results in the dispersal and divestiture of "self."[38] In The Confidence-Man, this process of dispersal might be better described as a strange proliferation, the production of excesses that highlights nothing so much as the fact that the self is never singular. Weber argues that "acting is no longer reducible, if it ever was, to some one, for instance, to an actor or an agent as individual or as subject."[39] As chapter 33 shows, neither is reading or beholding.

Theatricality opens a world—"another world, but one to which we feel the tie"—which undermines the first-person singular with its excesses, but which nonetheless produces a first-person plural. Another "we" appears after the passage through "more reality" and "nobody exactly" have revealed the difference and strangeness to be found in excesses of the same. The first "we" of the chapter seems to mark a certain expansiveness claimed by the narrator ("and with this class we side"), but that "we" grows, gathering more and more to its "side," ultimately creating an audience staring together into this other world. What is this other "we"? Emerging from a chapter of persuasion, is it the "we" of some suspect consensus? Does it require a "they" who have yet to sit by "our" side? Coming as it does after the tautological phrase, "more reality than real life itself can show," has eroded the sameness of the "real" to itself, this "we" appears after the possibility of "identity" has also been compromised. Perhaps, then, this is a "we" of strangers, of "nobodies exactly" whose plurality can never be reduced to a common sameness. The fact that Melville's tautological phrasing here is an echo of an earlier instance in the text of a thing defined through an excess of its basic quality—the "strangers still more strange" who feed the riverboat *Fidéle* like the waters that feed the "Rio Janeiro fountain"—suggests just this possibility.

* * *

"[T]hough always full of strangers, she continually, in some degree, adds to, or replaces them with strangers still more strange" (*Confidence-Man*, 8). *The Confidence-Man* opens with an attempt to imagine a collection of strangers irreducible to any collective identifier. Contained without being defined, this collection is human—Chaucer's Canterbury pilgrims, a piebald parliament, even an Anacharsis Cloots Congress (9). It is vegetable—"as pine, beech, birch, ash, hackmatack, spruce, bass-wood, maple interweave their foliage in the natural wood; so these varieties of mortals blended their varieties of visage and garb." And always it remains a river—"whose type is the Mississippi itself." Opening with such a chain of figures, which the narrator implies is endless (especially in light of the text's final line), entry into the text is conditioned on the acceptance of the simultaneity and congruence of strangeness.[40] This strangeness is more than the difference or diversity of parts to each other; it is the strangeness of a whole to itself that arises from the endless and unanticipated entry of new parts. Melville's tautologies convey this more precisely than his chains of metaphor can: at once, "strangers still more strange" and "more reality than real life itself" name and perform through inexact replication a proliferation, a dispersal, and a pluralization that estrange. As the text propagates a strangeness in and through each chapter, what it imagines through its own aesthetic practice is nothing less than an ethics and a politics of living plurally.

To make this point more concretely—and to emphasize the congruency of the aesthetic with the political in Melville's twin phrases—I want to turn to a remark of Hannah Arendt's early in *The Human Condition*, where she roots the possibility of human agency in a conception of plurality that reads like a meditation on Melville's "nobody exactly":

> Plurality is the condition of human action because we are all the same, that is, human, in such a way that nobody is ever the same as anyone else who ever lived, lives, or will live.[41]

The only human "sameness" is found in the shared strangeness of everyone to each other—past, present, and future—thus everybody is the same as "nobody exactly." To acknowledge this strangeness, Arendt suggests, is to understand life itself as plural, and it entails a duty to take only those actions that work for the good of that plurality through the strangers to come: "the task [is] to provide and prepare the world for, to foresee and reckon with, the constant influx of newcomers who are born into the world as strangers." In Melville's terms, regarding the world theatrically—that is, as "another world, but one to which we feel the tie"— makes it possible for everyone to be "nobody exactly"—precise copies of no one and inexact replications of everyone. Such an orientation, in turn, pluralizes everyone. It makes everyone strange to themselves, and it creates space for the arrival of "strangers still more strange," those strangers whom "we" must anticipate but will never know. With her emphasis on futurity, on preparing for the plural tides to come, Arendt also highlights the significance of the future to Melville's text and opens yet another reading of its enigmatic and long-debated final line: "Something further may follow of this Masquerade." If theatricality does make possible such strange pluralizations, what "may follow" from this masquerade is the possibility of living such a future.

Arendt's emphasis on the strangeness of the future as the basis for a democratic ethics and a democratic politics is by no means utopian or messianic. It marks for her the foundation of political activity by making "natality and not mortality . . . the central category of the political."[42] Certainly, a politics conditioned by natality and the strangeness of the future, over mortality and the power of life and death, runs counter to the assertions of a sovereignty that claims the right both to decide upon and to suspend exception. Indeed, as Arendt asserts later in the text, "sovereignty is contradictory to the very condition of plurality."[43]

To imagine a democratic public of strangers, who act not out of a sense of identity with each other, nor out of a belief in the singularity of the present, but with a knowledge of the "task" that Arendt defines as preparation for the strangers to come, is to imagine a public unburdened by the power of death with which sovereignty charges it. It is to imagine a democracy more radical than seems possible either in Melville's day or in our own. In March 1857, one month before the April 1st publication of *The Confidence-Man*, the burden of that sovereignty became acute with Taney's majority ruling in the *Dred Scott* decision. Enjoining the return of fugitives to the South and predicating the "sovereign people" on the constitutive exception of all blacks, free and enslaved, from the political community of the United States, Taney's democracy was "the truly warning spectacle of a man hanged by his friends."

When Tocqueville marveled over the consequences of a sameness so profound he could only speak of it redundantly as the "same likeness [that] leads [Americans] to place almost unlimited confidence in the judgments of the public" (*Democracy in America*, 435), he seemed to recognize it as a dead-end for democracy, the root of that "thing" which would blanket the public sphere with power and assume for its subjects "all the cares of living" by creating for some "a life worse than death." In rethinking democratic belonging as the promise of strangeness, Melville reimagines it, not as a zero-sum game of life or death, but as the radical and irreducible plurality of what is yet to come. To say that this plurality of "strangers still more strange" depends upon another world, one of "more reality than real life itself can show," is not to remove *The Confidence-Man* from history so much as it is to recognize the historical urgency of his aesthetic practice, to see in it a speculative politics that outruns even Tocqueville's.

# Notes

Introduction

1. Douglass, *Autobiographies*, 319.

2. Most famously, in the passage on slave songs reproduced from his 1845 narrative, Douglass designates no fewer than six positions from which the scene of slaves
singing on allowance day might be viewed, ending with the impossible position of a
spectator who, "in silence," stands in the woods to "thoughtfully analyze the sounds
that shall pass through the chambers of his soul" (*My Bondage and My Freedom*, in
*Autobiographies*, 185).

3. Douglass, *My Bondage and My Freedom*, 185 (first quote), 319 (second quote).
The beating of Douglass's Aunt Esther is, as Saidiya Hartman notes, the most fre-
quently cited and reproduced of these (see Hartman, *Scenes of Subjection*, 3–4; see also
Franchot, "The Punishment of Esther," 141–65).

4. Douglass, *Narrative of the Life of Frederick Douglass*, in *Autobiographies*, 18.

5. Douglass, *My Bondage and My Freedom*, 321–22.

6. Arendt, *The Human Condition*, 27–28.

7. Habermas, *The Structural Transformation of the Public Sphere*, 82.

8. Schudson, "Was There Ever a Public Sphere"; Fliegelman, *Declaring Independence*; Looby, *Voicing America*; Ruttenburg, *Democratic Personality*; Hill and Montag, *Masses, Classes, and the Public Sphere*; Berlant, *The Queen of America Goes to
Washington City*; Warner, *Letters of the Republic*; Warner, *Publics and Counterpublics*;
Castiglia, "Abolition's Racial Interiors and the Making of White Civic Depth."

9. See, in particular, Pease, *Visionary Compacts*; Berlant, *The Queen of America
Goes to Washington City*; and Castronovo, *Necro Citizenship*.

10. Novak, *The People's Welfare*, 9 (Novak's italics).

11. Ryan, *Civic Wars*, 8–9.

12. Ibid., 8.

13. Lefort, *Democracy and Political Theory*, 14.

14. Ibid., 15.

15. Toqueville, *Democracy in America*, 60.

16. Ibid.

17. Schmitt, *Political Theology*, 5; Foucault, *Society Must Be Defended*; Agamben, *Homo Sacer*, 28.

18. Schmitt, *Political Theology*, 5. Schmitt's account of sovereignty is emphatically a defense of the power that decides upon exception and declares the emergency suspension of law. Written in the early 1920s, *Political Theology* has often been read through the lens of Schmitt's later participation in the Nazi government after the disintegration of the Weimar Republic. In contrast to Schmitt's defense, Foucault, Agamben, and Derrida all write against the principle of a singular or unified sovereign power. As Foucault argues, "We should be looking for a new right that is both antidisciplinary and emancipated from the principle of sovereignty" (Foucault, *Society Must Be Defended*, 40).

19. Schmitt, *Political Theology*, 36.

20. See Schmitt, *Political Theology*, 48–49. Nancy Ruttenburg's *Democratic Personality* effectively undercuts Schmitt's characterization of democracy's equation of the people's voice with God's as a simple "aftereffect" of European political theologies. Uncovering the roots of democracy's invocation of invisible and divine power in Puritan theological debates and spectral evidence theory, Ruttenburg then traces its persistence in U.S. democratic discourse into the nineteenth century, in particular through the form and voice of the American novel (see Ruttenburg, *Democratic Personality*, esp. 180–89).

21. Foucault, *Society Must Be Defended*, 36–46. See also Foucault, *Ethics*, 59–61.

22. Ibid., 254.

23. Ibid., 259

24. Agamben, *Homo Sacer*, 142.

25. Ibid., 7–9.

26. Ibid., 9–10. Paul Downes characterizes the ambivalent place of "bare life" in the Declaration of Independence, the Bill of Rights, and the Constitution as "an ongoing confrontation between the discourse of the subject outside and before the law, the subject of the Bill of Rights, and the subject of the law's structures and concealments" in the Constitution (see Downes, *Democracy, Revolution, and Monarchism in Early American Literature*, 10).

27. For examples of what Derrida terms the "autoimmune" response, ranging from the suspension of the 1992 elections in Algeria to the post-9/11 United States and the homeland security state, see Derrida, *Rogues*, 33–34; on the circularity of sovereignty, see ibid., 13.

28. See Lefort, *Democracy and Political Theory*, 17. Lefort links this empty place to his assertion that power in Tocqueville's account of U.S. democracy belongs to no one, and contrasts this model with the monarchic embodiment of power.

29. Tocqueville is rather insistent on this point, repeatedly adding "in America" and "there" to his account of the sovereignty of the people (Tocqueville, *Democracy in America*, 58–60).

30. Douglass, *My Bondage and My Freedom*, in *Autobiographies*, 184.

31. Novak, *The People's Welfare*, 241–42. Novak follows historians like Morton Keller in considering Lincoln's presidency as heralding the emergence of a larger, more

forceful, and more central U.S. state in the second half of the century, but he does not assume that this state emerged out of a vacuum of sovereign power. He makes a clear distinction between acts of local "police power" and acts of state sovereignty, which he traces through the legal justifications made for regulation. In the latter chapters of his work, he argues that a pattern of justifying regulation by recourse to public health and morality in the antebellum era was gradually replaced by a recourse to state sovereignty and command.

32. See: Keller, *Affairs of State*, 21.

33. Agamben, *State of Exception*, 20–21.

34. Delany, *Blake; or, the Huts of America*, 61. Delany's Judge Ballard loosely paraphrases Roger Taney's majority decision in the *Dred Scott* case.

35. *Dred Scott v. Sandford*, 60 U.S. (19 How.) 393–633 (1857). Taney's decision is also excerpted in Finkelman, *Dred Scott v. Sandford: A Brief History with Documents*, 58. Not surprisingly, the Taney court was at odds with Lincoln throughout the early portion of the war, opposing the "activist character of the wartime government," as well as the war itself (see Keller, *Affairs of State*, 17).

36. *Dred Scott v. Sandford*, 405. Also at stake in Taney's ruling, of course, is the question of state sovereignty with respect to federal sovereignty. As Priscilla Wald points out, the *Dred Scott* case involved many of the questions of federal sovereignty over U.S. territories that the Marshall court had left unresolved in *Cherokee Nation v. State of Georgia* (1831) (see Wald, *Constituting Americans*, 40–41).

37. Best, *The Fugitive's Properties*, 81–85. Best reveals, in Taney's legal positivism and insistence upon the framers' intent, an almost hallucinatory quality, as the court finds, in words "too plain to be misunderstood," figurations of human property that, Best demonstrates, are nowhere present in the text of the Constitution: "In the poetics of property circa 1857, the work of the skilled translator on the word is hardly discernible from that of the skilled master on the slave" (ibid., 85). Tracing the roots of Taney's positivism to Hobbes, Best also shows how a Hobbesian conception of the sovereignty of law—its unity and homogeneity—guides the Court's insistence on the transparency of the text to the intent of its framers (ibid., 78–79).

38. *Dred Scott v. Sandford*, 423. In distinguishing these terms, I mean to suggest something quite specific: if assumptions of "exclusion" have focused public sphere theory on citizenship and the limited nature of political community, "exception" allows for those constitutive absences to be recognized as essential and shaping, which also leads to a focus on a more expansively defined public, one which contains and stages the battles over the sovereignty of political community. See Agamben's discussion of exception in Blanchot, Deleuze and Guattari (Agamben, *Homo Sacer* 17–20).

39. *Dred Scott v. Sandford*, 427.

40. As Best shows, Taney's ruling also burdens the fugitive, who is figured by law as one whose labor is owed to another. This figure of indebtedness creates a "ruse of consent" that confers on the escaped slave a form of consent through obligation, thereby masking the law's injury and theft of the slave's property in himself (Best, *The Fugitive's Properties*, 83). Also see Saidiya Hartman's discussion of the "burdened individuality" of the emancipated slave who becomes, through the legal debates over the Reconstruction Amendments, "the responsible and encumbered freeperson" (Hartman, *Scenes of Subjection*, 176–77).

41. Child, *An Appeal*, 121.

42. Ibid., 53.

43. Beaumont, *Marie; or, Slavery in the United States*, 73.

44. "Fate," in *Ralph Waldo Emerson: Essays and Poems*, 771. The passage begins with an even more explicit reference to death, making of this complicity a kind of cannibalism: "You have just dined, and, however scrupulously the slaughter-house is concealed in the graceful distance of miles, there is complicity."

45. Child, *Letters from New-York*, 145 (Child's italics).

46. Dickens, *American Notes, For General Circulation*, 252.

47. Tocqueville, *Democracy in America*, 255.

48. Foucault, *Discipline and Punish*, 216.

49. An anomaly of prison reform which Tocqueville also notes (see Tocqueville, *Democracy in America*, 250).

50. Joan Dayan makes a similar point in an essay that traces the legal history of solitary confinement through attainder and slave law, something I discuss in chapter 2 (see Dayan, "Legal Slaves and Civil Bodies," 64).

51. Reiss, *The Showman and the Slave*, 126–27. Reiss's study of P. T. Barnum's infamous Joice Heth exhibition gives a detailed account of how such phenomena achieved the status of mass cultural events. His reading of Heth's public autopsy as a "spectacle of inclusion and exclusion, masculinity and femininity, whiteness and blackness, social life and social death" provides an exemplary case study for what I call "democracy's spectacle" (ibid., 128).

52. Hartman, *Scenes of Subjection*, 26–28.

53. Debord, *The Society of the Spectacle*, 16.

54. Ibid., 15–22 (quotes at 15, 17–18, 22). For Tocqueville's description of democratic subjects as atomized and isolated, see his *Democracy in America*, 506.

55. DeBord, *Society of the Spectacle*, 14–19 (quotes at 14, 18, 19).

56. David Lloyd and Paul Thomas also make the point that the Debordian spectacle has a long prehistory—one which they trace through the positing of the spectator as the "exemplary, even heroic, type of political subjectivity," beginning with Rousseau (see Lloyd and Thomas, *Culture and the State*, 31–32).

57. This tendency is particularly evident in the first chapter of Donald Pease's *Visionary Compacts*, in which he responds to what he calls the "Cold War consensus": an emphasis by a generation of post–World War II scholars on individualism, which "equated any group interest with the demands of an oppressive power" (25), and created the somewhat contradictory pairing of a despotic general will with a passive public of spectators under a charismatic leader (30). Though Pease rejects the reliance by those critics on concepts of individualism and negative freedom, he preserves their association of "spectacle" with the passive crowd and the depoliticized public sphere.

58. Pease, *Visionary Compacts*, 30.

59. There are many excellent scholarly studies of the riots, beginning with the classic accounts of Richard Moody (*The Astor Place Riot*), and, more recently, that of Lawrence Levine (in *Highbrow/Lowbrow: The Emergence of Cultural Hierarchy in America*). But see also McConachie, *Melodramatic Formations*, 143–53; Lott, *Love and Theft*, 85; Ackerman, *The Portable Theater*, 34, 101–8; and Berthold, "Class Acts," 429–61.

60. The "hiss" became a central point of contention in the bickering between Macready and Forrest that was reported in the Philadelphia press in November 1848,

not because Forrest denied having done it, but because he gleefully admitted it (see Ackerman, *The Portable Theater,* 103).

61. *New York Herald,* 9 May 1849.

62. *New York Tribune,* 12 May 1849; *New York Herald,* 9 May 1849.

63. Berthold, "Class Acts," 432–40. Berthold also effectively traces the ambivalence of such distinctions through the shifting loyalties of the "Young America" circle, which included Duyckinck and Melville. Early boosters of Forrest's career as the first great American tragedian, their nationalism appeared to cede to other cultural and aesthetic judgments by the time they signed the Macready petition.

64. *New York Herald* 9 May 1849; *New York Tribune,* 9 May 1849.

65. Lott, *Love and Theft,* 65–67, 85. Lott's work dissects the intricate intersections of slavery and racial politics in popular theater and working-class culture as these played out in the Astor Place Riots.

66. *New York Herald,* 9 May 1849. Douglass was in New York that week for a meeting of the American Anti-Slavery Society.

67. *New York Tribune,* 9 May 1849.

68. *New York Tribune,* 12 May 1849.

69. Henry Bellows, *A Sermon Occasioned by the Late Riot in New York Preached in the Church of the Divine Unity on Saturday Morning, May 13, 1849* (New York: C. S. Francis, 1849), quoted in Berthold, "Class Acts," 349.

70. The events at Astor Place are often described in terms that concede one side or another—as either a riot or a massacre, with the antagonism between these groups characterized in terms of either democracy versus aristocracy or as a misguided populism versus the rule of law. Indeed, historians of Astor Place tend to become partisans of the actors involved. Those who sympathize with Forrest's appeal and his fan base generally accept the rioters' claims to "popular voice" (see Lott, *Love and Theft*; and Levine, *Highbrow/Lowbrow*), while those who defend Macready tend to do so out of desire to explain Melville's participation in what seemed an uncharacteristically classist petition (see Berthold, "Class Acts"; and Ackerman, *The Portable Theater*).

71. See Canetti, *Crowds and Power.*

72. My definition of the spectacular public draws in some ways on the relationships between crowd and public modeled by Ed White in his study of the colonial American backcountry (*The Backcountry and the City*), and by John Plotz in his study of the crowd in Victorian literature (*The Crowd: British Literature and Public Politics*). The public sphere does not precede such defining events as the Paxton riots (White) or the Chartist demonstrations (Plotz). Instead, it comes into being almost circularly in and through those events, by virtue of "what would come to count as public . . . at all" (Plotz, *The Crowd,* 10).

73. "Metonymy, *n.*," *Oxford English Dictionary,* 2nd ed., 1989. See *OED Online,* Oxford University Press, 7 July 2009, http://dictionary.oed.com/cgi/entry/00307897. I thank Bret Benjamin for pointing this connection out to me.

74. See Agamben, *Homo Sacer,* 84.

75. Tocqueville describes the part-for-whole structure of representational democracy this way: "In the United States, as in all countries where the people reign, the majority rules in the name of the people" (Tocqueville, *Democracy in America,* 173).

76. Thoreau, *Walden and Civil Disobedience,* 235.

77. Agamben, *Homo Sacer,* 9–10; Tocqueville, *Democracy in America,* 692.

78. Trish Loughran calls this the "golden age of U.S. nation building" (see Loughran, *The Republic in Print*, 304).

79. See Beaumont and Tocqueville, *On the Penitentiary System in the United States and Its Application in France*, 55. On the problem of "contagion" as it was addressed by U.S. penal reformers, see Meranze, *Laboratories of Virtue*, 87–127.

80. Dickens, *American Notes*, 111. As Thomas Dumm has argued, echoing the claims of Dickens and others, these institutions were "more, not less horrible for having been constituted as humanitarian reform" (see Dumm, *Democracy and Punishment*, 4).

81. Dayan, "Legal Slaves and Civil Bodies," 69. Recently, Dayan has also shown how the category of "cruel and unusual punishment" outlined in the Eighth Amendment to the Constitution has been interpreted so narrowly and with such discretion that abuse and torture throughout the penitentiary system in the United States have become "routine and entirely familiar." With this, Dayan demonstrates—contrary to Agamben's assertions in *Homo Sacer* (see p. 20)—that the prison does indeed represent a space where sovereign exception has found an enduring location within U.S. law and culture (see Dayan, *The Story of Cruel and Unusual*, 4–5).

82. For comprehensive studies of antebellum theater culture, see Ackerman, *The Portable Theater*; Bank, *Theatre Culture in America*; Levine, *Highbrow/Lowbrow*; Lott, *Love and Theft*; and McConachie, *Melodramatic Formations*.

83. Ryan, *Civic Wars*, 44–45.

84. Forrest's biographer notes that lines from two of his most famous roles— "Metamora cannot lie!" and Spartacus's war cry, "We will make the Romans howl!"— became catchphrases (see Alger, *The Life of Edwin Forrest*, 1:245).

85. Reiss, *The Showman and the Slave*, 126–27.

## 1 / "The thing is new": Sovereignty and Slavery in *Democracy in America*

1. Tocqueville, *Democracy in America*, 252–53 [hereafter cited in text].

2. See Derrida's discussion of democratic auto-immunity in Algeria (*Rogues*, 33–34).

3. For an example of the former, see Pease, "Tocqueville's Democratic Thing; or, Aristocracy in America." For an example of the latter, see Mary Ryan's introduction to *Civic Wars*.

4. Ryan, *Civic Wars*, 8.

5. Denning, *Culture in the Age of Three Worlds*, 205.

6. Political theorist Thomas Dumm describes this long passage as "among the masterpieces of political and social analysis" (see Dumm, *Democracy and Punishment*, 128).

7. Tocqueville's phrase—"the thing is new"—is echoed in the title of Pease's essay on Tocqueville, "Tocqueville's Democratic Thing; or, Aristocracy in America." While Pease's Lacanian analysis of the "thing" to which Tocqueville cathects is highly evocative, he does not discuss Tocqueville's own absorption with a "thing" at the end of *Democracy in America*, and Pease's "thing" is ultimately quite different from Tocqueville's. For Pease, analyzing a tradition of Tocqueville's reception as a celebrant of American exceptionalism, the "thing" becomes the alleged uniqueness of democracy in the U.S. that has eluded the French (30–32). Clearly, when Tocqueville comes to his own "thing" late in his text, he is far more skeptical about the forms of power that go

by the name of democracy, and far less liable to those readings which regard him as an uncritical apologist for U.S. political forms.

8. "Après avoir pris ainsi tour à tour dans ses puissantes mains chaque individu, et l'avoir pétri à sa guise, le souverain étend ses bras sur la société toute entière; il en couvre la surface d'un réseau de petits règles compliquées, minutieuses, et uniformes . . . ." (Tocqueville, *De la démocratie en Amérique*, ed. Eduardo Nolla, 2:266 [my translation]). The George Lawrence (Anchor/Doubleday) translation chooses "government" as the subject, rather than "sovereign," which has led even the most insightful readers of this passage to accept an equation of this power with a centralized state, a reading that somewhat oversimplifies what Tocqueville is theorizing through this tableau.

9. Indeed, in a footnote to this passage in the Nolla edition, the editors quote a manuscript note of Tocqueville's which says, "le despotisme administrative dont je parle est indépendente des institutions representatives, liberals, ou révolutionnaires, en un mot du pouvoir politique" (Tocqueville, *De la démocratie en Amérique*, ed. Eduardo Nolla, 2:266). In the note, Tocqueville seems to refine his idea of an administrative power that would become even stronger and more pervasive as political powers (kings, representative assemblies, etc.) waned, sometimes calling it an administrative despotism, sometimes an "administrative machine" (ibid.).

10. "Each of us puts in common his person and his whole power under the separate direction of the general will; and in return we receive each member as an indivisible part of the whole" (Rousseau, *The Social Contract and Discourse on the Origin of Inequality*, 18–19).

11. In a stirring reading of this chapter (discussed further in the next section), Dumm shows how the majority tyranny made possible by popular sovereignty develops seamlessly into what he calls "democratic despotism" and centralization in the final section of *Democracy in America*. Dumm accepts that the site of this unnamed power is a centralized government, and he argues that it develops as a result of the tendency toward uniformity, which centralization both profits from and encourages: "People come to seek an image of themselves in the political state. The state comes to inform them of what is right and wrong, of what they are capable of doing and failing to do" (Dumm, *Democracy and Punishment*, 133). What is ultimately at stake for Dumm—and more useful, I think, for his provocative and enabling reading of Tocqueville—is his focus on the mechanics of this power, its disciplinary roots and its operation on "the modern soul" (134).

12. Foucault, *Society Must Be Defended*, 243–44.

13. Ibid., 253.

14. Ibid., 247.

15. In the Doubleday edition, the translation reads: "It covers the whole of social life with a network of petty, complicated rules that are both minute and uniform" (Tocqueville, *Democracy in America*, 692).

16. Dominick LaCapra makes the point in *History and Reading* that Tocqueville and Foucault echo each other particularly strongly through their analytical methods, approaching questions of power through "the relations among customs, institutions, practices, affect, and thought," and tracing the "genealogy of practices and discourse analysis" (11). One of LaCapra's goals in calling for a "Tocquevillean" model of reading that stands with a "Foucauldian" model is to emphasize the radical potential of

Tocqueville's critical method that is too often suppressed by long-standing efforts to secure his place within a liberal tradition (9).

17. Foucault, *Society Must Be Defended*, 247, 254. There is a distinction in Foucault's lectures between what he calls "the juridical notion of sovereignty," in the *précis* for the lectures (published in *Ethics, Subjectivity, Truth*), and the right to kill, which he describes in the final lecture (in *Society Must Be Defended*). In the *précis*, juridical sovereignty refers to the social contract under which subjects consent to be ruled. Foucault argues that such a model "presupposes the individual as a subject of natural rights or individual powers; it aims to account for the ideal genesis of the state; and it makes law the fundamental manifestation of power" (*Ethics*, 59). Although Foucault argues that a juridical concept of sovereignty which presupposes the subject is not compatible with "a concrete analysis of power relations" (59) Tocqueville's definition of popular sovereignty in the U.S. as "the cause and the end of all things" is nevertheless the beginning of just such a "concrete analysis." First, Tocqueville does not assume that anything precedes the constitution of the sovereign, and second, he demonstrates that juridical and political sovereignty are very closely aligned in the United States (I'll discuss this further in following section). On Foucault's interest in norm rather than law in these lectures, see also Stoler, *Race and the Education of Desire*, 64.

18. Habermas, *The Structural Transformation of the Public Sphere*, 82, 137–40.

19. Schudson, "Was There Ever a Public Sphere?," 146; Fliegelman, *Declaring Independence*, 128; Ruttenburg, *Democratic Personality*, 3–4; Looby, *Voicing America*. Fliegelman and Ruttenburg have addressed the reliance on print forms and rationality in Habermas, calling into question the assumption that publics only emerge through deliberation and debate among the enfranchised citizenry, and in particular the assertion that the abstraction of print is essential to such a sphere. Paul Downes has sought to reconcile the apparent split in the scholarship of the Early Republic, arguing that the subject of democracy is a subject of both print and oratory. This contradiction is emblematic, for him, of the ambivalence within the "two bodies" of a democratic subject that emerges as the mirror image of the very monarch whom it is imagined to oppose (Downes, *Democracy, Revolution, and Monarchism in Early American Literature*, 10).

20. Hill and Montag, *Masses, Classes, and the Public Sphere*, 6–8.

21. Warner, *Publics and Counterpublics*, 68. Michael Warner's recent work seeks both to defend the usefulness of Habermas for the analysis of the American public sphere and to clarify Warner's own difference from him, specifically through the theorization of "counterpublics": publics which are constituted in explicit critique and opposition to the totalizing, normative public sphere.

22. Ibid., 65–124.

23. Warner clearly acknowledges the possibility of such domination, seeing in the subject's participation in public life a constant movement between identification and alienation, but he leaves open the question of whether a dominant or coercive public is a perversion or a perfection of the classic public sphere (ibid., 176– 86).

24. See Berlant, *The Queen of America Goes to Washington City*; Dayan, "Legal Slaves and Civil Bodies"; Castiglia, "Abolition's Racial Interiors and the Making of White Civic Depth."

25. Castiglia, "Abolition's Racial Interiors and the Making of White Civic Depth," 34.

26. Reading this section of *Democracy in America*, Claude Lefort writes: "Power was embodied in the prince, and it therefore gave society a body. And because of this, a latent but effective knowledge of what one meant to the other existed throughout the social. This model reveals the revolutionary and unprecedented feature of democracy. The locus of power becomes an empty place" (Lefort, *Democracy and Political Theory*, 17).

27. See Dumm, *Democracy and Punishment*, 34.

28. Ibid., 15 (quoting Foucault).

29. Ibid., 115.

30. Ibid., 120. The investment of Americans in problems of perfectibility and citizenship explains for Dumm how prison reform came to be the intensely contested question that Tocqueville and Beaumont encountered in the 1830s, as the debates over the New York and Pennsylvania systems intensified. Despite the fact that there was near consensus on the principle of isolation as the basic element of all penal discipline, Dumm argues that the difference between the Pennsylvania and New York models came down to a fundamental choice between a system that sought to reform the "inner" dispositions of inmates and one that aimed to alter their exterior habits (119). In tracing the influence of both systems on Tocqueville's conception of democratic discipline, Dumm privileges New York's Auburn Prison over the solitary system of Eastern State. Where the isolation of Eastern State might exacerbate tendencies toward individualism, Dumm argues, the Auburn model provides Tocqueville with an apt image for the subjection of men under conditions of equality. However, in asserting Auburn as Tocqueville's model for the "despotism" that threatens democracies, Dumm ultimately downplays the role of interior formation as a mechanism of democratic power and focuses on the reform of subjects through behavior and habit.

31. Ibid., 140 (quoting Tocqueville).

32. Lefort, *Democracy and Political Theory*, 17.

33. Ibid., 17–19.

34. Downes, *Democracy, Revolution, and Monarchism in Early American Literature*, 9–12.

35. "[M]ais dans les républiques démocratiques, ce ne point ainsi que procède la tyrannie; elle laisse le corps et va droit à l'âme" (Tocqueville, *De la démocratie en Amérique*, ed. Eduardo Nolla, 1:200).

36. This is what Dumm emphasizes in his reading of the passage (*Democracy and Punishment*, 134).

37. Agamben, *Homo Sacer*, 28 (Agamben's italics).

38. Ibid., 6.

39. Ibid., 124.

40. This is what Downes calls "the indissociable but never quite identical coincidence of the general subject of rights and laws . . . and the individual citizen" (Downes, *Democracy, Revolution, and Monarchism in Early American Literature*, 55).

41. "Il ne persuade pas ses croyances, il les impose et les fait pénétrer dans les âmes par une sorte de pression immense de l'esprit de tous sur l'intelligence de chacun" (Tocqueville, *De la démocratie en Amérique*, ed. Eduardo Nolla, 2:22).

42. Denning reads the absurdity of Tocqueville's claims about "equality of condition" as "simply wrong," and suggests that the text's central premise ought to be rejected (Denning, *Culture in the Age of Three Worlds*, 199). But such a move risks missing

the significance of what Tocqueville calls its "generative" function. Below, I show how "equality of conditions" might be rejected as an empirical fact in Tocqueville's study, while still being read as generative of the kind of ideological fantasy that structures the "reality" of social relations.

43. Schoolman, *Reason and Horror*, 272–76 (quoting Tocqueville).

44. Lefort, *Democracy and Political Theory*, 189, 195, 15.

45. Perhaps even in terms of a sublime object of ideology: Slavoj Žižek describes a duality—specifically, a split between a material and an immaterial, or transcendent, corporeality—as the basic character of the "sublime object," and he gives the examples of money and the tortured body of Sade's Juliette. "Equality" might be said to operate in this way, insofar as its ostensibly material quality—its alleged description of the material and political conditions of democratic society—cedes to its far more potent immaterial quality—the idol or pedagogy that forms democratic citizens (Žižek, *The Sublime Object of Ideology*, 18). See also LaCapra's reading of liberty in Tocqueville; for LaCapra, it is "liberty" that carries this imaginary, iconic status, not equality (LaCapra, *History and Reading*, 106–7).

46. Žižek, *The Sublime Object of Ideology*, 32–33.

47. "Ces objets, qui touchent à mon sujet, n'y entrent pas" (Tocqueville, *De la démocratie en Amérique*, ed. Eduardo Nolla, 1:246). Lawrence translates this as "These objects are like tangents to my subject" (316).

48. A distinction that Rey Chow, paraphrasing Foucault, describes as follows: "Some humans have been cast as objects, while other humans have been given the privilege of becoming subjects" (Chow, *The Protestant Ethnic and the Spirit of Capitalism*, 2).

49. Tocqueville's 1841 "Essay on Algeria" is a brutally calculating blueprint for war in Algeria: "Domination is the necessary means for achieving tranquil possession of the coast and a colonization of part of the territory" (Tocqueville, *Writings on Empire and Slavery*, 65). Jennifer Pitts's introduction to this volume thoroughly contextualizes Tocqueville's writings on empire with his work as an early theorist of liberal democracy. See also LaCapra, *History and Reading*, 92–93. I owe a debt of gratitude to Robert Fanuzzi, whose 2006 American Studies Association presentation on Tocqueville's Algerian writings alerted me to the crucial link between *Democracy in America* and the Algerian writings.

50. Pitts, Introduction to *Writings on Empire and Slavery*, xvi.

51. Tocqueville was fairly explicit about this: "I do not think France can seriously think of leaving Algeria. In the eyes of the world such an abandonment would be the clear indication of our decline" (Tocqueville, *Writings on Empire and Slavery*, 59).

52. LaCapra, *History and Reading*, 94.

53. Etienne Balibar's work on the "cycle of historical reciprocity" between nationalism and racism is instructive here. Cautioning against a reduction to simple causality or formal dependence, he argues that racism and nationalism are better understood in terms of a mutually reinforcing relationship that shifts over time (see Balibar and Wallerstein, *Race, Nation, Class*, 52–53).

54. See Arthur Riss's disciplined historicizing of the U.S. liberal tradition. While liberalism may posit itself as a "coherent metaphysical system" for all time, Riss argues, its central subject, the "person," is constantly being produced through history according to shifting imperatives. For this reason, he argues, nineteenth-century Americans

did not simply deny the latent "personhood" of the enslaved, thereby causing "social death." The assumption of U.S. law was that the enslaved were dead, because the category of personhood which would bring them to life did not apply. Riss argues that the reading of U.S. literature as "haunted" by the repressed personhood of the enslaved represents the persistence of liberal faith in the transcendence of the category of the person (see Riss, *Race, Slavery, and Liberalism in Nineteenth-Century American Literature*, 8–13, 28–30).

55. Denning notes that one-third of all the anecdotes in both volumes appear in this chapter (Denning, *Culture in the Age of Three Worlds*, 204).

56. Jefferson's haunting of this chapter becomes most peculiarly evident in an anecdote Tocqueville tells of "an old man who had lived in illicit intercourse with one of his Negro women. He had several children by her, who became their father's slaves as soon as they entered the world. . . . I saw him prey to the agony of despair, and then I understood how nature can revenge the wounds made by the laws" (Tocqueville, *Democracy in America*, 362).

57. Jefferson, *Notes on the State of Virginia*, 145.

58. Foucault, *Society Must Be Defended*, 15.

59. Melville, *The Confidence-Man*, 3.

60. While Tocqueville—along with the French Situationist Guy DeBord—merits only parenthetical mention in Agamben's study, he clearly places Tocqueville in a genealogy of figures who are theorizing the politicization of life that leads to Foucault and Agamben himself (Agamben, *Homo Sacer*, 10).

61. See Debord, *The Society of the Spectacle*, 12, 19.

62. Schoolman, *Reason and Horror*, 285; Lefort, *Democracy and Political Theory*, 198.

## 2 / Color, Race, and the Spectacle of Opinion in Beaumont's *Marie*

1. *Marie; or, Slavery in the United States*, trans. Barbara Chapman, 4 [hereafter cited in text]. First published in two volumes in 1835, Beaumont's *Marie*, went through five printings in France and was awarded the Prix Montoyn by the Académie Française, but it was not published in book form in America until 1958, when an abridged version of the novel was issued by Stanford University Press (that edition was reissued in 1999 by Johns Hopkins University Press). However, between July 1845 and May 1846 a translation of the novel was serialized in the *National Anti-Slavery Standard*, which importantly places it in a tradition of American abolitionist writing.

2. Although Tocqueville scholars do note the importance of Beaumont's novel, they invariably see it as a kind of footnote to the *Démocratie*. George Wilson Pierson, who makes a strong case for Beaumont's influence on Tocqueville's thought and work, dedicates only thirteen pages of his eight-hundred-page study to Beaumont's novel. Pierson lists the novel's failures as "too romantic, too sentimental and too interrupted, too much concerned with social issues and too little with political. . . . As a novel . . . the intended masterpiece [leaves] even more to be desired" (Pierson, *Tocqueville in America*, 522–23). Even recent critics, like Nathan Glazer and Gerard Fergerson, who appreciate Beaumont's concern with social issues, tend to see its importance only in its relation to Tocqueville's omissions. Glazer is particularly patronizing, arguing that Beaumont's novel served as a kind of good conscience for Tocqueville, allowing him to "put aside" the issues of slavery and Indian removal because Beaumont,

who was "more indignant" about such injustices, intended to dedicate his entire work to them (Glazer, "Race and Ethnicity in America," 96). Only Werner Sollors treats Beaumont's novel as a project independent of Tocqueville's work. Indeed, although he devotes a scant six pages of his encyclopedic study of interracial literature to a reading of *Marie*, Sollors significantly repositions Beaumont as one of the earliest authors in a tradition of interracial literature that gains immense popularity in Europe and the United States in the nineteenth and twentieth centuries. Sollors argues, albeit somewhat tongue-in-cheek, that the entire literary tradition associated with the Tragic Mulatta figure might be better redefined as "[the] representation of male and female mixed-race characters in the manner popularized by Beaumont's *Marie*" (Sollors, *Neither Black Nor White Yet Both*, 240–41, 257–60).

3. Sollors shows that, like the woman in the theater, the interracial figure in literature often stands as "a most upsetting and subversive character who illuminates the paradoxes of 'race' in America" both by revealing the insufficiency of the categories of black and white and by revealing the constructedness of "race" (Sollors, *Neither Black Nor White Yet Both*, 234). The paradoxes to which Beaumont responds begin with a notion of race that is made to transcend even skin color, an "inward racial essentialism" that would be totally implausible, Sollors argues, according to codes of difference which date back to antiquity, and which continued to operate in much of the world in the nineteenth century. Sollors argues that nineteenth-century American concepts of racial difference amounted to a virtual reversal of the attitudes of Classical authors (as well as contemporary European writers like Pushkin), for whom skin color could amount to little more than atavism, an accident of birth. He argues that "American School" racial scientists, like Josiah Nott, "virtually had to stand on its head the Classical distinction between 'essential' and 'accidental' qualities: whereas skin color had been the prototypical accidental trait in antiquity, it now became the sign of essential difference" (63–70). Nancy Bentley remarks that Sollor's claims about the peculiarity of U.S. racial beliefs may be the only form of cultural exceptionalism that has survived recent critical skepticism (Bentley, "The Strange Career of Love and Slavery").

4. In a footnote, Beaumont tells an anecdote of "a Creole from Santo Domingo" whose tanned face incites another American audience to "color" him and then expel him from a New York theater, suggesting that virtually anyone may be subject to this accusation which carries the status of a proof (*Marie*, 5).

5. For a discussion of whiteness in Melville's *Moby-Dick* and Edgar Allan Poe's *The Narrative of Arthur Gordon Pym*, see Morrison, "Unspeakable Things Unspoken"; and Morrison, *Playing in the Dark*.

6. Daphne Brooks's phrase "racial phantasmagoria" aptly captures this phenomenon. She coins the term to describe the spectacularization of cultural alienation in black performance in the nineteenth-century transatlantic, using it in particular in the context of a white spectator's response to an octaroon woman. In that spectator's emphatic insistence on the woman's blackness, he "makes the violence of his white supremacy spectacularly visible" (Brooks, *Bodies in Dissent*, 19–20).

7. "Il me paraît certain qu'ils ne forment pas une race distincte de la race européenne: la conformation de leur corps, la coupe de leur figure, la nature de leur physionomie, n'ont avec le nôtre aucune différence marquée. On ne saurait en dire autant des nègres qui, plus on les examine, paraissait avoir reçu une organization particulière" (Beaumont, *Lettres d'Amérique*, 110 [my translation]).

8. "Ce qui surtout te ferait rire ce sont les grosses figures noires des nègres qui sont si laides, si laides que chacun d'eux a l'air d'un diable. . . . Car ces Noirs ont une âme comme nous et tout leur crime est d'avoir une très vilaine couleur." (ibid., 178 [my translation]).

9. For discussions of the ubiquitous ethnological inquiry of the nineteenth century, see Sollors, *Neither Black Nor White Yet Both* (62–70); and Otter, *Melville's Anatomies* (especially 101–26).

10. Noting the legality of slavery in Baltimore, Beaumont writes of his intention to make copious notes on the subject toward a work that will "immortalize" him (Beaumont, *Lettres d'Amérique*, 175–77). In his introduction to Chapman's 1958 translation of *Marie* (reprinted in the Hopkins edition), Alvis Tinnen dates Beaumont's "compassionate interest" in slavery and freed blacks to his 12–18 October 1831 visit to Philadelphia (xxxi). While Pierson laments that no letter or diary entry describes the exact experience that Beaumont relates in the foreword, he also suggests that it occurred in Philadelphia (Pierson, *Tocqueville in America*, 512–13).

11. Sollors summarizes the critical treatment of black characters in the "tragic mulatta" tradition, beginning with Sterling Brown's 1933 essay "Negro Characters As Seen By White Authors," which outlined six elements of the "tragic mulatta complex": its cliché, its elision of more serious treatments of slavery and race, the problematic division in gender, the racialist division of the characters' "warring blood," its "flattery" of white readers, and its use, more often than not, by white writers. However, Sollors complicates Brown's catalog of the tradition by showing that the figure changes depending on whether it is used in a racialist context or in an anti- or non-racialist context, and he argues that Brown's criticisms all adhere to a realist standard of aesthetics, judging these figures exclusively against "realistic" portrayals of either black or interracial characters (Sollors, *Neither Black Nor White Yet Both*, 220–34). For treatments of the figure of the Tragic Mulatta in nineteenth-century white-authored fiction and popular theater, see Kinney, *Amalgamation!*; Paulin, "Representing Forbidden Desire"; Berlant's discussion of the stereotype in "National Brands/National Bodies"; and Jackson, *Barriers between Us*, 2–3.

12. A relatively unusual argument, though similar to one made by Lydia Maria Child in her 1833 *Appeal in Favor of That Class of Americans Called Africans*. According to Karen Sánchez-Eppler, Child's call for the repeal of anti-miscegenation laws centered on her point that the prohibition of interracial marriage and the social sanctioning of illicit interracial unions between white men and black women served primarily to secure white men's freedom in choosing their sexual partners. But where Beaumont frames his argument around a white man's right to legitimize his love for a black woman, Sánchez-Eppler argues that Child's argument implicitly articulates the untold "story of white women's desire for the black man" (see Sánchez-Eppler, *Touching Liberty*, 36–37; see also Weierman, *One Nation, One Blood*).

13. "Quelques personnes m'ont paru regretter que j'aie exposé dans l'avant-propos, un fait dont la révélation affaiblit . . . l'intérêt du Roman. Voici le motif qui m'a fait agir. L'odieux préjugé que j'ai pris pour sujet principal de mon livre est si extraordinaire et tellement étranger à nos mœurs, qu'il me semble qu'on croirait difficilement en France à sa réalité, si je bornais à l'exposer dans le texte d'un ouvrage auquel l'imagination a eu quelque part" (Beaumont, *Marie, ou l'esclavage aux États-Unis*, 1:vi [my translation]). In the *National Anti-Slavery Standard*'s 1845 translation of *Marie*,

the translator takes this footnote to heart and declines to relate this entire episode, in order not to "mar the plot by anticipation," since "no American reader would be disposed to doubt" the racial barriers that Beaumont intends the episode to illustrate (see the *National Anti-Slavery Standard*, 17 July 1845). This omission is quite remarkable; for the editors of the *Standard*, the demands of fiction apparently trump Beaumont's impulse to authenticate and authorize his novel with this anecdote, so they excise it. In so doing, not only does the *Standard* manage to cut one of Beaumont's more searing indictments of "public opinion" as the force behind racial prejudice in America, they also remove the scene which, as I argue below, provides the foundation for his critique of race as a spectacle of consensus.

14. "Bien résolu d'offrir à mes lecteurs un tableau fidèle et sincère, j'ai dû les prévenir de la vérité de mes peintures, et leur montrer d'abord, dans toute sa nudité, le préjugé que j'allais décrire, et dont je ferais ressortis les tristes conséquences sans les exagérer" (Beaumont, *Marie, ou l'esclavage aux États-Unis*, 1:vi [my translation]).

15. Beaumont's manuscript pages and notes for the fictional portions of *Marie* bear out the impression that the novel was not written in any linear fashion. While his appendices and notes are written out in draft form almost exactly as they appear in the printed text, the draft pages for the novel are almost illegible for all of his changes. The fictional portions clearly went through multiple drafts, which show that he rearranged scenes and chapters several times, renamed all of his characters, and made constant excisions and additions. Beaumont's notes and draft pages of the manuscript are held in the Yale Tocqueville Manuscripts, Beinecke Rare Book and Manuscript Library.

16. Sollors, *Neither Black Nor White Yet Both*, 259.

17. E.g., Jean-Christophe Agnew describes the theatrical worldview as posing a series of questions about the transparency, consistency, and stability of the subject in a world conceived as a "placeless market." Agnew argues that writers in the theatrical tradition (from Jonson to Melville) launch a particular critique of the instabilities of market culture by highlighting the epistemological ambiguities produced when social relations are governed by commercial exchange. In such a world, abstractions (like the formless nature of capital or the artfully performed character) achieve the status of "second nature," lived fictions that produce incredible and "disquieting" contingency (Agnew, *World's Apart*, 195–203; see also Hadley, *Melodramatic Tactics*, 15–31). For the theatricalization of the public sphere in post-Revolutionary America, see Jay Fliegelman's *Declaring Independence*, in which the author argues that the republican public, like the market culture in Agnew's study, also privileged a vision of the "natural" public self that was, at its essence, a performance.

18. Dumm, *Democracy and Punishment*, 140. Making a similar point, Joan Dayan describes the prison book as a "dark gloss to Tocqueville's *Democracy in America*" (Dayan, "Legal Slaves and Civil Bodies," 54).

19. See Thorsten Sellin's introduction to Beaumont and Tocqueville, *On the Penitentiary System in the United States and its Application in France*, xviii.

20. Foucault notes that in France in the first half of the nineteenth century, there were countless studies commissioned of other nations' prison systems (including two separate studies of American prisons in the 1830s alone), as well as numerous inquiries into the French system. He also notes that the idea of "prison 'reform'" is virtually contemporary with the idea of the prison itself"; the institution designed to reform its

inmates is equally subject to constant scrutiny and change (Foucault, *Discipline and Punish*, 123, 234).

21. Beaumont and Tocqueville, *On the Penitentiary System in the United States and its Application in France*, 55.

22. See Dayan, "Legal Slaves and Civil Bodies," 71–72.

23. Beaumont and Tocqueville, *On the Penitentiary System in the United States and its Application in France*, 96.

24. "Jeté dans la solitude, il réfléchit. Placé seul en présence de son crime, il apprend à le haïr: et si son âme n'est pas encore blasée sur le mal, c'est dans l'isolement que le remords viendra l'aissaillir" (Beaumont and Tocqueville, *Système pénitentiare aux États-Unis*, 109 [my translation]).

25. See, in particular, Tocqueville's transcribed interview with a man designated only as "Inmate No. 20," in Appendix no. 10: "At first, he says, solitude was insufferable, but custom overcomes gradually the horror" (Beaumont and Tocqueville, *On the Penitentiary System in the United States and its Application in France*, 188).

26. Foucault, *Discipline and Punish*, 237–38. Although this language implies a separation between the prisoner and the power "exercised over him," it is worth noting that the prisoner is always the instrument of his own punishment in Foucault's account. In a reading of *Discipline and Punish*, Judith Butler describes subjection in Foucault as "the making of a subject": "the individual is formed or, rather, formulated through his discursively constituted 'identity' as a prisoner," and thus his agency derives entirely from his subjection (Butler, *The Psychic Life of Power*, 84). But given that the "subject" is a product of subjection, Butler goes on to ask what escapes subjection or resists normalization in Foucault if not the "soul" or the "psyche." She argues that it is power's need to repeatedly constitute subjects, its iterability, that "becomes the non-place of subversion. . . . In other words, the law turns against itself and spawns versions of itself which oppose and proliferate its animating purpose" (ibid., 99–100).

27. Beaumont and Tocqueville, *On the Penitentiary System in the United States and its Application in France*, 72.

28. Foucault, *Discipline and Punish*, 237–38. Foucault reiterates Beaumont and Tocqueville's claim that, whereas the wardens of New York prisons must create an apparatus of discipline in order to enforce silence and maintain order when the prisoners gather, the Pennsylvania model is a self-maintaining system in which each cell is a prison unto itself (see Beaumont and Tocqueville, *On the Penitentiary System in the United States and its Application in France*, 73). In the end, Beaumont and Tocqueville also argue, the New York system creates citizens submissive to the law, while Pennsylvania produces "hommes hônnets" (*Système pénitentiare*, 152).

29. Foucault, *Discipline and Punish*, 200–201.

30. Ibid., 58.

31. Ibid., 216–17.

32. Dayan, "Legal Slaves and Civil Bodies," 64.

33. Ibid., 55.

34. Ibid., 65–69 (quotes at 65, 67, 69).

35. Beaumont and Tocqueville, *On the Penitentiary System in the United States and its Application in France*, 63.

36. To judge from their account, the minutiae of the prison's operations—from its

expenses to the efficacy of its program of reform—amounted to a national diversion, with detailed reports published annually in major newspapers and tours available to anyone who wished to inspect a facility. Beaumont and Tocqueville note that the only thing that prison tourists in Philadelphia are kept from inspecting are the prisoners themselves, since this would run directly counter to the principle of total solitude that the public has mandated as the basis of reform (see Beaumont and Tocqueville, *On the Penitentiary System in the United States and its Application in France*, 64). But even this exception is not absolute, judging from the extensive interviews that Tocqueville and Dickens were granted with the inmates of Eastern State.

37. Foucault, *Discipline and Punish*, 216.

38. Beaumont is not alone in understanding hallucination as a form of punitive visuality. Charles Dickens condemns the method of Eastern State as a "slow and daily tampering with the mysteries of the brain," which results in a particular form of madness: Dickens imagines a prisoner tormented by hallucinations of shadowy figures that represent other inmates and still ghostlier figures, "silent somethings," which become his constant companions (Dickens, *American Notes, For General Circulation*, 110–12).

39. "[E]lle s'approchait du lit, la phthisique prenait sa main, y déposait une larme: 'Ne pleurez point, ma bonne demoiselle,' disait la pauvre femme . . . " (Beaumont, *Marie, ou l'esclavage aux États-Unis*, 1:84 [my translation]).

40. Yale Tocqueville Manuscripts, box 1, folder 1, Beinecke Rare Book and Manuscript Library.

41. In this way, Beaumont's interpretation of post-Revolutionary America substantiates Foucault's claim that "racism is, quite literally, revolutionary discourse in an inverted form." Although Foucault is clearly speaking here of the French Revolution, there is an analogous narrative in the deployment of anti-revolutionary discourse in the United States. The difference between what Beaumont describes (and, to a lesser degree, Tocqueville) and Foucault's account is that, for Foucault, this marks the first appearance of State Racism (see Foucault, *Society Must Be Defended*, 81–82), whereas Beaumont and Tocqueville downplay the centrality of the state.

42. Pierson, *Tocqueville in America*, 13–33.

43. "M. Nelson lisant la Gazetter—George rêvant profonde, et soulent [illegible] quelquefois de la reverie pour admirer sa soeur" (see Yale Tocqueville Manuscripts, box 1, folder 1, Beinecke Rare Book and Manuscript Library).

44. Beaumont, *Marie, ou l'esclavage aux États-Unis*, 1:124 [my translation].

45. "Ainsi vous dites souvent des hommes; mais les Américains sont égaux.—Vous ne reconnaissez qu'une égalité nationale. En France, l'égalité Philosophique universelle est [illegible] moins couverte par les moeurs que l'égalité politique. Il me semble que vous vous prenez peur de force de la morale: peuple égoiste, vous invoquez des principes quand vous en avoir besoin pour être égaux & libre—et vous fouler [?] aux pieds [?] des lois quand vous veulent [?] vous ayez des esclaves" (Yale Tocqueville Manuscripts, box 1, folder 1, Beinecke Rare Book and Manuscript Library).

46. Primarily, I'm referring to Jay Fliegelman's theses in *Prodigals and Pilgrims* (especially 93–122), and in *Declaring Independence*. In *Prodigals and Pilgrims*, Fliegelman examines eighteenth-century discourses of filial debt and natural freedom as a crucial intellectual context for the rhetoric of American independence. He shows how Revolutionary iconography frequently depicted parental tyranny and abuse as metaphors

for an unnatural colonial authority against which rebellion was not only legitimate but also necessary to the natural independence of the colonies, imagined as children justly seeking self-sufficiency. In the later work, *Declaring Independence*, he describes that act as an oratorical one of "self-assertion and self-concealment." Other studies of the American Revolution focusing on the centrality of linguistic performativity include Looby, *Voicing America*; and Ruttenburg, *Democratic Personality*.

47. Douglass, *Autobiographies*, 302.

48. Jefferson, *Notes on the State of Virginia*, 145. See also Fliegelman's discussion of Jefferson's *Notes*, in which he makes it clear that the "oratorical revolution" was less invested in the "abstract" citizen than in the eloquence and transparency of an explicitly white speaker (Fliegelman, *Declaring Independence*, 192–93).

49. Where Bakhtin's heteroglossia refers to the dialogic voices speaking out from a text (see Bakhtin, *The Dialogic Imagination*, 272–73), the representation of speech as dramatic dialogue might be said to signal an inverse movement, where voices may enter the text. The combination of Nelson's use of the first person plural and the representation of speech as dramatic dialogue suggest that Beaumont's narrative device is politicizing just such an idea of the competing centripetal and centrifugal forces of language.

50. In a scene that becomes the text's most literal exposure of the racial specificity of public discourse, d'Almanza manages to invalidate an entire election by exposing George, who had passed as white in order to participate in the classic activity of abstraction—casting a vote (*Marie, ou l'esclavage aux États-Unis*, 117–18).

51. In *To Wake the Nations*, Eric Sundquist argues that the reference to figures like Turner and L'Ouverture as models for black rebellion by Frederick Douglass and other abolitionists often signaled "not necessarily the erosion of the ideology of the American Revolution, but rather its transfer across the color line" (36). However, he also notes that William Wells Brown, in his speech "Santo Domingo: Its Revolutions and Its Patriots," isolated Toussaint as the better model for the slave rebellion that would complete the failures of the American Revolution. When Beaumont turns to these figures as models for George Nelson's plotted revolt, he seems more clearly to turn away from the American model which George has apparently exhausted, and toward an idea of revolution that is drawn from the combined histories of Europe and the Caribbean—specifically, Haiti, as Sundquist describes in his reading of Melville's "Benito Cereno" (ibid.,135–39; see also Sundquist, *"Benito Cereno* and New World Slavery").

52. The play in question, written by Charles Dupeuty, was first performed in Paris in 1830.

53. Sundquist, *To Wake the Nations*, 31, 40–41.

54. Brown, "St. Domingo: Its Revolutions and Its Patriots," 500–502. Brown also notes that Napoleon's exile in St. Helena, the site of the second part of the Dupeuty play, forms a parallel to the exile of Toussaint: "Napoleon transferred Toussaint from the warm and sunny climate of the West Indies to the cold climate of the north of France; the English transferred Napoleon from the cold climate of France to the warm climate of St. Helena. This was indeed retribution" (ibid., 501).

55. See Yale Tocqueville Manuscripts, box 2, folder 1, Beinecke Rare Book and Manuscript Library.

56. A thorough account of the political context and key events of the riots can

be found in Richards, *Gentlemen of Property and Standing*, 113–22. See also Wilentz, *Chants Democratic*, 264–66; Bank, *Theatre Culture in America*, 156–58; and Lott, *Love and Theft*, 131–35.

57. In contrast to coordinated actions against the American Antislavery Society in 1835 and 1836, Richards describes the July 1834 riots as unplanned, unorganized, and largely unimpeded by city police, but he also argues that the crowds did not behave either "spontaneously" or "capriciously" (Richards, *Gentlemen of Property and Standing*, 113, 120). See also Trish Loughran's discussion of the organized actions against Arthur Tappan's 1835 pamphlet campaign, in Loughran, *The Republic in Print*, 347–48.

58. E.g., Rosemarie Bank refers to the "Farren Riots," and puts the events in the context of both theater history and more-broadly-defined cultural performances, calling them a "displaced play" that touched on issues of labor, nationalism, popular governance, race, and gender (Bank, *Theatre Culture in America*, 156–58). In contrast, Sean Wilentz discusses the riots in the context of earlier working-class riots and presents their stakes, in part, in terms of an emerging political culture of the streets, as opposed to the unions (Wilentz, *Chants Democratic*, 264–66).

59. Richards, *Gentlemen of Property and Standing*, 116.

60. *New York Commercial Advertiser*, 8 July 1834, and 9 July 1834.

61. Lott notes that the crowd at the Bowery Theatre was ultimately placated and prevented from doing further damage with a blackface performance of "Zip Coon," providing a test for his thesis that blackface minstrelsy mediated the contradictions of white working-class and black cultures (Lott, *Love and Theft*, 132).

62. Though, Wilentz notes, they spared a portrait of George Washington (Wilentz, *Chants Democratic*, 265).

63. Richards, *Gentlemen of Property and Standing*, 50.

64. Ibid., 120.

65. Lott, *Love and Theft*, 132.

66. Beaumont's sources and notes on the riots are collected in the Yale Tocqueville Manuscripts at the Beinecke Rare Book and Manuscript Library. Interestingly, many of the newspaper reports on the riots that he consulted appear side-by-side with eulogies for his wife's grandfather—General Lafayette—who had died on 21 May.

67. Trish Loughran offers a compelling account of how the paranoid specter of "amalgamation" operated in the 1830s as a "local reaction to a national conflict" over slavery, finding in the discourse around amalgamation a coherent resistance to federal consolidation and expanding national power (Loughran, *The Republic in Print*, 352). One great irony of this "local" response, however, is its ubiquity; anti-amalgamation and anti-abolitionist rioting asserted the resistance of particular localities in remarkably similar ways across vast distances.

68. Richards, *Gentlemen of Property and Standing*, 114.

69. *New York Commercial Advertiser*, 7 July 1834. Not surprisingly, the ad does not appear to have been printed in the *Liberator* as the editors of the *Advertiser* claimed. Such ads figure frequently in nineteenth-century fiction: Charles Chesnutt invokes a newspaper announcement as the pretext for the riot in *The Marrow of Tradition*, emphasizing how powerful white editors and political figures manipulate the specter of interracial marriage to extend the reach of their power. In James Kinney's study of "amalgamation" in nineteenth-century novels, he describes the use of a proposed interracial marriage as a pro-slavery political tool in G. M. Flanders's novel, *The Black*

*Idol* (1861), in which the abolitionist parents of a New England girl seek to marry her to a fugitive slave against her will. The parents are treated as insane fanatics in the novel, in much the same way as the editors of the *Advertiser* treat the man in the advertisement (see Kinney, *Amalgamation!*, 60).

70. In part this is because the "tragic mulatta" tradition is one that Marie may indeed have founded: Sollors argues for *Marie* as a kind of source text in the tradition of male and female mulatto characters, and he places them in a category "beyond" the stereotypes (Sollors, *Neither Black Nor White Yet Both*, 241).

71. "[C]ette population moitié européenne, moitié indienne, n'est point désagréable. Il y a dans les physionomies indiennes quelque chose de farouche que se mélange adoucit; les yeux du sauvage ont une vivacité naturelle que je n'ai vu chez aucun blanc; leur défaut est d'être en même temps durs et sévères, mais ce feu qui brille dans leur regard est d'une grande beauté, lorsque sans cesser *d'être* aussi vif, il perd quelquechose de sa rudesse primitive: c'est ci qui arrive par l'union de l'Indien et l'Européen. Les Canadiens appellent métiches (métis) ceux qui sortent de cette double origine. J'ai vu des jeunes filles métiches qui m'ont paru d'une beauté remarquables" (Beaumont, *Lettres d'Amérique*, 122–23 [my translation]).

72. Bentley, "The Strange Career of Love and Slavery" (quotes at 465, 462).

3 / "The Hangman's Accomplice": Spectacle and Complicity in Lydia Maria Child's New York

1. For more on these events, see Richards, *Gentlemen of Property and Standing*, 62–65.

2. See Karcher, *The First Woman in the Republic*, 100; Richards, *Gentlemen of Property and Standing*, 1–46.

3. Karcher, "Censorship, American Style," 285 (my emphasis).

4. John Plotz's definition of the relationship of crowd and public in Victorian England is instructive here; like the British public sphere between 1800 and 1850, the U.S. public sphere of the 1830s and 1840s was "the subject of a violent contest to determine what sorts of discourses would count as central to public speech and performance" (Plotz, *The Crowd*, 10).

5. See, in particular, Lydia Maria Child to Ellis Gray Loring, 31 August 1841, 24 November 1841, and 6 March 1843, in the Lydia Maria Francis Child Papers, 1838–78, Manuscripts and Archives Division, New York Public Library.

6. See Karcher, "Censorship," 294. The forty letters collected in Child's 1843 book represent a condensed and rearranged version of the fifty-eight letters originally published in *The National Anti-Slavery Standard* between 19 August 1841 and 4 May 1843. Of the original fifty-eight letters, twenty-two are excised from the book, some completely, while others are spliced and pasted into other letters; four of the collected letters did not appear in the *Standard* at all and are comprised entirely of portions taken from excised originals. For this reason, the numbers of the letters in the book do not correspond to the numbers of originals in the newspaper, and often, Child even altered the dates. Because I will cite from both the original letters (cited in text as "Letters from New-York") and the collected letters (cited as *Letters*), I will follow the numbering convention of both texts, using Roman numerals to denote letter numbers in the collected volume and Arabic numerals to denote letters cited directly from the *Standard*.

7. Loughran, *The Republic in Print*, 306–10, 388; Richards, *Gentlemen of Property and Standing*, 20–30.

8. Richards describes how the AASS made use of the exponential increases in printing capacity that came in the 1830s with steam presses and paper cutting machines (Richards, *Gentlemen of Property and Standing*, 71–75).

9. Child, *Letters from New-York: 2d Series*, 257. Child's *2d Series* followed the original collection by a year, and was comprised of letters written for the *Boston Courier*, not the *Standard*.

10. Karcher, *First Woman of the Republic*, 191–92, 183. The pain of this period is still evident several years later in Child's letters to Ellis Loring; see, e.g., her letter of 17 February 1839, in the Lydia Maria Francis Child Papers, 1838–78, Manuscripts and Archives Division, New York Public Library.

11. See Habermas, *The Structural Transformation of the Public Sphere*, 51–54; Tocqueville, *Democracy in America*, 254–59.

12. Loughran, *The Republic in Print*, 304–55 (quotations at 333). Loughran describes the success of what she calls the "national simultaneity argument," which involved the AASS's claim that "slavery was not local, but national, and that all citizens were responsible for it" (ibid., 388).

13. Ibid., 245.

14. Child, *An Appeal in Favor of That Class of Americans Called Africans*, iv [hereafter cited in text as *Appeal*]. Child's plea was, evidently, not heeded; according to Karcher, a rival of David Lee Child's "hurled the *Appeal* out the window with a pair of tongs" (Karcher, "Censorship, American Style," 192).

15. "It is worthy of observation that this slave representation [in determining the population of states] is always used to protect and extend slave power; and in this way, the slaves are made to vote for slavery; they are compelled to furnish halters to hang their posterity" (Child, *Appeal*, 104).

16. Child's language of crime and complicity is echoed in the language of an 1839 non-resistance resolution, and forms the basis of Garrison's policy of disunion, discussed below: "That every man thus consenting to the civil government of this country is responsible to God and man for the evils, and is accessory to the crimes, which are the necessary consequences of those false principles, when made the basis of legislative action, of which responsibility he can only divest himself by immediately repenting of his participation in this system from which these crimes and evils flow, and instantly abandoning it" (quoted in Fanuzzi, *Abolition's Public Sphere*, 33).

17. Karcher calls Child's argument against anti-miscegenation laws a "bold" transformation of the debate from one of racist standards of "decency" to one of individual choice and taste (Karcher, *The First Woman in the Republic*, 189). Karen Sánchez-Eppler takes the question of taste one step further, arguing that Child's statement in the *Appeal* comes closer than any contemporary text to telling "the story of the white woman's sexual desire for the black man" (Sánchez-Eppler, *Touching Liberty*, 36–37).

18. Sánchez-Eppler, *Touching Liberty*, 36–37.

19. Fanuzzi, *Abolition's Public Sphere*, 33.

20. Ibid., 50. As Fanuzzi shows, this problem chiefly manifested itself in the controversy over the editorial voice of the *Liberator* and the agency behind this declaration of right: "[W]ho had entitled Garrison to publicize the cause of disunion? And for whom was Garrison speaking?" (ibid., 51).

21. On Garrison's focus on the states, see Karcher, "Censorship, American Style," 285; and Fanuzzi, *Abolition's Public Sphere*, 34.

22. Ryan, *Civic Wars*, 48.

23. See ibid., 105; Barnum, *The Life of P. T. Barnum, Written by Himself*, 213.

24. Ryan, *Civic Wars*, 105–6.

25. Barnum describes his decision to give up the life of an itinerant showman in chapter 9 of his 1850 autobiography; lacking the funds to purchase the building and collection of Peale's Museum in late 1841, he gleefully recounts how he secured financing, in part, by putting up "Ivy Island," a worthless five-acre inheritance, as collateral (*The Life of P. T. Barnum, Written by Himself*, 213–18).

26. Ibid., 225.

27. Ibid., 226.

28. Ryan, *Civic Wars*, 85.

29. Indeed, Child's collected *Letters* is one of Ryan's sources (see Ryan, *Civic Wars*, 27, 39, 52, 54).

30. She opens the collected Letter II with the account of the Washingtonians from Letter No. 22 in the *Standard*, originally printed on 21 April 1842, and closes with the story of the dog killers from the original Letter No. 2 (26 August 1841). See also Bruce Mills's annotations in the University of Georgia Press edition, especially notes 1, 4, and 7 (208–10).

31. The book's Letter I is one of few that is almost identical to its counterpart in the *Standard*.

32. Heather Roberts notes how Child's characterization of her former view of New York resonates with the popular "mysteries and miseries" novels, and describes her new view as "allegorical," suggesting that Child's two views are also mediated by literary genres (Roberts, "The Public Heart," 757–58).

33. *The Works of Washington Irving*, 3.

34. Hamilton, *America's Sketchbook*. Hamilton isolates Irving's *Sketch Book* and Mary Russell Mitford's *Our Village* (1824–32) as the foundational texts of the form, whose conventions of perspective come to be picked up by later sketch-writers, including those explicitly associated with reform movements. Hamilton argues that the "public expression of private experience" defines the sketch's primary function, even when it becomes associated with political movements like the improvement of factory conditions at Lowell. The detached gaze, Hamilton argues, enables a similarly detached mode of assessment and judgment that appeals to personal preference, thereby privileging "a newly dominant conception of values as privately held" as the means by which a sincere and disinterested self might be expressed to a public readership (ibid., 21). The "insider's view" takes readers on literary tours of scenes in which the author is deeply interested; authority thus derives from the proximate view and intimate knowledge of subjects made to be part of the author's private sphere (23).

35. *The Works of Washington Irving*, 44–46.

36. Hamilton, *America's Sketchbook*, 29.

37. Brand, *The Spectator and the City in Nineteenth-Century American Literature*, 89. Brand traces the significance and particular development of the *flâneur* figure in the United States prior to the Civil War, making a strong case for the onset of an urban modernity in America decades earlier than critics and historians typically assume. He further shows how popular writers like Nathaniel Parker Willis had so

conventionalized the type of the *flâneur* that Poe's narrator "lays the groundwork for [its] transcendence."

38. Poe, *Complete Tales and Poems*, 475–81.

39. Brand, *The Spectator and the City in Nineteenth-Century American Literature*, 85.

40. E.g., McDonald Clarke in Letter XV, or the fugitive child in Letter XXX, to whom she explicitly compares herself (*Letters*, 147).

41. Roberts, "The Public Heart," 749–68 (quotes at 752, 753, 755, 768).

42. Esteve, *The Aesthetics and Politics of the Crowd in American Literature*, 25–43 (quotes at 36, 43). Not surprisingly, given Esteve's insistence on the political as a narrow and discrete realm of rational human activity, separate and apart from private, intimate, and aesthetic spheres, she dismisses Poe scholars like Jonathan Elmer who have turned to Tocqueville in order to argue for a more broadly conceived understanding of the political in the nineteenth-century U.S. (ibid., 44–45).

43. "Unlike the passerby who resides elsewhere, the vagrant has being only in the public sphere. . . . Insofar as citizenship describes a purely public persona, therefore, the beggar or vagrant appears to be the essential unit of the state, rather than evidence of its malfunction" (Langan, *Romantic Vagrancy*, 18).

44. Macdonald Clarke is the text's best example of the vagrant as a figure of public interiority; a man of radical, self-negating sympathy, Clarke lives to help others, but with "a nerve protruding from every pore," he is incapable of caring for himself. "Something ought to be done for me. I can't take care of myself. I ought to be sent to the asylum" (*Letters*, 68).

45. Her claim of effortless variety is also belied by what Mary Ryan has shown to be the carefully managed forms of ethnic and religious diversity around which both social and political life in mid-century New York organized (see Ryan's second chapter, "The Performance of People in Association," in *Civic Wars*).

46. Heather Roberts makes a similar connection between Child and Clarke (Roberts, "The Public Heart," 766).

47. Dana Brand remarks upon the ubiquity of descriptions of Barnum's Museum in writing from the 1840s and 1850s; along with the Royal Exchange in London, he writes, "these spaces appeared to spectatorial narrators to be the most representative spaces in their respective cities" (Brand, *The Spectator and the City in Nineteenth-Century American Literature*, 75).

48. See Harris, *Humbug*, 57–89.

49. Otter, *Melville's Anatomies*, 165–68.

50. See, in particular, Reiss, *The Showman and the Slave*.

51. "Song of Myself" (1855), in Whitman, *Complete Poetry and Selected Prose*, lines 843–44. For a discussion of what Karen Sánchez-Eppler calls Whitman's "poetics of merger and embodiment," which she argues is grounded historically in ideas of miscegenation, see her chapter, "To Stand Between," in *Touching Liberty*. Otter argues that Child, along with Melville, stages this desire for inside knowledge with a difference; although neither can escape the racialism that shapes their desires, both "seek ways of knowing without owning" (Otter, *Melville's Anatomies*, 168). See also Otter's chapter on Melville's *White-Jacket*, "Jumping Out of One's Skin," in the same volume, for a reading of how analogies of garments to bodies and skin elaborate fantasies of cross-racial identification in antebellum fiction and political writing.

52. Hartman, *Scenes of Subjection*, 17–23. Hartman emphasizes the implicit pleasure in such scenes of empathy designed to heighten terror and elicit feelings of sorrow. She also asks pointedly: "What does it mean that the violence of slavery or the pained experience of the enslaved, if discernable, is only so in the most heinous and grotesque examples and not in the quotidian routines of slavery?" (21).

53. What Child adds as a postscript in Letter XXXVI—the only such supplement in the edited volume—is initially published in the *Standard*'s Letter No. 54 two weeks after her original account of the exhibit in No. 52. In No. 54, Child speaks at greater length on the deaths of Do-Hum-Me and No-No-See, blaming the "avarice" of everyone involved in the exhibit, including the performers themselves, and she finds herself torn between a patronizing sense of their victimization and a recognition of their partial complicity in the show. "I find it hard to forgive the insatiable avarice which hurried these noble children of the forest from one scene of exhibition to another, till it pushed them into the grave. If they themselves were tempted by money to prolong their stay, oh how the bleeding heart of that young chieftain will have the yellow dust for which he sold a life so precious!" ("Letters from New-York No. 54").

54. Porter, *Seeing and Being*, xii–xviii, 30–32.

55. See, e.g., *Letters*, 133. Child also quotes a line from Emerson's "Friendship" twice in the *Letters from New-York*, and writes in her personal correspondence of attending his lectures. While she is clearly an admirer, her comments on his lectures are not always favorable. Writing to Loring about a lecture of Emerson's she attended in New York, she calls it "refreshing as a glass of soda but, as usual, not satisfactory." Specifically, Child criticized Emerson's evasion of slavery in a lecture on southern manners: "He gave, in one of the lectures, such a glowing and graceful picture of Southern manners and character that I might have supposed he considered arbitrary power one of the most beautiful influences on man" (Child to Loring, 21 February 1843, Lydia Maria Francis Child Papers, 1838–78, Manuscripts and Archives Division, New York Public Library).

56. *Ralph Waldo Emerson: Essays and Poems*, 772.

57. Otter compares Child to Melville (Otter, *Melville's Anatomies*, 166).

58. Cadava, "The Guano of History," 137–65 (quote at 143).

59. Ibid., 146; for the Emerson quote, see *Ralph Waldo Emerson: Essays and Poems*, 771.

60. Child combined two letters on Blackwell's Island which she originally published in the *Standard* (Nos. 38 and 39) into a single letter for the book, Letter XXIX.

61. This man, too, seems recognizable as John C. Colt, whose trial and execution for the murder of a business associate prompt Child's critique of capital punishment. Child became a defender of Colt's before his execution, and she tried to help his new wife escape to Brook Farm (see *Letters from New-York*, ed. Bruce Mills, 241n2).

62. This sentence originally appeared before the passage quoted above in her second letter on Blackwell's Island (see "Letters from New-York No. 39"), but she moves it to Letter XXXII on capital punishment, showing how clearly her thoughts on punishment and complicity in these letters are linked.

63. See Agamben, *Homo Sacer*, 28–29, 110–11; see also Downes, "Melville's 'Benito Cereno' and the Politics of Humanitarian Intervention."

## 4 / The Spectacle of Reform: Theater and Prison in Hawthorne's *Blithedale Romance*

1. Hartman, *Scenes of Subjection*, 26–28.

2. See Castiglia, "Abolition's Racial Interiors and the Making of White Civic Depth," 33–59. Reading Garrison's notion of sympathy through Adam Smith, Jeremy Bentham, and Foucault, Castiglia shows how "a form of surveillant discipline—what we might call sympathetic discipline" develops, which promises to reform the interior characters of both whites and blacks, while internalizing both racial difference and social hierarchy (37).

3. Nathaniel Hawthorne, *The Blithedale Romance* (New York: Bedford Books of St. Martin's Press, 1996) [hereafter cited in text].

4. The best of these include Brodhead, "Veiled Ladies"; Coale, *Mesmerism and Hawthorne*; and Castronovo, *Necro Citizenship*.

5. See, in particular, Brodhead, "Veiled Ladies," 278–80; and Castronovo, *Necro Citizenship*, 110–11.

6. Hawthorne, *The Letters*, 576 [hereafter cited in text].

7. Quoted in Gitter, *The Imprisoned Guest*, 4.

8. A claim often supported by reference to "The Custom-house." See, in particular, Castronovo, *Necro Citizenship*, 137–42; and Cain, Introduction to *The Blithedale Romance*, 14–20.

9. Dickens, *American Notes*, 41.

10. Ibid., 40, 43. Dickens quotes extensively from Howe's writings on his work with Bridgman, taking up nearly half of his chapter on Boston with Howe's story of Bridgman's early education at the Institute. Dickens's source is the Ninth Annual Report of the Perkins Institute.

11. Quoted in ibid., 45.

12. Gitter, *The Imprisoned Guest*, 102–24 (quotes at 106, 115). Gitter quotes Carlyle on page 103, and the poem attributed to "W. Holmes" on page vii.

13. Dickens, *American Notes*, 42.

14. Gitter notes that at precisely the time, in the spring of 1845, when Howe began to impose solitude and controlled visits on the fifteen-year-old Laura, his faction was losing ground in the Boston Prison Discipline Society (Gitter, *The Imprisoned Guest*, 190–92).

15. Dickens, *American Notes*, 111. Though Dickens extolled Howe's humanity in his chapter on Boston, his scathing account of Eastern State in his Philadelphia chapter shows he did not share the American's views of penal reform.

16. Howe, *An Essay on Separate and Congregate Systems of Prison Discipline*, 3–4, 33. Dickens called the process of blindfolding or hooding prisoners "an emblem of the curtain dropped between [the inmates] and the living world" (Dickens, *American Notes*, 113).

17. Howe, *An Essay on Separate and Congregate Systems of Prison Discipline*, 4–40 (quotes at 38–39, 19, 26).

18. Ibid., 67.

19. Ibid., 39.

20. Dayan, "Legal Slaves and Civil Bodies," 72.

21. In the Bedford Cultural edition of *The Blithedale Romance* (1996), William E.

Cain includes selections from Howe's *Essay on Separate and Congregate Systems of Prison Discipline*, implying that Howe served as one of Hawthorne's sources for Hollingsworth (along with Theodore Parker and others). Picking up on Cain's juxtaposition, Cassandra Cleghorn speculates that Hawthorne may have based Hollingsworth on Howe, in her 1999 essay on Howe and Bridgman (Cleghorn, "Chivalric Sentimentalism," 164).

22. Gitter, *The Imprisoned Guest*, 123.

23. Mary T. Peabody Mann to Sophia Peabody Hawthorne, [5] October 1842, in the Berg Manuscript Collection, New York Public Library. The letter is torn, and some of this section is obscured, but the full passage reads: "Do you mean to say lovey that [?] Mr. H. is not going to stay [?] here at all, nor you going to Salem at all? — E. thinks Dr. Howe will be most happy to render up any documents he has about Laura for the sake of having Mr. Hawthorne write a memoir of her. I meant to have L. and the Dr. here when Mr. H. came. I guess he can spare one night for the sake of that - can't he?" For recent scholarship on Sophia Peabody Hawthorne and her sisters, see Valenti, *Sophia Peabody Hawthorne, A Life*; and Marshall, *The Peabody Sisters*. For Meghan Marshall's speculations on the relationship between Nathaniel Hawthorne and Elizabeth Peabody, see her article, "The Other Sister: Was Nathaniel Hawthorne a Cad?" in *The New Yorker*, 21 March 2005.

24. Coverdale opens his narrative by invoking the clairvoyant mystic: "The evening before my departure for Blithedale, I was returning to my bachelor-apartments, after attending the wonderful exhibition of the Veiled Lady . . . " (*Blithdale*, 40).

25. Bumas, "Fictions of the Panopticon"; Brand, *The Spectator and the City in Nineteenth-Century American Literature*; Gable, "Inappeasable Longings"; Millington, "American Anxiousness"; Greven, "In a Pig's Eye"; Grossberg, "The Tender Passion Was Very Rife Among Us"; Tanner, "Speaking with Hands at Our Throats"; Mills, "'The Sweet Word' Sister."

26. See Hutner, *Secrets and Sympathy*, 117; Berlant, "Fantasies of Utopia in *The Blithedale Romance*,"; Brodhead, "Veiled Ladies," 283, 274. Michael Gilmore briefly recounts the recent critical history of Hawthorne's political "inactivism," before offering his own intervention to "deepen and complicate our understanding" of Hawthorne's relationship to the political, namely, that "Hawthorne's politics of pacification always contain an unpacified dimension" in both the unruliness of his narrators' language and in the leaks that keep popping open between the imaginative and the political (Gilmore, "Hawthorne and Politics (Again)," 33). Stacey Margolis also writes against this tendency in Blithedale scholarship, arguing that Coverdale's retreat to Blithedale is "a move . . . away from privacy and toward politics," which she defines as an "attempt to organize a heterogeneous community of individuals . . . to replace competition with intimacy." More precisely, she reads the politics of the text through mid-century debates about partisanship and sectionalism (Margolis, *The Public Life of Privacy in Nineteenth-Century American Literature*, 23–24).

27. Castronovo, *Necro Citizenship*, 103–5 (quotes at 103, 105). What is not entirely clear from Castronovo's reading of *Blithedale*, however, is whether he believes that the romance "tells an important story about the death of political life" or whether the romance is somehow implicated in this death: "Hawthorne's romance, in effect, reduces the republican consciousness associated with the public sphere to private desire" (106). This is a crucial distinction in a "diagnostic" reading, since it concerns whether the

text is just another symptom of the death of politics or has something of significance to say about that death. See also Berlant, *The Queen of America Goes to Washington City*.

28. Castronovo, *Necro Citizenship*, 111.

29. David Greven has also argued for a reconsideration of visual relations in the text, examining the primacy of the gaze at Blithedale through Kaja Silverman's readings of Lacan. He argues that gazes do not prescribe power relations in expected ways in Hawthorne's romance, instead exposing subjects' vulnerabilities. Although he wisely notes that the vulnerability of the subject is no mark of its subversion, Greven finds a "potential radicalism" in Hawthorne's commitment to both the mutuality and the psychic costs of the gaze (Greven, "In a Pig's Eye," 131–32).

30. Several scholars have noted how much Hawthorne's definition of romance owes to the phenomenon of mesmerism generally and to the Veiled Lady in particular; see, e.g., Coale, *Mesmerism and Hawthorne*, 108. And for an alternative reading to Coale's, see Castronovo, *Necro Citizenship*, 113.

31. See, in particular, Hutner, *Secrets and Sympathy*, 106; Carton, *The Rhetoric of American Romance*, 240–41; and Millington, "American Anxiousness," 563. Recently, David Greven, Douglas Anderson, and Stacey Margolis have sought to synthesize these readings. Greven argues that Coverdale "transforms his inviolate sanctuary into a theatre in which his scopophilic spectatorship has full voyeuristic reign" ("In a Pig's Eye," 133), while Margolis argues that "there is no refuge that will make his individuality inviolate" (*The Public Life of Privacy in Nineteenth-Century American Literature*, 47). For Margolis, the hermitage is the key emblem of the text's contradictory accounts of association—one characterized by choice and inviolate identity, one by coercion and vulnerability—a contradiction which the text does not attempt to resolve (ibid., 46–47).

32. Howe, *An Essay on Separate and Congregate Systems of Prison Discipline*, 67.

33. Both Greven and Margolis rightly note that the visual relations at Blithedale cannot be reduced to the single form of panoptic surveillance generally associated with Foucauldian discipline (see Greven, "In a Pig's Eye," 133; Margolis, *The Public Life of Privacy in Nineteenth-Century American Literature*, 49). For a reading that argues for somewhat closer parallels between Foucault's theories and Hawthorne's romance, see Bumas, "Fictions of the Panopticon," 121–45.

34. Beaumont and Tocqueville, *On the Penitentiary System*, 55. See also Meranze, *Laboratories of Virtue*.

35. Howe, *An Essay on Separate and Congregate Systems of Prison Discipline*, 39.

36. Bender, *Imagining the Penitentiary* (quotes at 202, 201).

37. Bumas uses Hawthorne's three American romances to counter Bender's claim that the novel is a form of supervision and containment. He argues that Bender's limitation is that he "uses Foucault to condemn the genre of the novel," in short, refusing to acknowledge "the autonomy of works of art" (Bumas, "Fictions of the Panopticon," 137). While I agree that Hawthorne's romance complicates Bender's account of the novel as a genre of total transparency and knowledge, I would argue that the limitation of Bender's study has less to do with his reliance on Foucault than with his reliance on the aesthetic theory of Michael Fried and his consequent privileging of absorption in the development of the novel, to the exclusion of other aesthetics.

38. Bender, *Imagining the Penitentiary*, 231–33.

39. Fried, *Absorption and Theatricality*, 71–105 (quotes at 131, 104). Fried's terms are echoed in Lloyd and Thomas's reading of Rousseau's *Lettre á D'Alembert* in *Culture and the State*, though where Fried's interest is in designating an aesthetic form that conceals the relations of representation on which it still relies, Lloyd and Thomas are seeking in Rousseau a fundamental critique of representation and mediation in general (Lloyd and Thomas, *Culture and the State*, 31–58).

40. Bender, *Imagining the Penitentiary*, 227.

41. Brodhead, "Veiled Ladies," 279.

42. Coverdale may indeed have something to fear from Zenobia; she basically condenses his entire narrative into seven pages, without his many gaps and with a more accurate account of the relationship between the two women. For a study of the rivalry between Zenobia and Coverdale as a battle for the authorship of Blithedale, see Tanner, "Speaking with Hands at Our Throats."

43. Diderot, *Le paradoxe sur le comédien*, 310, While Coverdale's praise mirrors the discourse of Le Premier in Diderot's *Paradoxe sur le comèdien*, whose skill allows her to double herself and remain supremely aloof from both her role and her audience, what he comes to realize is that the Veiled Lady is actually the kind of actress described by Le Deuxième, who annihilates herself in a way that Diderot describes explicitly in terms of mesmerism (369–70).

44. Castronovo makes Coverdale's confession of love for Priscilla the text's key instance of the privatization that, he argues, cloaks material inequalities, but his claims hinge on the presumed equivalence of Priscilla and the Veiled Lady, "the very stuff of an ideology that mystifies hierarchical social structures by turning to the spiritual" (Castronovo, *Necro Citizenship*, 121).

45. I borrow this formulation from Svetlana Boym, whose re-reading of Viktor Shklovsky's concepts of defamiliarization and estrangement raises questions about aesthetics and politics closely related to those, I argue, are posed by theatricality (see Boym, "Poetics and Politics of Estrangement").

## 5 / Theatricality, Strangeness, and Democracy in Melville's *Confidence-Man*

1. In the Northwestern–Newberry Edition of *The Confidence-Man*, Harrison Hayford and Hershel Parker give an extensive account of the efforts made by critics to identify the two manuscript pages that comprise "The River." They argue that both external evidence—paper type, ink, and provenance—and internal evidence—thematics and "verbal carryover"—strongly support the thesis that it was originally written as a chapter of the text (possibly the first) and later removed. The primary evidence against this is the fact that the sketch is given only a title and no chapter number, which is inconsistent with the rest of Melville's surviving manuscript pages for *The Confidence-Man* (see "Manuscript Fragments," in Melville, *The Confidence-Man*, ed. Harrison Hayford and Hershel Parker [hereafter cited in text], 402–10, 495–518).

2. Hayford and Parker address the lack of critical consensus on this point in their "Historical Note," but as Peggy Kamuf points out, they manage to dismiss half of the debate, noting only that some critics doubt "even whether he is a singular character" (257). For Kamuf's critique of "a certain mainstream of Melville scholars" who hold to the view that "*The Confidence-Man* is held together by the notion of a self who is self-same," see Kamuf, *The Division of Literature*, 169.

3. This passage appears in the first chapter of part 2, on the principle of sovereignty

of the people. Though this section of volume 1 ends with the chapters on majority tyranny, it begins with rather hopeful remarks that the people's will is effectively represented throughout the government by the agency of a majority that Tocqueville describes as "peaceful" and "sincerely desir[ing] the well-being of the country" (Tocqueville, *Democracy in America*, 173).

4. With this image, Melville also partially inverts Thomas Paine's famous filial metaphor of the island empire ruling a continent, suggesting a geographical analogy for unjust usurpation in response to Paine's assumption that geography dictates just revolution: "Small islands not capable of protecting themselves, are the proper object for kingdoms to take under their care, but there is something very absurd in supposing a continent to be perpetually governed by an island" (Paine, *Common Sense*, 90–91).

5. Kamuf elaborates on this "collapsing the narrative of time" in the second half of *The Division of Literature* (202).

6. As several critics have noted, the opening scene both stages and performs an invitation to interpret, enclosing the act of reading the text within the text. For this reason, the reader cannot be imagined as transcending the text in any way, thus there is no privileged position from which to view the man as some sort of "avatar" or "incarnation" to be unmasked, deciphered, and identified. Whether critics have read him as Christ, Satan, or the "confidence-man" in whiteface, the traditional critical assumption is generally that the deaf mute—like the Guinea, the man with the weed, and every other character that appears on the decks of the *Fidèle*—conceals another identity beneath his exterior appearance. Michael Rogin, Peter Bellis, Peggy Kamuf, Rachel Cole, and others have convincingly shown that it is a mistake to assume that "identity" rests securely inside or underneath "character," "costume," or "masquerade." See Rogin, *Subversive Genealogy*, 242; Bellis, "Mevlille's *Confidence-Man*"; Cole, "At the Limits of Identity."

7. As David Mitchell and Sharon Snyder note in "Masquerades of Impairment," this spectacle of strangeness also functions as an engine of normalcy, producing and confirming the crowd as "the realm of the normal." Focusing on the man's deafness and muteness, Mitchell and Snyder argue that corporeal disability "comprises a degree of difference that cannot be accommodated among even this motley crew" (41), though I would add that disability is a form of bodily variation that does accompany others (such as skin color in the Black Guinea episode) and does not always result in total estrangement (such as the one-legged man who instills doubt about Guinea, or Thomas Fry, whose "sugared" version of his disability allows him to be incorporated into a nationalist narrative).

8. In *Crowds and Power*, Elias Canetti notes that rivers commonly serve as figures for just such an idea of a crowd's momentum: "The unresisting and uninterrupted flow of its waters, the definiteness of its main direction—even if this changes in detail—the determination with which it makes towards the sea, its absorption of other, smaller streams—all this has an undeniably crowdlike character" (83).

9. See Watson Branch's summary of the more allegorical readings of these figures, beginning with Elizabeth Foster's Christian interpretation in 1954 and H. Bruce Franklin's response a decade later, both in the Norton edition of *The Confidence-Man* (316–17). What is surprising is that more recent critics, while abandoning the strictly Christian framework, continue to impose a certain allegorical model of reading on these figures when they regard them as "avatars" of the confidence man. Carolyn

Karcher is self-conscious about the consequences of such a reading: by presuming that the Black Guinea is the first avatar of a masquerading confidence man—and that the mute is his counterpart—one buys into a clear racial diabolism, and thus falls prey to the racist typing that the text satirizes (Karcher, *Shadows over the Promised Land*, 195).

10. Ryan, "Misgivings."

11. Schmitt's 1922 definition of sovereignty—"he who decides on the exception"—turns on this "decisionist" character, which is precisely what he argues democratic governments, with their emphasis on deliberation and debate, checks and balances, lack. He counters the image of the sovereign "decider" with that of the "neverending conversation" of German romanticism (Schmitt, *Political Theology*, 48, 53). For a revelatory reading of Schmitt's admiration for Melville, see Elmer, *On Lingering and Being Last*, 78–117. Elmer's book, which demonstrates how sovereignty and racialization become essentially linked in the political and literary traditions of Atlantic modernity, appeared as I was finalizing this project, and I regret that I was not able to give it the attention it deserves.

12. Jefferson, *Notes on the State of Virginia*, 145; Tocqueville, *Democracy in America*, 341–42.

13. Though the *Fidéle*, like the *Pequod*, contains an Anacharsis Cloots congress, Melville uses the metaphor quite differently in *The Confidence-Man*. When Ishmael invokes it, he calls the Pequod's crew an "Anacharsis Cloots deputation," describing the collective mission, "accompanying Old Ahab in the Pequod to lay the world's grievances before that bar from which not many of them ever come back." There is no such "deputation" aboard the *Fidèle*, no single voice speaking either to or for the varieties of strangers gathered under its name. At its most contained, the *Fidèle* is an "Anacharsis Cloots congress," a space where the "multiform pilgrim species" gathers, debates, scrutinizes, but declares nothing—neither allegiances nor grievances—collectively (Melville, *Moby-Dick*, 107). Michael Rogin also notes Melville's repetition of the "Anacharsis Cloots" metaphor (Rogin, *Subversive Genealogy*, 236).

14. Halttunen, *Confidence Men and Painted Women*, 153–61, 188–90.

15. Karcher and others also remark upon the affinities between these characters. Karcher goes so far as to suggest that they may be the same character in different disguises (Karcher, *Shadows over the Promised Land*, 206–8). While I resist the interpretation that sees these figures as "avatars" of a singular confidence-man, I do argue that they are fundamentally linked as iterations of related problems. I'll use a term borrowed from Ulysse Dutoit and Leo Bersani—"inexact replications"—to describe the relationship between these figures (see Bersani and Dutoit, *Arts of Impoverishment*).

16. The herb-doctor specifically diagnoses Fry as "much such a case as the negro's" (99).

17. Karcher notes that the Guinea and Fry episodes expose parallel violations at the hands of the state, arguing "that the racial distinctions on which the slave system is based provide no security against oppression for whites" (Karcher, *Shadows over the Promised Land*, 208).

18. Bersani and Dutoit, *Arts of Impoverishment*, 40–41.

19. Weber, *Theatricality as Medium*, 7 (Weber's italics); Bersani and Dutoit, *Arts of Impoverishment*, 85.

20. Barish, *The Antitheatrical Prejudice*, 80–130 (quotes at 92, 257–58, 117).

Antitheatricalism sometimes makes strange bedfellows, linking scholars like Michael Fried to materialist critics, like David Lloyd and Paul Thomas, who embrace Rousseau's transparency as a means of imagining the eradication of representation as the sole ground of social and political belonging. In their reading of Rousseau, representation and mediation are the problems to be overcome, and Rousseau's idealization of transparency offers an imaginative path before the advent of a modern political subject that is coextensive with the capacity for representation (see Lloyd and Thomas, *Culture and the State*, 35–46).

21. Fried, *Theatricality and Absorption* (quotes at 5, 104).

22. Stendahl, *Racine et Shakespeare*, 28. The story is quoted in Genette (*The Aesthetic Relation*, 17–18), and cited by Cavell (*Must We Mean What We Say*) with no attribution; and is also found in Reiss ("Psychical Distance and Theatrical Distance"). Stendahl's version seems to be the original. Though he claims that the event occurred in Baltimore, Maryland, in August of 1822, no earlier account of it has been found. In 1946, the theater historian C. Wesley Bird scanned the Baltimore newspapers from that summer for a mention of the incident and discovered only that Baltimore's two theaters were closed in August (see Bird, "Stendhal's 'Baltimore Incident': A Correction").

23. "Il ne sera jamais dit qu'en ma présence un maudit nègre aura tué une femme blanche" (Stendahl, *Racine et Shakespeare*, 28).

24. "Ce soldat avait de *l'illusion*, croyait vraie l'action qui se passé sur la scène" (ibid.; Stendahl's italics).

25. Ibid., 29; Genette, *The Aesthetic Relation*, 18.

26. Genette, *The Aesthetic Relation*, 18–19 (Genette's italics).

27. Cavell, "The Avoidance of Love," in *Must We Mean What We Say*, 257–356 (quotes at 330, 339). I am highlighting Cavell's phrase here despite the reservations he expresses about theatricality, so it is important to add that, according to Cavell, this other present which theater introduces arises from a conviction of the beholder's "absence" from the play. Citing Fried's "Art & Objecthood" in a footnote, Cavell basically endorses Fried's call to "defeat theater" with a model of absorption, and in doing so, he suggests that the very condition of theater—its constitutive relationship with an audience—must be suppressed. However, it seems that the power of this other present, the space where a "time and space" opens up that is in no way possessed by an "I," is made possible by theatricality's opacity, its reminder that—in Melville's words—this is "another world, but one to which we feel the tie." As with Fried's emphasis on theatricality's "estrangement," I read Cavell's point that it opens another present as evidence of theatricality's value not its mediocrity.

28. Kamuf discusses this temporality as the "collapsing of narrative time" (Kamuf, *The Division of Literature*, 201–2).

29. Pippin, "Authenticity in Painting, 575–98 (quote at 591).

30. Derrida, *Rogues*, 11–12.

31. Ibid., 11 (Derrida's italics).

32. Shklovsky, "Art as Technique." Shklovsky's term, *ostranenie*, is generally cited as the most influential model of aesthetic estrangement, though Carlo Ginzburg argues for a longer history to this device. While Ginzburg effectively historicizes the practice of "making things strange," he nonetheless assumes a certain transhistorical continuity to the practice, in particular, in its institution of a "detached gaze."

Equating estrangement with defamiliarization, Ginzburg argues that the naïve, outside observer is its typical subject (Ginzburg, "Making Things Strange"). See also Naiman, "Shklovsky's Dog and Mulvey's Pleasure"; and Smoliarova, "Distortion and Theatricality."

33. Ginsburg allies estrangement with a gaze that is "critical, detached" (Ginsburg, "Making Things Strange," 15), which Svetlana Boym describes as an inappropriate depoliticization of Shklovsky's concept (Boym, "Poetics and Politics of Estrangement," 599).

34. Cameron, *Impersonality*, 181.

35. Renker, *Strike through the Mask*; and Renker, "'A—!' Unreadability in *The Confidence-Man*."

36. Boym, "Poetics and Politics of Estrangement," 584–605 (quotes at 584, 599, 602).

37. In an insightful close reading, Rachel Cole links this passage to the model of mimetic realism articulated in chapter 14, to claim that the aesthetic imperative of both chapters is tied to a "freedom from convention" in both aesthetic and social terms. However, where she finds in Melville's invocation of theater a "hidden depth, the shape of selfhood," which she allies with interiority, my emphasis on the aesthetics of theatrical estrangement moves in the opposite direction, toward an understanding of social relations in the text as opaque, external, and irreducibly strange (see Cole, "At the Limits of Identity" 393–97).

38. Bersani and Dutoit, *Arts of Impoverishment*, 85, 7.

39. Weber, *Theatricality as Medium*, 46.

40. Here, I would argue, collective character in *The Confidence-Man* shares the same radical openness that Sharon Cameron finds only in *Billy Budd,* as she analyzes the tendency of character to bleed out its defining traits and properties, not only beyond individual persons but beyond the human as well (Cameron, *Impersonality*, 199–200).

41. Arendt, *The Human Condition*, 8–9; also quoted in Boym, "Poetics and Politics of Estrangement,"600.

42. Arendt, *The Human Condition*, 9.

43. Ibid., 234.

# Select Bibliography

Ackerman, Alan L. *The Portable Theater: American Literature and the Nineteenth-Century Stage.* Baltimore: Johns Hopkins University Press, 1999.

Agamben, Giorgio. *Homo Sacer: Sovereign Power and Bare Life.* Translated by Daniel Heller-Roazen. Stanford, CA: Stanford University Press, 1998.

———. *State of Exception.* Translated by Kevin Attell. Chicago: University of Chicago Press, 2005.

Agnew, Jean-Christophe. *World's Apart: The Market and the Theatre in Anglo-American Thought, 1550–1750.* New York: Cambridge University Press, 1986.

Aiken, George. "Uncle Tom's Cabin." 1852. In *American Melodrama,* edited by Daniel C. Gerould. New York: Performing Arts Journal Publications, 1983.

Alger, William Rounseville. *The Life of Edwin Forrest, the American Tragedian.* 2 vols. Boston: B. Blom, 1972.

Althusser, Louis. "Ideology and Ideological State Apparatuses." In *Lenin and Philosophy and Other Essays.* New York: Monthly Review Press, 1971.

Arendt, Hannah. *The Human Condition.* Chicago: University of Chicago, 1998.

———. *On Revolution.* New York: Penguin, 2006

Auerbach, Jonathan. *The Romance of Failure: First-Person Fictions of Poe, Hawthorne, and James.* New York: Oxford University Press, 1989.

Baer, Mark. *Theatre and Disorder in Late Georgian London.* New York: Clarendon/ Oxford University Press, 1992.

Bakhtin, M. M. *The Dialogic Imagination.* Austin: University of Texas Press, 1981.

Balibar, Etienne, and Immanual Wallerstein. *Race, Nation, Class: Ambiguous Identities.* Translated by Chris Turner. Verso, 1991.

Bank, Rosemarie. *Theatre Culture in America, 1825–1960*. New York: Cambridge University Press, 1997.

Barish, Jonas. *The Antitheatrical Prejudice*. Berkeley: University of California Press, 1981.

Barnum, Phineas T. *The Life of P. T. Barnum, Written by Himself*. Urbana: University of Illinois Press, 2000.

Baym, Nina. "*The Blithedale Romance*: A Radical Reading." *Journal of English and Germanic Philology*, no. 67 (1968): 545–69.

Beaumont, Gustave de. *Lettres d'Amérique*. Edited by André Jardin and George Wilson Pierson. Paris: Presses Universitaires de France, 1973.

———. *Marie; or, Slavery in the United States: A novel of Jacksonian America*. Translated by Barbara Chapman. Baltimore: Johns Hopkins University Press, 1999.

———. *Marie, ou l'esclavage aux États-Unis: Tableau de Mœurs Américaines*. 2 vols. Paris: Charles Gosselin, 1835.

Beaumont, Gustave de, and Alexis de Tocqueville. *On the Penitentiary System in the United States and Its Application in France*. Translated by Francis Lieber. Carbondale: Southern Illinois University Press, 1964.

———. *Système pénitentiare aux États-Unis*. 3rd ed. Paris: Charles Gosselin, 1845.

Behn, Aphra. *Oroonoko*. Edited by Catherine Gallagher. New York: Bedford/ St. Martins, 1999.

Bell, Millicent, ed. *Hawthorne and the Real: Bicentennial Essays*. Columbus: Ohio State University Press, 2005.

Bellis, Peter. "Melville's *Confidence-Man*: An Uncharitable Reading." *American Literature* 59, no. 4 (1987): 548–69.

Bender, John. *Imagining the Penitentiary: Fiction and the Architecture of Mind in Eighteenth-Century England*. Chicago: University of Chicago Press, 1987.

Bennett, Jane. *The Enchantment of Modern Life: Attachments, Crossings, and Ethics*. Princeton, NJ: Princeton University Press, 2001.

Bentley, Nancy. "The Strange Career of Love and Slavery: Chesnutt, Engels, Masoch." *American Literary History* 17, no. 3 (2005): 460–85.

Bercovitch, Sacvan. *The American Jeremiad*. Madison: University of Wisconsin Press, 1978.

Bercovitch, Sacvan, and Myra Jehlen, eds. *Ideology and Classic American Literature*. New York: Cambridge, 1986.

Berlant, Lauren. *The Anatomy of a National Fantasy: Hawthorne, Utopia, and Everyday Life*. Chicago: University of Chicago Press, 1991.

———. "Fantasies of Utopia in *The Blithedale Romance*." *American Literary History* 1, no. 1 (1989): 30–62.

———. "National Brands/National Bodies: *Imitation of Life*." In *Comparative American Identities: Race, Sex, and Nationality in the Modern Text*, edited by Hortense J. Spillers. New York: Routledge, 1991.

———. *The Queen of America Goes to Washington City*. Durham, NC: Duke University Press, 1997.

Bersani, Leo, and Ulysse Dutoit. *Arts of Impoverishment: Beckett, Rothko, Resnais*. Cambridge, MA: Harvard University Press, 1993.

Berthold, Dennis. "Class Acts: The Astor Place Riots and Melville's 'Two Temples.'" *American Literature* 71, no. 3 (1999): 429–61.

Best, Stephen. *The Fugitive's Properties: Law and the Poetics of Possession*. Chicago: University of Chicago Press, 2004.

Bhabha, Homi K. *The Location of Culture*. New York: Routledge, 1994.

Bird, C. Wesley. "Stendhal's 'Baltimore Incident': A Correction." *Modern Language Notes* 61, no. 2 (1946), 118–19.

Bird, Robert Montgomery. "The Gladiator." 1831. In *Early American Drama*, edited by Jeffrey Richards. New York: Penguin, 1997.

Boucicault, Dion. "The Octoroon." 1859. In *Early American Drama*, edited by Jeffrey Richards. New York: Penguin, 1997.

———. *The Poor of New York*. 1857. In *American Melodrama*, edited by Daniel C. Gerould. New York: Performing Arts Journal Publications, 1983.

Boym, Svetlana. "Poetics and Politics of Estrangement: Viktor Shklovsky and Hannah Arendt." *Poetics Today* 26, no. 4 (2005): 581–611.

Brand, Dana. *The Spectator and the City in Nineteenth-Century American Literature*. Cambridge: Cambridge University Press, 1991.

Brodhead, Richard. *Hawthorne, Melville, and the Novel*. Chicago: University of Chicago Press, 1976.

———. "Veiled Ladies: Toward a History of Antebellum Entertainment." *American Literary History* 1, no. 2 (Summer 1989): 271–94.

Brooks, Daphne. *Bodies in Dissent: Spectacular Performances of Race and Freedom, 1850–1910*. Durham, NC: Duke University Press, 2006.

Brooks, Peter. *The Melodramatic Imagination: Balzac, Henry James, Melodrama, and the Mode of Excess*. New Haven, CT: Yale University Press, 1995.

Brown, Charles Brockden. *Edgar Huntly*. New York: Penguin, 1988.

———. *Memoirs of Carwin*. New York: Penguin, 1991.

———. *Ormond*. New York: Burt Franklin, 1970.

———. *Wieland*. New York: Penguin, 1991.

Brown, Sterling. "Negro Characters As Seen by White Authors." In *Interracialism: Black-White Intermarriage in American History, Literature, and Law*, edited by Werner Sollors. Oxford: Oxford University Press, 2000.

Brown, William Wells. *Clotel, or the President's Daughter*. Edited by Robert S. Levine. New York: Bedford/St. Martin's, 2000.

———. "St. Domingo: Its Revolutions and Its Patriots." 1855. In *Clotel, or the President's Daughter*, edited by Robert S. Levine. New York: Bedford/St. Martin's, 2000.

Bumas, E. Shaskan. "Fictions of the Panopticon: Prison, Utopia, and the

Out-Penitent in the Works of Nathaniel Hawthorne." *American Literature* 73, no. 1 (2001): 121–45.

Burke, Edmund. *Reflections on the Revolution in France*. New York: Oxford University Press, 1999.

Butler, Judith. *Antigone's Claim: Kinship between Life and Death*. New York: Columbia University Press, 2000.

———. *Bodies that Matter: On the Discursive Limits of "Sex."* New York: Routledge, 1993.

———. *The Psychic Life of Power: Theories in Subjection*. Stanford, CA: Stanford University Press, 1997.

Butler, Judith, Ernesto Laclau, and Slavoj Žižek. *Contingency, Hegemony, Universality: Contemporary Dialogues on the Left*. New York: London, 2000.

Cadava, Eduardo. "The Guano of History." In *Cities without Citizens*, edited by Eduardo Cadava and Aaron Levy. Philadelphia: Slought Foundation, 2005.

———. *Emerson and the Climates of History*. Stanford, CA: Stanford University Press, 1997.

Cain, William E. Introduction to *The Blithedale Romance*, by Nathaniel Hawthorne. New York: Bedford Books of St. Martin's Press, 1996.

Calhoun, Craig, ed. *Habermas and the Public Sphere*. Cambridge, MA: MIT Press, 1989.

Cameron, Sharon. *The Corporeal Self: Allegories of the Body in Melville and Hawthorne*. New York: Columbia University Press, 1991.

———. *Impersonality: Seven Essays*. Chicago: University of Chicago Press, 2007

Canetti, Elias. *Crowds and Power*. New York: Viking Press, 1962.

Carton, Evan. *The Rhetoric of American Romance: Dialectic and Identity in Emerson, Dickinson, Poe, and Hawthorne*. Baltimore: Johns Hopkins University Press, 1985.

Castiglia, Christopher. "Abolition's Racial Interiors and the Making of White Civic Depth." *American Literary History* 14, no. 1 (2002): 32–34.

Castronovo, Russ. *Necro Citizenship: Death, Eroticism, and the Public Sphere in the Nineteenth-Century United States*. Durham, NC: Duke University Press, 2001.

Castronovo, Russ, and Dana D. Nelson, eds. *Materializing Democracy: Toward a Revitalized Cultural Politics*. Durham, NC: Duke University Press, 2002.

Cavell, Stanley. *Must We Mean What We Say? A Book of Essays*. New York: Scribner's, 1969.

Chesnutt, Charles. *The Conjure Tales and Stories of the Color Line*. Edited by William L. Andrews. New York: Penguin, 1992.

———. *The Marrow of Tradition*. Edited by Eric Sundquist. New York: Penguin, 1993.

Child, Lydia Maria. *An Appeal in Favor of That Class of Americans Called Africans*. Edited by Carolyn Karcher. Amherst: University of Massachusetts, 1996.

———. *The Collected Correspondence of Lydia Maria Child, 1817–1881*. Edited by Milton Meltzer and Patricia G. Holland. Millwood, NY: Kraus Microform, 1980.

———. *Hobomok, and Other Writings*. New Brunswick, NJ: Rutgers University Press, 1986.

———. *Letters from New-York*. New York: C. S. Francis & Co., 1850.

———. *Letters from New-York*. Edited by Bruce Mills. Athens: University of Georgia Press, 1998.

———. *Letters from New-York: 2d Series*. New York: C. S. Francis & Co., 1845.

———. *A Romance of the Republic*. 1867. Reprint, Lexington: University Press of Kentucky, 1997.

Chow, Rey. *The Protestant Ethnic and the Spirit of Capitalism*. New York: Columbia University Press, 2002.

Cleghorn, Cassandra. "Chivalric Sentimentalism: The Case of Dr. Howe and Laura Bridgman." In *Sentimental Men: Masculinity and the Politics of Affect in American Culture,* edited by Mary Chapman and Glenn Hendler. Berkeley: University of California Press, 1999.

Coale, Samuel. *Mesmerism and Hawthorne: Mediums of American Romance*. Tuscaloosa: University of Alabama Press, 1998.

Cole, Rachel. "At the Limits of Identity: Realism and American Personhood in Melville's *Confidence-Man*." *Novel: A Forum on Fiction* 39, no. 3 (2006): 384–401.

Cooper, James Fenimore. *The Deerslayer*. New York: Penguin, 1987.

———. *The Last of the Mohicans*. New York: Quality Paperbacks, 1993.

———. *The Pioneers*. New York: Penguin, 1988.

Davis, David Brion. *The Problem of Slavery in the Age of Revolution*. Ithaca, NY: Cornell University Press, 1973.

Dayan, Joan (Colin). *Haiti, History, and the Gods*. Berkeley, CA: University of California Press, 1998.

———. "Legal Slaves and Civil Bodies." In *Materializing Democracy: Toward a Revitalized Cultural Politics*. Edited by Russ Castronovo and Dana D. Nelson. Durham, NC: Duke University Press, 2002.

———. *The Story of Cruel and Unusual*. Boston: MIT/Boston Review Books, 2007.

Debord, Guy. *The Society of the Spectacle*. Translated by Donald Nicholson-Smith. New York: Zone Books, 2002.

Delany, Martin. *Blake; or, the Huts of America*. Boston: Beacon Press, 1970.

Delbanco, Andrew. *Melville: His World and Work*. New York: Vintage, 2005.

Denning, Michael. *Culture in the Age of Three Worlds*. London: Verso, 2004.

Derrida, Jacques. *Dissemination*. Translated by Barbara Johnson. Chicago: University of Chicago Press, 1981.

———. *Rogues: Two Essays on Reason*. Translated by Pascale-Anne Brauly and Michael Naas. Stanford, CA: Stanford University Press, 2005.

———. *Sovereignties in Question*. Translated by Thomas Dutoit and Outi Patterson. New York: Fordham University Press, 2005.

———. *Without Alibi*. Translated by Peggy Kamuf. Stanford, CA: Stanford University Press, 2002.

Dickens, Charles. *American Notes, For General Circulation*. New York: Penguin, 2000.

Diderot, Denis. *Le paradoxe sur le comédien*. Paris: Èditions Gallimard, 1994.

Dix, Dorothea. *An Address by a Recent Female Visitor to the Prisoners in the Eastern Penitentiary of Pennsylvania*. Philadelphia: Joseph and William Kite, 1844.

———. *Asylum, Prison, and Poorhouse: The Writings and Reform Work of Dorothea Dix in Illinois*. Edited by David L. Lightner. Carbondale: Southern Illinois University Press, 1999.

———. *Remarks on Prisons and Prison Discipline*. Montclair, NJ: Patterson Smith, 1967.

Douglas, Ann. *The Feminization of American Culture*. New York: Knopf, 1977.

Douglass, Frederick. *Autobiographies*. New York: Library of America, 1996.

———. *My Bondage and My Freedom*. Edited by William L. Andrews. Urbana: University of Illinois Press, 1987.

———. "What to the Slave is the Fourth of July? An Address Delivered in Rochester, New York, on 5 July, 1852." In vol. 2 of *The Frederick Douglass Papers*, Series 1: *Speeches, Debates, and Interviews*, edited by John W. Blassingame et al. New Haven, CT: Yale University Press, 1982.

Downes, Paul. *Democracy, Revolution, and Monarchism in Early American Literature*. New York: Cambridge University Press, 2002.

———. "Melville's 'Benito Cereno' and the Politics of Humanitarian Intervention." *South Atlantic Quarterly* 103, no. 2/3 (2004): 465–88.

Dumm, Thomas L. *Democracy and Punishment: Disciplinary Origins of the United States*. Madison: University of Wisconsin Press, 1987.

Dupeuty, Charles. *Napoléon, ou, Schoenbrunn et St-Hélène: Drame historique en deux parties en neuf tableaux*. La France dramatique au dix-neuviéme siècle series. Paris: N.p., 18—.

Eagelton, Terry. *Ideology*. London: Verso, 1991.

———. *The Ideology of the Aesthetic*. London: Blackwell, 1990.

Elmer, Jonathan. *On Lingering and Being Last: Race and Sovereignty in the New World*. New York: Fordham University Press, 2008.

———. *Reading at the Social Limit: Affect, Mass Culture, and Edgar Allan Poe*. Stanford, CA: Stanford University Press, 1995.

Emerson, Ralph Waldo. *Ralph Waldo Emerson: Essays and Poems*. Edited by Joel Porte, Harold Bloom, and Paul Kane. New York: Library of America, 1996.

Equiano, Olaudhah. *The Interesting Narrative of the Life of Olaudah Equiano, or Gustavas Vassa, The African.* Edited by Wernor Sollors. New York: W. W. Norton, 2000.

Esteve, Mary. *The Aesthetics and Politics of the Crowd in American Literature.* New York: Cambridge University Press, 2003.

Fanon, Frantz. *Peau noir, masques blancs.* Paris: Éditions de Seuil, 1995.

———. *Les damnés de la terre.* Paris: François Maspero, 1974.

Fanuzzi, Robert. *Abolition's Public Sphere.* Minneapolis: University of Minnesota Press, 2003.

———. "Taste, Manners, and Miscegenation: French Racial Politics in the U.S." *American Literary History* 19, no. 3 (2007): 573–602.

Finkelman, Paul. *Dred Scott v. Sandford: A Brief History with Documents.* New York: Bedford Books, 1997.

Fliegelman, Jay. *Declaring Independence: Jefferson, Natural Language, and the Culture of Performance.* Stanford, CA: Stanford University Press, 1993.

———. *Prodigals and Pilgrims: The American Revolution against Patriarchal Authority.* New York: Cambridge University Press, 1982.

Foucault, Michel. *Abnormal: Lectures at the Collége de France, 1974–1975.* Translated by Graham Burchell. New York: Picador, 2003.

———. *Discipline and Punish: The Birth of the Prison.* Translated by Alan Sheridan. New York: Vintage, 1995.

———. *Ethics: Subjectivity and Truth.* Edited by Paul Rabinow; translated by Robert Hurley and others. New York: The New Press, 1997.

———. *Language, Counter-memory, Practice.* Translated by Donald E. Bouchard. Ithaca, NY: Cornell University Press, 1977.

———. *Security, Territory, Population: Lectures at the Collége de France, 1977–1978.* Translated by Graham Burchell. New York: Palgrave, 2007.

———. *Society Must Be Defended: Lectures from the Collége de France 1975–1976.* Translated by David Macey. New York: Picador, 2003.

Franchot, Jenny. "The Punishment of Esther: Frederick Douglass and the Constitution of the Feminine." In *Frederick Douglass: New Literary and Historical Essays,* edited by Eric J. Sundquist New York: Cambridge, 1991.

———. *Roads to Rome: The Antebellum Protestant Encounter with Catholicism.* Berkeley: University of California Press, 1994.

Fried, Michael. *Absorption and Theatricality: Painting and Beholder in the Age of Diderot.* Chicago: University of Chicago Press, 1988.

Fuller, Margaret. *Woman in the Nineteenth Century.* New York: W. W. Norton, 1971.

Gable, Harvey L., Jr. "Inappeasable Longings: Hawthorne, Romance, and the Disintegration of Coverdale's Self in The Blithedale Romance." *New England Quarterly* 67, no. 2 (1994): 257–78.

Gallagher, Catherine. *Nobody's Story: The Vanishing Acts of Women Writers in the Marketplace, 1670–1820.* Berkeley: University of California Press, 1994.

Gebauer, Gunter, and Christoph Wulf. *Mimesis: Culture, Art, Society.* Translated by Don Reneau. Berkeley: University of California Press, 1995.

Genette, Gérard. *The Aesthetic Relation.* Translated by G. M. Goshgarian. Ithaca, NY: Cornell University Press, 1999.

Gilmore, Michael. "Hawthorne and Politics (Again)." In *Hawthorne and the Real: Bicentennial Essays,* edited by Millicent Bell. Columbus: Ohio State University Press, 2005.

Gilroy, Paul. *The Black Atlantic: Modernity and Double Consciousness.* Cambridge, MA: Harvard University Press, 1993.

Ginzburg, Carlo. "Making Things Strange: The Prehistory of a Literary Device." *Representations,* no. 56 (1996): 8–28.

Girard, René. *Deceit, Desire, and the Novel: Self and Other in Literary Structure.* Baltimore: Johns Hopkins University Press, 1965.

———. *Violence and the Sacred.* Translated by Patrick Gregory. Baltimore: Johns Hopkins University Press, 1977.

Gitter, Elisabeth. *The Imprisoned Guest: Samuel Howe and Laura Bridgman, The Original Deaf-Blind Girl.* New York: Farrar, Strauss, and Giroux, 2001.

Glazer, Nathan. "Race and Ethnicity in America." *Journal of Democracy* 11, no. 1 (January 2000): 95–102.

Godwin, William. *Caleb Williams.* New York: Penguin, 2005.

Greven, David. "In a Pig's Eye: Masculinity, Mastery, and the Returned Gaze of *The Blithedale Romance.*" *Studies in American Literature* 34, no. 2 (2006): 131–59.

Grimstead, David. *Melodrama Unveiled: American Theater and Culture, 1800–1850.* Berkeley: University of California Press, 1987.

Grossberg, Benjamin Scott. "'The Tender Passion Was Very Rife Among Us': Coverdale's Queer Utopia and *The Blithedale Romance.*" *Studies in American Literature* 21, no. 1 (2000): 3–25.

Habermas, Jürgen. *The Structural Transformation of the Public Sphere.* Translated by Thomas Burger. Cambridge, MA: MIT Press, 1995.

Hadley, Elaine. *Melodramatic Tactics: Theatricalized Dissent in the English Marketplace, 1800–1885.* Stanford, CA: Stanford University Press, 1995.

Halttunen, Karen. *Confidence Men and Painted Women: A Study of Middle-Class Culture in America, 1830–1870.* New Haven, CT: Yale University Press, 1982.

Hamilton, Kristie. *America's Sketchbook: The Cultural Life of a Nineteenth-Century Literary Genre.* Athens: Ohio University Press, 1998.

Hardt, Michael, and Antonio Negri. *Empire.* Cambridge, MA: Harvard University Press, 2000.

———. *Multitude: War and Democracy in the Age of Empire.* New York: Penguin, 2004.

Harris, Neil. *Humbug: The Art of P. T. Barnum.* New York: Little, Brown, 1973.

Hartman, Saidya. *Scenes of Subjection: Terror, Slavery, and Self-Making in Nineteenth-Century America.* New York: Oxford University Press, 1997.

Hawthorne, Nathaniel. *The Blithedale Romance.* New York: Bedford of St. Martin's, 1996.

———. *The Celestial Railroad and Other Stories.* New York: Signet, 1980.

———. *Hawthorne's Lost Notebook, 1835–41.* Edited by Barbara S. Mouffe. University Park: Pennsylvania State University Press, 1978.

———. *The House of the Seven Gables.* New York: Penguin, 1986.

———. *The Letters.* Edited by Thomas Woodson, L. Neal Smith, and Norman Holmes Pearson. 6 vols. Columbus: Ohio State University Press, 1984–88.

———. *The Scarlet Letter.* New York: W. W. Norton, 1988.

Hill, Mike, and Warren Montag, eds. *Masses, Classes, and the Public Sphere.* London: Verso, 2000.

Howe, Samuel Gridley. *An Essay on Separate and Congregate Systems of Prison Discipline, Being a Report of the Minority of the Special Committee of the Boston Prison Discipline Society.* Boston: William D. Ticknor & Co., 1846.

Hutner, Gordon. *Secrets and Sympathy: Forms of Disclosure in Hawthorne's Novels.* Athens: University of Georgia Press, 1988.

Irving, Washington. *The Works of Washington Irving: The Sketch Book and Abbotsford.* New York: The Century Company, 1910.

Jackson, Casssandra. *Barriers between Us: Interracial Sex in Nineteenth-Century American Literature.* Bloomington: Indiana University Press, 2004.

Jacobs, Harriet. *Incidents in the Life of a Slave Girl.* New York: Signet Classics, 2000.

James, C. L. R. *The Black Jacobins: Toussaint L'Ouverture and the San Domingo Revolution.* New York: Vintage, 1989.

Jefferson, Thomas. *Notes on the State of Virginia.* New York: Penguin, 1999.

Kamuf, Peggy. *The Division of Literature; or, the University in Deconstruction.* Chicago: University of Chicago Press, 1997.

Karcher, Carolyn. "Censorship, American Style: The Case of Lydia Maria Child." In *Studies in the American Renaissance,* edited by Joel Myerson. Charlottesville: University Press of Virginia, 1990.

———. *The First Woman in the Republic: A Cultural Biography of Lydia Maria Child.* Durham, NC: Duke University Press, 1994.

———. "Lydia Maria Child's *A Romance of the Republic*: An Abolitionist Vision of America's Racial Destiny." In *Slavery and the American Literary Imagination,* edited by Deborah E. McDowell and Arnold Rampersad. Baltimore: Johns Hopkins University Press, 1989.

———. *Shadows over the Promised Land: Slavery, Race, and Violence in Melville's America.* Baton Rouge: Louisiana State University Press, 1980.

Keller, Morton. *Affairs of State: Public Life in Later Nineteenth-Century America.* Cambridge, MA: Harvard Belknap, 1977.

Kinney, James. *Amalgamation! Race, Sex, and Rhetoric in the Nineteenth-Century American Novel*. Westport, CT: Greenwood Press, 1985.

LaCapra, Dominick. *History and Reading: Tocqueville, Foucault, French Studies*. Toronto: University of Toronto Press, 2000.

Lacoue-Labarthe, Philippe. *Typography: Mimesis, Philosophy, Politics*. Translated by Christopher Fynsk. Stanford, CA: Stanford University Press, 1998.

Langan, Celeste. *Romantic Vagrancy: Wordsworth and the Simulation of Freedom*. New York: Cambridge University Press, 1995.

Lefort, Claude. *Democracy and Political Theory*. Translated by David Macy. London: Polity Press, 1988.

Levine, Lawrence. *Highbrow/Lowbrow: The Emergence of Cultural Hierarchy in America*. Cambridge, MA: Harvard University Press, 1988.

Linebaugh, Peter, and Marcus Rediker. *The Many-Headed Hydra: The Hidden History of the Revolutionary Atlantic*. London: Verso, 2002.

Lippmann, Walter. *Public Opinion*. New York: Harcourt, Brace, 1922.

Lloyd, David, and Paul Thomas. *Culture and the State*. New York: Routledge, 1998.

Looby, Christopher. *Voicing America: Language, Literary Form, and the Origins of the United States*. Chicago: University of Chicago Press, 1996.

Lott, Eric. *Love and Theft: Blackface Minstrelsy and the American Working Class*. New York: Oxford University Press, 1995.

Loughran, Trish. *The Republic in Print*. New York: Columbia University Press, 2007.

Malone, Anne Righton. "Sugar Ladles and Strainers: Political Self-Fashioning in the Epistolary Journalism of Lydia Maria Child." In *Women's Life-Writing: Finding Voice/Building Community*, edited by Linda S. Coleman. Bowling Green, OH: Bowling Green State University Press, 1997.

Margolis, Stacey. *The Public Life of Privacy in Nineteenth-Century American Literature*. Durham, NC: Duke University Press, 2005.

Marshall, David. *The Figure of Theater*. New York: Columbia University Press, 1986.

———. *The Surprising Effects of Sympathy*. Chicago: University of Chicago Press, 1988.

Marshall, Meghan. "The Other Sister: Was Nathaniel Hawthorne a Cad?" *The New Yorker*, 21 March 2005.

———. *The Peabody Sisters: Three Women Who Ignited American Romanticism*. New York: Houghton Mifflin, 2005.

Marx, Karl. *The Eighteenth Brumaire of Louis Bonaparte*. New York: Mondial, 2005.

———. "On the Jewish Question." In *The Marx-Engels Reader*, edited by Robert C. Tucker. New York: W. W. Norton, 1978.

Mason, Jeffrey. *Melodama and the Myth of America*. Bloomington: Indiana University Press, 1993.

McConachie, Bruce. *Melodramatic Formations: American Theatre and Society, 1820–1870*. Iowa City: University of Iowa Press, 1992.

Melville, Herman. *Billy Budd and Other Stories*. New York: Penguin, 1986.

———. *The Confidence-Man: His Masquerade*. Edited by Hershel Parker. New York: W. W. Norton, 1971.

———. *The Confidence-Man: His Masquerade*. Edited by Hershel Parker, G. Thomas Tanselle, and Harrison Hayford. Evanston, IL: Northwestern University Press and The Newbury Library, 1984.

———. *Israel Potter*. Evanston, IL: Northwestern University Press, 1982.

———. *Moby-Dick; or, The Whale*. Berkeley: University of California Press with the Arion Press, 1979.

———. *The Piazza Tales*. Evanston, IL: Northwestern University Press, 1987.

———. *Pierre; or, The Ambiguities*. New York: Library of America, 1984.

———. *Typee, Omoo, Mardi*. New York: Library of America, 1982

———. *White-Jacket; or, The World in a Man-of-War*. New York: Modern Library, 2002.

Meranze, Michael. *Laboratories of Virtue: Punishment, Revolution, and Authority in Philadelphia, 1760–1835*. Chapel Hill: University of North Carolina Press, 1996.

Millington, Richard H. "American Anxiousness: Selfhood and Culture in Hawthorne's *The Blithedale Romance*." *New England Review* 63, no. 4 (1990): 558–83.

Mills, Angela. "'The Sweet Word' Sister: The Transformative Threat of Sisterhood and *The Blithedale Romance*." *American Transcendental Quarterly* 17, no. 2 (2003): 97–121.

Mitchell, David T., and Sharon L. Snyder. "Masquerades of Impairment: Charity as Confidence Game." *Leviathan: A Journal of Melville Studies* 8, no. 1 (2006): 35–60.

Moody, Richard. *The Astor Place Riot*. Bloomington: Indiana University Press, 1958.

Morrison, Toni. *Playing in the Dark: Whiteness and the Literary Imagination*. Cambridge, MA: Harvard University Press, 1992.

———. "Unspeakable Things Unspoken." *Michigan Quarterly Review* 28, no. 1 (1988): 1–34.

Naiman, Eric. "Shklovsky's Dog and Mulvey's Pleasure: The Secret Life of Defamiliarization." *Comparative Literature* 50, no. 4 (1998): 333–52.

Novak, William J. *The People's Welfare: Law and Regulation in Nineteenth-Century America*. Chapel Hill: University of North Carolina Press, 1997.

Okun, Peter. *Crime and the Nation: Prison Reform and Popular Fiction in Philadelphia, 1786–1800*. New York: Routledge, 2002.

Otter, Samuel. *Melville's Anatomies*. Berkeley: University of California Press, 1999.

Paine, Thomas. *Common Sense*. New York: Penguin, 1986.

———. *Rights of Man*. New York: Penguin, 1984.

Parker, Hershel. *Herman Melville: A Biography*. 2 vols. Baltimore: Johns Hopkins University Press, 1996.

Patterson, Orlando. *Slavery and Social Death: A Comparative Study*. Cambridge, MA: Harvard University Press, 1982.

Paulin, Diana. "Representing Forbidden Desire: Interracial Unions, Surrogacy, and Performance." *Theatre Journal* 49, no. 4 (1997): 417–39.

Pease, Donald. "Tocqueville's Democratic Thing; or, Aristocracy in America." In *Materializing Democracy: Toward a Revitalized Cultural Politics,* edited by Russ Castronovo and Dana D. Nelson. Durham, NC: Duke University Press, 2002.

———. *Visionary Compacts: American Renaissance Writings in Cultural Contexts*. Madison: University of Wisconsin, 1987.

*Performativity and Performance: Essays from the English Institute*. Edited with an introduction by Andrew Parker and Eve Kosofsky Sedgwick. New York: Routledge, 1995.

Pierson, George Wilson. *Tocqueville in America*. Baltimore: Johns Hopkins University Press, 1996.

Pippin, Robert. "Authenticity in Painting: Remarks on Michael Fried's Art History." *Critical Inquiry* 31, no. 3 (2005): 575–98.

Pitts, Jennifer. Introduction to *Writings on Empire and Slavery,* by Alexis de Tocqueville. Baltimore: Johns Hopkins University Press, 2001.

Plotz, John. *The Crowd: British Literature and Public Politics*. Berkeley: University of California Press, 2000.

Poe, Edgar Allan. *Complete Tales and Poems*. New York: Vintage, 1975.

Porter, Carolyn. *Seeing and Being: The Plight of the Participant-Observer in Emerson, James, Adams, and Faulkner*. Middletown, CT: Wesleyan University Press, 1981.

Reiss, Benjamin. *The Showman and the Slave: Race, Death, and Memory in Barnum's America*. Cambridge, MA: Harvard University Press, 2001.

Reiss, Timothy J. "Psychical Distance and Theatrical Distance." *Yale French Studies* 46, no. 1 (1971): 5–16.

Renker, Elizabeth. "'A—!' Unreadability in *The Confidence-Man*." In *The Cambridge Companion to Herman Melville*, edited by Robert Levine. Cambridge: Cambridge University Press, 1998.

———. *Strike through the Mask*. Baltimore: Johns Hopkins University Press, 1997.

Reynolds, David S. *Beneath the American Renaissance: The Subversive Imagination in the Age of Emerson and Melville*. New York: Knopf, 1988.

———. *Walt Whitman's America: A Cultural Biography*. New York: Knopf, 1995.

Richards, Leonard L. *Gentlemen of Property and Standing: Anti-Abolitionist Mobs in Jacksonian America*. New York: Oxford University Press, 1970.

Riss, Arthur. *Race, Slavery, and Liberalism in Nineteenth-Century American Literature.* New York: Cambridge University Press, 2006.

Roach, Joseph. *Cities of the Dead: Circum-Atlantic Performance.* New York: Columbia University Press, 1996.

Roberts, Heather. "'The Public Heart': Urban Life and the Politics of Sympathy in Lydia Maria Child's *Letters from New York.*" *American Literature* 76, no. 4 (2004): 750–75.

Rogin, Michael P. *Blackface, White Noise: Jewish Immigrants in the Hollywood Melting Pot.* Berkeley: University of California Press, 1996.

———. *Fathers and Children: Andrew Jackson and the Subjugation of the American Indian.* New York: Knopf, 1975.

———. *Ronald Reagan, the Movie, and Other Episodes in Political Demonology.* Berkeley: University of California Press, 1987.

———. *Subversive Genealogy: The Politics and Art of Herman Melville.* New York: Knopf, 1979.

Rousseau, Jean-Jacques. *Le contrat social et De l'inégalité parmi les hommes.* Paris: Éditions 10/18, 1973.

———. *Lettre à M. D'Alembert sur les spectacles.* Edited by M. Fuchs. Lille: Giad, 1948.

———. *The Social Contract and Discourse on the Origin of Inequality.* Translated by Lester Crocker. New York: Washington Square Press, 1967.

Rowson, Susannah. *Charlotte Temple and Lucy Temple.* New York: Penguin, 1991.

———. *Slaves in Algiers; or, A Struggle for Freedom.* Edited by Jennifer Margulis and Karen Poremsky. Acton, MA: Copley Publishing Group, 2001.

Ruttenburg, Nancy. *Democratic Personality: Popular Voice and the Trial of American Authorship.* Stanford, CA: Stanford University Press, 1998.

———. *Dostoyevsky's Democracy.* Princeton: Princeton University Press, 2008.

Ryan, Mary. *Civic Wars: Democracy and Public Life in the American City during the Nineteenth Century.* Berkeley: University of California Press, 1997.

Ryan, Susan M. "Misgivings: Melville, Race, and the Ambiguities of Benevolence." *American Literary History* 12, no. 4 (2000): 685–712.

Sanborn, Geoffrey. *The Sign of the Cannibal: Melville and the Making of a Postcolonial Reader.* Durham, NC: Duke University Press, 1998.

Sánchez-Eppler, Karen. *Touching Liberty: Abolitionism, Feminism, and the Politics of the Body.* Berkeley: University of California Press, 1993.

Sansay, Leonora. *Secret History; or, the Horrors of St. Domingo.* Edited by Michael Drexler. New York: Broadview, 2007.

Schmitt, Carl. *Political Theology: Four Chapters on the Concept of Sovereignty.* Translated by George Schwab Cambridge, MA: MIT Press, 1985.

Schoolman, Morton. *Reason and Horror: Critical Theory, Democracy, and Aesthetic Individuality.* New York: Routledge, 2001.

Schudson, Michael. "Was There Ever a Public Sphere? If So, When? Reflections on the American Case." In *Habermas and the Public Sphere*, edited by Craig Calhoun. Cambridge, MA: MIT Press, 1989.

Sennett, Richard. *The Fall of Public Man*. New York: Knopf, 1977.

Shamir, Milette. "Hawthorne's Romance and the Right to Privacy." *American Quarterly* 49, no. 4 (1997): 746–79.

Shklovsky, Viktor. "Art as Technique." In *Four Formalist Essays,* translated by Lee T. Lemon. Lincoln: University of Nebraska Press, 1965.

Smith, Adam. *The Theory of Moral Sentiments*. Edited by Knud Haakonssen. New York: Cambridge University Press, 2002.

Smoliarova, Tatiana. "Distortion and Theatricality: Estrangement in Diderot and Shklovsky." *Poetics Today* 26, no. 4 (2005): 3–32.

Sollors, Werner. *Neither Black Nor White Yet Both: Thematic Explorations in Interracial Literature*. Cambridge, MA: Harvard University Press, 1997.

Stendahl. *Racine et Shakespeare*. Paris: André Delpeuche, 1927.

Stoler, Ann Laura. *Race and the Education of Desire: Foucault's* History of Sexuality *and the Colonial Order of Things*. Durham, NC: Duke University Press, 1995.

Stowe, Harriet Beecher. *The Minister's Wooing*. New York: Penguin, 1999.

———. *Uncle Tom's Cabin*. New York: Norton, 1994.

Sundquist, Eric J. "*Benito Cereno* and New World Slavery." In *Reconstructing American Literary History*, edited by Sacvan Bercovitch. Cambridge, MA: Harvard University Press, 1986.

———. *To Wake the Nations: Race in the Making of American Literature*. Cambridge, MA: Harvard/Belknap, 1993.

Tanner, Laura. "'Speaking with Hands at Our Throats': The Battle for Artistic Voice in *The Blithedale Romance*." *Studies in American Fiction* 21, no. 1 (1993): 1–19.

Taussig, Michael. *Mimesis and Alterity: A Particular History of the Senses*. New York: Routledge, 1993.

Teeters, Negley K. *They Were in Prison: A History of the Pennsylvania Prison Society, 1787–1937*. Philadelphia: John C. Winston, 19—.

Thoreau, Henry David. *Walden and Civil Disobedience*. New York: Signet Classic, 1980.

Tocqueville, Alexis de. *De la démocratie en Amérique*. Edited by Eduardo Nolla. 1re éd. historico-critique, rev. et augm. 2 vols. Paris: J. Vrin, 1990.

———. *Democracy in America*. Edited by J. P. Mayer. Translated by George Lawrence. 2 vols. in 1. New York: Anchor/Doubleday, 1969.

———. *Ouvres et correspondences inédites de Alexis de Tocqueville*. Edited by Gustave de Beaumont. Paris, 1861.

———. *Writings on Empire and Slavery*. Translated and edited by Jennifer Pitts. Baltimore: Johns Hopkins University Press, 2001.

Tompkins, Jane. *Sensational Designs: The Cultural Work of American Fiction, 1790–1860*. New York: Oxford University Press, 1985.

Twain, Mark. *The Adventures of Huckleberry Finn*. Edited by Gerald Graff and James Phelan. New York: Bedford/St. Martin's, 1995.

———. *Pudd'nhead Wilson*. New York: Penguin, 1986.

Tyler, Royall. *The Algerine Captive*. Edited by Caleb Crain. New York: Modern Library, 2002.

Updike, John. "Hawthorne Down on the Farm." *New York Review of Books*, 9 August 2001.

Valenti, Patricia Dunlevy. *Sophia Peabody Hawthorne, A Life*, Vol. 1, *1809–1847*. Columbia: University of Missouri Press, 2004.

Wald, Priscilla. *Constituting Americans: Cultural Anxiety and Narrative Form*. Durham, NC: Duke University Press, 1995.

Walters, Ronald G. *American Reformers, 1815–1860*. New York: Hill & Wang, 1978.

Warner, Michael. *Letters of the Republic: Publication and the Public Sphere in Eighteenth-Century America*. New York: Cambridge University Press, 1990.

———. *Publics and Counterpublics*. Cambridge: MIT/Zone Books, 2002.

Webb, Frank. *The Garies and Their Friends*. Baltimore: Johns Hopkins University Press, 1997.

Weber, Samuel. *Theatricality as Medium*. New York: Fordham University Press, 2005.

Weierman, Karen Woods. *One Nation, One Blood: Interracial Marriage in American Fiction, Scandal, and Law, 1820–1870*. Amherst: University of Massachusetts Press, 2005.

White, Ed. *The Backcountry and the City*. Minneapolis: University of Minnesota Press, 2005.

Whitman, Walt. *Complete Poetry and Selected Prose*. Edited by James E. Miller Jr. Boston: Houghton Mifflin, 1959.

———. *Franklin Evans; or, The Inebriate*. Edited by Jean Downey. New Haven, CT: College & University Press, 1967.

———. *The Gathering of the Forces: Editorials, Essays, Dramatic Reviews, and Other Materials Written by Walt Whitman as Editor of the Brooklyn Daily Eagle in 1846 and 1847*. Edited by Cleveland Rogers and John Black, New York: Putnam, 1922.

———. *Leaves of Grass: The Original 1855 Edition*. New York: Dover Thrift, 2007.

———. "November Boughs." In *Complete Prose Works*. New York: Mitchell Kennerly, 1914.

Wiebe, Robert. *The Opening of American Society*. New York: Knopf, 1984.

Wiegman, Robyn. *American Anatomies: Theorizing Race and Gender*. Durham, NC: Duke University Press, 1995.

Wilentz, Sean. *Chants Democratic: New York City and the Rise of the Working Class, 1788–1850*. New York: Oxford University Press, 1984.

Williams, Linda. *Playing the Race Card: Melodramas of Black and White from Uncle Tom to O.J. Simpson*. Princeton: Princeton University Press, 2001.

Winkfield, Unka Eliza. *The Female American*. Edited by Michelle Burnham. New York: Broadview, 2000.

Wolin, Sheldon. *Tocqueville between Two Worlds: The Making of a Political and Theoretical Life*. Princeton, NJ: Princeton University Press, 2001.

Wollstonecraft, Mary. *A Vindication of the Rights of Man and A Vindication of the Rights of Woman*. New York: Cambridge University Press, 1985.

Zanger, Jules. "The 'Tragic Octoroon' in Pre-Civil War Fiction." *American Quarterly* 18, no. 1 (1966): 63–70.

Žižek, Slavoj. *The Sublime Object of Ideology*. London: Verso: 1989.

# Index

abandonment, 53–55, 68, 81, 87–89, 200. *See also* Agamben, Giorgio; ban

abolition, activists, 112, 121–22; discourse of, 16–17, 130, 149, 158, 233n1; national movement of, 126–28; and public opinion, 122–26, 130–31. *See also* slavery

absorption, as aesthetic mode, 178–82, 186, 211–15, 248n37, 249n39, 252n27; as stance of spectator, 140, 175, 182, 189–91, 212–13. *See also* Fried, Michael

Abu Ghraib, 159

affect, in public sphere, 4–5, 47–48, 65, 73–74, 146–47. *See also* intimacy; sympathy

Agamben, Giorgio, and the "aporia" of democracy, 10–11, 28, 72, 137; and ban, 54, 154–55; and "bare life," 54–55; and sovereignty, 8, 10–11, 224n18; and the "state of exception," 13–14, 16, 225n38, 228n81

Algeria, 62–63, 224n27, 232n49, 232n51

amalgamation. *See* interracial marriage

American Anti-Slavery Society (AASS), 114, 123–24, 127–30, 242n12

American exceptionalism, 38–39, 155, 228n7, 234n3

American Museum, 27, 32, 133–34, 137, 144, 147–51, 157. *See also* Barnum, Phineas T.

American Revolution, as anti-patriarchal, 103–4, 238n46; as compared to French Revolution, 97–98; as oratorical, 103–4, 238n46; as unfinished, 31, 96–97, 104;

and slavery, 104, 107, 111, 239n51; and sovereignty, 52, 96

anti-abolitionism, 111–13, 121–23, 132, 240n57, 240n67

antislavery. *See* abolition

Arendt, Hannah, 4, 216, 221–22

Astor Place riots, 21–25, 29, 132, 215, 226n59, 227n70

Auburn Prison, 231n30. *See also* New York System

ban, 7, 54–55, 68, 154–56, 197

Bakhtin, Mikhail, 239n49

Balibar, Étienne, 232n53

Barnum, Phineas T., and the American Museum, 27, 32, 133–34, 144, 147–51, 157; and humbug, 134, 147–48, 204–5; and race, 147–48; and spectacle, 29–30, 134–35, 144, 151–52, 155, 163, 226n51, 224n47

Barrish, Jonas, 211–12, 251n20

Beaumont, Gustave de, and the 1834 New York Race riots, 111, 113–15, 117; and American literature, 30, 233n1; *On the Penitentiary System in the United States and its Application in France*, 28, 31, 50, 86–93, 237n28, 237n36; and prisons, 18, 28, 88–93; and majority tyranny, 16, 31, 88; and public opinion, 87, 92–93; and race, 74–76, 80–82, 88, 234n3; and slavery, 16–17, 31; and spectacle, 19, 74, 77, 92–93; and Tocqueville, Alexis de, 19, 30–31, 50, 74–77, 81–82, 86–88, 97–98,